the Group Theatre, and the government-funded Federal Theatre Project. America had arrived on the world stage, and its achievements in the arts—once considered derivative of European traditions—won independent recognition and international acclaim. A concise history of the genre, *American Drama between the Wars* is essential reading for students and scholars interested in one of the great eras of American culture. A selected bibliography, a detailed chronology of world events and major plays, and a dozen photographs recording groundbreaking theatrical productions are included.

THE AUTHORS

Jordan Y. Miller and Winifred L. Frazer, professors emeriti of English at the University of Rhode Island and the University of Florida, respectively, have published extensively on American drama. Miller is the author of *American Dramatic Literature* and the editor of *The Heath Introduction to Drama.* Frazer is the author of *The Theme of Loneliness in Modern American Drama, Mable Dodge Luhan,* and *E.G. and E.G.O.: Emma Goldman and the "Iceman Cometh."*

American Drama between the Wars:
A Critical History

TWAYNE'S
CRITICAL HISTORY
OF
AMERICAN DRAMA

Jordan Y. Miller
GENERAL EDITOR
University of Rhode Island

American Drama between the Wars: A Critical History

Jordan Y. Miller
University of Rhode Island

Winifred L. Frazer
University of Florida

Twayne Publishers ◇ Boston
A Division of G. K. Hall & Co.

American Drama between the Wars: A Critical History
Jordan Y. Miller and Winifred L. Frazer

Twayne's Critical History of American Drama Series

Photographs by Vandamm, courtesy of the Billy Rose Theatre Collection, the New York Public Library for the Performing Arts, Astor, Lenox and Tilden Foundations.

Copyright 1991 by G. K. Hall & Co.
All rights reserved.
Published by Twayne Publishers
A division of G. K. Hall & Co.
70 Lincoln Street
Boston, Massachusetts 02111

Copyediting supervised by Barbara Sutton.
Book design by Gabrielle B. McDonald.
Typeset in Electra with Optima and Meridien display faces
by Huron Valley Graphics, Inc. of Ann Arbor, Michigan

10 9 8 7 6 5 4 3 2 1

The paper used in this publication meets the minimum requirements of American National Standard for Information Sciences—Permanence of Paper for Printed Library Materials, ANSI Z39.48-1984. ∞™

Printed and bound in the United States of America.

Library of Congress Cataloging-in-Publication Data

Miller, Jordan Yale, 1919–
    American drama between the wars : a critical history / Jordan Y.
Miller, Winifred L. Frazer.
        p.   cm. — (Twayne's critical history of American drama
series)
    Includes bibliographical references and index.
    ISBN 0-8057-8950-2 (alk. paper)
    1. American drama—20th century—History and criticism.
I. Frazer, Winifred L., 1916–   . II. Title. III. Series.
PS351.M5   1991
812'.5209—dc20   91-2757
                                                                CIP

contents

Prologue   *vii*

1   *The Revolt against Tradition: Little Theaters and*
        Women Downstage Center   *1*

2   *Some "-isms," the Guild, and the Son of Monte*
        Cristo   *27*

3   *Eugene O'Neill: From Nobody to the Nobel*   *46*

4   *Sturm und Drang, American Style*   *98*

5   *A Cry of Playwrights*   *120*

6   *Imitation, Mimicry, and Modification: Variations on*
        a Realistic Theme   *169*

7   *Seeing Ourselves as Less than We Are: The Great*
        Age of American Comedy   *210*

8   *The Fanciful Flights of Fantasy*   *232*

9   *Drama in the Folk Tradition*   247

Epilogue   263

Chronology   266
Notes and References   271
Selected Bibliography   290
Index   318

prologue

the new spirit, 1912–1920

Historical lines of demarcation in the arts cannot be established with any precision. Changes in taste, style, and technique do not suddenly emerge full-blown but develop over extended periods of time. No clear dividing line can be drawn between the late medieval morality plays of the fifteenth century, with their purely religious emphasis, and the magnificent secularism of the Elizabethan drama that evolved over the next hundred years, often, in character and theme, reflecting, however subtly, the earlier form. Jeremy Collier's berating of the theater in his *Short View of the Immorality and Profaneness of the English Stage* (1698) may have given pause, but the rhetoric of his outraged discoveries ignores the fact that the tenor of the theater he attacked was noticeably changing: the wild gallants and hero-rakes so prevalent after 1660 had already begun to yield to the sentimentalities that were to mark the eighteenth century. In no way can Collier be credited with bringing Restoration comedy to a halt. Victor Hugo's revolt against the tedious and stultifying tragedies of his day with the overt romanticism of *Hernani* (1830) may have caused riots in the theater, but the neoclassic tradition did not fall instantly by the wayside. And Nora's door slam in A *Doll's House* (1879) may have provided a point from which to mark the beginning of modern realism, but the overlapping influence of nineteenth-century well-made romantic plays remained everywhere evident in this as well as in other Ibsen plays.

There are, however, occasions when the normally elusive dividing line can be drawn with considerable accuracy. The clean break with the tradition of the Elizabethan-Jacobean stage in all aspects of dramaturgy, staging, and audience evidenced by the British theater after 1660 is one of the clearest examples of an abrupt artistic change that owed virtually nothing to, nor suffered any significant carryover from, the past.

A more contemporary example is evident in the development of American theater and drama. Neither as abrupt nor as clearly defined as that of the seventeenth century, the American break with the past in the eight years before, during, and after the First World War remains, in its way, just as significant as its British precedent. The changes were considerably more than cosmetic. The departure from the comfortably predictable styles of writing and staging of the nineteenth and early twentieth centuries, which had maintained a theater of polished, traditional popular entertainment, was absolute.

A combination of forces, rather than any single factor, prompted the new direction. The most obvious was the global catastrophe of the Great War itself—unwanted, easily avoidable, but an almost inevitable result of the unwieldy alliances and the stupefying miscalculations of the leaders who forged them. There is some validity in pointing to the conflict as the single most important factor in bringing about a permanent rupture with the previous complacent age. After all, America lost much of its idealistic innocence through its involvement in this "war to end all wars," and Europe, of course, saw a whole generation of its male youth slaughtered at the Somme and before Verdun, while its social and political geography was forever altered.

Artistically, insofar as the drama is concerned, the war was more of a catalyst than a direct influence. It provides a convenient historical marker that permits easy delineation of pre- and postwar trends. The extensive social upheavals of wartime prompted a swift departure from the past; but, like all catalysts, the war contributed to the process without becoming an integral part of it. The conflict itself faded into the background. There were isolated exceptions, namely Maxwell Anderson and Laurence Stallings's *What Price Glory?* (1924) (discussed in detail later), and Irwin Shaw's grim antiwar drama *Bury the Dead* (1936), in which a group of soldier corpses refuses to obey orders to lie down and be buried, thus providing a powerful indictment of war's pointlessness and stupidity. But on the whole, the war was largely ignored by American dramatists in developing their ideas and themes. In contrast, the legacy of the war's second half 20 years later, with the unfathomable horror of the Holocaust and the immediate aftermath of two giant powers staring each other down, provided material for endless artistic searches for sense or meaning in it all—something totally lacking after 1918.

The *direct* influences on the drama were not associated with the conflict itself. The social and political revolutionary movements that culminated in the Russian overthrow of the Romanovs had already existed before the war in Europe and to a lesser degree in America. The prewar period was also a time of considerable artistic ferment, which was especially notable in the European theater, predating the war but certainly accelerated by it. American dramatists, however, had paid little attention to the radical changes taking place on the stages of France, Germany, and Russia.

Before 1914 there were no American counterparts to André Antoine, whose Théâtre Libre in Paris began in 1887 to offer short, unconventional pieces, daring in their display of nontraditional, often unpleasant subject matter that was shunned by the established producing companies. There was no American equivalent of the Freie Bühne, begun in Germany in 1889, nor of Max Reinhardt's Berlin Kleines Theatre of 1902; absent were any creative artists who might establish anything resembling Konstantin Stanislavsky's Moscow Art Theatre of 1898, or the Abbey Theatre of Dublin, brought by William Butler Yeats and Lady Gregory to international fame by 1904. All of these groups presented imaginative, stimulating, and often highly controversial drama that was frequently disturbing to their audiences; this was illustrated by the initial unfavorable reception of Anton Chekhov's *The Seagull* in Moscow in 1896, or the violent outbursts that greeted John Millington Synge's *The Playboy of the Western World* at the Abbey in 1907.

The American drama, for all the radical stirrings overseas, continued on its well-established, commercially successful path, with only momentary excursions into the new ways of Europe. James A. Herne's *Margaret Fleming* (1890), treating marital relationships and the unique problem of a "fallen" man with realistic seriousness, and William Vaughn Moody's *The Great Divide* (1906), contrasting the old, conservative New England with the new and liberated West, gave some promise of change. For the most part, however, the successful American writers at the turn of the century, such as Clyde Fitch, Edward Sheldon, or

Eugene Walter, while paying lip service to the social realism of the Ibsenesque problem play, put their characters through stock situations, solving everything with preposterously happy endings or equally unconvincing melodramatic posturings.

If there was any single event signaling the drama's permanent abandonment of the past, it must be the arrival of Eugene O'Neill. Whatever we may assert about the influence of the war and the artistic upheavals of Europe, it remains tempting to regard the coming of O'Neill as the advent of the messiah who suddenly led the American drama out of the wilderness, instantly creating a modern American theatrical art. There is some basis for this view, to be sure. There is a fairly clear-cut pre-O'Neill and post-O'Neill American drama, as any study of modern American theater can attest, but O'Neill did not arrive Venus-like from the sea foam, nor did he spring fully armed, like Athena, from the head of Zeus. He came from as traditional a nineteenth-century theater background as one could possibly find, and he continually had to struggle to overcome the heritage of his father's ultraromantic *Count of Monte Cristo* sensationalism. He was important as a rebel against this heritage, and his single-minded devotion to the theater as an arena for serious artistry ultimately succeeded in bringing international acceptance and respectability to the American drama. Thus, with O'Neill as the central figure, by the beginning of the century's third decade an American drama of increasing artistic merit was emerging. Backward glances were few; those who led the way followed their own instincts without apology and without fear.

The drama, however, did not effect its changes within an otherwise static environment. The occasion that most clearly signaled the early twentieth-century shift in the American cultural climate occurred in painting and sculpture when the Armory Exhibition—the International Exhibition of Modern Art—opened at the 69th Regiment Armory in New York on 17 February 1913. If the overused term *landmark* can fit any early twentieth–century American artistic event, it is wholly appropriate to this remarkable display, which still retains its historical importance as the point from which modern art in America is measured.

Two unique aspects of the Armory Exhibition were its choice of artists and the widespread sensation it created. Probably the most controversial items on view were the paintings, virtually all of which were imports. The American public was being asked to look upon and to consider seriously the innovations of the European impressionists and expressionists such as Cézanne, Van Gogh, Picasso, Brancusi, Gauguin, and Matisse, all far removed from the American traditions of Thomas

Eakins, Winslow Homer, and James McNeill Whistler. When the exhibition moved elsewhere, to the Art Institute in Chicago, or to Copley Hall in Boston, the shock-wave reactions were the same as in New York. People stared in puzzled fascination, often horrified by what they saw, questioning how any of it could be called art. Duchamps's now familiar cubistic *Nude Descending a Staircase*, for instance, became the focal point for cartoon humor, belittled as the picture of a "fearful explosion in a lumberyard." In a manner similar to the notorious *Salon des impressionistes* exhibit of 1874 in Paris, mounted in revolt against the entrenched establishment of the French Academy, the Armory Exhibition jolted the public into a new way of thinking about and creating art.

The change in attitude fostered by the Armory Exhibition was emphasized by the insignia on the buttons worn by the members of the Association of American Painters and Sculptors who held the show. Imprinted in large letters under the upraised branches of the symbolic pine tree from the days of the American Revolution appeared the exhibitors' affirmation: THE NEW SPIRIT. This legend reflected more than the esprit of the exhibition; it also echoed what was happening at the same time in other artistic media, albeit less sensationally. The concentration of the exhibition's display under one roof was, by its very nature, more immediately visible to the public, creating its instant furor in the midst of a number of other no less remarkable, if somewhat overshadowed, events. New ideas, all part of the new spirit, were evident in poetry, music, dance, photography, architecture, and the drama as old barriers to artistic invention and freedom of expression rapidly began to fall.

In his autobiography, Floyd Dell, editor of the left-wing, worker-oriented journal *The Masses*, pointed to 1912 as an extraordinary year in American culture.[1] Politically, in a voter display of serious discontent, the year witnessed the election of the professorial idealist Woodrow Wilson. Culturally, it saw the establishment of "little" theaters by Maurice Brown in Chicago and Winthrop Ames in New York and the founding by Harriet Monroe of the immensely influential *Poetry: A Magazine of Verse*, which welcomed Ezra Pound and others equally controversial who dared to express themselves in the subtler cadences of free verse, outside the rigid forms of traditional metrics.

It was, as well, the time when Isadora Duncan, returning from Europe, practiced her theories of freedom of expression in bodily movements by abandoning the established dress of classical ballet and dancing barefoot in free-flowing Grecian-style robes. Anathema to the traditionalists, she found welcome acceptance from a public now becoming acquainted with the new artistic spirit. Already, throughout the previous decade, Alfred Stieglitz, an enthusiastic backer of the Armory Exhibition, had promoted the art of photography in his Studio 291 and in his publication *Camera Work*.[2] In architecture Frank Lloyd Wright's insistence that form should follow function helped, along with equally untraditional concepts by Walter Gropius and others, to create a new fluidity in design through the integration of terrain into a building's structure, as well as a newly imaginative use of space and light.

Women were uttering their cry for political and social equality and freedom. Although the constitutional amendment giving women the right to vote was not ratified until 1920, suffragists had aroused the national conscience in the early years of the century. In 1906 anarchist Emma Goldman began publishing her monthly periodical, *Mother Earth*, not only to promote political and economic justice but also to combine social ideals with various art forms, including poetry, fiction, and particularly drama. Like many others, Goldman recognized that the loosening of the strictures that had bound the arts coincided with a movement toward greater political freedom as well.[3]

Not insignificantly, underlying all was America's growing confidence in her industrial and political might as the new century began. In 1900, following the sudden acquisition of an empire in the Spanish-American War of 1898, Theodore Roosevelt sent the U.S. Navy on a round-the-world cruise to establish America's new international presence. Growing demographically as well as geographically (Arizona became the forty-eighth and final mainland state in 1912), the country's population in the 1910 census was approaching 100 million, nearly double the count in 1880. No longer a sprawling frontier nation but a rising world power, with its rapidly expanding wealth and military prowess, America had arrived at a time when its achievements in the arts, independent of its European forebears, could be recognized as easily as its formidable line of battleships. The motto on the lapel buttons of the Armory Exhibition, symbolizing the new spirit evident everywhere, was more than mere wishful thinking.

1

The Revolt against Tradition

Little Theaters and Women
Downstage Center

Given the nature of the drama, it is probably inevitable that its movements tend to lag behind movements in the other arts. Those who write the play and those who mount it, all of whom may hold widely divergent artistic views, must exert a unique cooperative effort if this composite form of art is to succeed. Faced with a generally conservative mass audience, it is the exceptional playwright who can suddenly break through the well-established limitations on what can be said and how it is expressed. Moreover, there are further artistic restrictions imposed by others of equal importance who design, direct, produce, and perform, as well as by the physical capacities of the theater building itself. Fortunately, the way was open in the pre-World War I years for a drama that took advantage of the contagious air of freedom of the new spirit, and there were those prepared to embrace it, both in writing and staging.

If American drama were to seize the spirit of the times, it needed a burst of native energy to abandon the worn-out molds of the past. The inertia was formidable. The American theater at the end of the nineteenth century was in the seemingly unbreakable hold of businessmen who had slight interest in the merits of drama as an art but were very aware of the theater's possibility for financial reward. The theater at the start of the new century was strictly a commercialized popular art of transitory value, little more than a means of making money for theater managers and a limited number of leading actors. In a system geared to profit as its sole means of survival, any idealized concept of dramatic art was necessarily sacrificed to money-making.

Monopolistic control of theatrical production, well established at the end of the nineteenth century, had long maintained the commercial safety of familiar formulas geared to second-rate dramatic writing. For a national public beginning to awaken to the possibility of high-quality original American drama, there was little to choose from. Almost every first-class house throughout the country was controlled by either the syndicate of Marc Klaw and A. L. Erlanger or the theater trust operated by Sam, Lee, and J. J. Shubert; playwrights and star actors alike found themselves caught between two powerful booking agencies that often ruthlessly exploited their talents.

Cracks in the monolith were evident before the war, and by its end the collapse was complete. The erstwhile highly profitable touring companies rapidly declined, as mediocre talent and repetitive plays no longer drew supportive audiences; increased pay scales and higher railroad rates, together with the inroad of motion pictures, sharply reduced the profits. Challenged by independent producers and actors, notably David Belasco and Minnie Maddern Fiske, and weakened by their own fierce competitiveness, the monopolies were losing their once-feared prowess. The artists themselves lashed out in force; in 1917 a bitter but successful strike by Actors' Equity closed down all New York theaters and for the first time brought performers the power to negotiate their own salaries.

With the increasing erosion of the restrictive influence of the business-oriented, formula-bound producers, American drama, late as it was, began to change in directions that could even be termed revolutionary. Gradually realizing their growing influence, actors, dramatists, directors, and designers began to develop a rapport among themselves that soon led to the formation of independent theater companies dedicated not to the business of money-making but to the creation of a meaningful art.

The Little Theater Movement

The companies that began to move into the breach created by the failure of American theater to keep step with the other arts were defined by a variety of terms to fit their social and artistic aims. Designations such as "art," "intimate," and "independent" were familiar tags. "Insurgent," suggesting rebellion against the big-business materialism of the Broadway establishment, was not unknown. Amateur, nonprofit "community" or "civic" theaters were increasingly popular. The most familiar term, regardless of company size, and still the most convenient, remains simply "little."

The growth of the little theater movement that began the rapid turnaround of American drama received a powerful impetus when the Abbey Theatre brought its troupe of Irish players to this country in 1911. For the first time Americans were provided with a direct demonstration of what the evolving artistic ferment in Europe was all about. The Abbey's successful tour, including Chicago as well as New York, may not in itself have prompted all that soon followed, but it revealed what seemed to many to be a truly revolutionary style of writing and production. The 22-year-old Eugene O'Neill attended every performance he could and by his own acknowledgment never forgot their powerful effect.

Encouraged by the visible presence of the Abbey, as well as by the continuing success of the art theaters in Germany, Russia, and France, determined Americans ventured, however belatedly, to follow the well-established lead. By the end of World War I little theaters zealously devoted to abandoning the old entrenched positions had been organized throughout the United States. As early as 1909 an attempt was made in New York to found a permanent "art" repertory company at the New Theatre under the direction of Winthrop Ames. Though technically very advanced, it undertook an ambitious program of star-studded productions that relied too heavily on European imitation without ever becoming a part of American artistic life. It failed within two seasons. Immediately afterward, and on his own, Ames founded the Little Theatre in New York in 1912, only to experience another quick failure. In the same year two other noteworthy, if short-lived, groups were established with the same anticommercial artistic standards. Chicago's Little Theatre was opened by Maurice Brown and would last for five seasons. Mrs. Lyman Gale's Toy Theatre in Boston endured for little more than two years.

In 1916 the Cleveland Playhouse, at first strictly amateur but soon fully professional, began its long and influential career. In the same year Gilmore Brown founded the prestigious Pasadena Community Playhouse, and Sam Hume began the important Detroit Arts and Crafts Theatre. In the Deep South the Petit Théâtre du Vieux Carré appeared in New Orleans in 1919. Others of varying distinction and endurance sprang up around the country, the best known including the Indianapolis Little Theatre, the

Wisconsin Players, and the Los Angeles Little Theatre. While isolated from each other and relatively few in number, totaling at most 50 groups across the nation, these professional and semiprofessional little theaters were indicative of America's growing interest in creating its own native art theaters paralleling those already established in Europe.

On the academic level, experimental groups, often known as workshop theaters, were also playing their part in fostering a more respected attitude toward native American drama. The most influential was created in 1905, first at Radcliffe and then at Harvard, by George Pierce Baker, who began a playwriting course called English 47. Its real purpose, to train students in dramatic and theatrical techniques, was at that time too daring to admit openly. The semantic evasion notwithstanding, English 47 evolved into the famous 47 Workshop, whose function was to offer a production outlet for student scripts. Finding Harvard unwilling to acknowledge the importance of what he was doing by providing adequate facilities, Baker moved to Yale in 1925, where he was given a new, fully equipped, professional-level theater building for what has since become the Yale School of Drama, one of the nation's outstanding training facilities in every phase of drama and theater.

For all of the surge of devotion to the new spirit in these widely varied experiments, in following the course of modern American drama we must first turn to the three little theaters of New York, all dating from 1915—the Neighborhood Playhouse, the Provincetown Players, and the Washington Square Players. Appearing at the epicenter of the nation's theatrical activity, they presented their wares to the public as genuine alternative choices. Their impact was immediate, their influence permanent.

THE NEIGHBORHOOD PLAYHOUSE

A most unlikely source from which one might expect an important little theater to develop would surely be among the immigrant tenements of New York's Lower East Side. Furthermore, in an age when any kind of theater management rested almost exclusively in the hands of men, for such an enterprise to have begun in the first place and then to have been successfully maintained exclusively by women would seem to tax credibility. But this did indeed occur, and the Neighborhood Playhouse brought to the public the new and independent outlook of an imaginative alternative to the increasingly stultifying commercial theater uptown.

Alice and Irene Lewisohn, wealthy sisters who worked with the

Henry Street Settlement House, strongly believed in providing something more than material aid, vital and welcome as it was, to a population confined by towering buildings, narrow streets, and poverty. They were convinced that the introduction of an aesthetic experience into lives demeaned by their surroundings and marked by uninterrupted dullness was of almost equal importance. At first they directed lively annual spring festivals for the children of the area as well as pageantlike dramas for the adults, using native songs and dances of the various immigrant groups to help integrate into American society a population whose native language was not English. By 1912, however, organized as the Neighborhood Players, they had begun to mount full-length plays in such area venues as a trade-union hall, the Settlement gymnasium, and even the neighborhood streets. Then, after traveling to Europe to study continental theater design, the Lewisohns, through their own resources and those of others whom they persuaded to contribute, were able to construct a beautiful Georgian-style theater at 466 Grand Street. The Neighborhood Playhouse opened for its first production on 12 February 1915 with a dance drama, *Jephthah's Daughter*, based on an incident from the Old Testament.[1]

Between 1915 and 1927 the Neighborhood offered a diversity of theatrical fare truly remarkable in its daring and in its scope. There were productions of plays by dramatists as varied as Sheridan, Chekhov, Shaw, Lord Dunsany, Galsworthy, and O'Neill. More frequent were ventures into foreign and domestic works, some with music and dance, written or adapted by individuals virtually unheard of by the regular theater-going public. A Japanese No play, *Tamura*, translated in part by Ezra Pound, was staged during the 1917–18 season. One of the most outstanding successes was the 1924 production of the Hindu classic *The Little Clay Cart*. In 1925 *The Dybbuk*, by the Hebrew writer Solomon Ansky, portraying life among a mystical Hasidic sect of Russian Jews, was so successful that increasing numbers of people were turned away from each performance. Broadway managers offered an indefinite run uptown, but the Lewisohns, realizing the problems of creating an essentialy new production to meet Broadway standards, and recognizing their obligation to the subscribers supporting them, declined the lucrative offer.

A yearly highlight at the Neighborhood was the annual edition of the Grand Street Follies, which began in 1922 and extended through five seasons into 1927. These high-spirited spoofs took on the most sacred of the uptown productions, satirizing in song and dance the leading plays of the New York season. Their targets included John Barrymore's legendary *Hamlet*, the naturalistic drama of Sidney Howard and Eugene O'Neill (parodied in *They Knew What They Wanted under the Elms*), and mindless censorship (ridiculed in a bowdlerized version of Maxwell Anderson and Laurence Stallings's raucous bawdy war play, *What Price Glory?*).

The phenomenon of the success of the Neighborhood Playhouse in its 15 years of existence was all the more exceptional because the mainstays of the theater were all women. The participation of the Lewisohn sisters themselves went far beyond money and moral support. They assisted in adapting foreign texts and arranging some of the more experimental and nontraditional productions. They were very active, both separately and together, in the direction of plays and musicals. Lillian Wald, who ran the settlement house, was a prime mover in supporting the entire Neighborhood undertaking and used her many official contacts to push the enterprise along. The talented performer Sarah Cowell LeMoyne trained the actors and was instrumental in securing Agnes Morgan, a graduate of George Pierce Baker's 47 Workshop, as the technical expert who also became the major director. Esther Peck, who had helped with costumes and other aspects of earlier productions, especially those with children, became costume and scene designer. The well-known dancer Blanche Talmud worked as choreographer; pianist Lilly May Hyland arranged music and composed original numbers for the annual Follies. Helen Arthur, a lawyer, left her job with the Shuberts to become business manager, but beyond that she lured the most popular American and European stars, such as Ellen Terry, Yvette Guilbert, Ethel Barrymore, Ruth Draper, and Jacob Ben-Ami, to appear at the playhouse. These and other women of comparable talent made a tremendous contribution to the drab life of this blighted urban area, and their productions often outshone those of the commercial theater because they incorporated novel settings, new kinds of music and dance, and authentic folk drama from other parts of the world.

Great as the enlightenment brought by the Neighborhood Playhouse to lower Manhattan happened to be, the theater could not be sustained except by subsidy from the Lewisohns. Faced with the increasing difficulties of maintaining an ambitious repertory company, the Neighborhood was forced to close in the spring of 1927 with the last edition of the Follies. Alice Lewisohn best summarized the reasons: ". . . financial pressure, the increasing handicap of location, the realization that we had outgrown the physical dimensions of the building [and] the growing intensity of the work" (Crowley, 237). But the influence of the Neighborhood Playhouse did not end when it closed its doors. A School of Theater was begun the following year with nine students under

Rita Morgenthau and has continued ever since to train new generations of artists. The Costume Institute, established in 1937 by Irene Lewisohn and others, is now a part of a valuable collection in the Metropolitan Museum of Art. For some 15 years the Neighborhood had brought entertainment at the very small price that its audiences could afford and had trained innumerable young people to appreciate the best in art, dance, music, and drama, while also providing an imaginative alternative for uptown audiences bored by the commercial theater. The words of Joseph Wood Krutch in his introduction to Alice Lewisohn's history of the Neighborhood Playhouse well express what it had set out to do and what it did. Its goals, says Krutch, were "less concerned with intellectualized convictions, with morals, or sociology, or manners, more with song and dance and ritual as direct expressions of the beauty and joy of life, or, as one might sum it up, less interested in drama as literature than in what the theatre and theatrical presentation can accomplish as an independent art" (Crowley, xiv).

THE PROVINCETOWN PLAYERS

The Neighborhood Playhouse opened its doors in February 1915, and during the summer of the same year the Provincetown Players, operating in the living room and on the front porch of a house in the artist-colony village far out on the tip of Cape Cod, took its first uncertain steps as an alternative little theater. The differences between the two groups throughout their nearly parallel lives were substantial, yet each was a major force in reshaping the American theater and its drama.

From its inception the Neighborhood Playhouse was broadly eclectic; it mounted productions of familiar and not-so-familiar foreign and domestic classics, contemporary works by established playwrights, and innovative original scripts. Its endowed playhouse, commanding the attention of some of the most famous performing artists of the day, was built to its own specifications, and its audiences from the surrounding tenements, as well as from the more sophisticated streets uptown, were provided a unique opportunity to witness what no Broadway entrepreneur would dare touch. Furthermore, while its school and its donation to the Metropolitan Museum of Art are important legacies, the Neighborhood did not foster the development of any playwright, producer, or performer who would achieve the kind of recognition afforded some of the Provincetown's best-known figures.

Significantly, the Provincetown Players evolved not from the immigrant settlement-house surroundings of the Neighborhood but from the small group of artists, writers, and political activists who chose to escape the heat of New York summers by gathering to work, play, and interact in the tiny isolated community of Provincetown, Massachusetts, where radical ideas, unorthodox philosophies, and unconventional lifestyles could be practiced and accepted without inhibition. In addition, the participants diverged from the path taken by the Neighborhood in deciding to do only American works and to assume among themselves all of the responsibilities of staging as well as acting. And finally, the Provincetown is remembered for the enthusiastic support it provided to its most famous member, Eugene O'Neill.

It would be a mistake, however, to limit the historical significance of the Provincetown to O'Neill alone. Giant figure as he eventually became, there were others whose devotion to the group from its beginning was paramount in advancing its purpose: to further American dramatic art, in line with the new spirit, by encouraging new playwrights and eventually forcing commercial producers to make the Broadway stage increasingly innovative. Without the backing of everyone in this enthusiastic group, O'Neill's entrance upon the scene might have been very different.

Foremost, of course, are the names of George Cram Cook and his wife, Susan Glaspell. The story of their association with the Provincetown Players is fully told in Glaspell's book *The Road to the Temple*, which revealed the near-messianic fervor with which Cook approached his work, and in Helen Deutsch and Stella Hanau's *The Provincetown*.[2] Both Cook (who was always known as "Jig") and Glaspell "held firm, even fervent views about the place of art, especially the drama, in the early century American renaissance which they created and celebrated . . . a curious blend of anarchism (by which they seem to have meant individuals living intensely and acknowledging no authority), visionary socialism, and a mystical assertion of life against death."[3]

Joining the Cooks were others, many of them products of the intellectual and political ferment of Greenwich Village in 1915, who pursued a variety of not always compatible sociopolitical ideals but shared the same enthusiasm for new movements in the arts. The liberal journalists Hutchins Hapgood and his playwright-actress wife Neith Boyce, strong believers that art, like anarchism, makes humankind free, brought an air of bohemianism quite unlike the aesthetic idealism of the Lewisohn sisters and the Neighborhood. Terry Carlin, another who found answers in anarchism, introduced O'Neill to the group and later became the model for Larry Slade in *The Iceman Cometh*. John Reed, the Harvard-educated journalist whose *Ten Days That Shook the World* (1919) enthusiastically endorsed the Bolshevik Revolution, and his wife Louise Bryant, equally left-minded, were prominent associates. So were Max Eastman of the radical monthly *The Masses*, his wife Ida Rauh, who was to become fully involved in acting and directing, and the freethinking young poet Edna St. Vincent Millay.

The beginning of what was to become known as the Provincetown Players was inauspicious enough, coming as it did in what was little more than an impromptu performance in the Hapgoods' home of *Suppressed Desires* (1915), a brief two-scene satire on the Freudian fad of that time. It had been written by Cook and Glaspell and seemed to be an appropriate piece to begin with, especially since Cook was unable to sell its virtues to others in Greenwich Village with whom he had been associated and who were forming themselves into the Washington Square Players. After a second play, *Constancy* by Neith Boyce, was produced under the same limited circumstances, Cook moved the performances into a tiny fish shack owned by another Provincetowner, Mary Heaton Vorse. Dubbed the Wharf Theater, it seated, not very comfortably, about 60 spectators. Two more plays, neither of which gained any substantial recognition thereafter, completed the initial season of 1915.

Eight plays at the Wharf followed in the summer of 1916. Scripts were supplied by John Reed, Louise Bryant, Susan Glaspell, and others, but the play most often chosen to represent the beginning of modern American drama was provided by the young, shy, somewhat brooding Irish-American named Eugene O'Neill. His one-act "nonplay," as it had been termed earlier by none other than George Pierce Baker, *Bound East for Cardiff* (originally titled *Children of the Sea*), about a dying sailor on a nondescript tramp steamer, had been read to the group and enthusiastically received for precisely representing what the Provincetown Players felt they were all about. From then on, every season featured one or more plays by this new and highly original dramatic voice.

The ever-enthusiastic Cook, determined to carry into New York the Provincetown's ideal of fostering native American drama within a closely knit, nonprofessional organization, moved the group back to Greenwich Village and into a converted brownstone at 139 MacDougal Street, where, in the fall of 1916, the players opened the Playwrights' Theatre with a series of one-act plays. By the third winter season (1918–19) the Provincetown had moved into still another building—this one, at

133 MacDougal, a converted storehouse and stable that could seat over 200 patrons. Operating on a strict membership-subscription basis in order to avoid certain licensing and fire laws, they maintained their essentially amateur tradition for six full seasons through 1921–22, staging not only 16 plays by O'Neill and 11 by Glaspell but a grand total of 93 works by close to 50 American writers.

But developments at the Provincetown were not always to Cook's liking. He became increasingly distressed by a growing professionalism and a tendency, as he saw it, to veer away from the kind of intellectual and artistic purity he felt was so essential in combating the commercial theater. The sensational success in the 1920–21 season of O'Neill's *The Emperor Jones*, which eventually moved uptown into a full-size Broadway theater, and the Provincetown's increased notoriety eventually led Cook to forsake the entire project in 1922. He and Glaspell departed for Greece, and although his wife soon returned to America, Cook spent the rest of his life living at the source of the classic dramatic ideal that he had never been able to infuse into the Provincetown. He died in 1924 at Delphi, where he had worn native clothing and lived among Greek shepherds, whom he put into acting roles in the ancient Delphi theater.

At the end of the 1921–22 season, which had experienced another O'Neill sensation, *The Hairy Ape*, the Playwrights' Theatre suspended operations for what was at first assumed to be a one-year interim in anticipation of Cook's return. When it reopened for the 1923–24 season it was no longer the enterprise that the idealistic Cook had fought so hard to maintain. Under the direction of the so-called triumvirate of producer Kenneth Macgowan, scene designer Robert Edmond Jones, and Eugene O'Neill, the Provincetown Players abandoned their insistence on purely American scripts, a policy that had frequently compelled them to mount inferior plays by unknown and soon-forgotten playwrights. When the three were joined by James Light, another member of the original band of Players, ties with the past were quickly dissolved. They formed the Experimental Theatre, Inc., and from 1924 to 1926 operated in conjunction with the Greenwich Village Theatre as the Provincetown Playhouse. Productions varied from revivals of Molière, Congreve, and Strindberg to Gilbert and Sullivan and, of course, new works by O'Neill.

The triumvirate were now firmly committed to their own pursuits at the Greenwich Village, leaving behind only the remnants of the original Provincetown Players. As early as 1920 O'Neill had begun his move to Broadway, and by 1928 he would be permanently under the wing of the Theatre Guild. The Provincetown's manager, Eleanor Fitzgerald, and one or two others sought to maintain the old tradition, even going so far as to attempt a move uptown into the Guild's former home, the Garrick Theatre. But the center had collapsed with the departure of the group's biggest names, and the flanks could not hold. By the time the market crashed in October 1929, the Provincetown had ceased to exist.[4]

For all its sometimes amateurish innocence, and despite Jig Cook's single-minded restrictions on what it could do, the Provincetown forced the New York commercial theater to take a hard and beneficial look at itself. In addition to discovering O'Neill, it started America's first important woman playwright, Susan Glaspell, on her successful career. With Cook's constant delight in nontraditional stagecraft, the Provincetown built this country's first permanent solid-plaster stage dome to replace the conventional cyclorama, making possible the eerie and terrifying expressionistic projections of *The Emperor Jones*, the play that had provided the first opportunity for a black actor, Charles Gilpin, to achieve genuine stardom. And it furthered the careers of producer Kenneth Macgowan and Robert Edmond Jones, who became one of America's foremost stage-design artists. It is not without justification to say that the Provincetown was midwife to, if not actually the parent of, the modern American theater.

THE WASHINGTON SQUARE PLAYERS

The third of the major little-theater groups of 1915, and through its evolution into the Theatre Guild the most enduring, was the Washington Square Players. Its founders' attack on the unimaginatively routine Broadway theater took a different path from either the Lewisohns' Neighborhood innovations or the Provincetown's restriction to experimentation with American writers only. The intent of the dozen or so Greenwich Village organizers of the Washington Square Players was to produce plays, regardless of origin, that were being ignored by the Broadway establishment.

Those who undertook the venture included many who would become nationally famous as the force behind the Theatre Guild: Lawrence Langner, Theresa Helburn, Philip Moeller, and Helen Westley. Even Jig Cook had been an early member before he, and eventually Robert Edmond Jones, moved to the Provincetown. Accustomed to meeting regularly at the Washington Square Bookshop, owned by the publishers Charles and Albert Boni, they had developed a strong interest in modern English and American playwrights, and like the people behind the Provincetown, they were attracted to the one-act play because it was both artistically exciting and logistically feasible for a small company. What prompted Cook's early departure was the founders' fairly conservative outlook. They were eager to take up some of the Broadway theater's slack but avoided commitment to the outright experimentation so attractive to Cook. In addition, their aspiration was to become a professional theater in the full meaning of the term, a goal never seriously considered by the Provincetown.

The first production, *The Glittering Gate*, a one-act by the Irish playwright Lord Dunsany, was modestly staged in 1914 in a back room of the bookshop. Encouraged by the results, and formally organized as the Washington Square Players, the group rented the small Bandbox Theatre on 57th Street—very far indeed from Greenwich Village—where they opened a series of weekend bills, starting on 19 February 1915 with Maurice Maeterlinck's symbolic *Interiors*. Other successes included Edward Goodman's *Eugenically Speaking*, with its advanced ideas on mating, and Lawrence Langner's *Licensed* (written under the pseudonym Basil Lawrence), which criticized restrictive marital conventions.

Thus launched, the Washington Square Players increased their 1915 performances to four a week and then to eight the following year. Although lacking the experimental drive that Cook deemed so important, they were not afraid of original interpretations and imaginative sets, a combination that brought them initial critical approval. An ability to attract a substantial subscription audience ensured their survival and soon permitted expansion into the 700-seat Comedy Theatre on West 41st Street, in the heart of the Broadway theater district. Other attractions included occasional free lectures on the drama for the subscribers, plus special performances of little-known plays not considered suitable for the regular bills. The Players also expanded their scope by conducting a training school not only for actors but also for designers, directors, and playwrights.

Considering the short life of the Washington Square Players before their metamorphosis into the Theatre Guild, their record of accomplishments was remarkable. True, they produced no figure as large as O'Neill or as charismatic as Cook, and they were sometimes faulted for paying too much homage to foreign writers. Nonetheless, their presentation of quality productions of works that the commercial theater still hesitated to touch was praiseworthy, and successful as well. Though competing directly with established Broadway producers, the Washington Square Players consistently refused to be trapped into long money-making runs, not infrequently terminating a play at the height of its popularity to make way for a new production. The wide diversity in tone and style of their programs is illustrated by the authors represented over the three years of the group's existence (1915–18). Ibsen, Chekhov, Shaw, Molière, Musset, Wedekind, and Wilde appeared regularly, but the Players also produced American plays by Elmer Rice, Alice Gerstenberg, John Reed, Zoë Akins, and even two headliners from Provincetown, Susan Glaspell and Eugene O'Neill. O'Neill's *In the Zone*, the melodramatic playlet about a tramp steamer in the European war zone, received its premiere at the Comedy Theatre on 31 October 1917.

As America became fully involved in the European war, the demand on the group's members for services in uniform and in other support efforts brought about the end of the Washington Square Players, who closed with a final season of 11 plays in 1918. Like the Neighborhood Playhouse and the Provincetown Players, the Washington Square Players had expended remarkable amounts of time and talent, garnering little financial remuneration but gaining much in the aesthetic return that had permanently changed the climate of the New York theater. Audiences were beginning to appreciate the best of foreign plays, but more important, they were now starting to support the new American playwrights. By the time these three exceptional little theaters had passed from the scene at the end of the 1920s, their legacy was well established, and serious drama had become widely acceptable. In the words of Alice Lewisohn, with the coming of the little theaters "there lived and breathed for the first time on this continent a group spirit of the creative life" that made the forward-looking dramas they produced very different in motive and influence from those of the past (Crowley, 391).

Women in the Wings

In a letter to his publisher in January 1855, Nathaniel Hawthorne railed against what he regarded as unfair competition from the successful but clearly second-rate female writers of his time, such as Susan Warner, because of popular acceptance of their "trash" and their resulting financial rewards, which surpassed his own; he blasted them as a "mob of damned scribbling women." While he was certainly correct in assailing them as artistically inferior to himself, or Melville, or Whitman, his chauvinistic attack revealed his adherence to a strong underlying national prejudice that would take America a century or more to overcome. Jane Austen, the Brontës, George Eliot, and Elizabeth Barrett Browning may have held their ground against men in the history of English literature, but in American letters—excepting Emily Dickinson, whose genius remained undiscovered during her lifetime—the women of the nineteenth century stood in very minor esteem compared with their male counterparts.

If one is to search American drama for women playwrights of any stature before 1900, the list is sparse to the point of virtual nonexistence. Mercy Otis Warren? Her patriotic dialogues and sketches of the Revolutionary War period remain little more than historical curiosities. Anna Cora Mowatt? Hardly a name to contend with, her ever-popular social satire *Fashion* (1845) notwithstanding. Harriet Beecher Stowe? Her lasting contribution was a novel, *Uncle Tom's Cabin* (1852), adapted by others against her will into what became probably the most popular American play ever written.[5] Not until the new century was well under way did American women dramatists contribute anything worthy of attention. When they did appear, they were hardly the contemptible scribblers Hawthorne had complained of. While not all of them actually appeared onstage as performers, their contributions in writing and backstage labors, combined with the impact of the alternative little theaters for which they often wrote, were vitally important factors in moving the American drama into the artistic world of the twentieth century.

The Lewisohn sisters and their several coworkers did not undertake the Neighborhood Playhouse project as a conscious revolt against male domination. What they did work against was a theatrical system that through history had happened to be in the not always competent hands of men. Despite the odds against them, their artistic abilities and professional acumen made their success doubly unique, first because the Neighborhood was one of the few truly successful little theaters, and second, because its success was accomplished entirely by women, a phenomenon never duplicated since. Nor did any group of women playwrights consciously oppose the system simply for the cause of establishing their own place as women in a man's profession. They were an integral part of the overall revolt and found themselves in a position to exercise their talents at a time when what they had to say socially and artistically found a welcome reception. Their existence was a fortuitous if accidental product of the era; no similar grouping of women dramatists simultaneously putting out work of such quality and quantity would be repeated.

SUSAN GLASPELL

The contribution of Susan Glaspell to the Provincetown has always been acknowledged as one of the primary reasons for the organization's success. She and her husband were understandably regarded as the mainstays of the entire enterprise, but the more flamboyantly energetic Cook, with his dominating personality, received more attention—which Glaspell, in her praise of Cook in *The Road to the Temple,* did little to dispel. Glaspell, however, was almost Cook's equal in her own contribution to the operation of the Provincetown: assisting in the choice of plays, in their direction and design, and in the theater's financing. Even more important to the group's success was her writing.

The remarkable impact of O'Neill in his early one-act sea plays and the shock waves caused by *The Emperor Jones, The Hairy Ape,* and *All God's Chillun Got Wings* have tended to overshadow and thus conceal the less sensational but steady contribution of Glaspell as a writer. This long-term eclipse is unfortunate. Second only to O'Neill in productivity, she wrote witty, provocative scripts that supplied the Provincetown with some of its best material. It must be acknowledged that the success of the Provincetown Players owed about as much to her as to O'Neill.

A close study of Glaspell's plays reveals considerably more substance than has been acknowledged in later years. To look at her first effort, *Suppressed Desires,* written in collaboration with Cook, is to realize why it has remained playable for so long. Created as a satire on the fast-spreading fad of Freudian psychoanalysis, its two brief scenes still strike tellingly at the willingness of those who have nothing better to do than to embrace the latest cure-all for ills that in all probability don't exist in the first place. Frothy and tongue-in-cheek as they are, the antics of Henrietta Brewster (originally played by Glaspell) impart a clearly understood lesson. Suddenly and completely devoted to the new "science" of which she understands virtually nothing, Henrietta almost loses her sensible husband, Stephen (played by Cook), by finding within herself and Stephen a whole list of imagined problems, marital and otherwise. Faced with disaster, she wisely concludes, contrary to the prevalent psychoanalytical advice, that some desires should remain suppressed. Her abandonment of her destructive, literal acceptance of "correct" Freudian practices leads to what we assume is a happy-ever-after ending. Inconsequential as the play may be, *Suppressed Desires* catches the comic essence of the hilarious, but potentially hazardous, actions of the sudden convert.

Of greater substance, and certainly Glaspell's best short play, is *Trifles,* staged at the Playwrights' Theatre in 1916. Within the brief scope of the one-act form, which by its nature limits the development of plot or character, Glaspell created an intensely gripping piece of realistic drama that transcends the natural restrictions of the genre through careful plotting and the portrayal of ordinary yet sympathetic characters involved in a

hopeless situation. Most remarkable is the fact that the principal characters never appear on stage. The almost photographic detail of the setting
combines with the action and dialogue to create a dark, forbidding mood
equal to the best of O'Neill's sea plays, with which it had to compete and
to which it was inevitably compared.

Past acts of oppressive cruelty and deep frustration and suffering
are gradually revealed as the sordid story of the murder of John Wright
unfolds. Mrs. Wright is in jail on suspicion of killing her husband; the
sheriff and a neighboring farmer, together with their wives, enter the
kitchen seeking a motive. The men conduct a thorough search of the
entire house, but they find nothing. The observant women, remaining in
the kitchen, soon uncover the truth of a stark and dismal life pattern,
evidenced by the unwashed pans, frozen jars of fruit in a sticky mess on
the shelf, an erratically stitched quilt, and a sewing box that yields the
pitiful body of a canary, its neck obviously wrung by Mr. Wright. The
story is now clear. Isolated, childless, enduring a deadeningly lonely
existence with an abusive husband, Mrs. Wright had been driven beyond
endurance by the callous destruction of her one cheering possession and
had avenged herself in kind, strangling her husband while he slept. The
normally law-abiding women instinctively protect one of their own by
concealing the damning evidence of the bird. The men, after deriding the
inferior intelligence of their womenfolk, who could not possibly discover
anything of value in these "trifles," depart empty-handed.

Within the tradition of realistic slice-of-life dramatic writing, the
use of symbols in *Trifles* is highly effective. The caged bird, much like
Ibsen's captive wild duck, reflects the pitiful nature of its devoted owner,
entrapped in a life without hope of freedom. The broken cage door, the
broken neck, the strangled husband, the cracked fruit jars, and the literal
chill of the cold, unwelcoming kitchen unite as a powerful sequence of
images.

Trifles has justifiably remained a popular piece, but others, although important parts of each Provincetown season, have not endured.
Close the Book (1917) and *Woman's Honor* (1918) are satires not only on
conventionality but also on the self-conscious unconventionality of
Greenwich Villagers. *The People* and *The Outside* (both 1917) convey
more serious messages: in the first, that a radical newspaper benefits the
people, and in the second, that a woman who retreats from life to an
abandoned Coast Guard station is unjust to herself. *Tickless Time* (1918),
written with Cook, combines the idealism of Glaspell's serious plays with
the humor of her satires to prove that hard as a couple may try to live only

by the "true" time of a sundial, the "tick" of the house clocks is necessary in the modern world.

The Provincetown's restrictive inclination toward the one-act form normally precluded staging longer plays, but because of Glaspell's position and demonstrated ability, the group chose to stage her first full-length drama, *Bernice*, in 1919. It was a wise decision: the play immediately established her as a playwright of considerable importance. The Broadway theater would have regarded it as too talky and lacking in action, but the Provincetown provided Glaspell with the necessary latitude for this serious psychodrama. It treats a single question: did the recently deceased Bernice commit suicide, and if not, why did she wish it to be thought that she did? Regarded by some as overly sentimental, *Bernice* was nevertheless such a success that its author could no longer be overlooked.

During the last two Provincetown seasons, Glaspell's versatility in idea and style was well displayed in three more long pieces. *Inheritors* (1921) was the first play the group performed that dealt with a theme that would continually preoccupy O'Neill and would recur in a long line of plays by others as well: the deterioration of American ideals and the loss of traditional moral ardor. Glaspell's tracing of three generations of two Midwest families whose increasing stodginess moves them onto a rigidly conservative and prejudicial path becomes an almost epic view of the background of those twentieth-century Americans whose desire for wealth and prominence outweighs the idealism of their forebears. The intolerance demonstrated in their condemnation of a granddaughter who espouses the cause of three Hindu students deported for the subversive political act of embracing the principle of self-government in India becomes the ultimate irony. The play is marred by certain obvious delineations between good and evil, but it is an effective and still-pertinent social document in its uncompromising treatment of the subject.

Glaspell's willingness to try a variety of styles took her into the portrayal of a disturbed mind in *The Verge* (1921). The writing and the stage setting underline the psychological problems of Claire Archer, the central figure, as her desperate attempt to break away from traditional personal and social values into a new order of beauty and morality keeps her living continually on the verge of madness. Claire stays mainly in a surrealistic tower with odd curves and jagged lines suggestive of her emotional strain, all conveyed through clever lighting and stage design which made excellent use of the Provincetown's innovative plaster dome. The stylized scenery and the pseudoexpressionistic dialogue deftly emphasize the character's mental disintegration and final collapse. The strains of exotic plants that Claire breeds are symbols of her need to free herself from old molds; one of her creations, Breath of Life, glows from some kind of inner light. Another aspect of Claire's difficulty in adjusting her personal life is her inability to establish a satisfactory relationship with any of the three men who surround her: Tom, her lover; Dick, who occupies a "middle" ground; and Harry, her husband. Their names seem to represent Glaspell's attempt to portray them as abstract symbols of Claire's emotional problems. At least one, Tom, becomes more real than symbolic and, hence, more sympathetic when Claire, unable to save herself from tragic insanity at the end, murders him.

The Verge was acclaimed for its power and brilliance, including its Freudian symbolism and well-integrated setting, as well as its grasp of some serious contemporary human problems. It established Glaspell as a genuine force in the evolving American drama. She followed with the less effective realistic comedy *Chains of Dew* (1922), her last play for the Provincetown before she and her husband left for Greece and the O'Neill-dominated triumvirate took over in late 1923.

Glaspell's fourth full-length play, and the last she ever wrote, was *Alison's House*. Among her longer plays, it contributed the most to her permanent reputation. Staged by Eva Le Gallienne's Civic Repertory Theatre in 1930, this sensitive work, based loosely on the life of Emily Dickinson, won the Pulitzer Prize for 1930–31. Alison has died, and as in the case of Dickinson, her poems are only now being discovered. The play rings with psychological truth. Instead of being sentimental about self-sacrificing loneliness, it reveals the unhappy love affair of a withdrawn spinster who controlled her grief through the creativity of her brilliant poetry. The public did not support the play, but its staging uptown, far from the familiar Greenwich Village scene, had been made possible through the encouragement of those early theater groups whose aim had been not commercial but artistic.

As a woman playwright, Susan Glaspell was able to illustrate a new and more meaningful view of women characters. Men, to be sure, have long portrayed madness in women (Ophelia and Lady Macbeth lead a long procession), but Glaspell created in Claire Archer an important character sympathetically understood from the woman's point of view, something no man could conceive or execute. Likewise, as a woman, she was able to examine the woman's psyche of Bernice and to illuminate the mind of the absent Alison.

Not bound by any particular theatrical form, she was comfortable with conventional realism and unconventional stylization, with comedy, satire, and serious social ideas. But after the Provincetown's decline, Glaspell did not bridge the gap into a continuing career in the Broadway theater, as O'Neill was able to do. Her last plays for the Provincetown had been presented in the terminal season of 1921–22, and she did not appear again until eight years later, with *Alison's House*. That brief Glaspell "revival" was never followed up. She ventured briefly into the Federal Theater Project as director of the Midwest Play Bureau, but she had become almost completely forgotten by the time of her death in 1948. Her name seems destined to survive as that of an interesting if lesser figure from the beginning of the century, a writer of a few short dramas still popular with high school, college, and other amateur groups.

EDNA ST. VINCENT MILLAY

None of the other women writers of the era were as prolific as Susan Glaspell, and their names have not remained as familiar. The exception is Edna St. Vincent Millay, whose appealing and somewhat unorthodox poetic originality sets her apart, especially in the brilliantly stylized modern morality play *Aria da Capo*, staged at the Provincetown during the 1919–20 season.

The European war had recently ended, but the impact of its inconceivable slaughter was only beginning to be felt. The relatively young Millay, 27 when she wrote the play, was already familiar to the public as a youthful nonconformist through some of her best verse, published in *Renascence and Other Poems* (1917). Beautiful and sensuous, she was known as well to be generous with her affections, an early freethinking, "liberated" woman of the notorious postwar jazz age. Her talent in poetic expression made her a permanently important figure in American letters; as a dramatist, she is best remembered for her antiwar stance in *Aria da Capo*. A seemingly light fantastic piece, it is bitter and scornful about mankind's sad ineffectiveness in using reason to reconcile differences and avoid conflicts.

Unlike Glaspell's heavily realistic revelations of endurance and suffering, Millay's play was conceived in vastly different terms; it is well worth detailed attention. In format, *Aria da Capo* is closely related to the improvised drama of the Italian commedia dell'arte. The two principal characters, Pierrot and Columbine, dressed respectively in ruffled costumes of lilac and pink, and speaking mostly in free verse, sit on delicate, thin-legged chairs before a long table covered by a hugely checkered black-and-white cloth against a stylized black-and-white interior setting. Millay's condemnation of the callous degeneracy of the effete who ignore the horrors around them begins as Pierrot and Columbine feast on nightingales' tongues and converse in frivolous nonsense. Columbine's first line, "Pierrot, a macaroon, I cannot live / Without a macaroon," is followed by Pierrot's reply, "My only love / You are *so* intense . . . Is it Tuesday, Columbine? / I'll kiss you if it's Tuesday"; they debate the vital question, "Is this my artichoke / Or yours?"

Between this opening scene and the last, while Pierrot and Columbine continue in their oblivious way, two shepherds, Thyrsis and Corydon, play out a violent tragedy. At first they enter into a "game" involving the building of a wall between their claims of land. But they begin to tire of the monotony, and an argument ensues regarding the discovery of jewels claimed by both, of water rights for their sheep, and so on. The result is inevitable: Thyrsis administers poison to Corydon, who strangles Thyrsis; both fall dead beneath the table. Cothurnus, the masque of tragedy, who has held the promptbook and entered the action on occasion, now steps in to assist Pierrot and Columbine, who protest that they cannot play their final scene with the two dead bodies under the table. "The audience wouldn't stand for it," complains Pierrot. Cothurnus advises them to pull the tablecloth down in front to hide the bodies, adding, "The audience will forget." They do so, then merrily set their bowls back on the table, draw up their chairs, and begin the play exactly as before, in the manner of a da capo aria, from whence the title. And so the world goes on, with pointless slaughter in the midst of total indifference, the participants in their unconcerned dilettantism undisturbed by the corpses beneath their feet.

Millay was impressed by the qualities of commedia in Jacinto Benavente's *The Bonds of Interest* (1919), in which she had acted, as well as by *The Yellow Jacket* (1917), an imitation of a Chinese romance with its onstage prompter and make-believe props. Her own combination of these styles resulted in a unique production, not only in the costuming and verse dialogue but also in the fanciful, unrealistic setting. The stark black and white of the interior, its merry effect of a harlequinade, contrasting with the horrors actually taking place, is complemented by the inventive stage props. The rocks for the wall are woven strands of crepe paper. Varicolored confetti serves as the jewels, black confetti as the poison poured into a bowl. Corydon strangles Thyrsis with long strips of paper. The feast of Pierrot and Columbine is done entirely in stylized pantomime as they sit at their huge table on high, spindly furniture. Pierrot and Columbine themselves recognize the fantastic nature of what they are doing and what is going on around them: they are perfectly aware that they are in a play and that Thyrsis has died with paper strips around his neck. But, they acknowledge, he is just as dead anyway. The result is a stunning display of contrasts, something the audience, despite the assertion of Cothurnus, cannot readily forget. *Aria da Capo*, still as inventive and daringly imaginative as it was in its day, has remained a powerful dramatic indictment of human stupidities and indifference, as relevant and playable as ever.

As a figure in American drama Millay remains best known for *Aria da Capo*, but she did write two other historical blank-verse dramas: *The Princess Marries the Page* (1918) for the Provincetown, and *The King's Henchman* (1927), set to music the same year by Deems Taylor for the Metropolitan Opera. Neither has held much interest. Millay also composed a "moral interlude," *Two Slatterns and a King* (1918), about two reformed slatterns, one of whom marries the king. She and her sister Norma played the lead roles. Millay continued a fairly prolific career as a poet with several published volumes during the late 1920s and 1930s. She won the Pulitzer Prize for poetry in 1923, but her writing grew infrequent in the last decade before her death in 1950. Her poems, in their reflection of the times between wars, have remained important for their lyricism and spiritual penetration. She has gained her rightful status as one of America's major poets, but the lasting influence of *Aria da Capo* places her in an important niche of her own in the development of American drama.

RACHEL CROTHERS

While Susan Glaspell and Edna St. Vincent Millay were working with the Provincetown Players, other women were benefiting from increased opportunities in the commercial theater. One of the more important was Rachel Crothers, who devoted her life to the theater as a successful playwright, director, and producer of many of her own plays from 1908 until 1937. Her first major play, *He and She* (1911), was a success some five years before the Provincetown got seriously under way.

Crothers often chose to dramatize the conflicts between marriage and career that have plagued conscientious women of the twentieth century, but she frequently pulled her most effective punches through the compromise of having the woman sacrifice the promise of her talents for the sake of her family. Unfortunately, Crothers's conclusions tended to slip into romantic sentimentality at the expense of more believable or realistic endings. *He and She*, although it follows this pattern, has long been admired by feminist groups, mainly because of the excellent characterization of the artistic couple of the title. Ann Herford, a talented sculptor, makes the expected sacrifice, but her husband Tom is very understanding in his recognition and appreciation of what she is doing for him and their daughter in placing her career second to her responsibilities at home.

To the extent that she questioned the place of women in twentieth-century society and in her own personal choice of career over marriage, Rachel Crothers can be fairly easily categorized as a feminist, but this label is a bit misleading. She certainly had little in common with the more ideologically aggressive women who have become associated with the term. By not portraying women in overtly "unfeminine" roles, she was fulfilling the expectations of the typical Broadway audiences, who preferred that women enact more traditional characters. She refused to proselytize, no doubt partly because of certain limits set by the more conservative uptown theater. Even so, through natural-sounding dialogue and tightly plotted action, her plays advanced her more liberated ideas.

In a semihumorous vein, Crothers dramatized the subject of new freedoms for women in a number of commercially successful plays in the 1920s, from *Nice People* (1921), with its rich New York flappers seeking excitement, to *Mary the Third* (1923), involving the changing mores of a three-generation midwestern family of Marys, to *Expressing Willie* (1924), satirizing the fashionable devotees of Freud's theory of repression, and finally to *Let Us Be Gay* (1929), written long before the contemporary sexual connotation of the word, in which a merry divorcée lives a promiscuous life, much as her husband had done. Despite sophisticated subject matter and skillful propounding of some advanced ideas, in all her plays during this decade of Prohibition and "dancing daughters," Crothers stopped short of probing any extensive psychological depths and brought down the final curtains with the rebellious or profligate female experiencing "redemption." Each learns that a simple life with a faithful mate is more rewarding than high living. Crothers's popularity in the twenties is understandable: she was able to gratify the desire of her audiences for a happy resolution affirming long-held American values while putting her characters through the questionable antics of the new social freedoms available to postwar American women. The plays end in a manner that does not always follow the direction they seem to be headed; but the playwright was able to make a point and remain in the good graces of those who paid to watch, without becoming simply moralistic.

In her plays of the thirties Crothers showed she had learned from her earlier experience how to explore with better effect women's need for self-fulfillment, both sexually and socially. She still surrendered the underlying sophisticated realism of her comedy to sentimental endings, but improvement in her characterization of upper-class New Yorkers and well-to-do midwesterners helped her to be less frivolous and to remain more acceptable over the long run. *As Husbands Go* (1931) relies on the always popular subject of the contrast between European and American mores. The comedy of two Iowa women tourists involved with a young English writer and a continental dandy is counterbalanced by the more serious treatment of their need to be something more than the wife or even the widow of an unimaginative midwestern husband. As always, the focus is on the conservatism of the provinces—that is, anything west of New York or, at the farthest, Pennsylvania—in contrast to the liberal ideals of the East, reversing the point of Moody's *The Great Divide* 25 years earlier. Crothers handles the situation well.

When Ladies Meet (1932) offers a triangle plot with a somewhat novel twist: the wife and the "other woman" decide after consultation that neither of them really wants the man whom both have formerly adored and for whose affections they have competed. Crothers's most popular play, the one for which she will no doubt be longest remembered, is *Susan and God*, a rousing success that she produced herself in 1937. Introducing a rich society figure with the strong evangelistic belief that she should travel abroad and convert sinners, the play has a remarkable satiric tone of genuine high comedy. The bored heroine, Susan, a product of a society not normally given to missionary fervor, is driven more by her wish to escape her deadening social routine than by any deep-seated religious zeal. Consequently, Susan reaches the conclusion—and here we are once again back to the Crothers solution—that there is more godliness in returning to live with her husband and daughter than in venturing on a career of saving lost souls.

All the flaws notwithstanding, including a certain shallowness in her avoidance of hard-nosed solutions to the problems confronting her several heroines, Crothers succeeded in portraying psychologically believable characters rather than trapping herself in the creation of mere character types, a danger always lurking in her method. Her confirmation of traditional values was lighthearted, but she raised some pertinent questions about the role of women in her era. She knew the dilemmas facing them, and to her credit she was aware of those facing men as well. Working within the uptown theater as both writer and director, Crothers knew the kinds of audiences that supported her. She preferred to bypass the experimentation of her Greenwich Village contemporaries and refused as well to take any militant stance. Her safe middle ground has made it difficult to accept her as a serious and enduring writer of American drama; but all in all, she created a series of plays that reflected much of the turbulent early twentieth century. In her way, she held her audiences and made them listen to what she had to say.

ZOË AKINS AND OTHERS

Zoë Akins, less talented and less prolific than Crothers, and less able to probe emotional depths than Glaspell, established her name with *Déclassé*, one of the most popular plays of the 1919–20 season. In the highly romanticized *Camille*-like plot, Lady Helen kills herself just as the man she loves returns from South Africa to claim her. *The Old Maid*, the Pulitzer Prize winner for 1934–35, was adapted from a sentimental story by Edith Wharton about a woman who, having allowed her illegitimate daughter to be adopted at birth by her married cousin, becomes to the grown girl merely a sour old spinster. The grief of the real mother, who has kept silent through the years, is relieved at the end when the just-married daughter kisses her "cousin" last of all as she leaves on her honeymoon.

Some of the same problems that faced Crothers also plagued Akins. In spite of their basic realism, her plays border perilously on overdone sentimentality; initially popular, they have not been successfully revived. Still, like Glaspell and Crothers, Akins was able to create substantial women's roles that called for a new and more serious kind of realistic character interpretation.

There were momentary successes by other women playwrights who actively contributed to the rapidly developing new American theater. Alice Gerstenberg dramatized a split personality by using two actors in the Washington Square Players' production of *Overtones* (1915), a device to be developed with notable failure by Eugene O'Neill in *Days without End* some 20 years later. Clare Kummer's *Good Gracious Annabelle* (1916) helped establish a new kind of American comedy full of native banter and good humor. Zona Gale was another Pulitzer Prize winner, taking the 1920–21 award for *Miss Lulu Bett*, a dramatization of her own novel about a rebellious unmarried woman whose love for a married man gives her the courage to escape from her derisive family and hometown. Lulu Vollmer's deeply moving, intensely realistic folk play of the North

Carolina mountains, *Sun-Up* (1923) (discussed in detail in chapter 9), was first presented by the Provincetown before its year's run on Broadway. In 1928 the Theatre Guild produced *Machinal*, a startling expressionistic play by Sophie Treadwell, based on a famous trial of a wife who, in love with another man, had murdered her husband. Its limited, spotty dialogue, repetitive sound effects, and stylized sets impressively conveyed the terrifying situation of a loving woman trapped as much by machines as by machinelike people.

□   □   □

Female talent and ingenuity contributed immeasurably to the new American drama rapidly evolving within the new spirit. They brought to the overwhelmingly male-dominated profession some of the most important advances in every area of drama and theater. And it must not be forgotten that in this era of remarkably successful women playwrights, there were equally remarkable women heavily involved with the production and direction of many important theatrical undertakings. At a time and in a city not noted for its support of repertory, Eva Le Gallienne performed the remarkable feat of establishing and keeping alive her Civic Repertory Company for six years, from 1926 to 1932. She not only managed the company but also played many of the leading roles. Theresa Helburn and Armina Marshall were vital to the development and continuing success of the Theatre Guild. The Group Theatre could hardly have stayed afloat during the 1930s Depression without Cheryl Crawford, and Hallie Flanagan's outstanding contribution to the Federal Theater Project (discussed in chapter 4) is legendary.

Sadly, the survival rate of women playwrights into the second half of the period between the wars was low. Not only had they mostly disappeared by the early 1930s, but their plays had faded as well, infrequently revived in an American dramatic repertoire once again dominated by men. They did succeed in leaving their mark, however, through their willingness to take some daring steps in their use of unorthodox writing stylization, controversial subjects, and unconventional staging. Collectively, they won no less than three Pulitzer Prizes, and they tackled every kind of play, from folk drama, comedy, and biting satire to serious social drama. In their often new kind of writing and in their skill in the grubby mechanics of production and direction, as well as in acting, these women revealed what might be termed an "inner truth" that they had made their own in the early years of the century. This truth revealed that women not only could hold their own as artists against the men of their time but also could create a truthfulness in their female characters that has not easily been surpassed.

Even Hawthorne might well have been impressed.

2

Some "-isms," the Guild, and the Son of Monte Cristo

The little theater movement had opened a lot of doors. By the end of World War I the stylistic variations already established in Europe had appeared everywhere. Audiences became more sophisticated and no longer automatically accepted the shallowness of the commercial theater's conventional fare. Even those who did not write for the little theaters were becoming aware of this change and began to adapt accordingly, but maintaining the momentum of the new spirit and vigorously pushing it into the mainstream of American drama rested most notably with two rising voices. The first was that of a producing company, the Theatre Guild, and the second was that of a single playwright, Eugene O'Neill. At first going their separate ways, they eventually formed a union of lasting influence. Separately and together, the Theatre Guild and O'Neill were arguably the most important forces in the permanent alteration of American dramatic art.

The momentum was initially slow; the postwar changes in the commercial theater occurred only after some powerful inertia was overcome, nowhere more apparent than in the rigid style of writing and treatment of subject matter that prevailed through the end of the nine-teenth century and into the first decade of the twentieth. Successful playwrights were certain of what their audiences would accept, and only a few dared venture beyond the established rules.

Bronson Howard, the first American to make his living solely by writing plays, explicitly spelled out these rules in a lecture on playwriting at Harvard in 1886. He held that plays must be "satisfactory" to an audience: for example, the death of a pure woman on the stage could not be termed satisfactory unless the play rose to the dignity of tragedy. One of his most bizarre assertions concerned the fate of those involved in a love triangle:

> There are axioms among the laws of dramatic construction as in mathematics. One of them is this—three hearts cannot beat as one. The world is not large enough, from an artistic point of view, for three good human hearts to continue to exist, if two of them love the third. If one of the two hearts is a bad one, art assigns it to the hell on earth of disappointed love; but if it is good and tender and gentle, art is merciful to it, and puts it out of its misery by death.[1]

The flaws in Howard's reasoning are so obvious that one can only wonder how in the world they were at one time so obediently followed. Anyone seriously involved in artistic creativity knows that "laws," how-ever clearly defined, can never be applied in this inflexible fashion. Attempting to apply the laws of science to art reduces the whole artistic process to rigid formulas—a practice, alas, only too common in How-ard's day. Howard and others judged what audiences "wanted" or would "permit" on the same misguided principles so uniformly apparent in mass entertainment in cinema and television, the modern replacements of popular theater. Audiences *accept* what they get because, with limited exceptions, that is *all* they get.

The escape from Howard's straitjacket involved the embrace of three dominant aesthetic styles in dramatic and theatrical art developing in both Europe and America. By war's end the Theatre Guild and O'Neill had so changed the concepts of what playwrights might create and audiences might welcome that the artificial limits of Howard's axioms were put aside for good. Further discussion of American drama between the wars cannot, therefore, proceed without establishing some reasonably serviceable definitions of these concepts.

Realism

By the end of World War I in 1918, three aesthetic styles of realism, its close relative naturalism, and the imaginative departure of expressionism began to turn the drama of Europe and, somewhat more slowly, that of America away from the romance and sentiment that had so consistently prevailed up to that time. Given that the history of any art represents a continuum from one era to the next, the changes evident in early twentieth–century American drama were not sudden or disturbing upheavals. In the case of realism, for instance, there had been exceptions within the existing patterns, indicating a growing awareness by American dramatists of the message from Europe.

The plays of James A. Herne had succeeded in remaining close to the common life and everyday existence within the urban middle class and among simple farm folk. Though unable to avoid completely Howard's "axioms" or some fairly stock plot complications, Herne had still been able to turn things around in *Margaret Fleming* (1890), with its convincing portrayal of a "fallen man" whose injured wife, remaining with him (not in the original version but in a subsequent revision by Herne's wife, who had created the role of Margaret), refuses to forget and forgive in an ending substantially devoid of conventional sentimentalities. Ahead of its time and ill received by contemporary audiences, the play still remains, for all its creakiness, surprisingly realistic in its treatment of an important domestic theme.[2]

The popular and prolific Clyde Fitch had portrayed more affluent levels of society. In *The Climbers* (1901) and *The City* (1909) his awareness of the sounds and patterns of actual speech and his comprehension of his characters' personalities provided his audiences with a startling picture of themselves and their often ridiculous and shallow behavior. Unfortunately, Fitch's treatment was pseudorealistic at best; his central figures were too often mere stage types, and he resorted to traditional melodramatic plots and happy endings. The standard Broadway fare was best represented by David Belasco, the greatest commercial producer of the era, whose meticulous attempts to reproduce the trappings of reality in his staging could not elevate his hack dramas (he wrote and mounted some 50 plays) into portrayals of truly believable action or character. Belasco's sole claim on posterity is the short romantic tragedy *Madame Butterfly* (1900), written with John Luther Long and now totally obscured by Puccini's more famous opera.

Their serious flaws notwithstanding, at the close of the nineteenth century Herne and Fitch, together with others such as Steele Mackaye and William Vaughn Moody, were important contributors to the changing attitudes about what might be staged. They were beginning to introduce into American drama an emphasis in story and theme that was based directly upon the often unsavory problems of contemporary society, already present in Europe in the controversial plays of Ibsen and to some extent in those of Shaw.[3] Stilted, stagey dialogue and set patterns of behavior were fast disappearing as characters increasingly talked and acted the same as anyone walking the streets outside the theater. Full acceptance by American writers and by the public was slow in coming, but the trend by the end of the war was irreversible.

This dramatic evolution was accelerated by the increasingly subtle use of electric stage lighting. Illumination by gas had existed since 1817 and by the 1880s had developed into a fine technique capable of brilliant effects controlled from a central panel. Limelights and the noisy, sputtering arc lights had been used as spots and floods as early as 1846, but with the advent of the incandescent bulb and its safe and more sensitive control through resistance dimmers, lighting entered the modern era with the first electric illumination of a stage in London's Savoy Theatre in 1881.[4] Now the stage technician could produce startling realistic illusions. Furthermore, while darkening the auditorium was not unknown with gas, electric lighting could instantly place the house in total darkness; as a result, the actors abandoned the custom of playing outward to a visible audience and turned inward to each other on the fully illuminated stage. The movement and stance of their characters became more natural, more representational, and less consciously and artificially theatrical.

The basic premise of stage realism is the depiction of the lives of ordinary people in ordinary settings, speaking and acting in what the audience will accept as an ordinary fashion. The entire stage picture thereby becomes a kind of photographic image very close to what is captured by even the simplest camera. Realistically detailed interior settings (exterior scenes have always been, and still remain, notoriously difficult to present as real) become the environment *within* which the actor performs. The entire mise-en-scène of the illusionistic setting puts Coleridge's "willing suspension of disbelief" to its most difficult test; but once the convention of the missing fourth wall is accepted, the audience can believe or, in Coleridge's term, not disbelieve, that the scene is reality itself. One may certainly argue that it is unrealistic to pretend that so artificial a situation, however photographically reproduced, is real, but stage realism does require that the scene and the characters be accepted as recognizable figures from the world out of which the audience has come and into which it will return.

Rapid changes in social conditions during and after World War I contributed to the strong public interest in this new kind of drama about the problems of ordinary individuals. The war had permanently ended the status and privilege of crowned heads and inherited nobility. Power, even in the vicious dictatorships that soon arose, emerged from currents of unrest and revolution deep within the base of society rather than at the top of the pyramid. The former absolutes of virtue and vice, the once clearly drawn lines between personal heroism and villainy, became indistinct and mostly irrelevant. The more fully conceived dramatic characters bore qualities of good as well as bad. The stage villain, as Ibsen had made evident in his realistic problem plays, was no longer just a human evil but also a social one; society itself, with its entrenched mores, controlled lives and exacted sacrifices from those who refused to fit into its traditional patterns. Individual heroes or heroines in the romantic sense had no legitimate place in realism. With characters behaving within the bounds of human nature as believable products of the society in which they lived, the outcome of a realistic play was often indeterminate or ambiguous, as in life, in which nothing really ever "comes out in the end."

With its unheroic characters, important only to themselves and those around them, and with its contemporary and frequently mundane themes, the realistic drama is not tragic in any classical sense of the term. Nor is it particularly comic. It stands somewhere in between, a "middle genre," as some have termed it. It can become the "problem play," sometimes with tragic overtones, sometimes with comic, but with emphasis on neither.[5] Whatever it may be called, it remains essentially a *realistic* play, its characters and ideas meant to be interpretations of the *realities* of life. As the twentieth century began, the changes in dramaturgy and theatrical effects had thus combined to assist in the rapid development of the artistic style defined as *realism*, identified in America and elsewhere as the dominant dramatic form for the last hundred years.

Naturalism

There is some truth in the not uncommon assertion that naturalism is no more than a variety of realism, and the two terms are often used interchangeably. True enough, the writer of dramatic naturalism shares the realist's interest in contemporary characters and themes; the "reality" of action and dialogue is very much the same, and stage settings maintain their realistic integrity. Dramatic realism and naturalism have distinctive qualities, however, and allowing as always for the inevitable crossing of boundaries, they can be readily differentiated.

The realistic view holds that society is the product of those who live within it and control it. In the naturalistic view, society itself is the controlling factor, and those who live within it are at its mercy. In realism the problems are created by the vagaries of human behavior, and any resolution comes about through the energies of the human beings involved. The exertion of human will controls the situation and determines the outcome. In naturalism human behavior is the product of social and natural constraints, including psychological forces beyond human control. Characters are trapped within their hereditary nature and within their surrounding environment. More pessimistic than the realist, the naturalist has a far bleaker view of human nature. Social and natural forces stacked against the characters render any struggle fruitless. The free will of the realist does not exist; the outcome is predetermined. Since their spiritual natures are submerged by their physical natures, characters act not through the freedom of sanctioned moral choice but because of irrepressible amoral drives.

The romanticist, believing in the inherent natural goodness of humankind, insists that beneath the veneer imposed by civilization lies a purity of thought and action that can be made visible by sending the characters into some real or symbolic Arcadia. In stripping away that veneer, the naturalist reveals the repellent beast motivated by instinctive animalistic drives. With unemotional objectivity the naturalist analyzes and dissects, treating the characters as little more than subjects for scientific scrutiny. The naturalistic world is a savage jungle where redeeming romantic love becomes destructive sexual lust and where rational human behavior is replaced by unrestrained primitive emotions.

In carrying the point forward, the naturalist often turns to the darker side of the human environment and has been accused of displaying the repugnant underbelly of existence for its own sake. It is an unfair accusation, for the conscientious naturalistic dramatic artist is far more interested in what is revealed about human behavior under social or economic deprivation than in the unattractiveness of the milieu. Still, the argument remains, and the opinion expressed by Henrik Ibsen summarizes an all-too-common outlook. Criticizing the sordidness of Emile Zola's late nineteenth–century naturalistic novels and plays, Ibsen is reported to have said words to this effect: "When I go into the sewer, I go to clean it out. When Zola goes into the sewer, he takes a bath."

Expressionism

The dramatic realist, freed from the false delicacies of the romantic, portrays the actual world of contemporary men and women, but at once serious questions arise: Can this kind of attempt to convey the literal truth be, in fact, art? Is this form of stage picture any more artistically viable than a photograph of the same thing? What room is there for genuine artistic individuality in presenting reality, other than a display of ingenuity in creating the illusion? The questions can be, and have been, endlessly debated, with no definitive resolution possible.

The means by which dramatic creations could be presented on the playwright's own terms were found in the simultaneous development of the nonrealistic aesthetic style of expressionism, not infrequently practiced by dramatists widely known for their realism. Furthermore, the increasing technical marvels available to the scene designer, permitting the introduction of ultrarealistic stage pictures, could just as easily be turned around to create scenes far removed from any attempt at verisimilitude. Heretofore held within the relatively neutral ground of impersonal objectivity needed to create a realistic illusion, playwrights discovered that they could subjectively *express* their viewpoints in a manner as unrestricted as they might wish. The subject matter was the same, but the writer's inventiveness and originality removed it from the literal or photographic, and thus possibly inartistic, style of realism.

For the first time in theater history, the stage became the artist's canvas, whereon a thoroughly personal interpretation of theme and idea could develop in a manner limited only by imagination and the physical restrictions of the stage. The expressionistic play sets no prescribed boundaries. Scenery may be sparse and distorted, with slanted walls, twisted doorways, and grossly exaggerated props. Lighting and sound may be equally distorted. Scenes may succeed each other in cinematic overlapping, and action may at times spill far out into the auditorium and among the audience. Characters can become automatons, their movements and speech equally mechanical, or they may appear as cartoonlike caricatures.

The prototype of expressionistic drama is generally considered to be *The Dream Play* (1902) by August Strindberg of Sweden.[6] It is a complex and confusing play, very difficult to stage, as action, scenery, and even characters follow the incoherent pattern of a dream; true to all dreams, there is no rational plot. Nonetheless, taken as a whole, *The Dream Play* makes sense as a vivid expression of the writer's picture of the nightmare of human existence, constantly emphasized by the statement that to be a man is a pitiful thing. During and after the war expressionism was best articulated by Georg Kaiser and Ernst Toller of Germany. Kaiser's *From Morn to Midnight* (1916), his *Gas* trilogy (1917–20), and Toller's *Man and the Masses* (1921) with the senseless furor and mechanized horrors of modern industrialized society driving its inhabitants to suicide or blowing the universe to kingdom come, are comprehensible even amidst the seeming madness of expressionistic character behavior. The emphasis of these and other expressionistic plays is the portrayal of human figures as helpless insignificant creatures who lack individual identity in an impersonal mechanistic society. There seems to be no way out, and a terrible destruction appears inevitable. Expressionism, taken all in all, becomes a literature of despair.[7]

The irony of the expressionistic outlook lies in the realization that the horrifying problems in the universe are of mankind's own making. Commerce and industry, business and politics, all creatures of the human intellect, turn, like Frankenstein's monster, upon those who have created them. The contaminated environment becomes Strindberg's fetid Foulstrand; the search for absolute power leads to Kaiser's annihilating Gas that Kills. These are not the deterministic forces of the naturalist, but are inventions that humanity has perpetrated against itself. Given enough strength of human will, these disasters could be overcome and the onrushing destruction avoided, but the practicing expressionist sees very little hope of so unlikely an event.

Expressionism as an aesthetic style has as many variants as practitioners, but one limitation does exist. The expressionistic playwright may legitimately seek to present his subjective views as imaginative expressions of reality, but at the same time the audience must be able to comprehend the artist's social or psychological premise, distorted or even alien as it may be. Complete understanding may not always be possible, but the expressionist will convey nothing to the audience if the point of departure is too esoteric or obscure.

The Theatre Guild

Among the important American producing companies active between the wars, none achieved the long-term success and artistic stature of the Theatre Guild. When it eventually became the sole producer of Eugene O'Neill, the partnership was unparalleled in its impact upon American theatrical history. No study of O'Neill can be completed without involving the Guild, and, conversely, the story of the Guild lies incomplete without O'Neill.

The life of the Washington Square Players was among the briefest of all the little theaters, but unlike many of them, in one way or another faded and forgotten, the Players quickly reappeared to become in remarkably short order the nation's preeminent stage company. Their accomplishments between 1915 and 1918 had been phenomenal, but as with all the variously struggling little theaters, the overwhelming majority of their productions—62 out of 68—had been one-acts. Their remarkably eclectic selections notwithstanding, the very small number of longer pieces kept the group from being regarded as a major producing company. Therefore, when wartime conditions ended their activities, Lawrence Langner, Lee Simonson, and others became intent on forming a new art theater that would carry the work of the Players beyond their previous restricted scope. The hope of the half-dozen enthusiastic members who met to discuss the possibilities on 19 December 1918 was to establish a thoroughly professional company capable of mounting high-quality, full-length drama on a regular basis.

In the course of successive and larger meetings, a board of six managers was formed to organize and administer what was to be called the Theatre Guild. Without an appointed or elected head figure, they worked in the spirit of the medieval trade guilds from which they deliberately took their name, performing collectively all organizational and management tasks. Although their limited subscriber list provided them with less than $1,000, having already leased the small Garrick Theatre on West 35th Street, they opened their announced spring season on 14 April 1919 with *Bonds of Interest* by the Spanish playwright Jacinto Benavente.[8] Its cast, performing for $25 a week, included Augustin Duncan, Mary Blair, and Dudley Digges, all of whom would become well-known, regular Guild performers. Playing Columbine, soon to reappear in *Aria da Capo*, was none other than Edna St. Vincent Millay.

This first production offered by the Theatre Guild was unsupported by the public and closed after four weeks. Determined to meet their promise of a two-play season, the Guild tried again, this time with *John Ferguson* by the Irish socialist playwright St. John Ervine. The day the play opened, 12 May 1919, the Guild held a bank balance of $19.50. Those who watched backstage knew that failure meant the end of everything. Walter Prichard Eaton, the Guild's first historian, reported, "It must have seemed to them at the time like nailing their flag to the mast and going down with colors flying."[9]

The dream did not collapse. *John Ferguson* was an immediate success. By July it moved into the much larger Fulton Theatre, a step that some members decried as tainting the dream with the commercialism of Broadway. With solvency a necessity if a second season was to be attempted, however, economic realities prevailed. Thus began the Guild's regular policy of running a play as long as possible in a Broadway theater while producing another at the Garrick or, in later seasons, at their own Guild Theatre.

By 1924 the Guild had proven itself to be a group of versatile professionals capable of undertaking any dramatic or theatrical task. Its prosperity had grown to the point where it could undertake the construction of its own house; the million-dollar 930-seat Guild Theatre was opened on West 52d Street on 13 April 1925. The great lobby and lounge areas, the ample spaces between seats, and the elimination of box seating and overhanging balconies contributed to its gracious atmosphere. A 48-foot stage, twice the depth of most Broadway theaters, and a modern lighting system made productions an aesthetic pleasure. "It was," noted Eaton, "a monument to the valiant and uncommercial spirit of the new playhouse in America, a monument to the community support of sound, disinterested dramatic art" (Eaton, 77).

As America stumbled toward establishing its own dramatic identity, the greatest contribution of the Guild during its early years was to set before American audiences strong proof of the viability of the new European methods of writing, staging, and directing and to build public acceptance, while at the same time proving profitable. Most important was the Guild's association with the irascible George Bernard Shaw. At first not quite convinced that the Guild could do him the justice he knew he deserved, Shaw eventually granted it the rights to fifteen of his plays in as many years; five of them had never been staged in Britain. [10] The Guild often ended its season with a play by Shaw, and though the relationship had cooled by the early thirties, it had brought considerable prestige to both sides.

Relying as heavily as it did on foreign plays, the Guild's board did not mount a play by a major American dramatist until Elmer Rice's *The Adding Machine* in 1923, followed the next year by Sidney Howard's *They Knew What They Wanted*. By the middle and late twenties, however, the Guild was promoting some dozen American writers. Foremost among them was O'Neill, whose *Marco Millions* received a lavish staging in 1928. Others who enjoyed a mutually beneficial relationship with the Guild were Maxwell Anderson, Sidney Howard, Robert Sherwood, S. N.

Behrman, and Philip Barry, all playwrights of more or less conventional style; Elmer Rice, John Howard Lawson, and John Wexley, with highly expressionistic creations; and Dorothy and DuBose Heyward and Paul Green, with their southern folk plays.

By its tenth anniversary in 1929, the Theatre Guild boasted 75,000 subscribers across the nation. During its second decade it continued to develop the talents of American writers while also staging foreign imports and Shakespearean classics, such as the unforgettably rowdy version of *The Taming of the Shrew* with Alfred Lunt and Lynn Fontanne in the 1935–36 season. By the end of the thirties, however, competing companies such as the Group Theatre and the Playwrights' Company were mounting plays that often surpassed what the Guild had to offer and proved equally popular with audiences, and the Guild no longer held the dominant place it had enjoyed for some 20 years. It continued its high quality of production but no longer held the corner in talent or in challenging ventures. Nevertheless, its influence on the commercial theater remained substantial. A considerable amount of its prestige continued through radio and television productions between 1945 and 1963. After World War II the Guild had begun to function primarily as a conventional commercial producing company. Enthusiasm for the new and different moved south to the burgeoning off- and off-off-Broadway theaters of Greenwich Village, completing an artistic circle begun so many years before by the enthusiastic amateurs and hopeful professionals from whom the Guild itself had sprung.

Enter the Son of James O'Neill

The manifesto of the Washington Square Players, inherited by the Guild, was unambiguous in its determined call for the production of plays avoided by the commercial theater. By the mid-twenties, however, it was clear that the commercial theater, with frequent, surprising success, was undertaking the kinds of plays that the Guild had previously assumed the regular Broadway theater could or would not do. In the New York season of 1925–26 the performance by a studio group from the Moscow Art Theatre, revivals of Ibsen by Eva Le Gallienne, works by left-wing American dramatists such as John Howard Lawson and John Dos Passos, and O'Neill's mystifying but powerful drama of masks and double identities, *The Great God Brown*, all staged far from the Guild's sheltering wing, compelled the Guild to face the reality that the original guidelines no longer provided a monopoly.

In his history of the Theatre Guild's first ten years, Walter Prichard Eaton, with undisguised echoes of Pirandello, dubs the Guild's board of Lawrence Langner, Philip Moeller, Helen Westley, Lee Simonson, Theresa Helburn, and Maurice Wertheim as "six characters in search of an American author" (Eaton, 41), thus noting what was apparently the board's sincere wish to discover a native writer who could fit their stated purpose. Until 1928 there had been passing comments by some professional critics questioning the Guild's neglect of O'Neill, who was already the winner of two Pulitzer Prizes and fast becoming the dominant American dramatic artist. The Guild seemed to have a peculiar blind spot that needed correction. Eaton acknowledges that the Guild had been taken to task for its apparently mysterious lack of interest in the one native dramatist who was writing what it was supposedly dedicated to, but he explains that the situation was not entirely a conscious act of avoidance but one that was "a story of temperaments, of those differences of opinion among artists which . . . seem matters of artistic principle at the time" (Eaton, 101). In retrospect, this may seem a rather lame rationalization, but it remained a plausible explanation in the eyes of the Guild's board. As early as 1919 O'Neill was not entirely pleased with the Guild's attitude when he wrote to his friend and critic, George Jean Nathan, "The Theatre Guild have seen [The Straw] and rejected it. They said it was most excellent but not the kind of play for their public. . . . I'm afraid they've become woefully worried about the supposed tastes of 'their public.' . . . My God! The trouble seems to be that you can't eliminate the weakness of the old Washington Square Players by merely changing the name. In my opinion the Guild is doomed to fail through the same timid endeavor to please 'their public.' "[11]

Once the differences were resolved and agreements reached for staging *Marco Millions* in 1928, the Guild became O'Neill's sole producer for the rest of his life, giving him everything he wanted, including its best actors and stage designers, even when there might have been serious reservations about the possibilities of success. This joining of forces—America's preeminent playwright with America's preeminent producing company, both direct products of the new spirit of the little theater movement—brought the American theater between the wars full tilt into the twentieth century, and for nearly a quarter-century thereafter into undisputed world leadership.

Eugene O'Neill's earliest playwriting was an outgrowth of the enforced leisure of his five months at the Gaylord Farm Sanitorium in Wallingford, Connecticut, where, between 24 December 1912, and 3 June 1913 he began his serious interest in reading drama, especially Strindberg.[12] By August 1913 he had written and copyrighted his first recorded one-act play, A *Wife for a Life*, a contrived little romantic melodrama about two gold miners. By July 1914 he had copyrighted a manuscript, "Children of the Sea," the first of his plays to illustrate his deep feeling for the sea. The same year he copyrighted *Abortion* and *The Movie Man*. The less said about any of them, the better. In August 1914, encouraged by a family friend, the scholar and critic Clayton Hamilton, O'Neill's father underwrote *"Thirst" and Other One-Act Plays*, a slim, stillborn volume that also included *The Web* (possibly the first play he wrote), *Recklessness*, *Fog*, and *Warnings*. This collection of heartrending melodramas with clever or sensational endings that overwhelm any realistic characterization is now a rare and valuable collector's item.

Although these early efforts came to nothing and generally deserve their lasting obscurity, the 26-year-old O'Neill, still with no personal means of support and uncertain of his future, took himself seriously enough to enroll in George Pierce Baker's 47 Workshop in September 1914, having stated unequivocally in his application letter, "I want to be an artist or nothing." His presence in the course convinced his tutor, his classmates, and himself that he was a rebel against the dramatic conventions of the day as Baker taught them. When he departed in May 1915, his formal education was permanently ended.

Living at home in New London in the summer of 1915, and in near destitution in Greenwich Village on his father's $10 weekly dole during the 1915–16 winter and spring, O'Neill would seem to have been unproductive. But by the time he appeared at the home of Hutchins Hapgood and joined the newly founded Provincetown Players in the summer of 1916, he had somehow managed during that interim to write five more plays, some copyrighted, some destroyed, none worthy of mention. What he did bring with him, however, was the revised "Children of the Sea," now titled *Bound East for Cardiff*.[13] When the Provincetown Players heard it read aloud for the first time, "we knew," reported Susan Glaspell, "what we were for" (Glaspell, 254).

The first production of a play by Eugene O'Neill, on 28 July 1916, suggests an almost unreal romantic adventure. The brief, emotional portrayal of the final moments of the dying Yank aboard the tramp steamer *Glencairn* was staged in the tiny Wharf Theatre. The dismal fog in the play was uncannily matched by the same conditions outside the theater, and the Provincetown foghorn provided an eerily appropriate sound effect. The tidewater beneath the shack washed around the dock and sent salt spray through the holes in the floor. If ever an environment contributed to a play's success, this was certainly it, as audience and players joined in a new theatrical adventure. From then on, the plays of Eugene O'Neill formed the keystone around which each Provincetown season was built.[14]

When *Bound East for Cardiff* opened on MacDougal Street on 3 November 1916, it was totally ignored by the Broadway critics. On 13 November Stephen Rathbun of the *Evening Sun* praised the Players and the play, and on 30 January 1917 Heywood Broun of the *Tribune* found that a "rich vein" was struck in the portrayal of the seamen. And that was all. The crew of the *Glencairn* reappeared as part of the season's first bill of the Washington Square Players on 31 October 1917 in *In the Zone*, the second O'Neill play to receive any critical notice. This timely bit of melodrama about a spy scare among the apprehensive crew sailing through the German submarine zone was reviewed mostly by second-string critics from New York's 12 daily newspapers for whom the Washington Square Players, not O'Neill, were the attraction. Burns Mantle, first-line critic of the *Mail*, apparently unaware that *Bound East for Cardiff* ever existed, noted that the Washington Square Players were presenting James O'Neill's son as a new playwright, erroneously observing that "this boy's first play" was the best of the lot.[15] O'Neill's third play, *The Long Voyage Home*, about a shanghaied crew member, appeared at the Playwrights' Theatre on 2 November 1917 and received no attention at all. On 20 December 1918 his fourth, *The Moon of the Caribbees*, an interlude in which the seamen are overcome by the enticements of rum and native women, was dismissed in only two brief notices.

A much lesser sea play, *Ile*, set on a whaling ship whose captain refuses to be defeated in his search for oil, even though being so long at sea is destroying the sanity of the wife who has accompanied him, was totally ignored when staged by the Provincetown on 30 November 1917. Ironically, when a competing company, the Greenwich Village Players, presented it on the following 18 April, it received 17 considerably mixed notices, two of which once more called attention to this talented "son of James O'Neill."

By the time O'Neill entered the uptown commercial theater with *Beyond the Horizon* in 1920, two more of his sea plays had been produced by the Provincetown. None achieved the stature of the *Glencairn* cycle and, like *Ile*, have remained interesting pieces lacking most of the notable traits that so distinguish the other four. In *Where the Cross Is Made* (1918) the old sea captain is driven mad by his obsession with nonexistent buried treasure. *The Rope* (1918), set by the shore, involves the sea only indirectly as the receptacle for a fortune tossed playfully into it by a slightly retarded child who loves to see the gold pieces skip over the water. Relying less on effective characterization and more on artificial melodramatics and sensational surprise endings, these three can readily be bypassed in any serious critical study.

The four *Glencairn* plays, on the other hand, deserve pause, not only for their historical interest as the plays that launched O'Neill but also for their dramatic significance. As early as 1911 O'Neill had been profoundly impressed by the themes and style of Dublin's Abbey Players, and his reading of Strindberg and other European playwrights was a strong influence in his rebellion against Baker's workshop practices, which still clung to the technical patterns of the nineteenth century. While not consciously a part of the new spirit, O'Neill soon stood at the head of America's advance guard, and the Provincetown Players were convinced that they had discovered someone of profound importance. The *Glencairn* plays, more than any others prior to 1920, awoke critics and public alike to an awareness that exciting theatrical events were happening.

The most remarkable aspect of the sea plays is the playwright's astonishing advance in all elements of dramatic technique beyond his early attempts. O'Neill had stumbled badly in the more than 30 plays he wrote up to 1920, varying from excellent to simply awful, an artistic inconsistency that was to disconcert his admirers throughout his life. From what we know of the surviving works, it is probably fortunate that half of his total output never saw production and that much of it was destroyed.[16] To compare the *Glencairn* plays to what he had done before 1916 is to marvel at the rapidly developing grasp of effective playmaking that O'Neill acquired within less than three years. The distance between *A Wife for a Life* and *Bound East for Cardiff* is a vast chasm. The wooden characters and the banality of theme and idea in the former, as well as in *Abortion* and *The Movie Man*, seem to have originated in an altogether different creative world. The blatant contrivances of *Fog* or *Thirst* or *The Web* seem to exist, as in any nineteenth-century potboiler, simply for their own shock value. The bleakness of embittered marriage and suicide in *Before Breakfast* (1916), or the pseudo-Shavian *Servitude* (1914), with its overtones of Ibsen, suggest ineffective parodies of European realism.

With the *Glencairn* plays, by whatever revelation his muse may have brought him, O'Neill came to grips with, and proved himself a master of, the portrayal of thoroughly believable realistic characters within equally believable realistic scenes. The patterns of character behavior, emotional at times, or even irrational, are consistently human and function dramatically without the introduction of extraneous gimmicks or theatrical contrivances. The result in the *Glencairn* plays is the creation of an effective dramatic unity never attained in the early plays. O'Neill himself was not sure about this unity when he told his friend and early biographer, Barrett Clark, that *"In the Zone* substitutes theatrical sentimentalities for truth."* Clark disagreed and felt that the other three plays would be incomplete without it.[17] Clark's assertion is borne out by the example of the plays' cohesion in the 1940 film *The Long Voyage Home*, adapted and directed by John Ford. The action was updated to the Second World War, and the few additional liberties taken did nothing to damage the impact. Ford sent Smitty to a heroic death in an air raid at sea and saved Olson from being shanghaied, but at the sacrifice of Driscoll's death aboard the hated *Amindra*. One of the finest pictures ever made of O'Neill's work, *The Long Voyage Home* remains a classic, even though it failed to gain widespread popularity. More important, O'Neill praised it as an exceptional picture that avoided "obvious Hollywood hokum or sentimental love bilge."[18]

This unity, remarkable in itself, cannot sufficiently explain what made these one-act dramas initially so effective or what has continued to make them popular. The foremost quality that keeps the plays lively and appealing is O'Neill's ability to project onto the stage the immediacy of the scene, through his awareness of the sailors' feelings in the forecastle, on deck, or in the waterfront saloon; of their genuinely human fears, frustrations, and animal energy; and of their lives, constantly overhung by the ominous realization that their long voyage will never take them home. They are characters created by an artist who had lived with them and had experienced their mental outlook and physical hardship. The assorted Cockney, Swedish, Irish, Russian, and American sailors are drawn from a life the playwright knew well. They are types, of course, and the likelihood in real life of such varied nationalities and dialects all assembled at one time in this small crew is very slim. But they are not stereotypes; they possess individuality, and their behavior quickly reflects their believable, three-dimensional identities in a manner never before seen in such short stage pieces.

Equally important is their lack of any resemblance to the familiar bell-bottomed stage tar who sang funny songs and danced hornpipes. O'Neill's seamen speak in the rhythms and diction of their own native languages. They are uncouth, hard-drinking, often spoiling for a fight, contemptuous of the "old man" and his authority, sick of the eternal drudgery, but trapped in the hopeless cycle: long voyages; short, wild escapades ashore, where hard-earned wages evaporate; and passages back to sea again.

In *Bound East for Cardiff*, with its setting in the cramped, inhospitable forecastle, O'Neill relied entirely on his characters to bring to the audience a feeling of the rough, almost inhuman hardships faced daily on the long, dangerous voyages of the plodding freighter. The dying, delirious Yank, who would have preferred to be buried on land, recalling the excitement of past brawls ashore; the grieving Driscoll, clumsily offering comfort but helpless to ease Yank's suffering while grasping for a long-forgotten prayer; the noisy, offensive Cocky and others—all convey the painful strain and distress of this agonizing deathwatch within an almost completely static dramatic situation.

In the Zone, leaning as it does toward contrived melodramatics, is still powerful in its demonstration of the hazards of violating the mutual trust that crewmen must have during their long, forced confinement at sea, devoid of women's company. In the end this display of men's emotions roused by an almost hysterical fear is more dramatically striking than any attempt to demonstrate literally the physical hazards of a defenseless tramp steamer entering the submarine zone. As the weeping Smitty cries out against the desecration of his pitiful love tokens, all the others, having so recklessly violated the most personal intimacies of their companion's life, stare in agony, unable to find any words to compensate for their insensitive blundering. In these final moments the realization of the hopelessness of assailants and victim alike turns the play into dramatic realism of the finest sort.

Even the trite plot of the shanghaied sailor manages to achieve a sense of real life with the sequences in the London waterfront bar of *The Long Voyage Home*. The abduction itself, which, once initiated, is quickly and relatively quietly executed, does not command attention as much as the atmosphere of the sleazy dive and the skulduggery of its disreputable inhabitants in taking advantage of the trusting Olson. The ironies are not contrived but believably realistic as the roaring gang, supposedly respecting and protecting Olson's determination to remain sober and to leave the sea for good, recklessly dispense their wages in the immediate pleasures of whiskey and women and abandon their shipmate to the well-known horrors of the freighter *Amindra*. The callousness of Fat Joe and Nick, the touching quality of the sympathetic but trapped

Freda, combine to create an almost unbearable tension on stage while the audience fruitlessly hopes that Olson will somehow escape. The grip of the sea is too much. It has held out to Olson his longed-for chance to gain his freedom with his hard-earned accumulated wages, but in its sinister nature the sea has treacherously captured and destroyed him. It continues to do the same to all those who live by it or who would attempt to defy it.

The most original of the four *Glencairn* plays, and in many ways the most convincingly realistic, is *The Moon of the Caribbees*. The vignette of rough men in the thrall of a humid tropical night, unwillingly held to their ship without shore leave, does more than any of the other *Glencairn* plays to drive home an awareness of the nearly intolerable emotional pressures that can explode under these circumstances on just about any pretext. The crew find temptations of the flesh too much to ignore as the sensuous native women bring to the foredeck food and forbidden rum, as well as their accessible bodies. Release of pent-up frustrations is uninhibited; the resulting brief but bloody violence is inevitable. In its midst, the primitive crooning from the shore provides a striking contrapuntal effect. All is not centered on the crew's rowdy antics, however. O'Neill provides the contrast of the quiet discussion between the emotionally unstable Smitty, a plainly displaced person (perhaps O'Neill?) amid this crew, and the aging, philosophical Donkeyman—both of whom refuse to participate.

The full moon, the calm sea and motionless ship, the white coral beach fringed with coconut palms, and the mournful music would seem the proper idyllic background for sentimentality and romance. Not so, in O'Neill's view of things. The sailors are discordant here, as everywhere, forever moving as strangers from port to port, experiencing moments of excess in pleasure and many more hours of paying dearly for them. In this male world women are dreamed of as Smitty dreams of Edith, or vilified, as by the Donkeyman: "White, brown, yeller 'n' black. A whack on the ear's the only thing'll learn 'em." Or they are cheated, like the native women who are denied their pay for the food they have brought. It is a world where the romance of the sea has no place, where exotic ports of call are unfriendly and dangerous. It is O'Neill's picture of men without women, coping as they can with the sea to which they are almost hypnotically drawn, engaged in a deadly one-on-one struggle, placed in impossible defensive positions, always, in the end, overcome and controlled by the ocean's unassailable power.

The three other sea plays—*Ile*, *The Rope*, and *Where the Cross Is Made*—are inferior to the *Glencairn* sequence. Their melodramatics are too contrived, their characters too flat and undeveloped. Collectively, however, all seven stand far in front of nearly all the other plays written at the same time by the various practitioners of the new spirit. They remain the best of the genre and among the best plays, one-act or full-length, in this fledgling American theater.

O'Neill's last produced one-act play was *Exorcism*, written in 1919 and staged by the Provincetown on 26 March 1920. Based on his own suicide attempt in 1912 and too nakedly autobiographical, it was a deserved failure. O'Neill destroyed all copies, and it was never revived. By the mid-twenties, as the original Provincetown struggled through its reorganization traumas and other little theater groups disappeared, full-length plays had become much more common. In effect, with O'Neill's *The Dreamy Kid*, undertaken by the Provincetown on 31 October 1919, the era of the one-act play was at an end.[19]

It had taken years for this "young man" to stand entirely on his own, no longer in the shadow of his famous parent. Echoes of his father's long-running vehicle *The Count of Monte Cristo* were to follow him well into the future and, in some critical opinions, were never completely shed, but if this "son of Monte Cristo" was unable entirely to avoid them, he would soon be able to transform those echoes into dramatic substance commanding eventual worldwide attention and respect.

3

Eugene O'Neill

From Nobody to the Nobel

To refer to Eugene O'Neill before 1920 as a nobody is not as inaccurate as it might first appear. The effect of the new spirit, important as it was in the little theaters, had yet to make any meaningful impression on the commercial theater. The Neighborhood, the Washington Square, and the Provincetown, frequently mounting productions of near-professional quality, remained amateurs at heart. The Lewisohns were adamant in refusing to capitalize on their successes by moving them out of Grand Street, and Jig Cook never visualized the Provincetown as competitive with uptown.

O'Neill's unique qualities were recognized by those among whom he worked as a regular, albeit exceptional, member of his company, and he lived the hand-to-mouth existence of his peers. Reviews by those few critics who made the effort to get to Greenwich Village often noted his superiority over the others who shared the evening's bill, but his recognition by audiences beyond the little theater subscribers was virtually nonexistent.

Had O'Neill done nothing more after 1919 he would be remembered as the one who brought respect to the one-act genre, a factor of primary importance to the Provincetown Players. So far as the mainstream New York theater was concerned, however, he was for all intents and purposes a nobody. Once he moved into the longer forms, he quickly became the most widely discussed figure in the American theater. By 1936, just 16 years after his first Broadway appearance, Eugene O'Neill had been awarded an honorary doctorate from Yale and had received not only three Pulitzer Prizes but the Nobel Prize for Literature as well. His impact upon American drama and theater during that period was profound, extensive, and permanent.

O'Neill's abandonment of the one-act play did not make the quality of his work any more consistent than it had been during his four-year stay with the Provincetown. Dismal failures balanced phenomenal successes in almost equal numbers among his 21 produced plays. Nowhere was this contrast more apparent than in the last two prewar plays, the hugely popular *Ah, Wilderness!* (1933) and the roundly condemned *Days without End* (1934). O'Neill's constant experimentation in form and style puzzled, delighted, and infuriated critics and public alike, prompting more than one bewildered reviewer, racing to as many as four O'Neill openings within a single season, to cry "Hold, enough!" in an effort to persuade this overenthusiastic artist to slow down, to determine just who he was, and above all, to find some consistent pattern for his artistry. The cries, as usual, went unheeded, and O'Neill continued to astonish and confound his severest detractors.[1] Though often stung by a particular adverse reaction, he was never one to linger over his failures.[2] He proceeded on to the next task, trying new tacks, revealing himself in those plays that did succeed as a playwright with a masterful sense of theater that transcended his acknowledged shortcomings.

Because of his unpredictability, his broad oscillation between stylistic extremes, and his controversial subject matter—miscegenation, adultery, incest, madness, religious fanaticism—opinions about O'Neill were seldom if ever moderate. He was either praised, sometimes irrationally, or condemned in similar manner. One either embraced or detested him; there was rarely a middle ground. The award of the 1936 Nobel Prize settled nothing; limited but strong dissent countered the widespread approval.[3]

Two things kept O'Neill going regardless of the frequency of his falls from grace. On one side, the public, whose physical and emotional endurance he often taxed to the limit, always gave him another chance. Nobody was ever quite sure what a new O'Neill play might bring, so the anticipation of the unknown was a constant attraction. On the other and more important side was the willingness of his backers to ignore the recurrent slippage. Thus encouraged, O'Neill had a constant incentive to try again. First Jig Cook, then the triumvirate of Macgowan, Jones, and himself, and finally the Theatre Guild all led him to expect that whatever he wrote would be produced.

The Journeyman Experimenter: Greenwich Village and Uptown, 1920–1925

Eugene O'Neill's service under the tutelage of Jig Cook and the Province-town from 1916 to 1919 had provided this enigmatic but exceptionally talented dramatist with a successful four-year apprenticeship that gave him every opportunity to develop his unique creative skills and to find himself as an artist. By 1920 O'Neill was becoming increasingly willing and eager to take the important if risky step of moving uptown beyond the restrictions of the Greenwich Village little theaters. Once the step uptown was taken, he entered his journeyman years, not yet the full master of his trade but quite capable of proceeding on his own. The skills attained during the apprenticeship continued to develop, but wide variants in style and technique still prevented critics as well as audiences from determining precisely where his artistry fit in.

The move out of Greenwich Village was provided by producer John Williams, who had long been interested in getting O'Neill to Broadway. The move was an exasperatingly long time in coming, and O'Neill almost gave up. Williams's "dilatory tactics," as O'Neill described them in a letter to Nathan in 1919 (Roberts, 33), forced him to violate his earlier agreement that Williams would have first choice on future plays by giving his next, the first version of *Anna Christie*, to another agent. After several renewed options, Williams finally ceased procrastinating and staged O'Neill's first uptown opening and his first full-length play produced anywhere, *Beyond the Horizon*, on 2 February 1920. A grim near-tragedy of the thwarted lives of two brothers, set against the stark background of a New England farm, it featured a devastating fatal outcome with no hope of any happy conclusion, a sharp contrast to the less substantial fare of the Broadway norm.

Producing a work so markedly different, so strenuously against the tide, cautioned Williams to hedge his bet with limited matinee performances rather than making an all-out leap into the more traditional nightly run. Moreover, he chose not to risk sending his actors into this questionable undertaking without some backup of their own, so he assembled a cast already committed to regular evening performances elsewhere.

Success was immediate. The critical and popular acceptance of *Beyond the Horizon* and the resulting Pulitzer Prize mark 1920 as the turning point in the development of modern American drama. The play proved that a more mature audience was fully prepared to accept and appreciate serious, realistically conceived theater. O'Neill's former mentor, George Pierce Baker, was prompted to write: "A public which heartily welcomes *Beyond the Horizon* is not the old public."[4] *Beyond the Horizon* soon settled in for a respectable, regularly scheduled run.

Shortly before his death in 1920, James O'Neill, so often despairing of his son's future, was privileged to attend a performance. Although he was obviously pleased, and although he recognized that a new era in American theater was at hand, the old swashbuckling romantic hero objected strenuously to the hopeless ending. "What are you trying to do," he is reported to have asked, "send the audience home to commit suicide?" The plot of *Beyond the Horizon*, which bothered the elder O'Neill with its sordidness and inevitable catastrophe, was not the only break with the past. What O'Neill attempted to do dramatically with his characters and theatrically with his staging was equally important. The results were not entirely successful, but they served notice that O'Neill as a serious artist was determined that the behavior of his characters and the environment in which they appeared were to be believable and hence dramatically realistic.

There are no villains and no heroes in *Beyond the Horizon*. Actions and reactions are those of undistinguished, down-to-earth rural folk with emotions that rise naturally from what they are. Robert and Ruth, young and romantically impressionable, cannot see beyond the thrilling intimacy of their suddenly discovered love; their impetuous decision in the play's opening sequence to forgo their expected paths, he to make the voyage with his uncle, she to marry the steady, industrious brother, Andrew, is a believable consequence. The outrage of the offended father and the acceptance of the situation by Andrew may at first seem contrived in order to head the plot quickly toward its foregone conclusion, but such is not really the case. This drastic last-minute switch in long-established plans could easily send any family patriarch with the temperament of James Mayo into fury. Any brother as fond of his sibling as Andrew is shown to be could well be one to offer himself for the voyage, however unacceptable the compromise would be to the parent. Throughout the remainder of the play the characters continue to move without contrivance, coincidence, or arbitrary outside force. The strain of manual labor in keeping the farm in working order is too much for the weak-willed, weak-bodied dreamer Robert. His helpless inability to act drives Ruth to understandably angry recriminations as they lose their only child and sink into financial collapse and emotional despair. Andrew, on the other hand, corrupted by his fateful decision into becoming a cynical "operator" unable to see a single romantic attraction in the stinking ports of call into which he has sailed, returns to watch Robert die on the ruined farm and to hurl accusations against Ruth for what she has apparently done to his brother. These are not attractive scenes, but they are logical and real. All of the characters have their just claims on audience sympathy; each is equally wrongheaded and stubborn. Human compulsion, driving out reason, has set them on the path of death or emotional disaster. Nowhere can blame be put except upon this irrational but very human behavior.

Going beyond well-established dramatic realism in the characters and their motivations in his use of theatrical realism in the setting of *Beyond the Horizon*, O'Neill made a calculated effort to bring the stage picture directly into the play's development; he attempted to have it accomplish more than what his characters convey by themselves by visually augmenting the theme of deterioration and despair. Unlike the overwhelming naturalistic detail of a Belasco setting, *against* which the actor was forced to work, O'Neill asked that the setting become a coperformer, unobtrusive yet clearly participatory. In the first act the small sitting room of the Mayos' farmhouse is "clean, well-kept," showing "the orderly comfort of a simple, hard-earned prosperity enjoyed and maintained by the family as a unit." In each succeeding act the room reflects the disintegration of that family unit. At first a bit shabby and uncared for, by the final scene, corresponding to the desolation of Robert and Ruth after the death of their child, it "presents an appearance of decay and dissolution," with torn, dirty curtains, broken furniture, and blotched wallpaper. Physical as well as psychological ruin is now complete.

Less successful was the division of each act into alternating interior and exterior scenes. Reacting to criticism of this apparent clumsiness, which seemed to lengthen the play to no purpose, O'Neill explained that he had tried "to get rhythm, the alternation of longing and loss" into the play's basic physical structure. He felt that the audience unconsciously understood his point because "it is often easier to express an idea through such means than through words or mere copies of real actions" (Gelb, 411–12). O'Neill employed the exterior scenery in the same manner in which he had used the altered interior of the farm-house to reflect the altered situations of the characters. The same vista of a section of country road between grassy banks with gnarled apple tree, snake fence, and fields stretching toward the horizon is used for the opening scene with its ecstasy of love and for the last scene with its despairing welcome of death. As young love blossoms, so does the ancient apple tree, with the distant fields greening in the May twilight. In the final misery of the distraught family, the tree seems dead, and the fields lie brown in the autumn chill. The symbolic point that nature's pattern follows that of sorrowing humanity is plain enough, if a bit artificial. What is not so plain is any self-evident "alternation of longing and loss" through the awkward scenic switchbacks. O'Neill's assertion that audiences would know what he meant, even unconsciously, pre-sumed something more than most audiences would be willing to ac-knowledge. It is not clear just how O'Neill concluded that alternating scenes could be more impelling than words, since every character speaks plainly of the disappointment and disillusionment over what has taken place. Unfortunately, this was not the only occasion in which O'Neill was to learn that what he saw as obvious within his scheme was simply too subtle for even the most sophisticated viewer.

Beyond the Horizon shows, as well, some of the problems of a playwright not yet the master of the longer form. Characters are accept-ably well developed, and they move and speak with reasonable motiva-tion, but events, while logically worked out, are readily predictable. Furthermore, the physical decline of everything and everybody, including Mrs. Mayo's descent into crabbed and crippled old age, plus the loss of the child, come close to overdoing things just for the depressing effect. The final death scene on the grassy bank is strained and too painfully extended. The most striking point, however, is that O'Neill was able to force his audience to accept the death of the central figure without assum-ing that things will work out for the survivors. Robert is physically dead, but so are the spirits, if not the bodies, of Andrew and Ruth, each torn apart by anger, hatred, and greed. The play's ending is in the best realistic tradition, as the curtain falls on an indeterminate conclusion. Robert Mayo has died, his hand stretched toward his unattainable horizon, but nothing is resolved; the world and its problems go on. Williams's initial hesitation to produce the play can be understood; at the time, happy solutions and joyful endings of reconciliation, or even touchingly senti-mental romanticizations of death scenes, remained the prevalent denoue-ments. From the perspective of more than half a century later, however, with audiences more inured to the starkness of dramatic realism, *Beyond the Horizon* is far less grim than it initially appeared.

Two elements in character and theme, central to much of what O'Neill was to treat in later plays, are firmly established in *Beyond the Horizon*. The first is the portrayal in Robert Mayo of the idealistic, impractical dreamer, physically and emotionally out of place in the world around him, carrying within his soul the touch of the poet and often resembling in appearance and mannerisms O'Neill himself. (Smitty of *The Moon of the Carribees* comes immediately to mind.) Opposing him is the unimaginative and practical-minded Andrew, who functions as the world expects, not infrequently with mocking cynicism, and who is often no more successful in life's accomplishments than the dreamer. The second element is the ironic paradox of O'Neill's artistic theme: existence becomes meaningless without the dreams of the romantic ideal, for life, if faced head on in all its sordid realities, is unbearable; simultaneously, the dream, if improperly pursued, destroys. All too often, as well, the pursuer of dreams can find no acceptable place in a society that rejects this "impractical" unreality, and destruction can descend with equal force. But to do without the dream is to lose one's soul; one cannot live without the dream, and one cannot ultimately survive as a viable human being even with it. Robert sentimentally succumbs to a moonlight-and-roses moment he mistakes for love and pays dearly for it in abandoning his lifelong dream of an exotic world voyage. Andrew impetuously abandons his more sensible dream of a solid, productive life on the farm. Both, of course, pay for their follies. But would Robert have found the dream beyond the horizon? Probably not, for horizons have a disorienting habit of steadily receding. He might have found beauty and romance in distant ports, but he would have been unable to avoid the stench and misery that so appalled his brother. On the other hand, Andrew's unimaginative refusal to see the poetic beauty that could be found if he looked closely enough keeps him as shallow as the idealistic Robert. It is a dichotomy that constantly worried the artist in O'Neill, and he explored its ironies and contradictions throughout his career.

With public acceptance of *Beyond the Horizon*, the identification of Eugene O'Neill as the quintessential dramatic realist in all the commonly accepted meanings of the term appeared well established. But nine months after *Beyond the Horizon*, *The Emperor Jones*, staged at the Playwrights' Theatre on 1 November 1920, shattered all previous conceptions about the direction O'Neill's artistry was taking. Nothing of its kind had ever been seen or heard in the New York theater; nobody was prepared for it. Its notoriety quickly spread, and the demand to see it swamped the Provincetown's tiny facilities.

Aside from the stylistic aspects, exceptional enough, the extent of O'Neill's daring in *The Emperor Jones* was shown in his unprecedented creation of a black protagonist to be played not by a white performer in blackface but by a black actor. Theretofore, the best a black actor in New York could anticipate was a subsidiary role as a servant or slave, a bum or whore, or a shuffling, ludicrously comic figure. Outside of black theater strictly for blacks, there was no serious role available, no matter what the talent. O'Neill had experimented with an all-black cast in *The Dreamy Kid*, his last one-act play at the Provincetown, on 31 October 1919,[5] but there is nothing in this brief melodrama about a gangland fugitive called Dreamy, who refuses to abandon his dying grandmother as the law closes in, that marks the play as distinctively "black." It could be done equally well with any ethnic group or, indeed, with whites. Its uniqueness lies in O'Neill's decision to do it as a black drama that avoids all the usual stereotypes by presenting black characters with close emotional relationships in a deadly serious situation.

The Emperor Jones was a wholly different matter. This terrifying picture of the mental and physical deterioration of the once arrogantly proud self-styled Emperor, the former Pullman porter turned brutal and exploitive dictator, demanded a powerful black actor, whom the Provincetown was fortunate to find in Charles Gilpin. His electrifying performance as Brutus Jones stunned the normally blasé New York audiences.

It would be a major error to interpret *The Emperor Jones* as simply a presentation of what has come to be called the American "black experience," that is, the white man's prolonged and cruel subjugation of an "inferior" race. To be sure, that experience had placed Brutus Jones in a substratum of society wherein the most prestigous position available was to serve the "white quality" on Pullman cars, but the exploitive degradation of blacks as such, denying them human dignity by keeping them "in their place," is not the concern of O'Neill or his protagonist. Brutus Jones is no representative of the contemporary injured black driven to violence or other antisocial acts by the white society around him. The point is not that he is black but that he typifies *all* human beings whose veneer of civilization is very thin compared to the depth of primitiveness within them. In *The Emperor Jones* O'Neill made no effort to decry or condemn the specifics of the white man's behavior. He was not appealing on behalf of the black. The message is much broader and more universal, having nothing to do with race or racism. What O'Neill succeeded in doing so brilliantly was to make use of the relatively short history of the blacks' close association with Western civilization as a paradigm of all human experience. Humankind's rise from the primordial jungle to domination of the natural world was a matter of eons. As O'Neill saw it, this rise led not to ultimate liberation of the human spirit but, over the millenia, to the loss of human dignity and an eventual surrender to the underlying savagery that had remained beneath the surface, covered but not always kept subdued, as in the essentially pessimistic view of the naturalists, by the veneer of "civilization." For the enslaved blacks, ruthlessly torn from their natural and often highly civilized African roots, thrown into the outside white world, the process was a matter of but a few generations. They were initially subjected to the same destructive forces that dominated those who had dominated them. In the paradigmatic black experience shown in the play, humankind's progression from "savagery" to "civilization" was considerably foreshortened.

By his own admission, O'Neill repeatedly interpreted in his plays the biblical dictum that one cannot profit in gaining the whole world while losing one's soul. In *Jones* this idea receives its first and in many ways its most powerful expression. In his brief hour upon the stage, Brutus Jones not only proves its validity but projects O'Neill's often quoted insistence that he was interested not in the relationship of man to man but in that of man to God. Jones, in acquiring all of the worst traits of those from whom he learned his lesson in the parlor cars—greed, ostentation, lust for power, wily dominance—has set himself up as godhead. He has erected around himself the myth that he is impervious to any threats or dangers from his subjects, whom he regards with contemptuous scorn as "ignorant niggers," deprecating his own race and, ironically, his own pomposity. Having cheated and killed and brutalized his way to the top, he is totally devoid of any redeeming spiritual nature. In short, he has gained the world.

The chilling destruction, bit by bit, of the proud Emperor is a fascinating theatrical display of the loss of soul in one's constant insistence on relying wholly upon himself. As Jones faces the Little Formless Fears after plunging confidently into what he assumes is the protective forest, and then progresses through the frightening visions of his own past and his race's past, he has no inner strength to fall back on. He has boasted to Smithers, the oily and sinister trader in his palace, that he has "put my Jesus on the shelf"; it is no longer a useful adjunct to survival. Recognizing too late that some sort of spiritual basis is necessary, he cries out to the God that white "civilization" has taught him to rely on, but that

God is no longer there. Instead, it is the savage Witch Doctor who meets him with the pursuing alligator god, whom his bullets may frighten and cast out of his hallucinations but cannot finally eliminate. Jones has been reduced to a whimpering creature, crawling reptilelike on the ground, surrounded by his vengeful former subjects.

The Emperor Jones is essentially a monologue, bracketed by opening and closing sequences with Smithers and the natives, a plotless piece running without intermission for little more than an hour. In scene after scene the only speech is Jones's ongoing chatter to himself as he tries to control his steadily rising panic.[6] But the portrayal of Jones as a character was not alone in making *The Emperor Jones* the sensation of its day. It was O'Neill's theatricality in his use of the techniques of expressionism that overwhelmed audiences and established the play as a significant American theater milestone.

O'Neill never acknowledged any direct influence from European expressionism, but in his reading of Strindberg and others he would have encountered and been impressed by their break from traditional forms. Himself an innovator and never an imitator, O'Neill was able to use the tenets of expressionism while going his own way in *The Emperor Jones*, the first important American expressionistic play. It remains uniquely apart from its European forebears. Instead of becoming an automaton, a dehumanized end product of modern mechanistic society, Jones disintegrates into helplessness as a result of his own undermining pride, guilt, and greed. In a reversal of the more common expressionistic characterization, O'Neill keeps his protagonist thoroughly human. The jungle through which Jones flees is the real thing; his pursuers, his erstwhile subjects, are very real as well. What Jones sees, and what the audience sees, are projections of the images of Jones's mounting internal fears and his vivid recollections of a personal and racial past, all part of the workings of a rapidly failing mind collapsing under increasingly intolerable stress. The result is a harrowing *expression* of a character's self-annihilation.

The success of O'Neill's form of expressionism resulted from the Provincetown's determination, through Jig Cook, to convey everything on stage that O'Neill wanted. To do so demanded considerable ingenuity, but Cook was willing to try anything and to spend the money to do it. The Provincetown's meager facilities had been remarkably adaptable to the uncomplicated interior sets for the sea plays, but here was a brand-new challenge. O'Neill called for a background that could enhance the movement of light and shadow for his expressionistic projections. The creases and light absorbency of traditional cyclorama fabric made the effects very

The Emperor Jones *(Eugene O'Neill, 1920). The chain gang scene shows the remarkable use to which Cleon Throckmorton put the plaster dome of the Provincetown Playhouse. The curved surface, appropriately back-lit, gave an illusion of infinite depth, while the cut-out shadows projected against it created the entangling forest in which Jones is trapped.*

difficult to produce. Convinced that O'Neill's new kind of playwriting required entirely new staging, Cook happily emptied the Players' limited treasury of a few hundred dollars and took the gamble of building a device already familiar in Europe, the permanent solid plaster dome constructed on a metal framework surrounding the stage on three sides and replacing the cyclorama.

Against the dome's bluish, sandy surface, the lighting effects gave an eerie sense of infinite distance. Instead of complex dimensional properties, designer Cleon Throckmorton created silhouetted hangings that could be flashed on and off in sequence, eliminating distracting set changes for the rapidly shifting scenes. The threatening trees and vines of the jungle, the shadowy images of chain gang, murder, slave auction block, and slave ship, appeared and disappeared soundlessly as projected shadows combined with the stylized movement of silent, menacing human figures. Illuminated to indicate the rising moon, the dome threw a ghostly white glow on the doomed Jones, while the seemingly limitless sky highlighted the jungle's "relentless immobility." When darkened, the dome emphasized the horrors of the slave ship's hold, with its chained, suffering creatures. And under everything, punctuating the action, the incessant drumbeats, starting at normal pulse rate but rising in tempo and intensity to incite the hysteria of performers and audience alike. From the opening scene in the garish audience chamber, with its glaring whites and scarlets and overbearing throne, through multiplying hallucinations, to Jones's execution by the natives, O'Neill and his fellow artists had brought American stagecraft into the modern era with unprecedented suddenness. Cook's risk had paid off handsomely.

Presented in an era when blacks on the Broadway stage were held to secondary or minor character roles, and when Al Jolson could cover his face with burnt cork, paint on grossly thick red lips, and stomp the floor while belting out "Mammy," there would in all probability have been no objection to Brutus Jones in minstrel-style blackface. To his credit, O'Neill knew how that distortion could destroy his play, but there was still a considerable risk involved in what he chose to undertake. He could have been accused of racism in his portrayal of Jones, who almost becomes a caricature of the common view of the black as an ignorant, lodge-going simpleton strutting in his garish crimson getup. He could have been seen as furthering the stereotype of the superstitious, fearful black man panicking at shadows and surrendering without control to the "ha'nts" surrounding him. No such accusations have ever been made. Those who saw the play and wrote about it could accept it for what it was and praise its accomplishments without accusing O'Neill of any patronizing downgrading of the black as a human being. Oliver Sayler, writing in *Freeman* shortly after the play's opening, thought it failed because of O'Neill's "plunge into the field of Negro psychoanalysis," hardly an astute view of what the play was all about.[7] Hubert Harrison of *Negro World* was precisely on the mark in stating that it was aimless to criticize the play because it "does not elevate the Negro"; he recognized that it could have been written about any race anywhere.[8] The British critic John Shand, writing in the *New Statesman* after seeing Paul Robeson's London performance, objected to the play's episodic nature and concluded that it "will never be famous [because] there are so many plays with good ideas spoilt by wrong treatment."[9]

The Emperor Jones has remained a permanent fixture in the American theater, always a reminder of its creator's venturesome antiestablishment originality.[10] Its portrayal of what Jung saw as mankind's compulsion toward racial primitivism, its striking illustration of the results of human self-centeredness and lack (or loss) of faith, and its sheer riveting theatrical nature have kept it one of O'Neill's most permanently respected works. Demands on the actor, brief as the play is in elapsed time, are prodigious, and only the very best dare try it. But most important is what the play accomplished. In the words of Travis Bogard, "The technical excitements of the play, with its drums, its sustained monologue, its rapidly shifting settings framed into a single desperate action were almost blinding in their virtuosity and in their assurance of important theatrical things to come. Not only the literate American drama, but the American theatre came of age with this play."[11]

Within six months after *The Emperor Jones*, the up-and-down success-failure syndrome that was to dog O'Neill for the rest of his career resumed. On 27 December 1920, the day when *Jones*, no longer able to accommodate the demand in the Village, moved uptown to complete its run of more than 200 performances, the Provincetown offered *Diff'rent*. A limited nod from the critics prompted its uptown move in the hope of capitalizing on the support given *Beyond the Horizon* and *Jones*, but the shift proved fatal; audiences stayed away. It is surprising that it lasted 100 performances. It has never been successfully revived, and to read it is to wonder how any audience appeal could be assumed in this depressing story of an impossibly prudish New England spinster. The weakness of the play lies in its characterization, especially in the unimaginative rigidity of Emma Crosby. Her change from the puritanical, idealistic maiden who insists that her fiancé be "diff'rent" from other men into the repressed, coquettish old maid with painted face and dyed hair is totally unconvincing. Moreover, with the ludicrous personality change thrust suddenly at the audience in a second act set 30 years after the first, and with a concluding double suicide of the protagonist and her erstwhile fiancé, this pseudo-Strindbergian attempt at a naturalistic sex battle falls embarrassingly flat.

On 1 June 1921 an even more dismal creation called *Gold* appeared; it quickly disappeared after less than two weeks. It was a very early work (the one-act *Where the Cross Is Made* had been lifted from it), and its unabashed use of romantic devices would have been welcomed by the world of James O'Neill. Buried treasure, ghostly hallucinations infinitely inferior to those of *Jones*, and a mad sea captain should have shamed its creator into keeping it locked safely away.

Fortunately, recovery was complete. One year and one day after *The Emperor Jones*, O'Neill's second Pulitzer Prize winner, *Anna Christie*, opened on 2 November 1921. The abortive road tryout more than a year and a half earlier as *Chris* (it received two other titles, *Chris Christopherson* and *The Ole Davil*, before finally settling down) forced O'Neill to redo the whole idea, wisely removing the emphasis from the old sailor

Chris to his daughter Anna. A far more acceptable, realistic trio of characters—the sea-hating father, the land-hating daughter, and the burly stoker caught between them—emerged in a convincing plot line with an inherent sense of humanity, both serious and comic.

It could be said of this fairly traditional, well-made play that O'Neill's introduction of the sense of fate, of man's inability to manage his own destiny in the face of the immutable force of the "davil," the sea, is determinism in the best naturalistic tradition. It is true that old Chris's well-laid plans to save his only child from the fatefully debilitating effects of the sea backfire in the girl's "worse-than-death" experiences on land, and it is true that the sea in turn thwarts his best efforts to keep his daughter from its deadly grip by tossing up the castaway Mat Burke to confound him. It is difficult, however, to regard what happens as the imposition upon the unwary threesome of any predetermined naturalistic fate. What has been thrust upon them in past and present is the ironic result of Chris's shortsighted ignorance, Anna's personal determination to escape an intolerable situation among her insensitive relatives, and a not uncommon accident at sea that delivers Mat onto the barge. Nothing is beyond realistic credibility.

O'Neill's ability to be more true to life than to any particular dramatic style or form is well shown in *Anna Christie*. Chris's attitude toward the deadly powers of his old antagonist, the sea, is the same traditional fatalism of the sailors aboard the *Glencairn*. Burke is a full believer in free will, and Anna, though a realist in outlook, has a perfectly rational feeling that chance rules their lives. Burke at one point exclaims, "For I've a power of strength in me to lead men the way I want, and women, too, maybe, and I'm thinking I'd change you to a new woman entirely." Anna, less hopeful that her past can be wiped out, surmises that what happens in life is not anyone's fault. People "yust get mixed in wrong, that's all." Only Chris remains, on the surface, a fatalist, but by blaming the sea for his troubles he displays his own fears in facing himself.

O'Neill from time to time may have seen the sea as fatefully destructive, but he certainly felt its positive and uplifting qualities, so beautifully expressed years later in Edmund's lyric eulogy in *Long Day's Journey into Night*. In Anna he creates a character who confounds her father's dour pessimism by finding in the sea a naturally redeeming power that can cleanse her soul and strengthen her body, previously blighted by the ugly actions of ugly people ashore. Further, it brings her a fortuitous personal redeemer in Burke, who must test his own faith and his concepts of purity in finally accepting the tainted Anna. What is more, in the portrayal of the sinned-against Anna, O'Neill makes no apologies for her actions and attempts no papering over of her sordid past. Chris and Mat are understandably appalled, and O'Neill does permit Anna to give momentary thought to a return to her old ways as she encounters the two men's stubbornly narrow view of her, but she stands firm and shames them into accepting her as she is. O'Neill has made a heroine of a thoroughly fallen woman, and counter to all past traditions stated so unequivocally in Bronson Howard's "laws," her redemption holds firm. Neither man nor the gods can impose lasting punishment upon her. She survives, stronger than ever. Sorry about her past and wishing to forget it, Anna remains far from any ideal of a contrite, subdued female.

Anna Christie concludes in almost comic irony. The confused Mat, a born if not practicing Catholic, is nonplussed to find that the Lutheran Anna has sworn her fealty to him on his crucifix, thus, in this profane act, rendering the oath meaningless. But his good sense takes over, and after some moments of despair he concludes, "If your oath is no proper oath at all, I'll have to be taking your naked word for it and have you anyway." Not long thereafter Chris and Mat, erstwhile violent antagonists over Anna's future, find they have signed onto the same ship, leaving Anna to wait for them ashore to "make a regular place for you two to come back to." The public took the ending for a happy one, and critics who were disappointed that O'Neill had lapsed from his serious realism into sentimental romance chided his apparent surrender to popular taste. O'Neill disclaimed such a view by replying that he had done exactly what he had intended: to show life as it is, with the ambiguous ending merely a pause—a comma, as he put it, not a period—in the lives of his characters. He would not accept the assumption that everything had "come out in the end." Happy as the ending may seem, in the best realistic dramatic tradition O'Neill refuses to close the book, and questions remain. Old Chris's curtain speech should have left audiences wary about any genuinely happy resolution. He looks out into the night, shakes his head, and mutters, "Fog, fog, fog, all bloody time. You can't see where you vas going to. Only dat ole davil, sea—she knows."

Between November 1921 and March 1924, three thumping failures made clear that this journeyman playwright still had a long way to go before he could be unequivocally recognized as an acceptable interpreter of the life and times of contemporary society.

First to fail was *The Straw,* based on O'Neill's experiences while at the Gaylord Farm sanitorium in 1913. It opened on 10 November 1921 and lasted scarcely three weeks at the Greenwich Village Theatre. The love affair between two tuberculosis patients, with all the attendant clinical detail, repelled more than it attracted. The second, *The First Man*, staged by the Lewisohns' Neighborhood Playhouse on 4 March 1922, convinced no one. The contrivances served no purpose but to render the problems of Curtis Jayson and his wife artificial and dramatically unconvincing. Nothing worked. The gossipy, backbiting family and small-town characters were flat and unsympathetic. The harrowing offstage screams of the wife dying in prolonged agonies of childbirth added disproportionate physical and emotional violence. The third play, *Welded* (17 March 1924), a bumbling attempt at Strindbergian sex-battle naturalism with some unsubtle symbolism tacked on, was the triumvirate's initial production. It came and went in a matter of days. Its deadly serious we-can't-live-together-and-we-can't-live-apart struggle between husband and wife became a virtual parody of the war between the sexes as they poured out speeches of recrimination and excruciating soul-baring agony, redeemed by no significant action whatever. Whether composed as a result of O'Neill's own tumultuous marriage to Agnes Boulton or his admiration for the misogynist Strindberg, this talky, amateurish attempt to philosophize on how love binds its victims in a paradoxical web of hatred and desire bored everyone.

These three failures represent the nadir of O'Neill's playwriting and remain, by any critical standard, the worst he ever did. Except for one or two fleeting revivals, none worthy of note, all of them have remained undisturbed and quite rightly unmourned. After the wholesale rejection of these three plays, for the rest of his active career before the second war—with the exception of the atypical domestic comedy, *Ah, Wilderness!*—Eugene O'Neill abandoned any attempt to create a routine family-conflict play.

The intervening thunderclap of the Playwrights' production of *The Hairy Ape* on 9 March 1922 reverberated far beyond the limits of Greenwich Village. The uninhibited cursing in the dialogue called down the wrath of the New York district attorney, who tried his best to close the play. Its imaginative style puzzled its audiences and confused its critics. How was one to interpret what was going on? What was its message, if any? Was it a play at all?

At first glance, *The Hairy Ape* seemed straight out of the tradition of German expressionism, dramatizing the radical social and political theories of the clash between working and leisure classes. Left-wing American labor welcomed it as a powerful statement of their cause—a plausible reaction, since O'Neill was known to have been inclined toward radical social thinking. [12] O'Neill, however, had never seriously embraced any radical cause, and his aim in *The Hairy Ape* was much more philosophical than sociopolitical. To regard Yank as a routinely exploited worker in a capitalistic hell, doomed in his lonely battle against the system, is as much an error as to regard Brutus Jones as no more than an exploited black. Neither Yank nor Jones can be isolated as a representative of a class or race; they are independent, giant figures, both physically and emotionally. In the end they are hampered and destroyed not by socety's exploitive cruelties but by fatal limitations of the mind.

The theatricality of expressionism had proven itself in its visual demonstration of the emotional breakdown of Brutus Jones. In *The Hairy Ape* Yank Smith is driven into a jungle as destructive and overpowering as that encountered by the dethroned Emperor. Yank, too, has been thrust from his own throne in the stokehold into a world that barely acknowledges his existence; he may not panic in quite the same manner as Jones, but his confused mind breaks apart just as surely. Expressionism was a logical stylistic choice, and O'Neill's use of Yank as a symbol was completely consistent. The stoker represents humankind as the "naked ape," caught in the outside environment he cannot understand, needing to accept it but unable to control it.

In their assumption that the opening scene was meant to be a graphic naturalistic picture of the dehumanizing conditions of stokers in the bowels of a modern luxury liner, audiences were baffled at the apparent inconsistency of style. [13] Is this *really* the way it is? Must men stoop to move about, behaving like hairy, long-armed Neanderthals? Do engineers whip these "men" (read slaves) into action by incessantly whistling for more coal and more steam? Is their laughing, singing, cursing, and drinking, their uproar like the "battled defiance of a beast in a cage," a reflection of the real thing? Certainly not, and O'Neill never intended it to be, difficult as it was to convince those who still saw him as the ultimate realist. He complained that "the public saw just the stoker, not the symbol, and the symbol makes the play either important or just another play." [14]

O'Neill meant to keep *The Hairy Ape* as unreal as possible, and his stage directions are explicit; every scene, he explained, should "by no means be naturalistic." Although he assigns his characters specific names and gives them some limited individuality rather than depicting them as stylized types, their loud reaction to Yank's exhortations and his ludicrous attempts, à la Rodin, to "tink" things through is specifically intended to be unreal, to give a brassy, mechanical quality to their choral responses, as if they are projected through the morning-glory horn of an old phono-graph. The stoking scenes are almost balletlike in their execution; the coal is imaginary, the glaring stokeholes of the boilers designed to heighten the impression of existence in a fiery Hades.

Even topside on the ship's passenger deck, the portrayal of the effete, snobbish do-gooder Mildred Douglas is unreal. Her determination to descend to "hell" in her virginal white clothes, with the unlikely permission of the ship's officer, sets a tone of unearthly unreality. One would expect the proud Yank, who is "de ting in coal dat makes it boin; I'm steam and oil for the engines; . . . I'm steel-steel-steel," who knows he is the power that makes the ship go, to scoff at and ignore the terrified Mildred's whimpering cry, "Oh, the filthy beast!" Instead, this white apparition, whom he whirls around to face after bellowing curses on the unseen whistle-blower, sends him into gaping-mouthed shock. It is this inexplicable intrusion into Yank's closed kingdom that sets him off. Being called a beast (Mildred never does call him a hairy ape, despite the assertions of the stokers), "he feels himself insulted in some unknown fashion in the very heart of his pride." He hurls his coal scoop after her with a roaring "God damn yuh!" and subsequently sinks into his pro-longed depression. One cannot reason realistically but must explain what this trauma means symbolically. Yank is not a rationally thinking, realis-tic character. He is the creation of the environment in which he works, a greater-than-life symbol of the brutish human figures who have become part of the great machine that depends on them. Mildred, as well, is a symbol and, like Yank, a creation of her society, existing without depth of character, of only momentary use within the drama. Yank's desperate attempt to think, to figure it all out, is equally unreal.

Yank's subsequent ventures, particularly the Fifth Avenue se-quence in which the painted, simpering, marionettelike figures parade their gross finery and have no awareness of Yank's existence, maintain the play's expressionistic style. His final encounter with the caged ape is a thoroughly stylized conclusion. Those who might question how the cage was left unlocked and how Yank could have access to it in the first place are missing the whole point. There *is* no rational explanation, and the negligence of zookeepers is entirely irrelevant. In the end, will anybody notice the difference? One ape is exchanged for another, and who is in or out of the cage is immaterial.

Though admired in Russia and by all of the radical left, the play as a whole cannot be fairly judged as propaganda for economic or political reform. Yank is as much an outcast in the labor union hall as he is on

Fifth Avenue, receiving no recognition or assistance from either. He is imprisoned and hosed down not as a dangerous radical but as a screaming madman. Being crushed to death by the gorilla does not fit the role of the proletarian hero. One may assert that Yank was naively unaware of how viciously he was being treated by those in power and that his revolt and search for vengeance arose from his long-postponed recognition of his violently repressed social position. The problem with this viewpoint is that Yank thrives on what he does, scornfully confident that his grueling labor is more meaningful and rewarding than anything practiced by "dem slobs in de foist cabin." When Yank is personally challenged, his pride shattered, he seeks his vengeance against the insult to his prowess as the prime mover of the universe. He becomes at once a symbol of all who abandon their faith and seek to function in the world by pursuing false gods, who in turn abandon them. His search for a place to "belong" is a result of his own shortsightedness. He has a place, and he functions perfectly well within it. What destroys him is his sense of loss in the encounter with Mildred, which drives him into his determination to find somewhere to belong outside his well-established venue. He will have none of Long's rebellion against the "Capitalist clarss," nor will he accept Paddy's idealized recollection of life before the mast, when men had straight backs and clear eyes under the open sky and fought the sea one on one in glorious sailing clippers. Yank is modern man, a product of the industry that makes and runs the huge, pounding steamers, and he is proud of it.

Those who would regulate public morality were deeply offended by the cursing and blasphemous language that Louis Wolheim, in his ferocious performance, roared off the stage to roll over the heads of incredulous viewers, but all who worked with O'Neill stood their ground and fended off the clumsy bureaucratic efforts to shut down the play. In the end Wolheim's remarkable interpretation successfully brought audiences to regard Yank, violent and arrogantly dominating as he is, as a man suffering from lost faith in both mind and body, much more significant than a mere symbol of martyrdom to a debilitating social system.[15]

O'Neill was bothered by the public's constant attempt to pinpoint him as a practitioner of a particular dramatic style. As he complained to Quinn, "To be called a 'sordid realist' one day, a 'grim, pessimistic Naturalist' the next, a 'lying Moral Romanticist' the next, etc., is quite perplexing" (Cargill, 125). He was as perplexed as ever by public reaction when the Provincetown Playhouse (no longer the Playwrights' Theatre), after an unsuccessful dalliance with his *Ancient Mariner*, staged *All God's Chil-*

lun Got Wings in May 1924. O'Neill long insisted it was one of his very best, a play that would someday come into its own. It was the last of his "black" plays, and it at once ran afoul of more official stupidity and outright racial bigotry, which kept him on the front page for a far longer period than the play itself merited. It is difficult to believe that O'Neill was unaware of the prejudices that would be fueled by his story of the marriage of a black man to a white woman. He was defying the strongest of racial taboos, and no amount of elevated theme and dignified performances could alter the fact that even in as "liberal" a northern city as New York there would be passionately indignant outcries, particularly from those who responded only to rumor and knew absolutely nothing about the play.[16]

On the surface *All God's Chillun* would seem to affirm the commonly held attitude that all the evils of miscegenation mean the inevitable collapse of any interracial marriage, but O'Neill never wrote that simplistically. The disintegration of the marriage between Jim Harris and Ella Downey does involve a violent clash between two distinct ethnic backgrounds, but the conflict occurs not in the outside world of racial intolerance and hatred but entirely within the living quarters and the minds of those involved.[17] It is an increasingly violent psychological struggle, underlined, it is true, by racial mores, but it avoids any moral stand concerning the racial intermarriage itself. Opposition to it comes entirely from the black side, Jim's own family. There is no interference or intervention by any white faction whatever.

With Ella and Jim having gone through a childhood affection for each other, and with Ella now abandoned by her tough white boxer lover, the union would seem to offer mutual love and support. There is, however, an underlying flaw, socially inspired, in Jim's approach to the marriage. He knows that Ella is an increasingly depressed social castoff with no place to go, and he is fully prepared to give her the protection and security she desperately needs. His initial mistake is to place himself in the inferior position that will haunt him throughout the play. Instead of entering his relationship with her on an equal basis, he offers "to become your slave . . . your black slave that adores you as sacred."

Unfortunately, Jim's image of himself, whether he intends it or not, carries over into the reality of their union. It is soon apparent that the marriage has never been consummated; the slave has remained a slave. Facing life in a small flat symbolically hung with a black Congo ceremonial mask, the couple encounter the intrusion of the white world only in the confused mind of Ella, who wavers between an inborn hatred of black people, even Jim, and her paradoxical love for her husband as her only emotional support. Her eventually fatal struggle originates in the contradiction that is tearing her and her marriage apart, namely, her desire to make Jim fail in his study for the bar, thus keeping him firmly in his place as her inferior, against her hope that he will achieve his goals and thus prove that he is the "whitest of the white." In the end it remains clear in Ella's unbalanced mind that no matter how good, noble, or talented her husband may be, only whiteness has virtue. After a final irrational frenzy during which she almost murders Jim, Ella reverts hopelessly into childish fantasies of herself as "painty face" and Jim as the old family retainer. Now wholly her helpless slave, Jim promises to play with her right up to the gates of heaven. His subjugation is complete.

O'Neill's portrayals of Jim's mother and sister Hattie are rather remarkable anticipations of the black struggles of the 1950s and 1960s. The mother, opposing the marriage, holds views similar to those held by midcentury militant blacks who would not have black become white by assimilation into society. "Dere's one road where de white goes alone," she says, "and dere's anudder road where de black goes on alone." Sister Hattie, far more confrontational, wants Jim and Ella to fight the battle of prejudice head on. Neither woman prevails, and both in their individual ways mourn their frustrated hopes in Jim and, by extension, in their race.

The psychological realism is well shown in the characters' relationships as they speak and act as individuals in a contemporary urban society. Dialogue flows naturally, and behavior is believably realistic. Certain racial antagonisms are evident in the scenes of the first act in epithets such as "Jim Crow" and "nigger lover" and in the obvious social distinctions, which increase as the children grow into adulthood, but it is through the stylized settings that O'Neill makes clear the barriers that exist. The narrow streets that converge at the center of the stage are precisely demarcated as black and white; the voices, songs, and sounds from each side are equally distinguishable. When Jim and Ella emerge from the church into the cold reality of the two societies they have defied in their marriage and in which they will now be forced to live, blacks and whites stand apart on either side, neither more than superficially communicating with each other.

Even more striking is the constant shrinking of the apartment room of the second act. By the third scene the ceiling has been lowered until it "seems barely to clear people's heads," and, with Ella's increasingly disturbed mind, the walls shrink more tightly to constrict movements and to make "the furniture and the characters appear enormously magnified," while the black Congo mask looms ever larger.

All God's Chillun remains an original and important experiment, despite its limited success. The reactions of a racially mixed couple whose lives are torn asunder psychologically rather than physically by the traditions of a segregated society are perceptively dramatized. Rather than teaching a moral or sociological lession, the play provides its audience with an emotional catharsis through the characters' sufferings and through Jim's heroic acceptance of an inevitable fate.

The appearance, on 11 November 1924, of *Desire under the Elms* might suggest that O'Neill had abruptly returned to the formula of nonstylized, straight drama. Close study, however, reveals something distinctly different. *Beyond the Horizon* and *Anna Christie* were successful as ordinary, nonexperimental plays, the work of a playwright getting the feel of the longer dramatic form. Truly memorable characters were absent,[18] and the subject matter, though serious, was not exceptional. In *Desire under the Elms*, on the other hand, O'Neill created one of his most imposing figures in the rock-hard patriarch Ephraim Cabot, and for the first time he was praised for having written a tragedy approaching the strength and dignity of the tragedies of classical Greece.

In opening-night and subsequent reviews of O'Neill's early plays, the word *tragedy* had been tossed around here and there to define the fates of Robert and Andrew Mayo, or of Emma Crosby and even Curtis and Martha Jayson, and, of course, of Jones and Yank; but the term had been applied in a fairly loose sense. In *Desire under the Elms* the stature of the characters and the scope of the action, with impending fate hanging over everything as surely as the towering elms, combined in a drama of considerably more tragic substance. The play remains O'Neill's finest work before his affiliation with the Theatre Guild.

O'Neill's sense of theater served him well in this modern adaptation of the medieval simultaneous stage, providing a variety of acting areas visible at all times, each with a distinct function, as the action shifts frequently from exterior to interior and back again. The path to the gateway at far stage right serves to bring old Cabot and his bride into the scene and to enable Simeon and Peter to leave on their way to California as they mock their father, tear off the gate, and exit into the distance, singing and laughing in their release from their farm labors. In the area of the farmyard and the space in front of the house, Abbie first encounters the family and her immediate antagonist, Eben, while she gains a full view of her new "hum." At the end, the same space witnesses the arrival of the sheriff and the departure of the guilty lovers.

Of greatest importance, and one of O'Neill's most impressive uses of stage technology, is the two-story farmhouse itself, its breakaway facade capable of revealing singly any one, or simultaneously all four of the rooms, each with its individual symbolic function. The house thus becomes an effective stage within a stage for several of the key scenes. It is overhung by the enormous elms bending "their trailing branches down over the roof . . . a sinister maternity in their aspect, a crushing, jealous absorption." Tying all acting areas together is a stone wall running across the entire stage, revealed to the audience in front of the curtain before it rises.

Desire under the Elms readily fits the Greek tragic tradition. The theme of the semi-incestuous love of the voluptuous young Abbie for her stepson Eben, and her violent denunciation of him to the aging husband who had brought her in from the outside world, is a close parallel to the classic myth of Phaedra, Hippolytus, and King Theseus. Unlike Hippolytus, his modern counterpart Eben reciprocates his stepmother's love; but in the end both are destroyed, and Ephraim, like Theseus, is left to bear his fate alone. A secondary parallel is Abbie's murder of her child, Medea-fashion, although the awful deed is not an act of vengeance but is meant to prove her love. And whereas the children of Medea are at first brought onstage alive before their bodies are later displayed, O'Neill permits no audience identification with the infant, its presence consisting only of a bundle of prop rags buried in the cradle. There is more than a little of Oedipus's love for Jocasta in Eben's obsession with memories of his dead mother, but it is the Hippolytus legend that best describes the doomed Cabot household.[19]

Mythic parallels alone do not make *Desire under the Elms* a classic tragedy. It is, rather, O'Neill's use of nearly all the classical ingredients that places his characters in the grip of powers beyond their understanding, driving them inexorably toward the final catastrophe. These characters and what they do are, in the best tragic sense, larger than life. Ephraim, the septuagenarian, "ripe on the bough," has outlived two wives and claimed a third, while his astonishing physical strength maintains his unrelenting iron grip on the farm. He defies the forces that by this time should have taken him to his ancestors. He worships a pagan god of brute strength and rock-hard will; he has made the stones yield to him in bringing prosperity out of a rugged and forbidding landscape. Abbie is a woman at her strongest and most seductive, enduring her unloved mate while aggressively seducing her resisting antagonist. Her murder of her son, meant to prove her love for Eben, is a willful act, done solely on her own volition. Eben himself, determined to avenge his mother's suffering, though fighting nature in his resistance to Abbie's

Desire under the Elms *(Eugene O'Neill, 1924). This scene, well displaying the break-away farmhouse designed by Robert Edmond Jones, is the most electrifying moment in the play. Eben and Abbie stare at each other as if the intervening wall did not exist. Ephraim remains ignored and unheard as the sexual magnetism of the young people draws them to each other. Note the stone wall, always visible, as a part of the farm's rock-hard atmosphere.*

siren call, defies his father not only by uniting sexually with his step-mother but also by producing a son and reveling in the secret satisfaction of having cuckolded his parent. Then, at the end, having fled to get the sheriff, in horror at Abbie's deed, he faces the full realization of their deeds and returns to stand at Abbie's side to face the death that probably awaits them.

O'Neill's superb use of dramatic naturalism provides a sense of overpowering fate as unavoidable, as inescapable, as any pursuing gods or demons visited upon a fifth-century Greek tragic protagonist. These very large characters are direct products of their natural environment, evident in the suffocatingly close trees, the stone walls, and the ceaseless demands of the land. Unsophisticated, unlettered, and ignorant, driven by their passionate, almost animalistic desires, and isolated from most normal social intercourse, all perform at the lowest naturalistic level. The slow-witted, animal-like behavior of Simeon and Peter is emphasized in the description of them as they enter the kitchen: ". . . shouldering each other, their bodies bumping and rubbing together as they hurry clumsily to their food, like two friendly oxen." Moreover, they hate their father and grab quickly at the gold that will release them. Ephraim follows his hard god and runs the farm without mercy. His attitude toward the cows in the stable, where it is "wa'am" in comparison with the cold atmosphere of the house, and to which he retreats to seek relief from his loneliness, is an impressive symbol of his affinity to nature. His return with Abbie, following his god's order to go forth and once more seek a wife, is an act of impetuosity, lacking any feeling of love. Abbie, on her part, shares no love with anybody. Her passion for security and a home enables her to overlook the nature of her marriage. Her drive to acquire Eben's body is hardly more than an irresistible sexual urge to gain something unavailable from her aging spouse. Eben's almost unnatural attachment to his mother's memory is driven out by the raw sex literally thrown at him by the sensuous Abbie.

O'Neill's use of his setting imparts the sense of a passionate fate in one of the most dramatically gripping scenes he ever wrote. With the downstairs closed off and the two upstairs bedrooms opened up, Abbie sits disconsolately on the bed as her mate, speaking but unheard, lies beside her. She stares at the thin partition separating her from the equally disconsolate Eben on the other side. Once Ephraim departs for the barn, the two begin to sense the rising eroticism that will soon bring them together. Though separated, they move hypnotically toward each other, as if the wall were not there at all. Abbie's abrupt entrance into Eben's bedroom, her forcing her body against him, and the calculated effect of their uninhibited consummation in the parlor, so sacred to Eben's memory of his mother, are triumphs of dramatic sensuality and theatricality. Abbie's repeated insistence to Eben that she will now replace his "Maw" is spine-tingling in its implications.

Though driven by their primitive emotions, all three protagonists ultimately recognize what they are and accept their fates with dignity. Old

Cabot stoically faces his final loneliness as the least tragic of the trio, while Eben and Abbie, doomed, face their fate but stand up to it in defiant realization of what awaits them. The two walk "hand in hand to the gate . . . looking raptly in attitudes of strangely aloof devotion," united in love and facing such final judgment as god or man may bring them. As a final irony, despite the tragedy the farm has brought down upon all the Cabots, the departing sheriff, whose eye is not on the holy but on the mundane, exclaims, "It's a jim-dandy farm, no denyin. Wished I owned it."

Desire under the Elms has not been without its detractors. Its language and frank sexuality prompted the ever-alert bluenose censors, who seemed continually on O'Neill's trail, to attempt to close it. All their efforts, as usual, came to naught. Thoughtful critics found that the accumulated violence and unrelieved, heavy-handed story line came close to making the play a parody of many a rural hard-time melodrama. Melodramatic it certainly is, but O'Neill was able to create characters of sufficient stature and humanity to override the melodramatic distractions. Whereas many of O'Neill's earlier plays have faded, *Desire under the Elms* has endured as one of his most impressive and still playable journeyman efforts. [20]

Having sought for several years to write a poetic drama based on the story of Ponce de Leon, O'Neill produced *The Fountain* with Jones and Macgowan in late 1925, a diffuse mixture of philosophy and mysticism about the explorer and the various women in his life. O'Neill hoped that the poetic telling of the search for the fountain of youth would have a special audience appeal, but he finally agreed that the play lacked dramatic action and was hindered by hortatory and pretentious language. An overblown pageant ("trial by scenery," one critic put it) [21] in which neither romance nor adventure held interest, *The Fountain* quickly departed as yet another failed experiment.

The Great God Brown was O'Neill's last play before the Theatre Guild became his sole producer. It was the most successful of his career up to that time, as well as the most challenging and baffling for its audience. O'Neill had always maintained that human beings constantly wore a public face, in effect a mask, to conceal their interior selves. He was convinced that the stage could convey this deception by the use of actual masks. He had already used masks in the expressionistic Fifth Avenue scene of *The Hairy Ape* and in *All God's Chillun*, with its dominating Congo mask, but these, like the stylized masks in the unsuccessful *The Ancient Mariner*, were designed to intensify the theme or to emphasize certain aspects of theatricality, not to suggest aspects of character. In *The Great God Brown* he leaped headlong into use of the mask as an active device in the development of both story and character. The play was, and still remains, a fascinating tour de force.

O'Neill's characterization of the impractical dreamer and the practical doer of deeds receives its fullest development in *The Great God Brown*. Dion Anthony, withdrawn by nature, loving, sensitive, and artistic, wins the hand of Margaret, the personification of girlish beauty and womanly devotion, away from his close friend Billy Brown, the outgoing and eventually successful architect. But to win and keep her, Dion must act the part and literally wear the mask of a "defiant, gayly scoffing and sensual young Pan" in Margaret's presence. She is incapable of recognizing the real Dion, and she flees in terror when the mask is removed.

Only in the presence of the prostitute earth-mother Cybel, who wears the mask of her hardened profession over her real fresh-complexioned, dreamy-eyed face, can Dion safely remove his mask. She, in turn, can remove hers as the two recognize each other for what they really are. Brown, the prospering businessman, at first unmasked, is also a frequenter of Cybel's parlor, and she serves as confessor and counselor to both men as they seek relief from the daily challenges of their lives.

In *The Great God Brown* O'Neill shows most graphically the dual theme first apparent in *Beyond the Horizon* and carried through a large part of his later work. First is the problem of the sensitive artist who has no place in contemporary society. His dreams rejected, even by those who purport to love him, he is driven to fatal despair. Second is the fate of the person who amasses material wealth through skill in the marketplace and who becomes a soulless individual as isolated as the dreamer.[22] Neither can survive alone; each will be destroyed without the other. In this remarkable play O'Neill melds the dreamer and the materialist into a single identity, but the hybrid monster cannot survive; each half finds itself mortally corrupted by the other.

On the whole, O'Neill's experiment works well. The abject failure, Dion, whose outward persona of the cynical, mocking Pan keeps alive his relationship with the devoted Margaret while slowly destroying the sensitive soul underneath, is taken in as partner in Brown's architectural business. Here Dion's artistic talents turn Brown's unimaginative structures into veritable cathedrals. The firm prospers, but the success of Dion's contribution only drives the real person under the mask into increased despair as Dion realizes that his artistry is being corrputed in the grubby task of making money. Eventually, hopelessly dissipated, Dion

The Great God Brown *(Eugene O'Neill, 1926). After Dion Anthony has bequeathed Billy Brown his mask, Brown goes through agony before finally deciding to adopt the mask and live with Margaret. The actors could hold the masks in front of their faces using one hand, or the masks could be strapped around the actors' heads, leaving both hands free.*

dies in Brown's presence, but not before he has compelled his partner to face what each of them really is. Brown, "with sudden frenzied defiance," admits that he has always loved Margaret, to which Dion, "with a terrible composure," replies, "No! That is merely the appearance, not the truth! Brown loves me! He loves me because I have always possessed the power he needed for love, because I am love!" Enraged, Brown starts to throttle his adversary, who shouts triumphantly, "Ah! Now he looks into the mirror! Now he sees his face!"

Subdued and weak, Dion mockingly bequeaths his mask to Brown: "My last will and testament! I leave Dion Anthony to William Brown—for him to love and obey—for him to become me." As the mask falls to the floor, revealing "his Christian Martyr's face at the point of death," he begs forgiveness and says, "May you design the Temple of Man's Soul!" Brown at last realizes how much he had actually feared the Dion of the mask, and that Margaret had never loved the "poor weakling" whom he now sees dead and unmasked before him. He accepts the inheritance and wears it to become precisely what Dion had intended.

It is here that the play can begin to fall apart. O'Neill is on very fragile ground in this exchange of masks and all that follows. Up to this point it has not been particularly difficult for the audience to follow the uncomplicated portrayal of inner and outer personalities through the device of the masks. But from here on O'Neill demands something more. There must be a willingness to go beyond mere recognition of the various multiple personalities into an awareness of what the play is actually about. If that becomes impossible and the viewer attempts literally to figure out what is going on, the play can well collapse into meaningless gibberish.

If, however, the entire play is taken as an allegory of success and failure, of blindly impractical love and devotion, and of society's sad inability to recognize and reward the artist in its midst, the wild improbabilities of the subsequent action can be accepted. As Brown adopts the demonic, pagan-god outer face of Dion, he removes the physical body of Dion from the stage; thereafter, it is never seen again. For the rest of the play, wearing the Dion mask as needed, Brown maintains a dual personality, living with and loving Margaret *as* Dion, undetected by either her or her sons. As Brown, he goes on conducting his business as before. The mask, however, does not transfer the soul of the artist to its new wearer. With Dion and his artistry both dead, Brown's "cathedrals" become little more than ungainly mausoleums, themselves dead and unattractive failures. Beneath the mask Brown deteriorates into a desperate, driven man. Without the mask he is sought as the murderer of Dion and, shot by the police, dies in the arms of Cybel, who voices a prayer over him. The Dion mask is found and carried onto the stage as if a corpse, but the actual body is never recovered. Audience acceptance of this device is stretched to its furthest limits in the epilogue. Margaret, never having recognized the real Dion beneath the mask, returns to the spot where she and Dion first declared their love. She brings forth the Dion mask, speaks to it, and gives it a "timeless kiss."

In one of his few written statements about his work, O'Neill tried to explain the play's meaning in an item in the *New York Times* in February 1926. It was not successful; his preliminary explanation, followed by what he termed "an explanation of this explanation," only further muddied his reasoning. The clearest part of the essay is his rationale for the names. Dion Anthony is Dionysus and St. Anthony, the mask persona being the god of wine and revelry, eventually degenerating into the goatlike Pan, and the real persona beneath the mask becoming the saintly aesthete. Billy Brown is the plain, ordinary, unimaginative American businessman, ultimately the "god" that saves, yet destroys, the saint. Margaret, from *Faust's* Marguerite, is the eternal girl-woman, seduced by the devil in her husband's licentious Pan-mask, the perfect wife and mother who can never see beneath the surface to welcome and love the true man who married her. Cybel is the personification of the mythical Sibyl, eternally wise, living forever, outwardly professionally enticing, inwardly a saintly redeemer in her own right.

Well enough. But what of the two men, separate identities, yet all one? Are they Man? Do they represent the dichotomous nature of all men? (a question that can also be asked of the masked and unmasked Cybel and Margaret, perhaps representing all women). Are they the same person, one man in his several parts? (The two were once played by identical twins.) Is there no hope at all in the modern world for the sensitive creator of love and beauty? Must he always be destroyed by the practical and successful individual? Are we all doomed eternally to hide ourselves from others? Cannot true love see through it all and welcome the reality beneath? Why, as Dion cries out, must such as he "be born without a skin . . . that I must wear armor in order to touch and be touched?" These can be profound questions, and O'Neill, often cited for his less than lucid, sometimes bumbling, mystic philosophizing, raises them in this most intellectually stimulating of all his plays. *The Great God Brown* cannot be dismissed as a failure; the device of the masks, clumsy as it is, does work. It worked well in the original production, and it has worked well in subsequent revivals. Enigmatic and obscure the play may be, but when it is met more than halfway—a step frequently demanded in the plays of Eugene O'Neill—it says something about human relationships, something universal about men and women in their lives and loves, that can successfully hold an audience.

The Master Craftsman:
The Guild Takes over, 1928–1934

With *Desire under the Elms* a solid if notorious success, *The Great God Brown* running the better part of a year, and the *Glencairn* plays, *Jones*, and *Beyond the Horizon* doing well in assorted revivals, it was clear that if

Eugene O'Neill were to receive the kind of backing he deserved by virtue of his growing artistic stature, the Theatre Guild would have to provide it. The erratic roller-coaster pattern of his plays seemed irrelevant. Public and critics alike supported those that deserved support, and the dismal lesser efforts happily, and quickly, faded from mind. Eugene O'Neill was no longer just the experimenting eccentric but was fast becoming a true professional with a creative imagination that brought him fame (and notoriety, it must be admitted) in theaters throughout the world. Here was a playwright who dared to pursue ideas that were frequently controversial, clouded, mystic, and unnerving, but who could take those ideas and combine them in his best plays with his inborn sense of theater—that is, a sense of what would work on the stage—that enabled O'Neill to transcend his often labored language or dramatic redundancy. O'Neill had become a master craftsman, fully in control of what he wanted to say and how it was to be projected from the stage. Finally, the Guild, thoroughly aware of the playwright's erratic record and his propensity to stumble, was willing to take the risks and provide whatever he requested, even when there were serious doubts about the chances of success. Unfortunately, these doubts were borne out on more than one occasion, because Eugene O'Neill, even under the Guild's tender loving care, could still put together an occasional collapsing house of cards.

On 9. January 1928, two years after *The Great God Brown*, the Guild took on their first O'Neill play, *Marco Millions*. Placing their prestige as well as O'Neill's squarely on the line, they spared nothing in a lavish production. Its casting included top Guild performers such as Alfred Lunt, Morris Carnovsky, Baliol Hollaway, and the beautiful Margalo Gillmore, who had earlier been acclaimed as the bright spot in the otherwise rejected *The Straw*. Originally planned for performances on two successive nights, it was trimmed to a more acceptable one-night size. As might be expected, the Guild opened their first O'Neill play with considerable fanfare. The best way to summarize the fate of *Marco Millions* is to hedge a bit and say that it was not unsuccessful; it did little to damage either the playwright or the Guild and had a respectable three-month run.

For the first time O'Neill attempted an out-and-out satire in drawing Marco Polo as a shrewd modern-day commercial traveler who is at the same time a mercenary and self-centered antihero. The grimness of the lost souls of Jones and Yank, or of the suffering of Anthony and Brown, has given way to a comic figure: the shortsighted Venetian who brashly transfers his concept of Western commercialism onto an Eastern society unable to comprehend or accept it but equally unable to make any impression of its own values on this upstart intruder, who does not lose his soul in the pursuit of his narrow vision, because he never had one to lose in the first place.

Marco Millions, staged in a kind of grand-opera style and costumed accordingly in more or less authentic thirteenth-century dress, was at best a mildly instructive presentation of the contrasting religious faiths of East and West, first in a prologue consisting of a series of repetitious, pageantlike scenes depicting the Polos' encounters with a variety of orthodox faiths on their way to Cathay, and later in a thin plot lacking dramatic believability. Marco's thirteenth-century Babbitt is too much a caricature, with little depth to help convey the point of the underlying sadness of what he represents. That the sweet-souled young granddaughter of the great Kublai Kaan (as O'Neill spells it), the princess Kukachin, would die for love of this insensitive though clever and attractive Venetian boor seems incredible. The Kaan is altogether too perfect a ruler, and the ways of his court, all proper Eastern elegance and, by definition, presumably all wise and good, are unconvincingly unworldly. The Polo brothers, with their heavy sample cases and lewd jokes, are not-very-clever stereotypes of modern traveling salesmen.

Perhaps a larger flaw is lack of conviction, a certain fuzziness, in the play's definition of "the wisdom of the East," to which O'Neill had always been attracted (in later years he would name his California home Tao House). Unfortunately, O'Neill's knowledge of Hindu and Buddhist beliefs, as well as the tenets of Zoroaster, comes across as sketchy at best. There is some evidence in the Kaan himself that he "harmonizes opposing tendencies within his own nature," reconciling the rhythms of the Tao, and "the personality differences of Kukachin and Marco Polo correspond to those between *yin* and *yang*, faintly suggesting that they may in fact be united by larger cosmic forces,"[23] but a cogent dramatization of Eastern philosophy was beyond the playwright's powers.

Compounding this difficulty was O'Neill's inability to articulate great conceptual themes or historic events in his faltering language. Whereas he could write acceptable vernacular dialogue in his best realistic plays, his attempt at an elevated poetic style of language for these mythic figures falls embarrassingly flat. He had encountered the same difficulty in the dull and stodgy *The Fountain* and, to some degree, in certain speeches by Dion and Cybel in *The Great God Brown*. He did not improve to any noticeable degree in *Marco Millions*. Take, for instance, the Kaan's prayer at the end as he weeps for his granddaughter. The poetry needed to express an appropriate climax to Kukachin's pathetic fate is woefully lacking. "Know in your heart that the living of life can be noble! Know that the dying of death can be noble! Be exalted by life! Be inspired by death! Be humbly proud! Be proudly grateful! Be immortal because life is immortal!" One senses that O'Neill relied on the exclamation mark to accent his message where words themselves did not succeed. To Ruby Cohn this passage illustrates O'Neill's "wet sponge failing," which made him strain to squeeze the last ounce of meaning from language that was already dry.[24]

Taken as O'Neill's most comprehensive elucidation of his concern for the soullessness of modern society, *Marco Millions* is enjoyable and amusing. Marco's schemes of taxing every necessity of life (with the consequent heavy burden on the poor), repealing excess profits taxes ("Imagine a profit being excess. Why, it isn't humanly possible!"), creating a law that "every citizen must be happy or go to jail," and appointing 500 committees to carry on in a system where "brains are no longer needed" are timeless examples of politico-economic madness. His obsession with power, status, and material goods makes him oblivious to the deep love offered him by the desperate princess. As he delivers her to a loveless marriage on his way back to the fat-and-forty Donata, O'Neill's Marco Polo is the very picture of materialistic blindness.

Had O'Neill been the first to create such a figure, the play might have been more favorably received. His method was unique and held its own attraction, but what he said had been said before. Exposing "Babbitry" had become passé, and O'Neill's message covered familiar ground. The patchwork of satire (often quite funny and accurately aimed) and stylized lyrical scenes, held together by superficial philosophy, prevented *Marco Millions* from achieving dramatic unity and a clearly stated purpose.

Marco Millions had been running but a few days when the Guild assumed an even riskier undertaking in the nine-act, six-hour marathon of *Strange Interlude* on 30 January 1928. The gamble paid off; the play became the stage sensation of the year and earned O'Neill a third Pulitzer Prize. Its 426 performances ran for a year and a half, a record unequaled by any other O'Neill play between the wars. (José Quintero's production of *The Iceman Cometh* in 1956 ran for 565 performances, an all-time record for O'Neill, but it was produced in the tiny Circle-in-the-Square, where it was seen by a much smaller total audience.) The published version sold like a best-selling novel, and its royalties, combined with those from the stage production, made O'Neill permanently well off.[25]

With its contemporary setting and recognizable modern characters, its subject matter reflecting the era's fascination with psychoanalysis, and its dialogue and action straight from the society of its day, *Strange Interlude* would seem to fit every definition of a modern realistic play. Even the technique of having the characters speak their innermost thoughts out loud in an extended pattern of soliloquy asides, disconcerting at first, is assimilated into the action with surprising ease, slowing the forward progress of the action hardly at all. But it isn't actually a realistic play. Frederick Carpenter has given it one of the best definitions. *Strange Interlude*, he writes, "is best described, not as tragedy nor even as realistic drama, but rather as a modern myth or morality play. . . . Its curious combination of symbolic melodrama with psychological realism constantly suggests overtones of myth." Concluding that in spite of its faults, the characters have some of the "dramatic depth" of the psychological novel, he decides that "realism is converted into myth by the strange, devious intuitions of the heroine and her creator."[26]

Here lies the crucial point. Edwin Engel is quite right in his designation of *Everywoman* as an alternative title.[27] Nina Leeds is not a realistic character, and nothing that she says or does can routinely be defined as realistic. She is, like the play, a kind of monster creation, and like all monsters, she fascinates, repels, dominates, and devours all those around her. O'Neill has drawn a portrait of the ultimate power of Woman; he has placed within her every characteristic of the women whom he loved, feared, or hated, or who in one way or another dominated his life. Nina Leeds is O'Neill's single most imposing character; the term *monumental* is not inappropriate. Her stature approaches that of the giant female goddesses worshiped in primitive religions above the weaker and "unproductive" males. She is Diana of Ephesus; she is the destructive Kali of Hinduism; she is the temple prostitute; she is the Siren not to be resisted.[28]

Physically attractive, lithe in body and alert in mind, sexually desirable and seductive, Nina Leeds is, in most of the play, the model of everything perfect in the female human animal. To her father, pedantic and authoritarian, she replaces her dead mother, and she rouses in him an incestuous jealousy through her love for her fiancé, the absent but never forgotten Gordon. She has been the perfect obedient daughter, heeding her father's highly moral instincts. To Gordon, the unseen dead hero, she has been the perfect proper lover, desperately wishing to give herself but withholding, even as he goes fatefully to war, so that he may return to take her as his pure and faithful bride.

The trauma of Gordon's death, always vividly recalled, turns the perfect daughter-lover into the perfect whore. She surrenders to any and all of the mentally and physically maimed she purports to nurse, rationalizing her abandon as retribution for her denial of herself to Gordon. To the pitifully worshiping Sam she serves as wife, performing her conjugal duties without love but with a propriety that hides her antagonism from the blindly loving spouse. As the perfect daughter-in-law she obediently heeds the terrifying warnings of Mrs. Evans, violating her own body in the destructon of Sam's child. To Ned Darrell she becomes the perfect passionate mistress. She risks all to keep her lover, even to the point of the possible loss, in mind and body, of her unwitting husband. As the mother of the love child, Gordon the Second, she is at first the ideal parent, but she eventually attempts to absorb him in an oedipal obsession, violently jealous of his love for the intruding Madeline. Unfortunately, by the end of the play she has become the picture of the worst in a possessive mother and resentful mother-in-law. And to Marsden, dear old Charlie, she is the inaccessible wraith, available at last as the thoroughly exhausted, unsexed companion of his declining years, whom he can serve and protect as she "rots away" in peace.

   This formidable creation of female power controls or destroys every man she touches. This Everywoman may entice the men around her, who admire her and give her their affection, but what she becomes is the overpowering force of a sex to be held in awe and to be profoundly feared. She cannot be escaped. The death of Professor Leeds may not be directly attributable to any conscious overt act on Nina's part, but her unnatural grip on him and her later refusal to perform as he wishes can be regarded as contributing toward his death early in the play. Almost at the last minute her son Gordon does finally escape her clutches, but it takes Darrell's direct intervention to prevent her revealing all to Madeline in her frantic attempt to separate the young couple.

   The others, however, are not so lucky. Nina's grip on each is complete. In her beauty and outward femininity she parallels the ensnaring spider that devours her mate, who finds himself unable to escape and apparently unwilling to make the effort. The most chilling sequence O'Neill ever wrote is the infamous "my three men" scene, in which the conquering Nina speaks of her total superiority over her male admirers. The scene represents the epitome of O'Neill's views of the hypnotic powers that render the others so helpless in her presence. As the men obey her at the sharp command, "Sit down, all of you! Make yourselves at home! You are my three men! This is your home with me!" each reflects to himself on some of his private thoughts about his relationship with her,

Strange Interlude *(Eugene O'Neill, 1928). "My three men"—the play's single most memorable scene, in which Nina soliloquizes about her success in capturing and absorbing into herself the three male forces in her life. To her right is her husband, Sam; standing is Marsden; seated next to him is Edmund Darrell.*

after which Nina, "(more and more strangely triumphant)," speaks her own view: "My three men! . . . I feel their desires converge in me! . . . to form one complete beautiful male desire which I absorb . . . and am whole . . . they dissolve in me, their life is my life . . . I am pregnant with the three! . . . husband! . . . lover! . . . father! . . . and the fourth man! . . . little man! . . . little Gordon! . . . he is mine too! . . . that makes it perfect." Few scenes anywhere are as emotionally numbing as this total assimilation of three helpless grown men, "dissolved" in Nina's overwhelming possessiveness. It is a devastating indictment of the Everywoman whom O'Neill himself constantly seemed to fear.

In the end Nina's deception of her trusting husband, Sam, while it has brought him success in life, has actually destroyed him. His fortune is built upon a gross lie—his assumption that he has proven himself a man in fathering a son in the noble image of his youthful idol, the god-figure of Gordon Shaw. His corpulence and personal indulgence, the result of this false premise, send him to an early death by stroke; he is a victim whose innocent ignorance of the deceit against him renders him far less a man than he would imagine. Darrell's career is in shreds, a ruin brought upon himself by his inability to escape from Nina, no matter where in the world he ventures, and he is drawn against all common sense back into Nina's web, which has relentlessly entangled him. Marsden, the mother-fixated "old maid," passionless, terrified of anything sexual, plods faithfully along, unable to become his own master in his art or his person. Suspecting, agonizing, waiting until too late for any reciprocity from Nina, whose change of life is upon her, he gains only the empty shell of the ideal figure from whom he, like all the others, could never part.

There are intriguing questions raised by *Strange Interlude* and its protagonist. Did O'Neill, who claimed he knew little or nothing of Freud, consciously use Freudian sources for his characters? Or was his source Nietzsche's "superman" turned into "superwoman"? Instead of Freud or Nietzsche, was it Schopenhauer, as suggested in some of the earliest serious criticism by Doris Alexander and reiterated by the contemporary scholar James Robinson?[29] What of the strong biographical factors influencing the playwright? Was O'Neill attempting to cope with the recent deaths of his father, mother, and brother through the deaths of Gordon, Professor Leeds, and Sam, all closely related to the play's central figures, "all linked by the fact that the character closest to the deceased (that is, Nina) either has trouble feeling the death, or facing it," as he himself has experienced?[30] Was O'Neill, feeling betrayed by his mother's drug addiction, as Nina feels betrayed by her father's refusal to let her marry Gordon, disguising himself in the role of Nina, who momentarily hits bottom, as O'Neill had done? Or did the playwright perhaps rest in Charlie, haunted wherever he goes by the death of his mother? Is the Ned-Nina affair ("Oh, those afternoons!") a parallel to O'Neill's clandestine pursuit of the provocative actress Carlotta Monterey (Manheim, 64)? One must be wary in searching for sources in this manner or in ascribing any particular biographical or philosophical influences to any work of art. Ideas abroad in any culture must by the very nature of human behavior be subconsciously absorbed by artistic portrayers of that culture, and their own lives are bound to be reflected in their works, consciously or unconsciously. In the end, a question covering all of these speculations can seriously be asked: how much does it matter? The ultimate test of any play is how it works onstage, and *Strange Interlude* in its day worked magnificently.

Above all else hangs the question of the spoken thoughts. In the final analysis, how effective are they as a dramatic and theatrical device? For one thing, their use in revealing the "inner" person beneath the outward veneer has been well proven in performance to be better than the more intrusive device of masks, as in *The Great God Brown*. In the original production and in the limited revivals, the method of delivery has proven surprisingly successful. In situations such as Marsden's long opening speech, which is a series of random musings rather than a traditional soliloquy, during which a character is alone on stage, there is no particular problem. He moves about naturally, talking to himself rather than addressing the audience (or, in at least one production, not speaking, while a recorded voice-over indicates his thoughts). The presence of other characters, however, creates a different problem, solved by the simple process of having everyone freeze in a predetermined natural position while the speaker, using limited bodily movements in order to focus audience attention, delivers the thoughts in his or her natural voice. Time is thus made to stand still, permitting these spoken thoughts to occur simultaneously with those speeches meant to be heard by others. Though the play's progress is momentarily slowed, audience acceptance is generally gained quickly, and this modern version of the old "aside" becomes a viable theatrical device. Dramatically, however, the use of the spoken inward thoughts frequently contributes nothing to enlighten the audience beyond what it already knows. In fact, if a large portion of the spoken thoughts is eliminated, the gist of everything expressed in them can, through voice and body language, be conveyed by any competent actor.

O'Neill's bold stylistic experiment was heralded, sometimes rhapsodically, as rendering obsolete the established forms and customs of dramatic technique. Nothing would be the same again; a new era of theater was dawning. But, of course, nothing of the sort happened. As O'Neill found in trying the technique later in the failure *Dynamo*, it was a one-shot deal. Exciting as the experiment appeared, any subsequent attempt by O'Neill or anyone else to replicate it was bound to be anticlimactic; once done as extensively as in *Strange Interlude*, it could not be repeated. In truth, it replaced nothing, and the theater continued in its usual way, affected only temporarily by O'Neill's daring.

There are many aspects of *Strange Interlude* that would raise serious questions of logic in a more routinely realistic play. Underneath the sensation not only of the spoken thoughts but also of the subject matter so frankly (and to those who would condemn the play, so shockingly) presented are some very creaky, if not outright crude, plot devices.

The whole outrageous scene with Mrs. Evans taxes credulity with its tale of inherited insanity, the Gothic syndrome of the madwoman in the attic (shades of *Jane Eyre*), and the twisted reasoning of how to "save" poor Sam. How can a person of Nina's strength succumb to the wild insistence on abortion and adulterous deceit? What kind of mother *is* the one who would propose such a dreadful plan, or the expectant mother who would listen to it, let alone undertake it? The wicked Mrs. Evans serves as a sinister reverse deus ex machina introduced to complicate matters, not to resolve them. Once used, she disappears for good. How can any husband of any intelligence with any intimacy at all with the wife he so dearly loves be fooled, as is Sam, by Nina's "illness" and the subsequent events? It may be that Ned Darrell's infatuaton can force him to carry on as he does, or that Marsden's doglike devotion can keep him ever watching, ever hopeful; but to any casual observer, Nina Leeds, after more than 20 years of obsession with the dead Gordon, is quite mad. The healthy mind does eventually heal to enable pursuit of a normal and loving life with others. One would think that either Ned or Charlie or both would finally determine that Nina ought to be put away.

Looking at *Strange Interlude* two-thirds of a century later, one can still marvel at O'Neill's audacity. Doing little to change anything in American theater, in no fashion a "hewer of new ways," as one critic expounded, it was, for all that, tremendously exciting and emotionally powerful. The words of two of the most respected critics who witnessed the opening night are as appropriate these many decades later as they were in 1928. In the words of Joseph Wood Krutch, "It arrests and startles its auditors because it moves them in a new way . . . because, in short, it treats modern life in a fashion convincingly heroic." To John Anderson, "O'Neill tortures his characters with such searing woe, lashes them with so many fierce relationships out of their writhing inhibitions and agonizing complexes that his play wails upon the taut nerves and quivering emotions of clinical psychoanalysis," but in spite of its overlengthy philosophizing, it "does manage to be profoundly engrossing."[31]

In April of 1928 the Pasadena (California) Community Playhouse, a mostly amateur company, staged one of O'Neill's most extravagant and puzzling creations, *Lazarus Laughed*. It remains the only major O'Neill work that has never received a professional production. Even the Theatre Guild made an exception to the policy of taking everything O'Neill offered, wisely declining to tackle this sprawling pageant of muddled pagan and Christian philosophies posing as a play. True to form in his self-misjudgment, O'Neill admired it far more than his critics, but he did admit that this "Play for an Imaginative Theatre" was not likely to gain a regular commercial audience.[32]

The influences of Nietzsche's *Birth of Tragedy* and *Thus Spake Zarathustra* are plain enough in O'Neill's attempt to create a modern ritualistic pageant that also extols Zarathustra's yea-saying enthusiasm for the strong of heart. In explaining his intent, he wrote that the play was a "legitimate descendant of the first theatre that sprang, by virtue of man's imaginative interpretation of life, out of his worship of Dionysus . . . a theatre returned to its highest sole significant function as a Temple where the religion of a poetical interpretation and symbolical celebration of life is communicated to human beings, starved in spirit by their soul-stifling daily struggle to exist as masks among the masks of living!" (Cargill, 121–22).

O'Neill's high intent might be praiseworthy, but his execution of it suffers from overkill. All of the successive mob scenes, whether composed of Lazarus's friends, who consider him the embodiment of the god Dionysus, or his enemies, convinced he is the devil, fast become monotonous and lose their dramatic impact in the continuous "high, free, aspiring, exulting laughter" that infects them. O'Neill left no doubt that he wanted to involve the audience in a ritualistic Christian experience akin to what the ancient Greeks encountered at the Dionysiac festivals, but one important problem remains: in his emphasis upon laughter, precisely what was O'Neill trying to say about faith, be it Dionysiac, Christian, or other? After his resurrection Lazarus responds to the question mankind has always asked: "What is beyond?" As one who has been there and returned, he speaks in a voice of "loving exaltation": "There is only life! I heard the heart of Jesus laughing in my heart: 'There is Eternal Life in No,' it said, 'and there is the same Eternal Life in Yes! Death is the fear between!' And my heart reborn to love of life cried 'Yes!' and I laughed the laughter of God!"

In his postresurrection progress through the ancient world until his immolation in a Roman arena, Lazarus endlessly asserts not only that there is no death but that there is only the laughter of God. Unfortunately, the meaning of "there is only laughter," or "There is only God / We are his laughter," remains vague and puzzlingly obscure. In Lazarus's words, there appears to be only the superficiality of laughter; there is nothing else. The laughing god whom Lazarus describes is as uncontrolled and hysterical as those who practice the laughter on earth. Further, the laughter that Lazarus constantly reaffirms is nontransferable; for all its infectiousness as it is carried from mob scene to mob scene, nothing really happens. Once Lazarus has passed by, everything returns to normal, with absolutely no carryover. As Lazarus tells Caligula, and as Caligula reiterates in the play's last line, "Men forget!" We all know that; mankind never remembers from one point in history to another, but what are we forgetting in this case? All that has happened? God? Death? The "laughter of life"? The mystery remains.

Cyrus Day's observation may be of some help. He explains O'Neill's thesis of *amor fati*, or "love of necessity," as the attitude of Nietzsche's superman toward life and death, involving repression of pity and recognition of the eternal recurrence of all life; "Men pass. Man remains!" At the conclusion of *The Great God Brown*, Cybel as Mother Earth assimilates mankind, who dies happily in her arms, and in *The Fountain* Ponce de Leon is reabsorbed into the material universe, recognizing that "immortality means the cyclical regeneration of the biological abstraction Man."[33] Perhaps.

It is possible that Lazarus speaks to O'Neill's religious philosophy more specifically than character in his earlier plays, but given his ambivalence toward any faith, it is difficult to draw conclusions. *Lazarus Laughed* is probably best considered a part of O'Neill's continuing mysticism, his searching for but never finding the meaning of humankind's relationship to a divine being.

The last four plays appearing before his 12-year self-imposed retirement contained two of Eugene O'Neill's most successful works and two of his most abject failures. The Guild followed the triumph of *Strange Interlude* with a confusion of ranting sound and fury called *Dynamo*, another attempt to dramatize mankind's loss of faith in old gods and failure to find new ones. Opening in February 1929, it was lucky to stretch to 50 performances, the shortest O'Neill run since *The Fountain*. Little more than a decade earlier, Henry Adams, in "The Virgin and the Dynamo," had questioned the twentieth century's material worship of electrical energy, in contrast to the spiritual energy of paying homage to the Virgin in the Middle Ages. O'Neill, like Adams, deplored the diminution of human qualities in America's worship of machinery; if he was endorsing Adams's thesis, it was all but lost in the overblown Freudianism of this new play. Critics responded with outrage and audiences with incomprehension.

O'Neill demands too much in asking that we swallow the outlandish plot, in which the fundamentalist preacher's son Reuben Light renounces his father's faith, rapes and kills his sweetheart, and embracing the womb-shaped, humming dynamo he calls "Mother," electrocutes himself by grasping its agitators, which resemble female breasts. The horrors are compounded by weak dialogue, helped none at all by ineffective *Interlude*isms in spoken thoughts, and the characters are exaggerated beyond belief. Reuben's mad infatuation with the dynamo as an object of sexual desire, a Venus, gets hopelessly confused when he also prays before it as the Virgin Mother. The sexual aspect of Reuben's attraction to it is carried into O'Neill's stage directions describing the suicide. The dynamo has emitted a flash of blue light and almost stops when Reuben grasps it. "Simultaneously Reuben's voice rises in a moan that is a mingling of pain and loving consummation." If Oedipus is not onstage, he is directing behind the scenes.

The violent ending turns unintentionally comic and destroys all the intended serious effect. After his "violation" of "mother" by sexually uniting with Ada, Reuben goes mad, screams "Harlot" as he shoots her, and runs to the humming object of his worship. Then, with Ada's murdered body on the steel stairs above and Reuben burned to a crisp, Mrs. Fife, Ada's mother, herself near madness, having viewed the carnage, turns to the dynamo, once again humming at full speed, and shouts, "What are you singing for? I should think you'd be ashamed! And I thought you was nice and loved us!" She pounds on the generator "in a fit of childish anger" and utters the play's last line, "You hateful old thing you!"

O'Neill's dispute with the conventional view that machines mean progress is valid, for he sensed, as had the European expressionists before him, that machines entice us to our deaths. His concern about mankind's loss of god is equally valid. He has no more use for the Reverend Light's sterile fundamentalism than for the teachings and rituals of the Catholic faith of his background. *Dynamo*, however, cannot fill the vacuum; the man-made device that can bring light (enlightenment?) in what it creates is a hypnotic force without spiritual substance, capable only of destroying its worshipers. Reuben's religion is a worship of science, if you will, but O'Neill's attempt to find meaning in the search for faith in *Dynamo* results, unfortunately, in a profound nihilism. In this play, at any rate, he was unable to reconcile science and religion. There was probably the germ of a good idea somewhere, but O'Neill succeeded only in smothering it with hysterics and murky religious pronouncements. If he could have softened his plot line, created some appealing characters, and conveyed the overwhelming effect of the powerhouse, *Dynamo* might have been the success he always felt it should have been. [34]

After the failure of *Dynamo*, Eugene O'Neill did not return to the theater for more than two and a half years. The interim was a period of considerable turmoil in his life. In the winter of 1927 he had left Agnes and their family of two young children in Bermuda to attend rehearsals of *Strange Interlude* and *Marco Millions*. He never returned. His romance with Carlotta Monterey, who had once played Mildred in *The Hairy Ape*, had made him determined to marry her; he abandoned his writing when he embarked on a round-the-world voyage with her in February 1928. Best described as wild, the trip was marked by a tempestuous relationship involving an almost surreal pursuit of each other by separate ships through the Orient, compounded by illness, and made even more ludicrous by O'Neill's attempt to avoid publicity by traveling in disguise. By the end of July 1929 the couple settled in France after O'Neill's divorce was granted and they could finally marry. In May of 1931 they returned to the States for good, carrying the completed manuscript of the playwright's second marathon drama, *Mourning Becomes Electra*.

For nearly two years during his residence in France, O'Neill worked on what he called his "magnum opus." The many ideas that came and went, the creative roadblocks, the continued experimentation with stage techniques are all revealed in his work diaries. What opened in October 1931 was the end product of months of concentration, a climactic embodiment of his exploration of myth. No subtle references here, no suggestive interpretation, but a full-fledged adaptation of the classic fifth-century Greek trilogy by Aeschylus, *The Oresteia.*[35]

Discovering the surface parallels to the Greek tragedy makes an interesting exercise, but it is O'Neill's modernizing of the plot and his important change in emphasis that make his interpretation of the psychological and mystical elements of the myth uniquely his own. Underlying all is a sense of repressive New England puritanism and provincial isolation. Like the warrior-king Agamemnon in his hilltop Mycenaean palace, Ezra Mannon, the judge and general, is an awesome figure respected and feared by the local small-town populace. The Mannon family, like a noble Greek line, must maintain appearances, playing the part of a ruling nobility above reproach. They must, in short, play god, and like their Greek counterparts, isolated from fellow human beings, the members of this royal family are the victims of their own internal destructive forces.

Within the general classic parallels, O'Neill creates his characters in contemporary Freudian terms; the Oedipus and Electra complexes are more specific than those shown by Aeschylus or Sophocles. Most notable are the overwhelming incestuous desires. Christine may have taken a lover in Adam Brant, but her undisguised love for her son—whom she regards as exclusively her own, hating to admit that her despised husband

had anything to do with his procreation—is an unhealthy oedipal possessiveness. Orin, torn from his mother's smothering embrace to be sent off
to war against his will, welcomes her hysterical concern upon his return
from the battlefield, where, he admits, his dreams were almost entirely of
her. His murderous rage when he discovers his mother's sexual encounters with Brant shows more than a son's pure love for his parent. The
daughter, Lavinia, has sworn to keep herself virginal so long as her father
needs her solicitous care. Her determination to avenge his death is that of
the thwarted lover. Nor is there anything subtle or subdued about the
ensuing relationship of the siblings with each other. Offered "pure" love
by Hazel and Peter Niles, the surviving Mannons reject it. Instead, Orin
proposes that Lavinia and he remain in their tomb of a house on a more
intimate basis than brother and sister. Now grown to resemble his father,
he caresses the reddish hair of Lavinia, who has come to look like her
mother, and the incestuous transfer is complete. Lavinia's cry of "Adam!"
in the embrace of the unfortunate Peter is the shocking revelation of her
wish to substitute for her mother in loving Adam Brant, the replacement
father figure for whom she has always inwardly lusted.

    O'Neill's most important alteration of the Greek myth is his
choice of Lavinia, the Electra figure, as the dominant character. In his
notes he speculated on why Electra, "the most interesting of all women in
drama," should have escaped punishment. By the third play of Aeschylus's original trilogy Electra has disappeared completely, leaving the hapless brother to endure the consequences of her deeds. O'Neill felt it was "a
weakness in what remains to us of Greek tragedy that there is no play
about Electra's life after the murder of Clytemnestra."[36] The title also
underlines Lavinia's role in two ways: black mourning garments are *becoming* to her, the Electra figure, and she *becomes* the embodiment of
deep, continuing mourning. It is incumbent upon her to endure the final
punishment, since it is not for God but for the Mannons themselves to
administer.

    For what, in the end, is Lavinia being punished? Punishment as
such is not usually administered in tragedy, for that would imply some
form of justice and retribution, two elements that have no place in
tragedy. As George Steiner has so convincingly asserted, disinterested fate
and what is does to any tragic figure have nothing to do with justice.[37]
Justice is tied directly to a code of laws. If they are broken, if guilt is
established, appropriate punishment ensues. Society cannot function
without its laws and exacts retribution from those who defy them. Fate,
on the other hand, has no such laws. The most perfect law-abiding

citizen can be struck down by a madman's bullet or a speeding car. Those who cannot conceive of such a disaster without some meaning, some rationale behind it, supply that rationale by asserting that God or the gods are working out some sort of pattern, and thus the catastrophe is explained as "God's way." That explanation, however, is based on an assumption that God functions along understandable *human* lines, else there can be no meaning and God is capriciously arbitrary. That is precisely the point. In the classic concept of tragedy, fate *is* capricious, and any search for meaning is useless because it assumes that the sufferer *must* have done something to deserve punishment. Acceptance of this view is comforting in its assumption of reasonable behavior on the part of the god who has brought about the disaster, but tragedy permits no such comfort. Fate is completely disinterested; the thunderbolt may fall on sinner or saint—it makes no difference.

For what is Oedipus punished? For being born? Hardly his fault, and punishment for that "act" has no meaning. Oedipus does, however, violate human laws in the murder of his father and the incestuous marriage to his mother. The gods have warned Laius and Jocasta not to have a child because that child would destroy them. They choose to defy the warning. Very well, so be it, say the gods. What happens is now beyond us. Nothing can alter the verdict, even though its consequences fall on entirely innocent heads. Oedipus, therefore, cannot escape. No matter what he does to avoid it, he moves inexorably toward his doom. That is not justice as such; it is patently unfair. It is, however, tragic. Oedipus rises to great dignity in recognizing what he is as a man, and he punishes himself for violating the human code, unintentional as that act may have been. The gods—fate—have long since removed themselves from the case.

Neither is it the fault of Lavinia for having been *born* a Mannon, but she takes upon herself the sin of *being* a Mannon, for which she feels punishment is deserved. The Mannons are destroyed not by the indifferent fate of Greek myth but by the sins of the father, committed in the inescapable background of puritanical culture.

This background of a repressive kind of Christianity, so often associated with New England, distorts any family love into a destructive guilt. Generations of attendance at the white meetinghouse have condemned sexual love as a "vile thing." This kind of attitude has made the deadly sin of the earlier sordid sexual battle of the brothers over Marie Brantôme into a permanent curse. Lavinia herself, conceived in lust rather than love, must suffer the consequences. She may have fleetingly metamorphosed from Puritan maiden into sensuous woman aware of her natural eroticism while in the "blessed isles" of the Pacific, but the redeeming power of natural, uninhibited sexuality, which had momentarily saved Lavinia, vanishes. Orin, on the other hand, has maintained his puritanical inheritance. Guilt-ridden by his violence against his mother and disgusted by the naked native women, he remains, as he says, "too much of a Mannon after all to turn into a pagan."

In order to convey the inevitability of this Mannon fate, this inability to avoid or escape the Mannon curse, O'Neill toyed with spoken thoughts and masks. He quickly abandoned them and turned instead to masklike countenances and inherited facial resemblances. His description of the front of the house, with its temple portico facade "like an incongruous white mask fixed on the house," establishes at once what he was trying to do. In the interior scenes he retained the Greek model of a doomed family by placing on the walls the imposing portraits of ancestors who seem to exert a continuing malignant influence. The portrait figures are so dominating that they are directly addressed as if they were living presences. All the living family members resemble the portraits of the dead, each one having a masklike facial quality, appearing to be, as O'Neill describes them, "in repose," or more literally, as in death. Even Christine, not born a Mannon, has taken on the Mannon look, a curse in itself.

In *Strange Interlude* Nina Leeds, that mesmerizing personification of all of woman's primitive power, determines that human problems began with God the Father and therefore cannot be alleviated until God the Mother can take his place and allay the neuroses of human beings cut off from the joy of life by overbearing male domination. Dominant as the male Mannon line might wish to be, as Edwin Engel astutely observes, "the Mother is a primordial image" in *Mourning Becomes Electra*. Ezra, Orin, and Christine's lover Adam Brant all long for love and peace, which they associate with mother love, the peace of the womb, and with escape to a "blessed isle" of the South Seas, where the sun warms the lush growth, the sea croons in the ear "like a lullaby," and "a Garden of Paradise" allows love without puritanical fears and guilt. Orin, incapable of accepting the release of the "blessed isles," decides instead to reach his paradise through death. "It's the way to peace to find her again—my lost island—Death is an Island of Peace, too. Mother will be waiting for me there." It is an escape from "death-in-life, from the 'tomb' [the house] which Abe Mannon had built, to death-birth-peace, to the womb [i.e., the grave]" (Engel, 239–59).

In *Mourning Becomes Electra* death is never far away; it haunts the family from the beginning. The mansion is itself a house of death, erected to replace a previously desecrated dwelling. Orin, speaking to the corpse of his father, says, "Death becomes the Mannons! You were always like the statue of an eminent dead man." Orin is so inured to death by his battlefield experiences that it has become meaningless, but it does of course bring him the relief he needs to enable him to join his mother. Lavinia, turning the house into her living tomb, completes the picture. Orin's suicide has taken him quickly; Lavinia's will take much longer. It is a positive kind of suicide, undertaken not to save herself but to inflict a self-punishment for all the Mannon sins.

But is all this really tragic? Aeschylus saves Orestes by Athena's deus ex machina resolution, and the hopeless dilemma Orestes has found himself in is divinely lifted. There is no tragedy in his survival. Orin dies with his problem unresolved, and he has failed to achieve any kind of tragic dignity. If there is to be tragedy, Lavinia must make it happen. Her decision is a decisive and positive step, taken by a strong dramatic figure. The world outside returns to normal, becomes tranquil, as the Mannon secrets are interred with her; consequently, O'Neill has given his trilogy a more classic tragic denouement.

Still, there has always been a problem in judging O'Neill as a tragic writer because the consistent passive acceptance of death by his leading characters as a reward for and relief from suffering is not truly tragic. No tragic protagonist seeks death consciously or is pleased to die. The view of Edmund, O'Neill's surrogate in *Long Day's Journey into Night*, who sees himself as one who "must always be a little in love with death," cannot make for successful tragedy. But this idea of final peaceful release in death runs in varying depths as far back as Robert Mayo's wayside acceptance, even welcome, of death. Dion Anthony, though passing his mask along to Brown as a curse, is blissfully relieved to die, and his saintly real face reveals it. Nina Leeds welcomes a figurative death in the cool shade with Charlie, happy to surrender herself to a nothing-ness that can obliterate past suffering and to look forward to the real thing, however far in the future. The fact that mankind begins to die at the hour of birth, with this "strange interlude" of life in between, a life that can only lead to death's ultimate release, is constantly reiterated in O'Neill's plays and can prompt a depressing audience reaction of hopelessness and futility, quite contrary to the positive uplift of classical tragedy. It is diffi-cult to determine if O'Neill is pursuing a form of Christian doctrine, preaching the ultimate reward in heaven, or if he is negating the whole idea by looking at death as an achievement, a reward in itself, with no concern about what lies beyond. If the protagonist is to achieve any kind of tragic stature, there must be a positive assertion of human dignity in defying the fates and rising to superior heights as a living person before the finality of death.

Mourning Becomes Electra fails in many ways. Its multiple murders and suicides, the discovery by Lavinia of the wrong pills and her revelation of that discovery to her mother, the sometimes painfully obvious incestuous overtones, the constant reiteration of the past, including Brant's ancestry, and the overplayed curse make it difficult to have serious interest in any single character. In the context of its time, however, and taking into account O'Neill's brash daring in forcing the American public to look at the theater as something beyond mere entertainment, *Mourning Becomes Electra* is a major accomplishment. Whether seen as a "Christian tragedy" with a "keen sense of sin" more profound than in the original Greek model,[38] or as a confirmation of the latest "concepts of the psychology of mourning" with characters more vital than the originals,[39] or as an unworkable attempt to unite classical tragedy and puritan sensibility, O'Neill's modernization of the classic myth must still be admired for the attempt, if not for the ultimate result.

Two years were to elapse before the Guild mounted another O'Neill play. *Ah, Wilderness!* (produced in October 1933) was as much of a hit as anything else he ever wrote. Not only was it a family comedy full of romantic sentimentality, but it also starred one of New York's most famous song-and-dance men, George M. Cohan. Beyond that, for the first time the name of the star appeared on marquees above that of O'Neill.

Ah, Wilderness! was first taken to be O'Neill's fond recollection of his Connecticut childhood and youth. The nostalgic picture of the Miller family on a turn-of-the-century Fourth of July seemed to be the picture of the ideal American nuclear family. Nat Miller, wise, tolerant, understanding small-town editor, personifies the best in husbands and fathers. Essie, his wife, properly frets over her children, sees danger in their youthful ways, and keeps her place, never quite sure what is going on. Yale student Arthur; rebellious Richard, teased and annoyed by younger sister Mildred; firecracker-shooting, brattish Tommy; spinster schoolteacher Aunt Lily; boozing Uncle Sid—all are here, coming and going, eating and drinking, attractive human characters caught in the day-in-the-life-of pattern of wistful memory.

The truth, of course, is that *Ah, Wilderness!* is a wonderful might-have-been. Nat Miller is no parallel to James O'Neill, and Essie Miller and Ella O'Neill have nothing in common. The restless Richard, however, shows behavioral traits of the young O'Neill himself, and Uncle Sid, the hard-drinking, jolly-spirited, hale fellow who cannot hold a job, has a lot in him of O'Neill's brother Jamie. Family resemblances stop there. Nat actually seems to be a composite of some of the people of New London whom O'Neill knew during his brief stays in the town, especially the editor of the newspaper on which he worked. Muriel has qualities of one of O'Neill's early girlfriends, Maibelle Scott, and the town, its holiday celebrations, and the shabby beachfront bar have a lot in common with turn-of-the-century New London.

Popular as the play is with high school and amateur groups, it conveys more than just a Norman Rockwell *Saturday Evening Post* cover. Within it, amidst the often amusing situations and funny lines, can be found elements of O'Neill's familiar world. When *Ah, Wilderness!* and *Long Day's Journey* are produced in tandem, using the same intimate setting closely patterned after Monte Cristo Cottage (the O'Neill family's New London summer home), and played by the same actors, the lighter play reveals a lingering edge of darkness.[40]

Richard is not quite the typical teenage rebel. His fight is more against the society he views as exploitive than against parental constraints. He sees the Independence Day celebration as a mockery that praises the "home of the slave," not the brave, caught under the grinding capitalistic heel. He would welcome the tumbril and guillotine for the likes of Pierpont Morgan. To the distress and shock of his parents, Richard gains his attitude toward love and social mores not from teenage light reading but from Ibsen, Wilde, Shaw, and Swinburne, those "dangerous" free-thinkers. There is a definite dark side to the temperamental, brooding son, ridiculous and naive as he often appears.

Richard does respect Muriel, the next-door girlfriend denied him by her intolerant and bigoted father, and the semierotic poems copied from his books are meant innocently enough. But O'Neill places Richard in a dangerously compromising situation in his encounter with the floozie in the beach hotel barroom, which ends with a drinking binge that almost gets everybody in trouble. It is a shocking bit of education for Richard; the sordid tone is typical of O'Neill in its underlying hardness. The next day Richard stumbles through a facts-of-life scene with his father that is not what one might expect. Nat exhibits far more tolerance than Richard anticipates. Instead of preaching on the sacredness of sex or roundly berating his inexperienced son for violating cherished family principles, he offers practical advice about how to handle "a certain class of women," who are to be used if necessary. "You just have what you want and pay 'em and forget it."

Ah, Wilderness! contains unmistakable criticisms of the family life its seems to extol, as well as satire of the idealized characters and their chauvinistic response to the Fourth of July. Each member of the family must play a role assigned by society, Nat as head of the household, the women and children as less important in the hierarchy. Richard's concern for those who have not felt the benefits of American prosperity is a source of amusement to his father and uncle, but he is showing an awareness of a serious reality of the time. The brutal treatment of the unfortunate prostitute by the bartender, who himself makes a precarious living, is the reflection of a life less wholesome than that of the Millers.[41] Still, if one chooses to ignore its more weighty aspects, the play remains a bittersweet period comedy done in very good taste. Everything comes out well in the end. Unpleasant things are happily forgotten. Richard and Muriel meet in a tender moonlight love scene, and as the curtain falls, Nat and Essie gaze out the screen door into the same moonlight, rejoicing in Richard's growth and their own continuing love. With convincing dialogue and the play's evocation of a simpler past, *Ah, Wilderness!* is saved in the end from maudlin sentimentality by characters who come alive, bringing the pleasure of easy audience association with all of them.

It is sad to leave O'Neill, the master craftsman, on a note of total failure, but that is the way with O'Neill. The commercial disaster of the controversial *Days without End* in 1934 was the last new O'Neill play before he faded from the New York theater scene for more than 12 years, with only the headlines surrounding the Nobel Prize in 1936 to remind the world of his existence. Burns Mantle, in his opening-night review, observed that the play would be "a thrill for the religionist"; he was absolutely right. The play was welcomed as O'Neill's finest piece by the religious press, both Catholic and Protestant, who praised the long-awaited return of the heretic to the fold. The protagonist lying prostrate before a crucifix in the final act, combined with the miraculous recovery of his wife, was proof enough that O'Neill, glory be, was now saved. Proselytizing may be welcomed by the church, but it is insufficient to bear the burden of convincing drama. There has to be considerably more than dramatizing the benefits of confession and the revelation of seeing the heavenly light if a play is to work for a lay audience. Predictably, *Days without End* was condemned by a solid majority of the secular critics as tedious, artificial, sophomoric, trite, and just plain bad.

O'Neill's supposed return to the church is simply a misreading. It is apparent from his working notes and from all evidence in his life after the play that O'Neill never considered *Days without End* a dramatization of his reconversion, or even, as in the more common Protestant expression, of his being "born again." John the novelist is O'Neill the dramatist, and his relationship with Elsa suggests the author's own tempestuous marital problems, but the play is no more literally biographical than many an earlier work.

Most of the play's techniques are unsuccessful throwbacks to a number of O'Neill's past practices. Endlessly talky, with no action to speak of, the play has unfortunate echoes of the tedious *Welded*, with its long discussions about how overpowering love imprisons, driving those caught by it into an almost uncontrollable desire to kill it. The final result is boredom in the extreme.

The use of the hideously masked doppelgänger named Loving, visible and audible only to John, has the possibility of good theater, but O'Neill muffs the chance. This cynical, satanic half of the protagonist's nature gambols, hisses, and interpolates remarks into the conversation in a manner initially disconcerting and ultimately extremely irritating. The technique is successful neither as a *Brown*ism nor as *Interlude*ism; it simply interferes ad nauseam. The pleasure in seeing Loving destroyed in John's "mystic exaltation" before the crucifix comes not because the Devil receives his due but because the audience is jolly well tired of him.

John's endless relating to Father Baird of his attempt to find himself through socialism, anarchism, Nietzsche, Marx, Taoism, Buddhism, Greek philosophy, numerology, and evolutionary scientific truth becomes grotesque. Desperately loving his wife, Elsa, he cheats on her with her best friend. Now she is dying. The predicament for John is intolerable, and so in fact is the play; Elsa's patently and unbelievably artificial miracle of recovery is the last straw. One almost hears the heavenly angels welcoming *Faust*'s Marguerite into paradise. The play becomes not a portrayal of faith but a parody. Lionel Trilling's comment neatly sums it all up. O'Neill, he sadly notes, "has crept into the dark womb of the Mother Church and pulled the universe in with him" (Miller, *Progress*, 119).

When Eugene O'Neill received the Nobel Prize for Literature in 1936, reaction was as sharply divided as ever. The respected editor of the *Saturday Review of Literature*, Bernard DeVoto, flatly asserted that O'Neill "can hardly be called an artist of the first rank; he is hardly even one of the first-rate figures of his own generation in America" (Miller,

Progress, 109). Some years later John Gassner echoed the positive side. Though O'Neill's power often exceeded his skill, he said, "still his craftsmanship was sufficient to carry him through some of the most ambitious projects attempted in the Western theater since Aeschylus wrote trilogies twenty-four hundred years ago."[42]

Although the Nobel award was far from unanimously acclaimed in America, given the theater for which O'Neill wrote and the risks he took, with his acceptance overseas often exceeding that at home, the prize was probably deserved. There was never a modern dramatist who remotely approached what he tried, for better or worse, and there has been none since. Judged from the perspective of his plays produced after the Second World War, widely acknowledged to be not only his greatest but also the work of a true artistic genius, the plays that gained O'Neill the prize are far less impressive. But hindsight is irrelevant; second-guessing the Nobel committee is fruitless. The best of O'Neill's prewar plays, in spite of repeated melodramatics and overconscious straining for effect, are still frequently played and increasingly studied, not just because they led to greater works but also because of their innovative techniques and undeniable inherent dramatic values that cannot be ignored.

As the second war approached, O'Neill continued to work on his multiplay cycle entitled "A Tale of Possessors Self-Dispossessed," treating several generations of an American family. In desperately bad health, he floundered in the magnitude of his task and became more and more depressed by the war news, which made his own efforts seem so trivial. Estranged from both surviving children, whom he disinherited, and trapped in the isolation of his California mountain home, he became the sad figure of a collapsed giant who regarded his own efforts as useless in the face of global disaster. To read his notes, diaries, and letters from his last years is a deeply saddening experience. Not until 1946 would O'Neill, obviously a dying man, again be seen in person, watching the rehearsals of the last of his plays produced in New York in his lifetime, *The Iceman Cometh*. Thereafter, the steadily decreasing news about him sounded like communications from a long-forgotten past.

4

Sturm und Drang, American Style

The pioneering little theaters that had brought the revolution of the new spirit to the American theater, introducing Eugene O'Neill and leading American audiences into the excitement and challenge of twentieth-century methods already familiar in Europe, had done their work within a relatively tranquil society. The unfathomable violence of the Great War had remained in a distant world, even after America became a participant. Unscathed by the conflict, its youth sacrificed in very small numbers, and suffering nothing of the upheavals that shattered Europe, the United States had become the dominant global power to which other nations looked and listened.

By the mid-1920s the little theaters, those prime movers in dramatic taste, had accomplished their task in peace, devoid of political overtones or social commentary. After the fifth edition of the Grand Street Follies, the Neighborhood Playhouse, its part of the artistic revolution accomplished, closed up shop in 1927. The Washington Square Players had long since become the Theatre Guild; its aim continued to be to bring the best drama to the American theater, with politics or social content incidental at most. There had been a smattering of politically far left and anarchic thinking among the Provincetown Players. One of them, John Reed, on the strength of *Ten Days That Shook the World* and his praise of the Soviet Revolution, was buried in the Kremlin. The fire that burned among the Provincetown group, however, was internal, seldom apparent in the productions the public came to see. Millay's quiet but pointed indictment of war in *Aria da Capo*, and O'Neill's *Hairy Ape* and *All God's Chillun*, were about all that could be labeled "social" or "political." After the Provincetown regrouped in 1923 under O'Neill, Jones, and Macgowan, and until the last season ended in the spring of 1927, the list of plays, both domestic and foreign, offered little to stir the collective social or political emotions.

There were rips within the postwar social fabric of America. The bogeyman of the bewhiskered, bomb-toting communist continued in the big Red Scare, which culminated in the disgraceful railroading of Nicola Sacco and Bartolomeo Vanzetti to the execution chamber. There was a moment of sharp recession as the decade of the twenties began. Unemployment was widespread, especially among returning veterans; labor strikes were numerous. Rejecting Woodrow Wilson's cherished League of Nations, the country withdrew into its shell of isolation, endured a scandal called Teapot Dome, then headed into a period of booming prosperity led by the passive, silent man from Vermont, Calvin Coolidge. The colossal failure of the great moral experiment of Prohibition introduced gang wars and that new source of pleasurable law-breaking, the speakeasy. The twenties roared on and chose to ignore the warnings of impending global economic disaster. Women finally got the vote, long after England had broken the barrier. Compared to some of its late allies and enemies, however, America experienced no storm and stress, no violent social upheaval.

This was a time when the American theater, its creative energies now centered exclusively in New York, began to acquire world dominance. By the thirties the theaters of Russia, Germany, and Italy faded under dictatorships, and British drama was mostly Shaw and the lesser Galsworthy. Playhouses flourished on every street in a 10-block area on either side of Broadway. With entertainment in the great motion-picture palaces still silent and radio in its infancy, new plays by the hundreds appeared season after season. American playwrights other than O'Neill soon began to share the spotlight and to command serious attention.[1]

Things abruptly changed after 29 October 1929. For the next ten years, before the second half of the great European conflict known as World War II, the world depression raised serious doubts about the ability of traditional capitalism to survive. The United States government began more and more to enter actively into the control of society. Strong voices of the far Left increased. The communist Soviet Union, hitherto regarded as the great Red menace, was formally recognized by President Roosevelt in 1933. It even became acceptable to place onstage characters who advocated the Communist party line, especially those who resisted the growing threats of Nazi Germany and Fascist Italy. Young American volunteers fought beside the Russian-supported Loyalists of Spain against the Fascist rebels of Franco.

By the mid-thirties conditions had altered rapidly within the American theater. Motion pictures now sang and talked; radio comedy and drama held audiences at home. It was no longer possible to ignore the increasing threats of world events; the storms and stresses of national unrest began to make themselves evident on the stage, sometimes subtly, not infrequently in the open. Radicalism was afoot, and the Theatre Guild, its successes and its prestige notwithstanding, encountered open challenges to its staid conservatism.

Early Rumblings: The New Playwrights' Theatre, 1927–1929

Before considering the independent breakaway faction that departed from the ways of the Theatre Guild, as well as other important companies of the 1930s, we need a quick look backward at the earlier New Playwrights' Theatre, the group that anticipated the tone soon to be set by more radical companies. From the spring of 1927 through the spring of 1929, like the little theaters before it, the New Playwrights' Theatre undertook experiments unfettered by the conventions of the commercial stage. Its difference lay in its pursuit of support by political radicals and industrial workers for its prolabor bias against the capitalist system. The original membership of self-styled "revolting" playwrights who wanted to reemphasize the "social realism" they felt had become seriously eroded, if not lost altogether, included the well-known names of John Dos Passos, John Howard Lawson, Michael Gold, Francis Faragan, and Emanual (Em Jo) Basshe.

Unfortunately, the New Playwrights' Theatre was ahead of its time. The reception from the radicals and the laborers toward whom it directed its social message was, at best, lukewarm. More important, the company did not recognize two facts of life: workers themselves were not theater-goers, and middle-class Americans, forming the bulk of theater audiences, eschewed propagandistic drama. In an era when capitalism seemed to be functioning very well, few people were attracted to this early attempt at what came to be called proletarian drama.

A further problem that would bedevil all subsequent radical producers was the avowed purpose of demonstrating social injustice at the expense of dramatic artistry. Intent on creating a theater that meant to shock its audiences into becoming strongholds of liberalism, the New Playwrights' found that the unconventional style of most of the ten plays it managed to produce pleased neither the regular and relatively conservative Broadway audiences nor the more radical readers of the *Daily Worker*. The succession of episodic and disjointed scenes with vaudevillelike characters may have represented virtuosity in scenic art, but they were sadly deficient in play construction. On the one hand, the unsubtle social emphasis in the realism they sought to capture was distasteful to the conventional theater-goer, while on the other hand, the desired impact on the Left was not strong enough. Thus, the productions fell between the Right and Left, leaving everybody unhappy.

The New Playwrights' Theatre cannot be faulted, however, for attempting to make its case in a variety of subjects. The first production, Lawson's *Loud Speaker* (1927), satirized machine politics. Paul Sifton's *The Bell*, the same year, involved an assembly line that turned workers into expendable robots. Basshe's *The Centuries* (1928) concerned Russian Jews who fled the pogroms only to end up in New York's ghettos and demeaning sweatshops. Lawson's *The International* (1928) dramatized the confict between Communist and Fascist forces. If these and the other productions made no memorable contribution to the history of the American theater, they added significantly to the experience of two of the group's members, Dos Passos and Lawson. The techniques they learned made a strong impact on the style used by Dos Passos in his great narrative trilogy, *USA* (1938). Lawson went on to formulate the aims of drama as a weapon in the battle between the proletariat and the bourgeoisie in his influential *The Theory and Technique of Playwriting*, published in 1936 and reissued in 1985.[2]

The Proletariat Finds a Voice:
The Group Theatre, 1931–1941

The Theatre Guild had been founded and had succeeded on the premise that European and American dramaturgy could compete in attracting audiences and proving profitable. In 1931 a group of fervent young Guild actors and directors who felt that the Guild was not living up to its promises broke away to form the Group Theatre. Influenced mainly by the example of the Moscow Art Theatre, their aim was to attempt ensemble playing and mutual artistic development along the lines of the Stanislavsky method of acting. Konstantin Stanislavsky, the directing genius behind the Moscow Art Theatre, had set down his acting theories in two widely influential books, *My Life in Art* (1924) and *An Actor Prepares* (1926). Simply put, he insisted that character portrayal involves recall of the appropriate emotion from the actor's past, enabling the performer to project to the audience the sense of the emotional actuality of the scene. Furthermore, he compelled the entire cast to act together as a unified ensemble, permitting the domination of no single star.

To the three leaders of the dissidents, Harold Clurman, Lee Strasberg, and Cheryl Crawford, the Stanislavsky method made eminent sense. The name given to the company implied a cooperative effort "to bring the actor closer to the content of the play," as Clurman explains.[3] Actors would not be hired for a specific part; there would be no stars, because the Group wished their distinction to reside not in the individuals but in the production as a whole. Although salaries were pitifully small, the same amount was paid to actors who took major or minor roles. Neither writers nor directors would be masters, but they would serve as guides to the company, which belonged equally to all.

Beyond their full embrace of what has ever since been known as "Method acting,"[4] the Group Theatre pursued two further ideals. The first was the desire to develop a sympathetic audience that they hoped to educate to become a part of the production by actively entering into the play's spirit. This somewhat vague concept is a bit difficult to explain precisely, since it assumes audiences must somehow become direct participants beyond their normal empathic responses. This viewpoint constantly faces the danger of breaking down all barriers of aesthetic distance so that the play becomes an actual happening, in keeping with the Method's attempt to create Stanislavsky's emotional actuality. The ideal can work under very limited circumstances, as the Group was to prove in Clifford Odets's *Waiting for Lefty*, but as a routine pattern of actor-audience relationship, it has its pitfalls.

Second, because they felt that drama should reflect the life from which it grew, pure romance, mere farce, or any play unrelated to American life was unacceptable. Moreover, the Group strongly favored plays showing that even deplorable conditions were susceptible to improvement by vigorous human action. Unfortunately, these self-imposed restrictions prompted the Group to turn down plays that later became minor classics. Maxwell Anderson's *Winterset* is a case in point. The play's doomed young lovers choose to die rather than live in an imperfect world, which, counter to the Group's ideal of social "improvability," they make no effort to improve. The Group may have avoided the romantic for fear of becoming involved in dangerously intrusive sentimentality, but holding the line by refusing to accept the possibility that a character like *Winterset's* Mio might fail resulted in a kind of romanticizing in itself that, in hindsight, appears almost naive.

The Group's determination to follow their ideals was shown in their first production, Paul Green's *The House of Connelly* (1931). In his original version, Green, so well versed in southern social tradition, emphasized the decadence of the old plantation South, ending the play with a vicious murder of the owner's wife, a tenant farmer's daughter, by two sybil-like black retainers. The Group preferred to look more optimistically toward the emergence of a new South from among the tenant farmers and prevailed upon Green to eliminate his initial conclusion. As Clurman explains, "Our own sense of perfectability of man, or, at least, the inevitability of the struggle against evil . . . made us impatient with the play's violent ending" (Clurman, 44). The Guild, having released the play to the Group, sharply disagreed and consequently withheld some of its originally promised financial support. Nevertheless, the Group stuck to their decision, and the play opened in September 1931 "under the auspices of the Theatre Guild," as explained in the program, for a successful if limited run. (See chapter 8 for a more detailed discussion of *The House of Connelly.*)

Success was short-lived. *The House of Connelly* was followed the same season by what has been called the first proletarian play, *1931 . . .* by Claire and Paul Sifton. Its obvious attempt to shock and anger in the episodic story of Adam, a working Everyman who falls from factory job to breadlines, attracted no audience. Maxwell Anderson's rather muddled verse tragedy of Spanish feudalism in New Mexico, *Night over Taos*, likewise went nowhere. Two more failures followed in the 1931–32 season, Lawson's *Success Story* and Dawn Powell's *Long Night*, both dealing with the perversity of the American success myth. Without its Guild support, cast adrift on their own, and unable to build an audience through an abortive subscription campaign, the Group had apparently collapsed.

Refusing to quit, the Group, nearly penniless, sat out the 1932–

33 season without a show. In September 1933 they pulled themselves together to stage Sidney Kingsley's hospital melodrama *Men in White*. Its instant success and one-year run were lifesavers, but to many Group members this long-running sentimentalizing of a doctor's life, so far removed from any proletarian concern, seemed a betrayal of their cause. It was a lesson in the practicalities of the New York stage, however; ideals had to be bent if the Group were to remain viable. Made financially sound by this momentary sacrifice of ideals, the Group were now able to continue as a vital part of the New York theater for another seven years.

The Group made no apologies for the leftish, proletarian slant of many of its productions. As the Great Depression wore on, the Group's subject matter, while not the transparent propaganda that others were undertaking, depicted a good part of the era's developing stresses. The public viewed the ensemble's close unity as communistic, a label the members stoutly denied. The denial may have been genuine, but it was a little suspect: a Communist cell did exist, separately but concurrently, within the Group. Among its membership for a short time was the Group's best-known playwright, Clifford Odets, whose seven plays brought the Group their greatest successes and their most notoriety. Odets's Communist connections and the subject matter of his plays did little to alter the public image of the Group as a far-Left, red-tainted, propagandizing organization.

Clifford Odets's first produced play, *Waiting for Lefty*, opened on 5 January 1935 for a series of benefit performances at the Civic Repertory Company. It received little notice from the professional critics, but through the theater world's underground grapevine it quickly gained an audience and became the season's out-and-out sensation. The play's undisguised vehemence and openly communist slant, and its closing with shouts from the audience to "Strike! Strike!" shot the young playwright to permanent fame. In March—combined with Odets's third play, the first American anti-Nazi drama, *'Til the Day I Die*—*Waiting for Lefty* entered a regular three-month run. More than any other play, it inspired the kind of direct audience involvement the Group had first dreamed of. According to Clurman's report on the opening night, "A shock of delightful recognition struck the audience like a tidal wave . . . a kind of joyous fervor seemed to sweep the audience toward the stage. . . . Audience and actors had become one" (Clurman, 138).

Lefty was followed almost immediately in February 1935 by *Awake and Sing*, Odets's full-length portrayal of the frustrations and bitterness of a lower-middle-class Jewish family caught up in the trials of the deepening Depression. *Paradise Lost* (1935), *Golden Boy* (1937), and *Rocket to the Moon* (1938), all explorations of the debilitating aspects of a variety of social pressures during the Depression, enhanced the Group's artistic reputation, though not always its coffers. After *Night Music* (1940), about two young lovers trying to find themselves, Odets ran off to the more lucrative offers of Hollywood. (See chapter 6 for a full discussion of Odets.)

By the time it disbanded in 1940 the Group had staged 23 plays of widely varied success that had brought new excitement into the Depression-ridden American theater, not only in playwriting but particularly in the impressive success of their ensemble acting. In addition to their excellence within the conventional style of contemporary realism, they willingly undertook variations, such as Paul Green and Kurt Weill's stylized antiwar musical drama *Johnny Johnson* (1936), William Saroyan's sentimental, almost mystical, dreamlike short piece *My Heart's in the Highlands* (1939), and Robert Ardrey's metaphysical fantasy of a lighthouse peopled by ghosts, called *Thunder Rock* (1939). In the long run, perhaps the Group's weakest link was a lack of sufficient suitable scripts. The dearth of new plays had always hampered other companies struggling to remain independent of Broadway commercialism, but perhaps none so seriously as the Group, which consistently attempted to seek the expression of American life through American authors. Nevertheless, the Group cast their influence over the American theater for years afterward through many of their outstanding members: Stella and Luther Adler, Morris Carnovsky, and Franchot Tone in acting and the teaching of acting; Lee Strasberg and Cheryl Crawford in the Actors' Studio and in producing and directing; Mordecai Gorelik and Donald Oenslager in scene design; and to be sure, Clifford Odets in playwriting.

The Government Gets into the Act: The Federal Theatre Project, 1935–1939

During the Great Depression the *Sturm und Drang*, the storms and stresses in American society, were popular dramatic subjects, with Clifford Odets and the Group among the more articulate voices. Some of the most audaciously outspoken and lively theatrical treatment of the strains that verged on tearing American society apart, however, came from a highly unlikely source: a theater created and subsidized by the United States government.

One of the more familiar and widespread of Franklin Roosevelt's "pump-priming" efforts—putting federal money, through deficit spending, into the economy in order to create jobs in hopes of reducing unemployment and increasing consumer spending—was the Works Progress (eventually Works Projects) Administration. Known everywhere by its initials as one of Roosevelt's "alphabetical" agencies (NRA, AAA, TVA, CCC, and others), the WPA was criticized for its many make-work projects, derisively termed "boondoggling" by its detractors. It was subject to ridicule and comedians' jokes for the seeming overkill of employing ten or a dozen workers to accomplish a task that could be handled by two or three. What is often overlooked is the major cultural impact of the WPA through its various arts projects for writers, artists, musicians, and performers. One of the largest, the Federal Theatre Project, was established during the depths of the Depression in the summer of 1935 as a relief program for all kinds of theater personnel whose unemployment rate more than equaled that of the general labor force. (During the worst of the Depression unemployment across the nation approached 30 percent.) At its height the Federal Theatre provided some 13,000 actors, directors, and technicians with a small but lifesaving income.[5]

Nothing like the Project had ever been attempted in this country. It involved direct federal subsidy of the performing arts, familiar enough in Europe but always avoided in America for fear of government interference and the constant danger of censorship. During the four years of its existence, however, the Federal Theatre Project was not only a phenomenal success but was also able to act as an independent organization, free, except on one or two occasions, of governmental intrusion. There were no limits on what was undertaken. Greek or Shakespearean classics, new and experimental plays and dance drama, musicals, pageants, and puppet shows, children's plays and foreign-language adaptations, and, even in those days of segregation, a separate black drama, were offered in towns and cities across the country. The inexpensive ticket prices created audiences in areas where live entertainment had hitherto been unavailable or even entirely unknown.

Such an ambitious program could very easily have foundered had the Project not made the fortuitous choice of director Hallie Flanagan from Vassar College, whose experimental theater had attracted wide attention. In addition, her visits to European theaters and Stanislavsky's Moscow Art Theatre made her extraordinarily well qualified. Of greater importance than her artistic qualifications was her unusual administrative ability, combined with the patience and tenacity so necessary in her many visits to Washington. There she was continually forced to rise above bureaucratic red tape and endless delays in prying appropriations from a not always sympathetic Congress. Fortunately, her persistence succeeded; with her integrity and her ability to explain and justify the Project's artistic aims, she was able to counter the criticism that productions were politically slanted toward socialism and to allay the misgivings of those in power who not only mistrusted the stage itself but questioned federal subsidy for a people's theater, or any theater at all, for that matter.[6]

When the Theatre Project was set up, WPA administrator Harry Hopkins had promised a free, adult, and uncensored theater, but in 1935, before things could get under way, the promise seemed empty and the future ominous. In one of those rare encounters with censorship, the New York unit was forced to withdraw its first scheduled production, *Ethiopia*, because Washington officials refused to allow the portrayal on stage of foreign individuals such as Italian dictator Mussolini or Ethiopian Emperor Haile Selassie. Thereafter, the Project was permitted to function with almost no interference.

Because the large number of unemployed actors who sought relief in the Project could not be accommodated in traditional plays with their normally small casts, the challenge was met by the inspired invention of the Living Newspaper. Sponsored by the Newspaper Guild of America, this vigorous newsreel form of drama made use of large casts in highly theatrical productions. Familiar with the driving impact and forceful journalistic style of the popular movie documentary series "The March of Time," audiences were stirred by the dynamic live performances dramatizing the natural, social, and economic stresses of the Depression crisis, which were affecting Americans everywhere. The fast-paced momentum of one melodramatic short scene following another across the stage, each spotlighted in turn, was enhanced by background music and voice-over editorial comment. Other nontraditional effects included unusual singing and speaking choruses, projected photographs, cartoons, and newspaper headlines, soliloquies, and pantomime. Restrictions were imposed only by the physical limits of the theaters themselves.

A mere summary of Living Newspaper productions hardly conveys the excitement this new form of drama generated. The fast and often furious pace made for powerful audience response; each performance consciously sought to encourage the viewers' involvement and to spur public action in support of the ideas and attitudes being promoted. Strong audience empathy was also gained through the emphasis on hope expressed at the end of each production. *Triple-A Plowed Under* (1936) concentrated on the plight of the farmers and closed to stirring music as impoverished farmers moved with outstretched arms toward hungry slum dwellers with cries of "We need you!"[7] Even more vivid was *One-third of a Nation* (1938). President Roosevelt had focused attention on the dehumanizing conditions forced upon the one-third of the nation whom he identified as ill clothed, ill housed, and ill fed. Staged in a lifelike setting of rat-infested slum rooms built atop each other, with a terrifyingly realistic fatal fire, this Living Newspaper production made its strong social point in the closing scenes about greedy landlords and overcrowded tenements, together with instructions on safety codes. *Power* (1937) was an appeal to support public ownership of utilities being developed by the Tennessee Valley Authority. It used direct audience involvement by a sudden theater blackout, cries from the house for "Light! Light!" and brilliantly spotlighted vignettes in such places as a hospital and a home with a sick child. *Spirochete* (1938) defied established taboos by dramatizing the battle against syphilis in order to foster a less hypocritical public attitude toward this serious social contagion. In some productions the audience was drawn in as part of the debate by actors seated in the auditorium and portraying legislators or other public figures.

The Living Newspaper's ability to create an impressive unified whole through its combination of widely variant styles, imaginative use of lighting, sound, and scene design, and very large casts was a remarkable theatrical achievement in itself. Even more important was its great success in creating through live theater not only an emotional experience for audiences mainly attuned to the motion picture but also a heightened public awareness of crucial social problems.

One of the most celebrated conventional plays of the Project was *It Can't Happen Here*, an adaptation of Sinclair Lewis's frightening novel about America's gradual takeover by a Fascist dictator who follows the simple expedient of silencing dissent instead of using brute force. Americans were slowly gaining awareness of what overseas dictators were doing to suppress basic human freedoms, and demagogues at home—Huey Long, Father Coughlin, and others—were capturing devoted followers while raising serious questions among the general populace about the influence of their charismatic performances in person and on the radio as they propounded their half-baked schemes to regain national prosperity. Those doing the play felt that a dramatization of the novel's sinister theme and terrifying consequences would carry a greater impact by being seen everywhere at once rather than here and there at different times. Therefore, on 17 October 1936, *It Can't Happen Here* opened simultaneously in 21 theaters, all of them outside New York, in 17 states. The positive public reaction proved the wisdom of this unique idea.

The Negro unit, always so identified because *black* at that time was a forbidden word, made good use of technicians denied membership in the Stagehands' Union because of race. They were the first to open a Federal Theatre production in New York following the cancellation of *Ethiopia*. Their play about a southern race riot, called *Walk Together Chillun*, received little notice from downtown critics when it opened at Harlem's Lafayette Theatre in February 1936. This indifference quickly changed with the tour de force *Macbeth* (1936) set in Haiti. This sensational version of one of the most well-known Elizabethan plays proved that Shakespeare could be successfully performed by black actors and could attract black and white audiences equally. (See further discussion below under Orson Welles.) The unit's *Swing Mikado* (1938) did well in Chicago, New York, and elsewhere before being taken over by private producers for extended runs.

The Federal Theatre Project's aim to reach all levels of society everywhere was realized in a manner no commercial organization could ever have accomplished. The Living Newspaper may have received most of the headlines, but the variety and scope of the Project's other ventures command a certain awe at what it achieved in so short a lifetime over such a broad area. The "legitimate theater," almost wholly limited to New York and a few other large cities, became available at very low cost to audiences who had never seen such things before, in productions of Greek classics and plays by Shaw, Ibsen, Chekhov, and Tolstoi, plus American works by O'Neill, Maxwell Anderson, Thornton Wilder, and Sidney Howard. Dickens's *A Christmas Carol* and medieval mystery plays traveled to churches and schools. The Radio Division brought hundreds of radio plays to those areas where live theater was impossible. Paul Green's symphonic drama *The Lost Colony* (1937), about early Virginia colonists, played annually on Roanoke Island. Ethnic audiences in major urban areas could attend some 80 productions in French, German, Spanish, Italian, and Yiddish. The cumulative breadth and variety made the Federal Theatre Project the first and only truly national theater the nation was ever to experience.

The Federal Theatre Project mounted some 1,200 productions nationwide during its brief four years. If the enthusiasm on both sides of the footlights had been the determining factor, some form of federal theater might still be in existence. Unfortunately, its fate was decided not by the Project's participants but by the politicians who were determined to end the experiment. Although the House Committee on Un-American Activities (HUAC), in investigating the Federal Theatre Project, never accepted any of Flanagan's official invitations to see any of the performances of any unit in any city, and although they found no immorality, subversion, or misuse of funds, their report, filed with the House of Representatives on 3 January 1939, charged that "a rather large number of the employees on the Federal Theatre Project are either members of the Communist Party or sympathetic to the Communist Party."[8] This gratuitous statement reinforced the perception by government watchdogs of a communist threat, and it combined with fears of southern congressmen that the strength of the Negro unit and the Project's policy of nondiscrimination might spread. Others of fundamentalist and far-right persuasion feared the Project might propagate radicalism and blasphemy. Congress caved in and on 30 June 1939 voted to discontinue support.[9]

With the immediate dispersion of all properties, costumes, scenery, and other goods of the Project, as ordered by Congress, the great experiment ended, but not before 30 million viewers and thousands of theater personnel in hundreds of theaters and school auditoriums, and on portable stages in parks and elsewhere across the country, had enjoyed between 1935 and 1939 a unique and valuable experience. Fortunately for posterity, some 6,000 plays and radio scripts, dozens of cabinets of photographs, crates of posters, clippings, and other Project records were found in 1974 stored in the Library of Congress. They were placed in the Research Library of George Mason University in Fairfax, Virginia, where they remain accessible to all scholars who wish to seek them out.

Much Sound and Fury:
The "Mad Genius" of Orson Welles

The one individual who made the most noise and received the most attention in the briefest time during the turbulent late Depression years was a driven, hyperenergetic young man named Orson Welles. Whatever he undertook as performer or producer on stage or on the air (and later on the screen) created a sensation, upon one occasion sending the nation into instant panic.

There is much of legend about Orson Welles. The tales of his brawls and debauches, his prodigious eating, his furious 20-hour working days, his habit of driving his casts to exhaustion, then demanding still more, his violent rows with his actors, were well known, but there was never any argument that the "boy wonder" of the American theater was justly acclaimed a genius. At 16, Welles had played leading roles at Dublin's Gate Theatre. In 1934, only 19, he was playing opposite Katharine Cornell in her national repertory company, creating a grimly fascinating, sick, and furious Tybalt in *Romeo and Juliet.* His uniquely vibrant, resonant voice commanded instant attention and became a hallmark throughout his career.

After being struck by Welles's exceptional Tybalt, producer John Houseman had cast him as a fiftyish industrialist-financier in Archibald MacLeish's anticapitalistic play *Panic,* presented in the spring of 1935 by the newly formed Phoenix Theatre. When Houseman was put in charge of the Negro unit of the Federal Theatre Project, he again sought Welles to collaborate on a major undertaking, the staging of *Macbeth* with an entirely black cast. By setting the play in Haiti and employing a troupe of genuine African drummers and an authentic witch doctor, the play soon became known as the "voodoo" *Macbeth.* The text was performed as written, with straightforward delivery of the Shakespearean blank verse and no attempt at Negro or other regional dialect.

Long before the play opened, the prospect of a Harlem-based Negro company doing a hyped-up *Macbeth* aroused all manner of curiosity, apprehension, and, of course, downright bigotry. Happily, the effort was worth it. The play opened in April 1936 and was performed before sellout houses for ten weeks at the Lafayette in Harlem and for two more months downtown. Critics were generally favorable, noting, as they had with O'Neill's *The Emperor Jones,* that the Negro now had a genuine opportunity to appear in major roles. In the words of Roi Otley, a militant Negro journalist, the Negro could "discard the bandanna and burnt cork casting to play a universal character. We attended the *Macbeth* showing, happy in the thought we wouldn't again be reminded, with all its vicious implications, that we were niggers."[10]

The Federal Theatre Project production of Marlowe's *The Tragical History of Dr. Faustus* once again inspired Welles to almost fiendish efforts. The Maxine Elliott Theatre was transformed by the addition of a stage thrust into the auditorium beyond the proscenium, full of murderously dangerous trapdoors from and into which characters appeared and disappeared to such a volume of smoke and flame that the New York Fire

Department threatened to close the play down. In sound, acting style, scenic conceptions, props, and compounded magic tricks, it was a vivid expression of Welles's very special talents. Welles played Faustus opposite the Mephistopheles of Jack Carter, who had taken the lead in *Macbeth*. According to Houseman, their combined stage presence was unforgettable. Welles and Carter were each around six-foot-four, with abnormal strength and a capability of sudden furious violence, but able to play with remarkable restraint. The press responded with praise, and *Faustus* ran from early January to May 1937 before standing-room-only audiences.

Houseman's account relates many of Welles's personal idiosyncracies, but his comment about Faustus bears repeating:

> The truth is that the legend of the man who sells his soul to the devil in exchange for knowledge and power and who must finally pay for his brief triumph with the agonies of eternal damnation was uncomfortably close to the shape of Welles' own personal myth. Orson really believed in the Devil. . . . This was not a whimsy but a real obsession. At twenty-one Orson was sure he was doomed. . . . [H]e was rarely free from a sense of sin and a fear of retribution so intense and immediate that it drove him through long nights of panic to seek refuge in debauchery or work. (Houseman, 235)

The production most directly associated with the storms and stresses of the Depression, and the most notorious for Welles before he formed the Mercury Theatre, was his staging of Marc Blitzstein's radical labor musical, *The Cradle Will Rock* (1937). There were resemblances to *Waiting for Lefty*—for example, vignettes and flashbacks were used to develop the theme of corruption—but Welles planned an elaborate series of settings rather than Odets's bare stage. There was a little bit of everything in *Cradle*, from mock operetta to marching songs, vaudeville sketches, recitatives and arias, declamatory speeches, and political caricatures. All were aimed at telling a loosely constructed story of Mr. Mister, the cigar-chewing boss of Steeltown, and his sycophants, Reverend Salvation and Editor Daily, collectively opposed to the blue-collar hero Larry Foreman and his fellow workers, who, in a rousing finale, sing "The Cradle Will Rock," predicting labor's triumph.

The story of the opening of *The Cradle Will Rock* has become almost legendary. In a time of serious social unrest, with sit-down strikes in the automotive industry, bloody violence in the Republic Steel strike, and martial law in Johnstown, Pennsylvania, there was genuine fear of what might result from such a radical antiestablishment satire. Afraid of adverse repercussions in Congress, which was considering appropriations for the next year, the WPA administration refused to sponsor the play, forcing Houseman and Welles to take it on themselves. Problems mounted as Actors' Equity denied permission for its members to perform outside WPA jurisdiction. Then on 16 June 1937, the scheduled date for opening, apprehensive civil authorities forcibly closed and locked the Maxine Elliott Theatre, elaborate scenery and all. As Houseman observes, there was now everything for doing the play—except a theater and a cast.

The solution was as spectacular as the problem. As restless crowds who had expected a show waited to see what would happen, Houseman and Welles learned that the old Venice Theatre some 20 blocks up Seventh Avenue was dark and immediately available. Thereupon, they led a parade of audience and actors, followed by a hastily secured out-of-tune piano, up Seventh Avenue and into the vacant house. There Blitzstein himself went through the entire production in a solo performance on the dusty stage, his silenced cast seated among the onlookers. On 18 June, after persuading the authorities to unlock the Maxine Elliott, *The Cradle Will Rock* opened an extended commercial run at full Equity rates. The entire event had been front-page news, but the professional New York critics never seriously reviewed the play until it opened in December for a special benefit performance at Welles's newly formed Mercury Theatre. Notices were predominantly favorable. The press of the Left hailed it; the organized Right hated it.[11]

Welles had strong hopes of establishing his own repertory company, and for a moment it appeared as if he might succeed. With his usual unchecked gusto and dreams far ahead of reality, with Houseman's help he planned the entire operation, secured the old Comedy Theatre, renamed it the Mercury, and in November 1937 launched the enterprise with a rousingly successful modern-dress production of *Julius Caesar*. The presentation of Caesar as a Fascist dictator, with soldiers in contemporary military uniforms, was a striking parallel to the threatening world situation, in which Hitler and Mussolini were stalking the globe. In the words of John Mason Brown, the critic of the *New York Post, Julius Caesar* was "by all odds the most exciting, the most imaginative, the most topical, the most awesome, and the most absorbing of the season's new productions. The touch of genius is upon it" (Houseman, 314).

The future of the Mercury seemed assured as *Julius Caesar* played the season to full houses. The reprise of *The Cradle* in an "oratorio" version began a regular run in January 1938 and lasted for nearly three months. An adaptation of Thomas Dekker's Elizabethan farce *The Shoe-makers' Holiday* opened the same month, with the double entendres and other comic aspects altered to fit a modern audience. By this time Welles was widely hailed as the great hope for a new American theater. His ultrarealistic staging of Shaw's *Heartbreak House*, an attempt to woo middle-class audiences as well as the more liberal supporters of the earlier plays, was followed by George Büchner's *Danton's Death* in November 1938. Its pessimistic view of the French Revolution and its expressionistic sets seemed irrelevant, baffling audiences of all classes. Neither produc-tion did well at the box office.

Suddenly, with audiences no longer out front, its treasury rapidly emptying, the Mercury Theatre found itself insolvent and unable to stage another play. Almost as quickly as it had appeared, the Mercury, after little more than a year, closed permanently. At the age of 24, Orson Welles had passed the peak of his acclaim and turned to Hollywood, where in 1940 his *Citizen Kane* would become one of the great cinema classics of all time.

Why did the Mercury zoom on and off stage so quickly? Views expressed in the *New York Times* attributed it to the cost of repertory and the egotism of its director; others blamed the "new fangled bohemianism and fundamental lack of seriousness" (Houseman, 409). More than anything else, the Mercury's brief life was probably the fault of the overambitious, tempestuous, self-centered, disorganized, at times almost mad genius who was in over his head in the practical world of New York theater. But the impact of the Mercury, however brief, was profound. Its special and some-times frenetic quality amidst all its difficulties brought a new kind of energetic excitement to the art of the stage that was attempting to hold its own in a society that seemed to be everywhere falling down.

No discussion of the Mercury Theatre can close without a brief comment about its most sensational performance, the broadcast of H. G. Wells's "The War of the Worlds" on the CBS Mercury Radio Theatre on 30 October 1938. It was aired so realistically that despite repeated state-ments by the announcer that it was only a play, panic reigned from one coast to another, especially throughout the Northeast. Hysterical citizens fled into the streets, uncertain what to do, but certain of one thing: the world was at an end. Meanwhile, all other radio stations blithely contin-ued their regular programming, which those in panic never seemed to notice. It was the Mercury's greatest success, and the nation's greatest embarrassment, as millions realized how utterly they had been taken in.[12]

Storms and Stresses on the Left:
The Agitprop Theaters of the Thirties

Most of what soon became known as "agitprop" (agitation-propaganda) theaters were far outside the mainstream of the legitimate theater of the 1930s. A study of American dramatic literature might, in fact, leave them out entirely, but to do so would be to ignore some of the liveliest and noisiest theater to be seen during the Depression.

Unabashedly left-wing, often to an extreme, and unashamedly propagandistic, agitprop theaters had their time and place, pushing their attacks on "the system" and raising some legitimate questions in the midst of the nation's trauma. One-sided and emotional, some of them were very exciting to watch, presenting a voice that any open society should permit and even listen to. The biggest drawback, however, was that once the message was presented, it stood a great chance of being worn out through repetition. And once the conditions on which their criticism thrived were changed by law or the passing of time, the agitprop theaters had no further reason to exist.

From the political standpoint, the Communist party was the most active in the presentation of agitprop theater. Notwithstanding congressional committees—in particular, HUAC and other agencies, including the FBI, bent on purging the nation of the Red threat lurking on every street corner—the Communist party was not outlawed and never has been. Through the *Daily Worker* and *The Masses*, which at one time listed Eugene O'Neill as a member of the editorial board, and through the channels of American politics, including the perennial presidential candidate Earl Browder, the party's activities were well known and widely tolerated.[13]

The party organized many of the short-lived agitprop theaters on somewhat different lines from those followed in Russia. In both countries the aim was to convince audiences that the virtues of the proletariat were superior to the evils of the capitalist state; but the Soviets, as in all their art, considered "social realism" best suited to furthering the Communist cause. To a large extent the American left-wing theater groups chose less orthodox methods, preferring experiments in a variety of forms. In the early twenties Michael Gold had said that the "class war" had long since been declared and that an art should be forged by the proletariat itself. He asserted that "the Revolution in its secular manifestation of strike, boycott, mass meetings, imprisonment, agitation, martyrdom, organization, is thereby worthy of the religious devotion of the artist," but as Trotsky himself warned, "Proletarian art should not be second-rate art" (Bigsby, 189–90, 192).

One of the earliest propaganda groups was the German-speaking Proletbühne (Proletarian Stage), actually formed in 1925 but reorganized in 1928, before the Depression. Modeled directly on the "committed" theaters of Europe, it drew very limited audiences. The Workers' Laboratory Theatre, founded in 1930, originally performed its short, stylized pieces on street corners, on docks, and at factory gates. Audiences were invited to participate by being directly addressed by the performers; subjects "discussed" varied from problems of striking Kentucky miners to criticism of New York's Mayor LaGuardia. Later, the Laboratory offered its wares in a large room with benches and a simple raised platform, over which hung a banner with the slogan "The Theatre Is a Weapon". One of its most effective pieces, *Newsboy*, exhorted the public to read Communist publications promoting peace rather than capitalist newspapers underwritten by munitions makers. In 1934 the Laboratory Theatre, reorganized as the Theatre of Action, abandoned the old agitprop style for a more professional approach to socialist realism. Many important names appeared on the theater's advisory council, including Moss Hart and Lee Strasberg. Elia Kazan was employed as director, and John Howard Lawson, at the time a party member, was on the executive board. A try at making the theater's case by transferring to Broadway failed completely. After 1936 the Theatre of Action ceased altogether.

Neither the Theatre Collective nor the League of Workers' Theaters, two radical companies operating between 1932 and 1936, was able to attract any significant audience. In contrast was the thoroughly professional Theatre Union. Between 1933 and 1937, in its call for reform, the Union's less hysterical plays were better suited to the sentiments of those who welcomed the challenges to government policies and social injustice. In 1933 the Union staged the first important antiwar play, *Peace on Earth* by Albert Maltz and George Sklar. The suffering of abused peace-seekers was shown as equal to that endured by workers in the class war. *Stevedore* (1934) by Maltz and Sklar, an early plea for racial cooperation among all workers, concerned a militant black longshoreman framed on a rape charge, whom white union friends try but fail to save. Sklar's *Black Pit* (1935) centered on a coal miner scab who suffers guilt and ostracism. In John Howard Lawson's *Marching Song* (1937), the most polemical of the Union's four American plays, the "hero" was the collective group of workers who finally unite against the villainous strike-breakers and sing their revolutionary marching song at the end. Not surprisingly, Broadway critics complained about the polemics, but Marxist critics praised this dramatization of society as an industrial battleground.

A major flaw, which should have been obvious from the first among those who attempted to propound their arguments in dramatic form, was the inability to make actors out of party zealots. The New Theatre League, the name adopted by the Collective in 1935, did discover one play that worked, Odets's astonishingly successful *Waiting for Lefty* at the Civic Repertory Theatre, but even that was far more a success of the Group Theatre than of the League or any other organization. These unprofessional groups did not achieve their hope of building wide audiences, even though they provided some new avenues of experimentation for writers, actors, and directors.

It was inevitable that the revolutionary solutions to all political and social problems suggested in the productions of the Union and others found less and less public favor. It was impossible to build an audience committed to supporting a Marxist theater; rapidly changing times were undermining everything. Liberals began to see hope in the strong measures of Roosevelt's New Deal, the Federal Theatre Project provided a better stage for experimental drama, and Communist ideology no longer seemed to be the only answer to unemployment and social upheaval. The most devastating blow to the Communist cause was the Stalin-Hitler nonaggression pact of 1939, which led directly to World War II. This was an incomprehensible act of betrayal that drove away a host of Marxist sympathizers. Having played their role at the height of America's flirtation with ideological resolutions of her difficulties, agitprop theaters, including the relatively successful Theatre Union, faded permanently from the scene.

The Communist party had made no headway in the American theater, but a more authentically American labor organization, the International Ladies' Garment Workers Union, succeeded with *Pins and Needles*, a lighthearted musical satire of capital and labor that became one of New York's longest running productions before World War II. Much less revolutionary than the Communist-sponsored theater, and using the motto "Dedicated to the Advancement of Workers' Culture," this group was not above making fun of socialist drama itself. Originally offered only on weekends, since the cast had regular duties during the week, the play became so popular that performers secured extended leave from their garment industry jobs. From its opening in June 1936 at the small Labor Stage through its Broadway stand at the Windsor Theatre until it closed four years later, *Pins and Needles* appeared more than 1,100 times in New York alone. Its national touring company fared equally well.

The Labor Stage, at first considered part of the so-called popular front, an uneasy alliance of socialists, communists, and other anti-fascist liberal groups working for peace, soon became anti-Soviet as well as anti-Nazi. Using satiric good humor in sketches and songs and a high-class professional production, the Labor Stage's agitprop effectiveness was greater than the lead-pipe assaults on the audience of the single-minded radical groups who, in the main, were preaching to the converted and turning off those they were supposed to convince. In an unusual gesture of recognition, if not full approval, President and Mrs. Roosevelt held a command performance of *Pins and Needles* at the White House on 3 March 1938.

Throughout the turbulence of the Great Depression—labor riots, soup lines, bloody strikes, and the natural catastrophe of the Dust Bowl—not a single agitprop production undertook to advocate what any genuine revolutionary would be expected to espouse: that is, the overthrow of the government and the rule of the proletariat. Characters often spoke with passion about the need to study and learn from Marx and Engels, and *The Communist Manifesto* was a visible prop in Odets's *Waiting for Lefty*; but the messages centered mainly on reform through humane and antidiscriminatory labor laws, the recognition of unions, and other social improvements for the oppressed. The nearest approach to a call to arms was in the shouting of "Strike! Strike!" at the close of *Lefty*. No appeal to man the barricades, to storm any symbolic Bastille, was ever made. Much of what was advocated arrived in legislation such as the Wagner Act and the establishment of Social Security, introduced by the rich, privileged, aristocratic president who, with his strong social consciousness, tried to turn things around. Then with the abrupt end of the Depression upon America's entry into the Second World War with the Soviet Union a full, if wary, ally, the causes of the radical theaters collapsed.

It was, nonetheless, a provocative and stimulating period in American theater history. The New Playwrights, the Group, the Federal Theatre, the Mercury, and the Labor Stage, the Sturm und Drang of their existence known and frequently applauded across the country, had greatly increased the range of drama that American audiences would accept. For the first time social awareness, long practiced in European theaters, was introduced onto the American stage more directly and more loudly than ever before. Even the more conventional and conservative playwrights and producers could now more easily do the same.[14] The agitprop theater groups had had their day as they performed on the edge of society and off the mainstream of the New York theater, but there was an inevitable truth that they could never escape: the marketplace of that very commercialized capitalistic stronghold, the Broadway theater, was the final arbiter of what would appear and succeed before a paying public.

5

A Cry of Playwrights

Would not this, sir . . . get me a fellowship in a cry of players?
—*Hamlet to Horatio, 3.2*

Eugene O'Neill's dominating presence from 1920 to 1934 cannot be challenged as the single most important factor in bringing American drama fully into the twentieth century. His 21 new plays within 14 years, successes and failures alike, were always newsworthy. Their impact was all the more remarkable, as they came from someone who was never a public figure, never a part of the "Broadway scene," a mystic, enigmatic, and intensely private in his isolated life on Cape Cod, in Bermuda, France, and Georgia.[1]

Furthermore, within the theater that he shocked out of uninspired commercial complacency, O'Neill never established a following or a school. None of his contemporaries between the wars was ever regarded as an artist "in the style of" Eugene O'Neill. The sometimes astonishing experiments that he so often sprung upon his audiences were not emulated, nor indeed could they be. Who would dare attempt the use of masks, ancient as the tradition might be, in any manner approaching O'Neill's? Who would plunge into the aside/soliloquy technique, which O'Neill himself discovered could not be effectively used more than once?

Who would be audacious enough to command that Broadway audiences endure nine acts in one long afternoon and evening performance? Who would embrace the task of placing on the contemporary stage the greatest of classic myths, explored in modern psychological terms, in a full-length trilogy? The answer is plain enough: nobody.[2]

What O'Neill accomplished, of course, was the release provided to his contemporaries and those who followed, enabling them to venture into any area of subject matter, style, and technique that struck their fancies. O'Neill early on had demonstrated the viability of serious, even tragic, drama, portrayed without sentimentality or debilitating romanticizing. He impressively showed the capabilities of highly stylized staging, and he proved that topics including incest, adultery, prostitution, violent love-hate relationships among husbands, wives, and children, and to some extent, religion and faith, could be not only explored in detail but also discussed in language far more frank than ever before. By the time O'Neill had retired from active participation in the artistic world he had so severely jolted, nothing was any longer taboo; everything seemed possible.

With this view of O'Neill, we can now consider the other major figures in American drama between the wars who established their own reputations independent of O'Neill's towering presence. Simultaneously with O'Neill, they created an American drama that was the unchallenged world leader, adopting all avenues of expression and forming a body of dramatic literature thoroughly respected at home and abroad.

Four of the most important playwrights contemporary with O'Neill, all writing for the Theatre Guild, began to encounter increasing problems with the Guild's operating procedures. Objecting to methods of casting and script revision, and strongly opposed to the Guild's close control of the subsidiary rights to their plays, Maxwell Anderson, Sidney Howard, Robert E. Sherwood, and S. N. Behrman, soon joined by Elmer Rice, decided in 1937 to found their own producing company.

The idealistic aims of the resulting Playwrights' Company were familiar echoes of those at one time expressed by the Guild itself in its own break with the New York theater establishment. They were, said Rice, "all concerned about the wastefulness and the limitations of the Broadway theatre; and all were deeply interested in the maintenance of high artistic standards of production."[3] The Company hoped to become a more genuine "artisan's guild" in which each member would be in sole charge of the production of his own plays, with profits going to the playwrights rather than into the producing organization (as was the case at the Guild).

From the beginning the Playwrights' Company expected to thrive within the framework of the commercial theater, not as a special interest or splinter group. In spite of dire predictions that a group of playwrights could not manage a company, their expectations were realized when the success of Sherwood's *Abe Lincoln in Illinois* and Anderson's *Knicker-bocker Holiday* in the 1938–39 season established the Company's importance. Although Howard died in 1938 and Behrman returned to the Guild in 1945, Rice, Anderson, and Sherwood kept the Company active for more than a decade, with all members benefiting from the association with each other and from the freedom to produce plays according to one's own vision. Most of the Company's output appeared after the Second World War and remains outside our purview here, but the rise to prominence of each member, whether with the Guild or independently, is directly pertinent.

Maxwell Anderson: Man of Many Muses

The only dramatist within the Playwrights' Company, and the only American dramatist between the wars who can be compared to Eugene O'Neill, is Maxwell Anderson. No other American playwright came close to their levels of productivity and skill; over thirty plays by each writer appeared during his active lifetime. Anderson left behind some 20 unpublished manuscripts, and had O'Neill not destroyed most of his own unfinished works, he would have left an equal or greater number. Both were serious theater professionals, conscientious artists of unquestioned integrity, driven by single-minded convictions of what they wanted to do and how they wanted to do it. They were strongly attracted to the tragic muse, while equally willing to explore wide variations in form, style, and subject matter. And both held within them an underlying touch of the poet.

The dissimilarities in the accomplishments of Eugene O'Neill and Maxwell Anderson, as well as in temperament and personality, were many and distinctive. The brooding, introverted O'Neill, exploring the ways of God to man in his often ponderous style, never catered to any popular taste. Once his career began, he wrote, with minor exceptions, nothing but plays. Frequently disappointed by public or critical rejection, he would express his unhappiness to friends but rarely made a public defense. In sharp contrast, Anderson wrote radio plays and film scripts as well as articles and books of essays about the theater. Outspoken in nature, Anderson was willing to argue publicly with any dissenting critic and sometimes purchased newspaper space to spell out his rebuttal. He displayed a facile theatrical skill expressed in poetry, prose, and even song. In the one artist there was the drive of genius; in the other there was the steady accomplishment of polished ingenuity.

Having taught briefly at Whittier College in California, Anderson remained throughout his career something of a professor in demeanor as well as in artistic practice. His knowledge of world literature was substantial, enabling him to write about characters in a range of time, place, and nationality from Socrates and Joan of Arc through Henry VIII, Elizabeth I, and Mary Stuart to Peter Stuyvesant and George Washington. At one time an active journalist, he was interested in and often dismayed by the American political and social system, which could exert pressures from the Left and Right to limit individual freedom and development. The results of his concerns were plays about the Sacco-Vanzetti case, racial prejudice in South Africa, and the destructive exploitation of the beauty of the upper Hudson River palisades. His dramatic theories were explained in his essays (*The Essence of Tragedy* still remains relevant), and he achieved notable, if limited, success by going against the grain of established twentieth-century realism in writing historical and contemporary dramas in verse.

The play that brought Maxwell Anderson his first widespread attention was *What Price Glory?* written with fellow journalist and combat-disabled veteran Laurence Stallings and thrust upon a shocked public in 1924. Its rousing depiction of cursing, hard-drinking, fornicating American fighting men permanently ended the long tradition of romanticizing war and glorifying its battles and its heroes. What Stephen Crane had done in *The Red Badge of Courage* to erase the same attitude from the novel, Anderson and Stallings did for the stage. For the first time a play attempted to portray as literally as possible the bloody filth, fear, hate, and suffering endured by men who must perform as beasts in a life monstrously insulting to human intelligence. Traditional gallantry and chivalry have no place here. Defense of flag and country does not concern these men, who pursue their sensual pleasures with the strumpet in the local bistro in primitive celebration of the fact that they have so far remained alive. Officers and men alike forgo any semblance of "gentlemanly" behavior. Captain Flagg and Sergeant Quirt carry on a personal feud in blasphemous roars, with military decorum reduced to utter meaninglessness. The battle-weary captain, leading his exhausted men, hardly fit for duty, back to the slimy trenches, explains himself to two spruce replacement lieutenants: "I'm the sinkhole and cesspool of this regiment. . . . I take chocolate soldiers and make dead heroes of them." Unimpressed by views of glorious death, his matter-of-fact approach is summarized thus: "When they tell you to die, you have to do it, even if you're a better man than they are." Quirt's famous penultimate line, "What a lot of God damn fools it takes to make a war!" is a fitting epithet for all those who send men off on the hideous work of killing each other.

The authenticity of the frontline picture in *What Price Glory?* prompted first-night viewers, though visibly taken aback at this depiction of "our boys" as little better than foul-mouthed, rutting beasts, to stand and cheer. Hardly six years after the end of hostilities, the play struck an immediate response in America's growing disillusion with the butchery that had purported to make the world safe for democracy, as well as with the country's growing isolationism. If any one passage played to these changing sentiments, it was probably Lieutenant Moore's verbal assault on Flagg in his passionate "What price glory now" speech, shouted hysterically as a mangled soldier dies in agony. The price of "glory" in any war is the brutal destruction of men's lives and the degradation of women, well shown by Flagg's description of the fought-over Charmaine as "a damn fine little animal," nothing more than a mere prize for a winning poker hand. The play may have offended, but nobody questioned the obvious: *What Price Glory?* was created by those who knew of what they wrote.

There are, however, problems. *What Price Glory?* makes use of ultranaturalistic staging in an attempt to re-create the horrors of battle-field existence, but in the end the play succumbs to the inevitable. No matter how well done, how grimly lifelike, the play runs head on into the impossible task of attempting the literal dramatization of battle, or, as in this case, the abomination of trench warfare, within the imposed limits and unavoidable artificialities of the proscenium stage. Further, the language is held back by restrictions of the times, which keep it from being an authentic transcription of soldiers' speech. Its earthy and relatively uninhibited vocabulary goes far beyond what had up to this time been permitted on stage, but it never crosses the line into the four-letter "latrine" vocabulary so common among all fighting men everywhere.[4]

More important are the character portrayals and the situations explored. The play may have permanently exploded the traditional stage image of the soldier, but it ultimately remains as romantic as anything out of the past that it meant to avoid. The men may ride greasy motorcycles instead of white chargers, and they may be stalemated in foul trenches instead of galloping forward in bugled attack formations, but they always come through in the end, their hearts of gold belying their coarse exteriors. As long as we have Captain Flaggs to fight our wars and proclaim that "there is some kind of damned religion" connected with the profession of arms, as long as Sergeant Quirts are ready to limp after the advancing ranks shouting "Hey, Flagg, wait for baby," all will be right with our world. Memorable as these characters are, however, they are not provided with the emotional depth so badly needed to convey the havoc that warfare creates in men's souls as they order others to die, or face violent death themselves. That havoc is suggested in Moore's outburst, but that is a set speech with little carry-over into the subsequent action. What finally comes across is too much alarum and excursion, too much noisy romanticizing of men and deeds, too much effect for its own sake. The play somehow lacks the gut-wrenching agonies and the deep emotional wounding that these men will permanently carry with them.

If the gods of war unleashed in *What Price Glory?* can be seen in the same light, as indifferent fate wreaking havoc on the helpless individuals struggling against deterministic forces that ultimately destroy, then the play can be judged within the broad definition of dramatic naturalism. But the romanticized, upbeat conclusion, combined with the fact that men in their stupidity blunder into war, the gods notwithstanding, considerably undermines the naturalistic effect. If *What Price Glory?* now appears to be a bit too pat, perhaps somewhat shallow, no longer able to move audiences emotionally, it still remains a significant and impressive play.[5]

After *What Price Glory?* Anderson proceeded on his own with three plays—*Outside Looking In* (1925), *Saturday's Children* (1927), and *Gypsy* (1929)—wherein he attempted to incorporate the sense of naturalistic determinism into contemporary social and economic subject matter. All three plays experienced varying degrees of failure and can be safely bypassed. Permanent recognition arrived in the unique historical dramas of the so-called Tudor plays, *Elizabeth the Queen* (1930) and *Mary of Scotland* (1933), joined 15 years later by the postwar *Anne of the Thousand Days* (1948). Here the muses of history and poetry combined to prompt Anderson to write of British Renaissance history in his own free verse. In the long run, aside from the contemporary tragedy *Winterset* (1935), it is for these three historical romances that Anderson will most likely be best remembered.

Americans have always exhibited great interest in the ways of British royalty, particularly the plots and counterplots of the Renaissance court, so the Tudor plays proved not unattractive to audience and critic alike, who were able to accept the historical liberties and to adjust to the unfamiliar poetic cadences. In each of them Anderson's treatment of history is respectful and, in the main, fairly accurate. There is always a temptation for the dramatic artist to tinker with the known facts of history or to fill in gaps with some wishful might-have-beens. Only the most narrow-minded pedant would fault Shakespeare for the liberties he takes in his history plays, and Anderson follows suit. His most glaring deviation, imitating Schiller in *Maria Stuart* (1800), is Elizabeth's tension-filled meeting with Mary of Scotland. It is fine theater as the two proud queens face each other, but historically, alas, it never happened.[6]

The plays' strengths lie in the dramatically attractive characters, who maintain throughout a high personal bearing. Audience sympathy for and understanding of the central figures of the queens are possible because of their development as real persons entrapped by human emotion, which must always be subject to rigid control because of their royal status. There remains, however, a serious challenge in the re-creation of history in this manner, because characters must so often be based on skimpy evidence, broad assumptions, or historical tradition. (Was Henry V really *that* good a king? Was Richard III really *that* deformed and wicked?) In this vein, Anderson chooses to present a serious love affair between Elizabeth and the much younger Essex ("I love you, my queen, madly, beyond all measure"), whose chauvinistic pride prompts him to inform the queen of her failures because "a woman cannot / Act and think like a man," and leads to his fateful rebellion and subsequent execution. Both are portrayed as stubbornly iron-willed, but Elizabeth does explain why she is forced to condemn him in admitting that the sovereign's rule must be "quite friendless, without mercy, without love." Her terrible self-recognition comes with the realization of what she has lost when Essex dies, refusing to accept mercy from the lover who has betrayed him.

In *Mary of Scotland* Elizabeth is directly involved in Mary's life by tricking her into marriage with the weak Catholic Darnley in order to separate her from her people. Like Elizabeth's presumed passion for Essex, Mary's love for Lord Bothwell is doomed, though he could probably save her and her throne. Displaying her own pride as sovereign, she informs Bothwell, "I, too, have a will—a will as strong as your own / . . . I will have my way in time / Though it burn my heart out and yours." Again, love is sacrificed to power, but Mary's understanding of herself brings recognition of her need for humility. In the end she triumphs, for it is her son who will succeed the childless Elizabeth.

The postwar *Anne of the Thousand Days* tells of the fate of Anne Boleyn in flashbacks after her imprisonment under sentence of death. The once clever and ambitious Anne realizes how power has corrupted the king, but she gains awareness that death is preferable to any kind of life she might be able to live in the future.

A final evaluation of the Tudor plays must recognize the dignity and sense of decorum that Anderson brought to the American theater but at the same time must acknowledge a lack of artistic depth. Granted, the character development and dramatic conflict in these plays elevate them far above Anderson's earlier plays, and the melodrama inherent in the situations never gets out of hand. The lofty themes are valid, and the choices of action and subject matter befit the poetic line, but the elevated themes and stately language cannot completely hide the evidence of superficial though skilled theatricality and facile ingenuity which make the plays good theater rather than great drama. The most serious problem is a sense of pretentiousness; to read the dialogue is to have an uncomfortable feeling that Anderson is consciously creating "poetic tragedy" through the simple expedient of placing excellent and rhythmic prose in a broken verselike line, while asking the audience to follow a series of pseudo-Shakespearean romantic intrigues to go with it.

All this being said, the Tudor plays retain their significance because of Anderson's demonstration of his own theory of tragic drama, not entirely unlike Aristotle's. In *The Essence of Tragedy* Anderson holds that the tragic protagonist, imperfect as he is, can change for the better through his self-recognition in discovering some new truth. This may not be an earthshaking interpretation of tragedy, but it is developed remarkably well in Anderson's modern rendition of the classic view. The destructive inevitability of the varied plot lines is intrinsically tragic in the Greek sense, and although the plays are, in the end, heavily romantic, falling short of the expected heights, Anderson's attempt at creating a kind of twentieth-century classic tragedy is eminently noteworthy.

By setting the Tudor plays in the remoteness of Renaissance England, Anderson had no problem justifying his use of verse, but his handling of contemporary subjects wholly or in part in verse can more easily be challenged. Two plays, *Night over Taos* (1932) and *The Wingless Victory* (1936), can be dismissed as minor efforts. The first is an uninspired look at the early semi-feudal Spanish culture of New Mexico, peopled with embarrassingly wooden characters speaking a stilted verse dialogue that does nothing to elevate the subject matter. The second transfers the classic tragedy of *Medea* to New England, where the intolerance of the sanctimonious Christians of Salem drives the East Indian princess bride of a ship captain to the double murder of her children and to suicide. Comparisons with O'Neill's *Electra* trilogy are inevitable, and they are consistently unfavorable. Anderson created a formidable Medea-like heroine of near-tragic stature in Oparre, but the petty stupidities of prejudicial and narrow-minded provincialism destroy her with none of the sense of the Olympian Fates or even the family curse of O'Neill. Of melodrama there is plenty, but there is not enough flesh and blood to cover the skeleton of the myth, while the verse is almost indistinguishable from the frequent prose passages. In *Valley Forge* (1934) the use of verse, though sparing, unfortunately clashes with the more conventional prose that tells the story of half-frozen scavenging rebels and the lofty, almost mythical character of Washington. It may have been possible to accept the verse of the Tudor plays because of some naive assumption that people at that time "talked that way." But not George Washington. Anderson's attempt to humanize him in his sharing of suffering and determination to carry on the fight makes verse seem entirely out of place.

  Winterset, a commercial failure, remains Anderson's master-piece. *Gods of the Lightning*, written in 1928 with Harold Hickerson, was an unsuccessful and overly propagandistic version of the injustices of the Sacco-Vanzetti case. *Winterset* avoids any direct allusion to the case itself but uses broad parallels to build a fictional account of what might have befallen Sacco and Vanzetti's survivors. A fortunate combination of Jo Mielziner's superb setting and Burgess Meredith's great performance with Anderson's most effective poetic diction and articulated tragic theme showed the playwright at his dramatic and theatrical best.

  Beneath the looming, ghostly presence of a stylized Brooklyn Bridge jutting out towards the audience, on a cold December day during the winter solstice, 17-year-old Mio reaches the end of his quest to find and punish those who had unjustly condemned his father. Here he encounters and falls in love with Miriamne, the sister of the very man he seeks, ultimately to gain from her the self-recognition that the highest good is to love. In the pattern of *Romeo and Juliet*'s star-crossed lovers, they find in each other a force transcending family hatreds. "I've lost / my taste for revenge if it falls on you," he tells Miriamne; "if you / love me . . . / teach me how to live and forget hate."

  Anderson's poetry in *Winterset* carries a conviction almost totally lacking in his other plays. It is not the "poetic" world of Tudor England nor that of Revolutionary America, but the hazy nightmare world of twentieth-century gangsters and crumbling tenements, a modern world of wild im-

Winterset (Maxwell Anderson, 1935). Jo Mielziner's stunning set was a stage designer's masterpiece: the beautifully stylized form of the looming pier of the Brooklyn Bridge dominated the scene, simultaneously emphasizing the overwhelming fate hanging over the protagonists. Here Mio and Miriamne hide from the thugs pursuing them. The Esdras tenement home lurks stage right.

probabilities, where murder victims seem resurrected and conscience-stricken mad judges hold court. It is a real-unreal world of injustice, violence, and pointless death, one we know but shudder to recognize, a world of the most unpoetic sort, inhabited by unfathomable evil; yet what it does to those in its grip can inspire poetry. Mio and Miriamne, experiencing instant love while hardly knowing its meaning, perfectly comprehend its death-bringing power, and they willingly die under the hail of bullets from the gangsters who have pursued them. *Winterset* adds up to a tremendously moving stage piece, tragic, touchingly romantic, unquestionably poetic.

Winterset comes closer to the classic concept of tragedy than any of the Tudor plays for two basic reasons. First is the believable humanity of the characters, and second is the success of the language. It is clear from the start that the play, even with its contemporary subject and setting, makes no pretense at a portrayal of contemporary reality. The characters, imaginative and original, immediately strike an empathic note. They behave and speak in a manner that is not incongruous with this Eliot-like wasteland. They become at once acceptable and sympathetic; their tragedy is today's, not the sixteenth century's. Their suffering and doom are identifiable and readily comprehended. Mio's discovery of himself through Miriamne's love is thoroughly convincing.

Winterset relies heavily on contrived melodramatics, but rather than intruding, they become an exciting and gripping aspect of the unfolding tragedy. The string of coincidences that brings everybody together as Mio stumbles upon the family against whom he seeks his vengeance—the new deranged judge who condemned his father, the gangster intent on silencing all involved, the ineffective policeman, and the apparently resurrected murder victim, all assembled as the elements rage around them, Lear-fashion—stretches all realistic credibility, but concern for credible realism is irrelevant. The remarkable result is a deeply moving modern poetic tragedy, well deserving the Critics' Circle Award for the 1935–36 season.

The muse of comedy that inspired *High Tor* (1936), Anderson's next verse play, drew audiences no more successfully than did *Winterset*, but *High Tor* contains almost every one of Anderson's skilled theatrical devices. The story of Van van Dorn, who must defend the beauty of the Catskills of his ancestors against knavish exploitive realtors and fleeing bank robbers, gets wound up within a web of whimsy, fantasy, slapstick, romance, and not a little melodrama. Although the disturbing confusion, involving bumbling gangsters, a dying Indian philosopher, highway patrolmen, and funny Dutchmen from a 300-year-old ghost ship, compels audiences to back and fill in order to close the gaps, *High Tor* succeeds in delighting more than it disturbs. Its message of dismal human shortsightedness, corruption, and brutality is plain enough, and the bickering lovers who fight over principles of natural beauty and ordinary human decency finally unite in a happy ending. Anderson's fanciful inventiveness and, once more, a verse style appropriate to the occasion, created a work of almost pure theater, winning once more the Critics' Circle Award.

Both Your Houses (1933) won Anderson his only Pulitzer Prize, but this cynical satire on American politics, involving an idealistic young congressman, McClean (the name itself is enough to raise eyebrows) who encounters corruption at every turn, is decidedly inferior to most of Anderson's prewar output. *The Masque of Kings* (1937), a look into the intriguing historic mystery of what happened at Mayerling, constantly threatens to fly off into the rarefied atmosphere of Viennese operetta. *Knickerbocker Holiday* (1938), loosely based on Washington Irving's tales of New Amsterdam and Peter Stuyvesant, is best remembered for Walter Huston's breathy rendition of Kurt Weill's perennially popular "September Song."

A closing discussion of Maxwell Anderson between the wars must necessarily go over the line far enough to include the four plays centering on the war itself, *Key Largo* (1939), *Candle in the Wind* (1941), *The Eve of St. Mark* (1942), and *Storm Operation* (1944), only one of which can sustain serious consideration.

Key Largo is not actually about World War II but is relevent because of its treatment of individuals involved in the Spanish Civil War, a conflict that was widely regarded as the dress rehearsal for the debacle soon to overtake all of Europe. The poetic line is not particularily noteworthy in this tale of the heroic redemption of King McCloud, whose cowardice in abandoning his men in Spain has driven him to the Florida key, where he gives his life to save a sister of one of his army buddies. *Candle in the Wind*, a slow and talky story of an actress and her French naval officer lover, whom she frees from the Gestapo at the cost of her own life, alludes to war's suffering but lacks the attractiveness of *Winterset*'s doomed Mio and Miriamne. The intrusion of a pair of touring American spinster schoolteachers in the midst of a European war is simply ludicrous. *Storm Operation*, set during the North African campaign, becomes even more unbelievable in the introduction of an Arab "slave girl" belonging to one of the Americans, an improbable love triangle, and a climactic battlefield wedding. The contrived situations and the overextended philosophizing by all the characters make for an uninteresting and essentially dull play that quickly failed.

The Eve of St. Mark, moderately successful on both stage and screen, is an interesting hybrid that on the one hand is almost maudlin in its sentimentality but that offers, on the other, one of the most appealing portraits of the World War II GI of any wartime play. Even-tempered, authentic, and compassionate, it displays a maturity of approach to the unnatural situations of men at war that underlines the shortcomings of the style of *What Price Glory?*

In *The Eve of St. Mark* back-on-the-farm episodes involving Quiz West, the central figure, together with his family and his girlfriend, alternate with stateside barracks-room and frontline sequences in which Quiz and his doomed companions hold out on a Pacific island. The scenes of those who keep the home fires burning, including a rather soggy encounter between the lovers in a dream, spoken in verse, can be ignored. The soldier sequences are another matter. Those who fight the war are shown for what the great majority of them were: the ordinary, decent men who made up this citizen army. The traps into which the playwright can easily fall when he succumbs to noise and sensation in the manner of *What Price Glory?* are successfully avoided.

There are character types in *The Eve of St. Mark,* but they are not stereotypes. The hulking Regular Army topkick Ruby, the only professional in the lot, is familiar enough, but he is not the iron-fisted, threatening image of Sergeant Quirt. Mulveroy, the boy from Brooklyn, is no comic fool but an understandable city product with a strong and ingratiating sense of humor. Quiz, the chaste nice guy from down the street (in this case, off the farm), remaining faithful to the girl he left behind, is no misfit outsider but an active member of the company, as brave as any. The drawling, soft-spoken southerner Francis Marion is one of Anderson's best characters, comic, philosophical, poetry-quoting, far removed from the too-familiar tall Texan or backwoods redneck. From top sergeant to private, everyone is healthy and emotionally stable; there are no fights or perversions, no sadistic officers who enforce brutal orders—in fact, there are no officers at all—and no girls are raped. The slightly tarnished, readily available Lil and Sal are no hardened camp followers but sympathetic, almost pitiful local products taking momentary advantage of the situation around them. Nobody is a coward; nobody is a hero. The audience is witness to the rowdy and profane world of the barracks and then the besieged Pacific outpost where these men fight a war that is a monstrosity they cannot explain but something they must endure and perish in while struggling to retain their basic human decency.[7]

The final estimate of Anderson's position in American drama must rest with the larger proportion of his work that appeared in the 1930s, although he continued to write until the mid-1950s.[8] Aside from the shared *What Price Glory?* few of his plays were sustained hits; the majority often faded after fewer than 100 performances. As a member of the Playwrights' Company, he tried to ensure successful runs through his own management, but the elevated nature of what he had to say did not command an extensive audience. In spite of all that, Anderson cannot be judged as a critical or artistic failure. Nearly everything he undertook gets high praise for the artistic integrity he brought to the growing body of American drama. He followed the muses of poetry, history, tragedy, comedy, and music with a considerable amount of daring. His use of verse was unique, and though devoid of rhyme, alliteration, assonance, or the meter of conventional blank verse in its broken-up prose line, he was able on occasion to adapt it to his characters with some measure of success. Was his range of style, setting, and plot weakened through pedantic moralizing? Possibly. Were his characters not as full-bodied as O'Neill's Nina Leeds or Lavinia Mannon? To some degree, yes. It is clear that Anderson's impressive body of works is the product not so much of a gifted thinker but of a gifted technician. The permanent universal appeal of great dramatic literature is not there; his dramatic theorizing gets in the way of his dramatic instincts, forcing the plays into molds that are unduly artificial. The plays remain as products of a studied ingenuity.

Sidney Howard's Brief Hour on the Stage

When Sidney Howard died in a tractor accident on his Massachusetts farm in 1939 at a relatively young 48, the American drama, as observed by Walter Meserve, lost a playwright of imagination and talent, with a new sense of realism and a new dignity in writing social drama.[9] The author of a number of short stories, more than 20 successful film scripts, including the award-winning *Gone with the Wind* (1939), some 20 original plays, and 15 adaptations and translations, Howard was a prominent theatrical figure with the promise of a long productive life. His fame, however, rests with but two plays from very early in his career. Revivals of his work have been only infrequently undertaken.

As a graduate of George Pierce Baker's 47 Workshop in 1916, Howard had looked forward to a career in playwriting, but he interrupted his plans with service as an ambulance driver and aviator in World War I. He returned to a combined career of journalist and dramatist, becoming a reporter for the liberal *New Republic,* then an editor of *Life* (at that time a humor magazine), and finally a feature writer for Hearst's *International.* His first play, *Swords* (1921), was an unsuccessful romantic-historical verse drama. Edward Sheldon, one of the big names in Baker's roster of early-twentieth-century dramatists, against whose nineteenth-century well-made social melodrama O'Neill had revolted while under Baker's tutelage, collaborated on *Bewitched* (1924), set in the Middle Ages. Howard, like O'Neill, quickly sensed that he was attempting plays in a style clearly out of date in postwar America and thereafter kept his own counsel in the development of a kind of contemporary stage realism centered on unglamorous characters whose social and personal problems were understood by a wide spectrum of Americans. In the view of critic (and namesake) Sidney Howard White, the playwright recognized that the "low key compromises of little people, making the best of what they have," could readily replace his long-nurtured literary vision of "grand heroics and larger-than-life principals."[10]

In each of his four plays between 1924 and 1926, Howard developed his "new sense of realism" with a wide range of characters who behaved as distinctive individuals with considerable inner strength. He successfully avoided placing them in situations controlled by existing hidebound conventions of social morality; nor did he show them as victims of overpowering social forces such as those that were soon to play so important a part in the thirties.

The first, *They Knew What They Wanted,* was produced by the Guild in November 1924. It is Howard's finest, overshadowing all else he accomplished in the 1920s. It ran for more than 400 performances and took the Pulitzer Prize for 1924–25.[11] This play about the common people in California's Napa Valley wine-growing district is the best example of what Meserve meant in his assertion about Howard's "new dignity" in writing social drama. It is not a social or problem play in the generally accepted sense. The characters are driven by instincts and desires unrelated to the pressures of society beyond the limits of Tony Patrucci's prosperous vineyards. The only outside force representing conventional morality is the ineffective and rather seedy Father McKee. The ultimate escape from the predicament in which the characters find themselves is accomplished entirely by practical reasoning and common sense, providing a solution that the laws of Bronson Howard or the traditional mores of the theater before the First World War would not have tolerated.

Howard had grown up in California and knew the territory of the Napa Valley very well. His intimate knowledge of the nonintellectual people who lived there enabled him to portray their emotions and their actions in a fashion that transcended the trite plot. The well-worn Miles Standish–John Alden–Priscilla Mullins triangle is modernized with the involvement of the 60-year-old wine grower Tony, his mail-order bride Amy, and the carefree young foreman Joe. Everything is transparently predictable as Amy, believing she has come to marry the handsome Joe, who has written the proposal letter and whose picture Tony, unknown to Joe, has foolishly included, discovers the awful truth immediately upon arrival. Furthermore, Tony, in his eagerness to meet her, has wrecked his car and fractured both legs.

The unpropitious situation could lead to disaster, and Howard lets his characters come perilously close. Everybody is at fault in what has happened, but nobody is really to blame. Joe's seduction of Amy on her wedding night could be regarded as underhanded in the extreme, but Howard has shown Joe as an honest and reliable friend, genuinely fond of the foolhardy Tony yet compassionate toward the stunned Amy, who has been devastated by Tony's cruel trick. The excess of wine at the wedding fiesta, the sudden panic of a beautiful and frightened girl, and the sheer chemistry of the moment combine with human weakness to overcome more prudent behavior. Tony's dishonesty is unforgivable; his blatant deceit of both Amy and Joe has brought about the whole mess, but his pathetic affection for Amy and his desperate fear of losing her have prompted his wild, unthinking act. Amy might appear mercenary in accepting the proposal in the first place, and equally foolhardy in abandoning such security as she already had for the total unknown, but faced with a dead-end job and willing to gamble, her move is understandable. The seduction is as much her fault as Joe's and, like his part in it, also understandable.

The resolution proves the basic sanity of three momentarily despairing individuals pushed to their emotional limits before reason takes hold. Over the three months of caring for the helpless Tony, Amy has come to love him but knows that the truth must out and she must leave. Her revelation to him prompts a hysterical outrage that leads to Tony's threats of murder by shotgun before he is subdued. Joe, true to his underlying honesty, offers to leave and take Amy with him, an act of fundamental decency that Amy accepts. But Howard refuses to end it all there, defying convention with Tony's overcoming his initial anger and false pride by deciding to welcome the coming child as his own and to accept Amy and Joe's contrition at face value. Howard turns the play away from catastrophe, and with each character's strength of purpose and honest determination to accept the others' good faith, he brings the whole thing around to a satisfactory ending with a convincing human sensitivity. It is an appropriate ending, one of good common sense. Each person is aware of what got him or her into this jam in the first place, and all three are sensible enough to see that the ending will bring what they wanted—Joe's freedom to move around the country unencumbered, Amy's secure future with Tony, and Tony's gaining a wife and heir. All have been gravely hurt, but such hurts do eventually heal.

The triangle plot of O'Neill's tragic *Desire under the Elms*, produced the same year, with its child murder and suggestion of incest, assumes punishment of the protagonists for their sins. In Howard's play the culprits go free. Yet it was *Desire* that brought down the wrath of censors, while Howard's play went unmolested. Howard's conclusion in the characters' acceptance of their situation somehow seemed more moral. It is a conclusion that would have been welcomed by, say, Henrik Ibsen, who always maintained that society's "morality" is often more immoral than individuals following their own consciences.

At the opposite end from *They Knew What They Wanted*, socially and geographically, but with the same problems of personal emotion and family relationships, is Howard's chilling indictment of maternal possessiveness, *The Silver Cord* (1926). We are in the presence of a prosperous, educated elite with interests in science, medicine, and architecture, living in elegant surroundings in an unnamed eastern city. The central figure of Mrs. Phelps, far more sophisticated than the bumbling Tony, while outwardly in control of herself, is a woman of great insecurity, desperately determined to control the lives of her two adult sons.

Howard's Mrs. Phelps is a brilliant practitioner of what has come to be called *momism*. Energetic realistic dialogue and awareness of Mrs. Phelps's serious psychological problems, explained in her condemnation by her daughter-in-law Christina, help to keep Mrs. Phelps on this side of caricature, but the line is perilously narrow. To keep the play from turning into an overly hortative warning against such dangerous parents, her interpretation must be carefully controlled to avoid becoming nothing more than a one-sided portrait of an unbelievably obsessed bitch. For the play to be taken seriously, there must be sufficient understanding of what drives Mrs. Phelps into her appalling behavior, and there must be equally sufficient understanding of what makes the two sons react as they do. It's a close call: Howard's message tends to be overstressed in some not entirely motivated sensationalism, but the final impact is stunning and not a little terrifying.

Mrs. Phelps's unhealthy attitude toward her sons is apparent as soon as they enter their old home—Robert, the younger, with his fiancée Hester, and David with his six-month bride Christina. Howard knows well the behavior pattern of the kind of woman Mrs. Phelps represents, beginning with her cold disregard of the two women in her protestations of welcome meant only for the sons. Her repeated assertions that she could not possibly interfere in her children's lives are transparently hollow, contradicted at once by her actions. She is immediately contemptuous of the quiet and unassuming Hester and within minutes has informed Robert that he could not possibly be in love with this creature most unworthy of him. At a complete loss to understand the significance of Christina's scientific interests as more than "puttering around," and determined to keep David at home so he can develop her suburban land, Mrs. Phelps points out Christina's inadequacies in considerable detail.

Mrs. Phelps's further tactics aimed directly at the sons, though crude, are familiar ploys of overprotective motherhood. One is the continual emphasis on the mother's great physical suffering in bringing her children into the world, plus all the tears and sacrifice of raising them. Another is the equally familiar plea that her sons deserve the best, which only she can offer, and of which no other woman is capable. She is determined to hold these men attached to herself by the invisible silver umbilical cord in a calculated process of unmanning them.

Howard's attempt to establish psychological justification for Mrs. Phelps's actions do not entirely escape making her a monster in two specific instances. The first, so barefaced as to be scarcely believable, is her singularly outrageous gesture of contempt for Christina by putting her daughter-in-law in a spare room and David in his old bedroom, where she coyly visits him, sits with incestuous suggestiveness on his bed, and advises him to meet Christina's "selfishness with firmness, her jealousy with fairness." This sequence alone can throw the play askew, and it demands a long stretch of audience credulity to hold things in place this early in the action. One must ask why David, not yet married a year, goes along unprotestingly, but an even more important question is how the otherwise strong-willed young wife can so easily acquiesce. One would normally assume that the danger signals are so glaring that Christina would refuse to accept such a gratuitous insult and would depart forth-with, husband or no.

The treatment of Hester is equally vicious. The distraught girl, her engagement to Robert shattered, tries to call a taxi in order to leave. A logical response would be to encourage her to do so, but for no apparent reason Mrs. Phelps rips the telephone wire from the wall, performing, as she says, the only "undignified" act of her life. She is then momentarily attached to Hester by a cord as hard and unyielding as herself. Hester at once flees in hysteria and in her flight slips into the partially frozen pond. As David and Robert rush out to save her, Mrs. Phelps's only worry is that her dear sons, improperly clad, may catch pneumonia.

As Christina prepares to leave with Hester, she makes the limited options clear to David: he must immediately choose between wife and mother. Christina's final counterattack, which horrifies Mrs. Phelps and shocks both sons, puts the separate-bedroom act in perspective: she tells her husband that his mother "refuses to believe that you're a grown man with thoughts for another woman. Grown man that you are, she still wants to suckle you at her breast," a doubly accurate shot in view of Mrs. Phelps's repugnance upon learning of Christina's pregnancy.

David, at last aware of the trap, runs off after Christina, but Robert is engulfed forever. His head on his mother's bosom, he hears Mrs. Phelps intone her "love" for the destroyed son. As the curtain falls she recites an ironic litany: "Mother love suffereth long and is kind . . . hopeth all things; endureth all things."

The Silver Cord makes wonderful theater. In spite of its threaten-ing flights of melodrama, it can hold an audience, even though one has to swallow hard to accept some scarcely credible moments. It is a tribute to Howard's ability to force acceptance through well-rounded characters, even including Mrs. Phelps herself. Her distorted view of motherly love comes from a distorted personality that can see nothing in her widowed life but her sons, a not unknown parental phenomenon. Robert's surren-der and the others' escape are logically motivated, and the ending is inevitable.

Howard's two other plays of the 1920s possessed many of the quali-ties of *They Knew What They Wanted* and *The Silver Cord* but lacked the same impact. *Lucky Sam McCarver* (1925) concerned an ambitious and materialistic nightclub owner, Sam, and his socialite hanger-on wife, Carlotta. Their frivolous, shady, and ultimately fatal life-styles prompted their comparison with Fitzgerald's Daisy Buchanan and Jay Gatsby. *Ned McCobb's Daughter* (1926) almost succumbs to nineteenth-century melodramatic clichés in the scheming of two rascally brothers, a philandering husband, and illegal bootlegging activities.

Howard continued to be active in the decade preceding his death, but his other plays never gained the public acceptance, even notoriety, of *They Knew What They Wanted* and *The Silver Cord*. Several were adaptations. Best known were *The Late Christopher Bean*, from a play by René Fanchois, about a treasure of art left behind by the deceased artist; *Dodsworth*, a version of Sinclair Lewis's novel; and *Yellow Jack*, an epic-style bare-stage production, taken from a chapter in Paul DeKruif's *Microbe Hunters*, about the conquest of yellow fever, all staged in 1934. Of his own original creations, *Alien Corn* (1933) was a great success for Katharine Cornell, but *Madame Will You Walk*, offered posthumously in 1958 by Jessica Tandy and Hume Cronyn, showed sharply diminished originality.

Howard served as president of the Dramatists' Guild of the Authors' League of America from 1935 to 1937 and was a member of the Playwrights' Company for only two years. The might-have-beens are tantalizing; the sense of realism in his important plays, with their well-drawn characters and well-developed dramatic situations, gave the idea of social drama a new sense of dignity. The theater and the country were heavy losers in his untimely death.

Robert E. Sherwood: Idealist in an Idiotic World

Robert E. Sherwood's service in World War I left him with physical and psychological wounds that led him into idealistic pacifism, not uncommon among those who had endured the senseless conflict. This idealism, while visible in his important plays, did not prevent his recognizing that civilized Western nations would be driven at some point to react with force against the rising dangers of Hitler's Germany. He soon became one of the earliest active interventionists and, as president of the Dramatists' Guild, urged his fellow artists to enter the fight. He joined the Committee to Defend America by Aiding the Allies soon after the Second World War began, and he quickly attracted the attention of President Roosevelt, who used his writing talents in the Office of War Information for the duration.

During his active playwriting career between the wars, Sherwood ventured not only into satire, historical romance, and comedy but also into serious explorations of the behavior of sensitive individuals in the face of the seemingly imminent national disintegration of the Great Depression and the second war. Frequently underlying all was his idealistic sense of human behavior amidst irrational forces of destruction. Even when his idealism became tinged with romance, he endowed his characters with qualities of speech and action that made them, whether historical, contemporary, or even allegorical, attractively believable figures.

Sherwood had established a firm reputation as a movie critic in the postwar heyday of silent pictures, when serious movie criticism held no particular status. He had written screen scenarios and dialogue titles for silent films in Hollywood for several years before independently producing *The Road To Rome* (1927), a play that had been rejected by the Guild.

One of the enduring historical mysteries has been the unanswered question: in 216 B.C. why did the brilliant Carthaginian general Hannibal, with Rome helpless within his grasp, abruptly withdraw and fail to enter the besieged city? Sherwood hypothesized a perfectly logical explanation: sex and seduction. The result was a sophisticated spoof of history, carrying serious antiwar overtones. Hannibal, in Sherwood's view, is so taken by the charms of his captive, Amytis, the beautiful Greek wife of the Roman dictator Fabius Maximus, that after a passionate night with her he is convinced by her reasoning that because Rome will perish through its own degeneracy, he will be a greater man for sparing rather than sacking it. As he departs, Hannibal slyly tells Fabius that he hopes the coming child "will inherit the qualities of greatness" so evident in his father. The unimaginative Fabius, unaware that he is the cuckolded butt of Hannibal's satiric remark, proudly claims to have saved Rome through "high moral purpose." Amytis, whose infidelity has really saved the city, gaily waves to Hannibal and his departing army.

One of the reasons for the play's success was its identification with prevailing antiwar sentiments, but the prosperous theater-goers in those pre-Depression times were also attracted to the spicy, suggestive humor of the central drama. Sherwood was able to use his comic effects, preposterous as the play's basic premise may have been, to offer an implicit comparison of decadent Rome to America of the Coolidge era, living high as it rode to the end of the twenties. More obvious is Amytis's frequent condemnation of the cruelty of war, with its clear theme of pacifism. Indeed, her power in overcoming Hannibal's initial inclination to destroy Rome is a fine demonstration of Sherwood's idealistic view that human reason would save mankind from destruction.

Well established by this initial positive reception, Sherwood floundered through four undistinguished plays. *The Love Nest* (1927) dramatized a Ring Lardner story; *The Queen's Husband* (1928) drew a moderately amusing picture of a henpecked husband. *This Is New York*, a melodrama of blackmail and scandal, flopped miserably in 1930. *Waterloo Bridge*, also 1930, was made into a sentimentally touching movie starring Vivien Leigh and Robert Taylor; it was more popular in London than in New York.

Sherwood's return to the source of his original success, the always intriguing titillation of a sex triangle in high places, restored his reputation. Set in one of the world's most romantic cities, *Reunion in Vienna* (1931), with all its sexual infidelities, still maintains a moralism that was to become even more apparent in later plays, and Sherwood's pacifistic overtones are apparent as well. The reunion is that of the exiled Hapsburgs, who, having been removed from power, hold a secret family gathering. These members of the old order, with its beauty and elegance, would very much like to return to power, a prospect that Sherwood clearly abhorred, for they are throwbacks to the time from which the catastrophe of the First World War had emerged. The clash, and union, of the old with the new in the dashing, romantic Archduke Rudolf Maximillian, now a taxi driver in Nice, and his former mistress, the beautiful Eléna, is the central theme. A carryover from the past, Eléna is married to Anton Krug, psychiatrist, a member of the new order that promises, through science and business, a far better world for Austria than the decayed monarchy could ever provide. Parallels to the earlier *The Road to Rome* are obvious, as Rudolph and Eléna, for old times' sake, renew their relationship in a single night of love, while Krug, as unaware of what goes on as was Fabius, is away trying to arrange Rudolph's escape. The irony of the situation is the possibility that a child born to this married couple may carry Hapsburg blood.

The sentimentalities of the lovers' reunion and the aura of romanticism that pervade both setting and action tend to suppress the message that Sherwood wants to convey—that is, the satire on the theme of love and honor and the emphasis on the rapidly changing social scene, which he so realistically portrays. Sherwood, like Anderson in *The Masque of Kings*, neatly avoids the threat of his play's becoming a Strauss operetta by establishing the hero and his lover firmly in the modern world, but there is much in the play to demonstrate not only the disillusionment of the fateful Hapsburg past (a metaphor for that historic era destroyed in the war) but also some discomforting uncertainties about the future. As Bigsby observes, Sherwood, in his contrast of old romanticism and new rationalism, was "setting side by side an effete, decadent culture and one which destroyed the spontaneous and undermined the moral conscience" (Bigsby, 39). Choosing the irrationalism of the Hapsburgs is unthinkable, but the uncomfortable choice of the world of Anton Krug, with its detached and cold analysis, raises troublesome questions as well.

Sherwood seems to deny his own strongly felt moralism in *Reunion in Vienna* through Eléna's blatant infidelity, which has none of the moral purposes that could excuse the relationship of Amytis with Hannibal, even though the affair may fit the overall situation the playwright has created. Further, the Hapsburgs receive a more sympathetic treatment than might be expected, considering Sherwood's repugnance at their past. But these objections do nothing to damage the importance of the play's picture of the realities of changing cultures. Sherwood may have given a nod to the nostalgia of the old, but the virtues of the new were fully acknowledged.

The Petrified Forest (1935), Sherwood's metaphor of the Depression and the attendant social and political sterility, even though seriously dated in many repects, remains the strongest expression of the playwright's concern for ordinary people in an American society gone awry. It is a time when idealism and human sensitivity seem to have no place but must surrender to violence at the end of a gangster's machine gun or to the blind and bigoted viciousness of superpatriotic "Americanism," all played out against the background of a barren and unproductive world of sand and petrification.

The situation at the Black Mesa Bar-B-Q, where "Today's Special" is always the same hamburger sandwich, represents the familiar dramatic "world in microcosm." In the midst of those who live and work here in this desolate spot on the edge of Arizona's great stone forest, representatives of the outside are assembled fortuitously but logically, their escape momentarily blocked. The natives are a varied lot. Paunchy Jason Maple, the superpatriot, fiercely proud of his American Legion uniform, operates the run-down filling-station oasis with his daughter Gabrielle (Gabby), who dreams of escaping by rejoining her war-bride mother, who has returned to France. Gramp Maple lives on his constantly recalled frontier exploits involving the romantic villain-hero Billy the Kid. The hulking, football-playing assistant, Boze, has little on his mind aside from a constant hope of rolling Gabby somewhere out there in the desert. Two telephone linesmen, wolfing Today's Special, talk of the revolution that will have to come if they are to gain "freedom," a discussion that revolts the all-American Boze.

In presenting the "outcasts" who are drawn into this closed bit of the universe, Sherwood has a lot to say about the broad and arid social desert that has produced them. Alan Squier, the cultured, world-weary writer, gentle and sensitive, can find no place in it. His talents are wasted, unwanted in a failing economy with no room for the unproductive aesthete. The cold-blooded Duke Mantee can secure what he wants by robbery and murder, but society has no more place for him than it has for Squier. The rich and arrogant Chisholms, in their chauffeured Dusenberg, are as alien and suspect to the majority of those in the society in which they live as are the others. Together, insiders and outsiders alike illustrate the philistinism of Americans that depresses Squier and prompts Gabby's hope of escape.

The resolution devised by Squier for himself and the romantic Gabby, whose paintings and love of French poetry have made him determined to help her, produces a conclusion that is shockingly brutal but still within possibility. Upon her promise to go to France, Squier signs over his $5,000 life insurance policy to Gabby and strikes a deadly bargain with Mantee. As the mobsters depart, Mantee fulfills the bargain by shooting Squier as requested, stunning those onstage as well as in the audience. No argument about the theatrical effectiveness of the shooting, but it raises the question that perhaps Squier has overdone the romantic heroics in giving his life for Gabby's sake. Signing over the policy in this manner may well be illegal, and Squier's choice of death may indeed seem implausible, but as a sensitive intellectual confronted by the realities of the world, Squier plainly longs to die. His sudden decision to do so while freeing Gabby at the same time is not all that distorted. If Duke Mantee seems too obliging, the truth is that one more death cannot make him any more of an outlaw. Moreover, by the time of the climactic gunfire, Sherwood has shown that Squier and Mantee, the debased image of Gramp Maple's hero, Billy the Kid, are spiritual brothers, each understanding the frightening and debilitating isolation of the other in a world that casts them aside.

What makes the allegory of *The Petrified Forest* work so well is Sherwood's use of setting and characterization acceptable to the contemporary audience. Sad little roadside cafés like the Black Mesa Bar-B-Q were familiar across the country, and the individuals who people this one existed in the audience's immediate world. And the play does tenuously offer some hope, for it must be assumed that Gabby will honor Squier's sacrifice and rejoin her mother. The moralist in Sherwood would certainly expect her to do so. He might even have hoped, without saying it, that Mantee, very likely betrayed by the blonde he waited for, will escape

Jason's pursuing posse of legionnaires. Gramp Maple would like it that way.[12]

Sherwood won his first Pulitzer Prize for *Idiot's Delight* (1936), a seriocomic exposé of a topsy-turvy, idiotic world inexorably racing toward another bloody showdown. With terrifying accuracy he forecast the coming conflict, even though up to the last he sincerely felt it could be prevented. Once more the playwright assembles a wide variety of characters, this time in a second-rate Italian alpine resort. The setting may not be as forbidding as the desolation of a petrified forest, but the beauty of the surrounding mountains does not obscure the fact that all those gathered here are in a forbidding spot from which escape may be difficult once the war that everybody expects but chooses to ignore begins. Similar to the central figures of his earlier plays, Sherwood's protagonists are a sophisticated couple brought together after a long separation for a final, brief affair as the world starts to blow apart. In this instance, however, death, rather than the creation of new and hopeful life, is the partner at the consummation.

Because this play, like *The Petrified Forest*, is an allegory of the time, some of the more preposterous elements cannot be condemned out of hand. Foremost is the situation involving Harry Van, an American "vaudevillian, hoofer, barker or shill" who has long capitalized on his powers of salesmanship, "none of them entirely honest." He and his bevy of dancing beauties have been touring Europe, oblivious to the mounting tensions, but are now trapped by a closed border. It is a ludicrous group that Van pulls together to perform a morale booster for the guests—a routine out of touch and absurdly inappropriate to the occasion yet, in Sherwood's hands, extremely funny. And what brings a honeymooning British couple to this frontier outpost, knowing well the imminent danger in a potential enemy country? Similar questions can be asked about the others, including the munitions maker Weber and his elegant "Russian" mistress, Irene, but as in *The Petrified Forest*, each character has a purpose in making Sherwood's point.

The pacifist condemnation of those who were held, in society's view, to be responsible for creating wars is centered on Achille Weber, the French munitions magnate. He is seen by Harry as one who "considers the human race as so many clay pigeons," to which Irene replies that Weber's is a necessary idiocy "for the sort of civilization that we have got." Sherwood's indictment of Weber's implication that mankind is helpless to alter the situation appears in an exchange between Irene and Weber as the war begins. Irene has just congratulated him on the "wonderful death and destruction" that he has made possible. Weber asserts that honor should be given "to Him—up there. . . . I am but the humble instrument of His divine will." Irene responds: "Yes—that's quite true. We don't do half enough justice to Him. Poor lonely old soul. Sitting up in heaven, with nothing to do but play solitaire. Poor, dear God. Playing Idiot's Delight. The game that never means anything, and never ends."

As the bombs start falling, Weber shows his true nationalistic self by hastening to return to France, where his abilities are now desperately needed. Having displayed little or no human compassion up to this point, he is even less humane in his abrupt abandonment of Irene to her own limited devices in escaping or even surviving. Others, as well, quickly abandon their individual identities and hurry off in response to the war's irresistible call. The young Englishman rushes back home to enlist, his promising career in art pushed aside. The German doctor, so near, perhaps, to a cure for cancer, must forget his hopes for a Nobel and the possibility of eliminating a curse on mankind, and return home to support his country's war effort. Humanity must take a far back seat.

Left behind in the fast-emptying hotel, the desolate Irene, dropping all her pretenses to Russian nobility, finally admits to Harry Van that she did spend that night with him ten years ago in an Omaha hotel and has always loved him as one who would never misunderstand her. Harry has sent his improbable troupe off on the last train to safety and returns to share Irene's fate. The snappy song-and-dance man sheds his showman's veneer and becomes a compassionate and caring human being.

The play's denouement abandons all pretenses of comedy and hits the audience's emotions with a throat-catching final sequence. Deserted by friends and by God, who cannot act to save anyone, Harry and Irene look out the windows at the idiocy of the destruction falling closer and closer around them. These two outcasts, sensing the futility of any rational act in the face of a world now utterly mad, admire what they see as "superb," as "positively Wagnerian," while Harry pounds out "The Ride of the Walkuries" on the piano. "Harry," says Irene, "do you realize that the whole world has gone to war? The *whole world!*" To this he replies, "I realize it. But don't ask me why. Because I've stopped trying to figure it out." Irene's response is a bitter and pointed one. "I know why it is. It's just for the purpose of killing *us* . . . you and me. Because we are the little people—and for us the deadliest weapons are the most merciful."

The bombs come nearer, and seated close together by the piano Harry and Irene sing loudly and defiantly the most militant of hymns, "Onward, Christian Soldiers" as the din increases and the curtain falls.

Where, Sherwood is asking, is the place for that "Cross of Jesus, going on before"? The hymn itself becomes the ultimate irony and the ultimate in idiocy.

In March of 1936 Sherwood wrote a postscript to *Idiot's Delight* before it appeared on stage, emphasizing his faith that the power of the world's decent people would prevent a repeat of 1914–18. Written by a man dedicated to peace but soon to become an active interventionist, it is worth quoting here because it demonstrates the hope that the "idiot's delight" of war could be ended once and for all.

> Let me express here the conviction that those who shrug and say, "War is inevitable," are false prophets. I believe that the world is populated largely by decent people.
>
> Of course . . . if decent people will continue to be intoxicated by the synthetic spirit of patriotism, pumped into them by megalomaniac leaders . . . then war *is* inevitable. . . .
>
> The megalomaniac, to live, must inspire excitement, fear and awe. If, instead, he is greeted with calmness, courage and ridicule, he becomes a figure of supreme insignificance. A display of the three latter qualities by England, France, the Soviet Union, and the United States will defeat Fascism in Germany, Italy, and Japan, and will remove the threat of war which is Fascism's last gesture of self-justification.

Sherwood's next Pulitzer Prize winner, *Abe Lincoln in Illinois*, was produced by the Playwrights' Company in 1938. E. P. Conklin's *Prologue to Glory* of the same year placed its emphasis on the familiar myth of Lincoln's supposed passion for Ann Rutledge. The only other important play about the Civil War president, *Abraham Lincoln*, written 20 years earlier by the British playwright John Drinkwater, was an episodic portrayal of historic events in Lincoln's life during his presidency. While a landmark against which dramatic treatment of Lincoln was long measured, it too furthered the traditional mythic aspects. Sherwood took a different approach, choosing to look at Lincoln as far less heroic and more human. Inspired by Carl Sandburg's extremely popular biography *Abraham Lincoln: The Prairie Years* (1926), Sherwood presents a Lincoln who is unsure of himself, who prefers to remain the ordinary small-town lawyer without political responsibilities—but he also shows Lincoln's steady, if sometimes reluctant, progress toward his recognition of what he has to do and his final acceptance of it. The play closes as Lincoln boards the train to depart Springfield. No national hero is yet evident; the new president is only an untried, 51-year-old, lanky frontier lawyer and legislator who faces the wrenching agony ahead of him with something of the heroic premonition of the fate that will prevent his return home.

Somewhat epochal in form, the play manages to avoid dramatic effects for their own sake, a strong temptation, considering the many well-known events in Lincoln's life that could be so used. For instance, Sherwood holds the Ann Rutledge relationship to a very few lines, keeping the traditional sentimental treatment at bay. The climactic scene with Seth Gale and his family on their way west is the moment when Abe recognizes what his own duties are; this recognition is close to Maxwell Anderson's dramatic theory of arrival at self-discovery, even though the play is not a tragedy. It is a well-drawn revelation of Lincoln's growing understanding and deep concern, but there is neither sudden conversion nor any evidence of flag-waving patriotic fervor.

Throughout the play, which includes his rather awkward courting of the ambitious and high-brow Mary Todd, and long passages of his debate with Douglas, Sherwood's Lincoln is consistently realistic. His wife may believe in his manifest destiny, but Abe himself keeps his sights lowered, determined to do "what is right—as God gives me power to see what is right." Emphasis on Lincoln's development as a person rather than reliance on the too-familiar and romanticized picture of him as a kind of god figure makes *Abe Lincoln in Illinois* an important historical drama, popular enough to be performed around the country during 1976, the bicentennial year.

Before America's entrance into the Second World War the Playwrights' Company produced Sherwood's third Pulitzer Prize winner, *There Shall Be No Night*, in 1940. The world had been shocked enough by the ruthlessness of the Soviet invasion and subjection of eastern Poland under the pact with Germany, but the attack on supposedly neutral Finland was in many ways more appalling. The heroic resistance put up by the tiny, superbly trained Finnish army literally froze the invaders in their tracks during the 1939–40 winter. Hopeless as it was, the defense by the Finns as they inflicted heavy casualties on the unprepared Russian troops gained worldwide admiration; unfortunately, nothing more than praise was forthcoming from those fighting Hitler or, like the United States, remaining outside.

Now a confirmed interventionist and increasingly fearful of the catastrophe a German victory would bring, Sherwood used the Russo-Finnish war as a metaphor for the stand he felt America must eventually take to halt the Nazi terror. During this stalemate period of the so-called phony European war, when most Americans felt confident that England and France would easily take the measure of the mad dictator and saw little need to act, they did welcome *There Shall Be No Night* and recognized the validity of its point that the principle of freedom, with its sacrifices, must be upheld against all odds. The neurologist and Nobel Peace Prize winner Dr. Haarlo Valkonen, who could no doubt flee to safety, remains behind to attend the wounded at the front, while his wife, Miranda, stays in Helsinki and his son, Erik, leaves to die as a ski trooper. Only Erik's pregnant wife, Kaatrin, escapes to freedom in America, where it is hoped the child will help a new generation build a better world. The human courage of Sherwood's characters far outshines their deaths, effecting a near-tragic catharsis. The play maintained its attraction even when altered to dramatize the equally heroic and equally briefly successful resistance of Greece against the invading Italians. Its universal message of the noble dignity of people caught up in an overwhelming struggle remained vivid and deeply moving.

As the world fell into the idiocy of another war, Sherwood's pacifism rapidly evaporated, but his commitment to the ideal remained in Alan Squier, Abe Lincoln, the Valkonen family, and, yes, Harry Van. By its very nature Sherwood's form of idealism, whether in sophisticated comedy or serious drama, was romantic at heart, sometimes in its historical perspective—ancient Rome, Vienna, the prairie village of Illinois—but most often in characterization. Still, the harsh, immediate realities of the Depression, a nation about to break in half in civil conflict, and a vicious war are all well treated in Sherwood's action and settings; sentimentality never becomes a problem. Not limited to the American scene, Sherwood's emphasis is cosmopolitan, with a universal appeal that kept his plays attractive to audiences far beyond his own time.[13]

The High Comic Sophistication of S. N. Behrman: Some Plot, Some Humor, but No Farce

The character of Mr. Fainall closes the prologue to William Congreve's exquisitely brilliant 1700 comedy of manners, *The Way of the World* in this wise, as he conservatively bespeaks the content of the comic drama we call "high":

> Some plot we think he has, and some new thought
> Some humour, too, no farce—but that's a fault.
> Satire, he thinks, you ought not to expect
> For so reform'd a town who dares correct?

The "he" is, of course, the playwright himself, who had been stung by the attack upon his plays by Jeremy Collier's earlier diatribe against the sins of the London stage. Thus, with tongue in cheek, Congreve purports to avoid the pointed barbs of satire, since the town, now reformed, needs no further correction.

Whether or not Congreve's play is really a satire is beside the point here, but Mr. Fainall's list of what makes up a comedy of this nature is entirely relevant. Of plot there is often more than "some" in intricately convoluted goings-on, as anyone who has read Congreve's masterpiece can attest. There is as well more than "some" humor in high comedy's constant display of sparkling wit. Of farce there is none. Mr. Fainall may see its absence as a "fault," but the well-drawn characters of good high comedy, performing within a cultivated hothouse of unreality, remain considerably removed from the cardboard figures of the low comic characters of farce.

Excellent modern high comedy is rare. Achieving its most dazzling display in the hands of those dilettante seventeenth-century playwrights Etherege, Farquhar, Vanbrugh, Wycherly, and the incomparable Congreve, and of the eighteenth century's Goldsmith and Sheridan, the high comic tradition has remained ever since the eminent domain of such British writers as Wilde, Shaw, and Maugham. Not until the plays of Samuel Nathaniel (S. N.) Behrman, the fourth of the original Playwrights' Company (and to some degree plays by Philip Barry), were there any American high comedies that could stand against their British counterparts.

Comedy at its highest level is a matter of *idea* rather than action. Its main appeal is to the intellect, and the reason for its rarity springs from its demand for objective detachment and intelligent insight on the part of the writer. The playwright must be skilled not only in character portrayal but also in the execution of a polished, highly artificial language that, while being far too effervescent and contrived to be real, must convey to the audience, willing to find amusement in the manners of sophisticated character behavior and clever dialogue, the sense of its absolute reality. Further, the successful high comic playwright must maintain throughout the ongoing frivolity practiced with utmost seriousness by the characters—a nonsentimental, nonromantic aura of *amorality*, especially in the lighthearted pursuit of sexual pleasure, performed entirely apart from any strict moral judgments.

   S. N. Behrman, writer for the liberal *New Republic*, the sophisticated *Smart Set*, and the *New Yorker*, editor and book reviewer for the *New York Times Book Review*, had collaborated unsuccessfully in lesser plays with others, among them Owen Davis, writer of formula melodramas. He was almost completely unknown before the Theatre Guild discovered him through its production of *The Second Man* (1927). Suddenly visible was a refined comic sense that was to become Behrman's hallmark. His privileged upper-class characters moved effortlessly through luxurious drawing rooms or sumptuous estates; they faced life as a game not to be taken too seriously, the major problems being whether or not to accept a weekend invitation, or who would be the most socially acceptable candidate to marry an eligible daughter. What his characters said and *how* they said it, not what they did, became paramount. These characters, as John Gassner so astutely observes in his introduction to *The Second Man*, "operated in a world where even folly wears the mask of good manners or at least polished ones, and where raffishness is *de trop.*"[14]

   The Second Man meets virtually every established criterion for high comedy. Its setting is the more than comfortable living room of a West Side New York apartment suite—the mandatory drawing-room milieu of high comedy—"its furnishings leaning a little to the exotic," inhabited by a short-story writer appropriately named Clark Storey, who finds himself deeply involved with the rich widow Kendall, five years his senior, and the nubile sex-kitten "flapper" Monica, at least a decade younger. The only other character, a prosperous doctor, Austin Lowe, helplessly in love with the elusive Monica, completes the tight little group. Of Congreve's action there is, in this case, some, but it is severely limited within the room and subsumed by the steady stream of Congreve's second proviso, humor, in the flashing, crackling wit of the conversation, derived mainly from Storey's flippant one-liners and often facetious responses to the others. Storey, as the central figure, would aspire to greatness as an artist and as a person, but he can't, and he knows it. His is the status of a kept man who accepts $500 support checks from Kendall without shame ("I suppose it's dreadful to take money from a woman. But why it's worse than taking it from a man I don't know"). He cannot survive on his own writing, which he knows very well is second-rate, and refuses to take what would clearly be the moral stand of artfully starving in a garret, which the idealistic Monica insists they could happily do until he "finds himself." He prefers, with a considerable amount of logical reasoning, to continue his life of ease under Kendall's support. He fends off any demand that he face reality by refusing to take things seriously. He does not deny that serious things exist, but his own common sense tells him that he cannot change them, and he unheroically takes the world as it is, survivable through intelligence and wit.

His opposite, the unimaginative Austin Lowe, whose ability to convey his love to Monica is near zero, takes the world with deadly seriousness, to his own constant disadvantage. Appealing to Storey for help in his love life by complaining, "If I could only talk like you," he receives the ultimate in advice as Storey replies, in the best of high comic epigrammatic tradition, "That's easy. Cultivate superficiality," followed later by, "Real emotion and real feelings are destructive. I've learned to do without them. That's civilization."

When faced with the reality of Monica's pressing presence, Storey reacts with understandable human emotion to her obvious attempt to seduce him: he momentarily surrenders to her innocent but alluring sexuality and admits, upon her stubborn insistence, that he loves her. But only momentarily. The physical attractions of a passing erotic moment are recognized for the trap they are.

The funniest and most revealing scene involving Storey's high comic control of the situation occurs in Austin's confrontation with Storey, who, he thinks, has ruined Monica. Driven by his panicky belief in Monica's transparently desperate ploy of announcing Storey as the father of her nonexistent unborn child, wildly out of control, soaking wet from wandering in the rain, a pathetic figure of vengeful justice, Austin produces a pistol, determined to eliminate his rival. Refusing to take him seriously, Storey faces the imminent possibility of his sudden end with the weapon he knows best, his wit, further infuriating his adversary:

STOREY (*without flinching*): Is it loaded? Am I facing death? The situation is novel, but not as thrilling as I might have expected. Do you really mean to kill me, Austin?

AUSTIN: Why do you think I brought it?

STOREY: Did you go home for that thing? You needn't have. I have one upstairs. I'd have lent it to you.

AUSTIN: You don't believe I'll do it. That's
               why you're so flippant.

STOREY: Oh, I suppose you will. I
               suppose—at the Threshold of the
               Great Unknown, as they call it—I
               should be solemn.

AUSTIN: Words!

STOREY: Force of habit. Sorry. You press
               that thing—and no more words.
               Death is probably very common-
               place. Disintegration. Resolution
               into original elements. Your prov-
               ince, Austin.

AUSTIN: Talker!

STOREY: Can't help it, old dear. It will wag.

. . . .

AUSTIN: Have you nothing else to say?

STOREY: Do you want a last speech? Dear
               me! I can't think of a thing. Isn't it
               funny? Now I'd like to say some-
               thing brilliant I can't. I've often
               wondered how all those great men
               engineered their death bed
               speeches. Made 'em up in ad-
               vance, I bet. (*Austin levels
               the gun.*) Wait! I've thought of
               something.

AUSTIN: Say it quick.

STOREY: His last words were: "Give my
               love to Monica."

AUSTIN (*wildly*):   Damn you! (*He fires.*)

Completely missing his target, Austin is reduced to wobbly helplessness
when he realizes what he has done. Storey, shaken but still in control,
suggests he go upstairs and sleep it off.

The "second man" of the title is Storey's inner self, described to
Monica as cynical, odious, grinning, and horrid, never letting him be,
mocking him even as he declaims his love, which the "second man"
knows is nonsense, but which Storey declares because she is young and

lovely, wonderful to touch. When Monica retorts that Storey is "fine and decent," the second man wisely prompts him to say that it is "the illusion of an adolescent, love-struck girl." Leaving "standards to the moralists," Storey maintains his cynical enunciation of his selfish love of comfort; ever the practical realist, he pushes Austin and Monica out the door together while he returns to woo back Kendall and share her upcoming trip to Europe.

In *Biography* (1932) Behrman created one of his most individualized characters in the self-sufficient, self-made portrait artist Marion Froud. Once more, in atmosphere, character, and dialogue, he achieved that lustrous polished quality of the spirit of high comedy. In her cluttered apartment, Marion lives happily independent of arbitrary convention, her own life unaffected by the preachments of hollow conformists. In the course of the play she is surrounded by those whose earnest concerns seem to be for matters most trivial, while aspects of a serious nature get light treatment. Kurt, the upstart radical who would reform Marion and the world through instant Marxism, is actually more concerned about the thirty minutes of his life wasted waiting for her, or that being close to Marion for too long, he may lose his fervor and become "tolerant." Leander Nolan frets more about a youthful indiscretion with Marion, so insignificant that she can hardly remember it, which could damage his coming campaign for office if she includes it in her proposed autobiography, than he does about the matter of making himself a worthy legislator. The cavalier unconcern of Marion and her close friend, the musician Feydak, toward their past transgressions—her openly acknowledged free love, often practiced, for personal gain, with those who have sat for her, and his blatant appropriation of a dead brother's fame—prevent any serious audience concern.

The more the leading characters talk of their own importance, the more they reveal their very ordinary, second-rate human qualities. Nolan, painting himself as another William Pitt, irritated at being called "Bunny," comes across as a conventional moralist, willing to share Marion's "shame" with her (a shame she refuses to recognize), constantly fearing others' opinions, while nowhere providing any convincing evidence that he is a gentleman or a statesman. Kurt, out to remake society in his own liberal but narrow image, is a pitifully ridiculous creature suffering hopeless delusions. Marion's mediocre actor friend Wilson has long since worn her unflattering nickname of "Tympi," after the drum with the large size and hollow sound. Marion knows what everybody is, including herself, and she has no pretenses about her own artistic limits.

She never permits the serious trivialities of those around her to alter her own sane and sensible—and comic—outlook, and her adroit handling of all their attempts to break through her defense is constantly amusing. But she can suffer; this is shown briefly near the final curtain, when she dismisses Kurt, for whom she has developed genuine affection, with equally genuine pain. She is, like Kurt and Nolan, a solid three-dimensional character, her feet on the ground considerably more firmly than the flippant Storey's. Neither cynical nor cruel, she can be earnest when the occasion arises, and her own emotional stability, more solid than Storey's, comes from her frank recognition that most things are not worth the trouble of anxious concern.

The repartee that bounces back and forth is, of course, wholly unrealistic, but it is delightful to hear and gives the illusion of complete spontaneity. Moreover, the neatly phrased high comic conversation is considerably more believable than the more one-sided quips, however brilliant, of Clark Storey.

MARION: But Bunny—Bunny dear—how important you've become! You look wonderful. You look like a—like a—Senator or something monumental like that.

NOLAN: That's a good omen. Your saying I look like a Senator. Because—I don't want to be premature—but in a few months I may be one.

MARION: A Senator! Do you really want to be a Senator or can't you help it?

NOLAN: What do you mean?

MARION: I'll paint you, Bunny. Toga. Ferule. Tribune of the People. I can see how successful you are, Bunny.

NOLAN: How?

MARION: White piping on your vest. That suggests directorates to me. Multiple control. Vertical corporations. Are you vertical or horizontal, Bunny?

NOLAN: I'm both.

MARION:	Oh, Bunny! You're sweet. You're so ingenuous. That's what I always liked about you.
NOLAN:	What do you mean?
MARION:	The way you look at me, the incredulity, the surprise. What did you expect to see? A hulk, a remnant, a whitened sepulchre . . . what? Tell me, Bunny, what? I won't be hurt.
NOLAN:	Well, naturally, after what I'd heard.
MARION:	What have you heard? Oh, do tell me, Bunny.
NOLAN:	Well, I mean—about your life.
MARION:	Racy, Bunny? Racy?
NOLAN:	If you're going to be flippant I suppose there's no use my saying anything—I might as well go, in fact.
MARION:	Do forgive me, Bunny. One gets into an idiom that passes for banter but really I'm not so changed. . . . I didn't know the news had got around so widely.
NOLAN:	I wish you wouldn't call me Bunny. My name is Leander.
MARION:	Really I'd forgotten that. Leander! Who was he—he did something in the Hellespont, didn't he? What did he do in the Hellespont?
NOLAN (*sharply*):	Beside the point.
MARION:	. . . Will I be burned for a witch if I go back home? Will they have a trial over me? Will you defend me?
NOLAN:	I should be forced, as an honest man, to stand before the multitude and say . . . it was I with whom this woman first sinned before God. As an honorable man that is what I should have to do.
MARION:	You're the holy man and I'm Thais! That gives me an idea for the portrait which I hope you will commission me to do. I'll do you in a hair-shirt.

Throughout the 1930s Behrman was one of the most active contributors to the Broadway stage, remaining with the Guild through his
1936 production of *End of Summer*. *Brief Moment* (1931) had preceded
Biography, but its story of a pretty blues singer married to a polished but
incompetent songwriter was a lesser piece of high comedy. As the prewar
decade wore on, however, Behrman's high comic tone began to be
blurred by his increasing concern about the political, social, and racial
conflicts that were compounded during the Depression and as the war
approached. The drawing-room, leisure-class atmosphere still prevailed,
but serious issues were given less lighthearted treatment than before. *Rain
from Heaven* (1934) has an English country-house setting, but its central
figure, Lady Wingate, encounters more than passing problems, none of
which are resolved, with a near-fascistic American southerner and a
refugee Jewish music critic from Germany. By the end, the comic aspect
has given way to some almost tragic complications. *Wine of Choice*
(1938), set on a luxurious Long Island estate, does not go particularly
deep; it revolves around a film star's ultimate rejection of her many
suitors, with too many echoes of *Biography*.

With the Depression at its greatest depth, *End of Summer*, set on a
large country estate in Maine and laying its emphasis on advantageous
marriages or business and political alliances, does raise questions about
the morality of inherited wealth and of being conspicuously rich in the
midst of the surrounding social crisis. The flighty, addlepated Leonie
(played, interestingly enough, by Ina Claire, who had originated the role
of Marion Froud) head of the household but unable either in dress or
behavior to outgrow her youthful enjoyment of wealth and amorous
escapades, is an object of comic ridicule as a throwback to a generation
that has no place within the contemporary society. Her daughter, Paula,
who will pair up with the young radical Will, out to destroy through
revolution the rich dynastic families represented by Leonie as well as
Paula, may represent a new and more concerned generation. By the end
of the play, however, after a lot of talk about the ills of the world, bantered
about in excellent high comic fashion, no fundamental social changes
seem imminent, and everybody leaves the stage very much as each had
entered it. Leonie has moved sufficiently into the present to offer financial aid to assist the far-left student publication being undertaken by Will
and his friend Dennis. Realizing that her assistance will (in theory, at
least) help to create a society its young sponsors admit will destroy her
kind forever, Leonie humorously asks if she will have nothing at all.
"Don't worry," Dennis tells her in the play's last line, "come the Revolution you will have a friend in high office."

In 1939, having left the Guild to help form the Playwrights' Company, Behrman was prompted by his increasing social awareness to write *No Time for Comedy*, in which he all but abandoned his lighthearted comic touch. As the world began to fall apart on the eve of the second war, Behrman, like others, considered it no time to undertake comedy. (O'Neill, on the other hand, refused to release his plays, contending that this was no time for the public to support tragedy.) In this possibly autobiographical portrait, Behrman creates a playwright "between ideas," unable to write the comedy for which his actress wife is waiting. Instead, he attempts a tragedy about the Spanish Civil War but finds himself equally frustrated. His idealism rapidly eroding, he realizes how bad his "serious" play is, and after toying with the idea of departing with the "other woman," he returns to his wife, who believes that "trivial comedy" is superior to "shallow tragedy." His grand and mostly shallow gesture of a trip to Spain to join the Republican side is abandoned, but the larger human issues raised by the play's argument are never satisfactorily resolved. True to the comic genre, all comes out well in the end; the stronger, more intelligent woman, the wife, wins out, and the vacillating artist makes his final decision by choosing not between social or political ideology but between two women. Whether or not the world really wants comedy is never decided. Absent are the finer touches of drawing-room comedy in amusing, if foolish, central figures speaking the unreal but fascinating dialogue of earlier plays. *No Time for Comedy* was one of Behrman's most successful prewar plays, featuring the major stars Katharine Cornell, Margalo Gillmore, and Laurence Olivier, but its dichotomy of purpose keeps it from being outstanding in the same fashion as *The Second Man* and *Biography* were.

S. N. Behrman, among all American writers of comedy, best embodies Horace Walpole's familiar observation that life is a tragedy to those who feel and a comedy to those who think. The artificialities of high comedy as Behhrman created them do not fully overshadow his thoughtful concern for the larger issues of his time. He peopled his plays with radicals of left and right, Jews and Gentiles, and other figures whose reasoning and common sense enable them to transcend the often ridiculous behavior and beliefs of those around them. As long as he retained the detached comic view, he wrote the best of drawing-room comedy; but when he became too closely involved with the issues of persecution and the rise of Nazi Germany, he gave way to an increasingly grave concern antithetical to the conventions of high comedy.

None have summarized Behrman's art and the art of high comedy better than Joseph Wood Krutch:

No person was ever so triple plated with the armor of comic intelligence as his heroes; no society ever existed in which all problems were solved—as in some of his plays they are—when good sense has analyzed them. . . . No drawing-room ever existed in which people talked so well or acted so sensibly at last, but this idealization is the final business of comedy. It first deflates man's aspirations and pretensions, accepting the inevitable failure of his attempt to live by his passions or up to his enthusiasms.[15]

Elmer Rice: Searching for a New Dramatic Language

Elmer Rice, active in the establishment of the Federal Theatre Project, cofounder of the Playwrights' Company, and composer of more than twenty-five produced plays, four novels, and two theater books, was, with some justification, referred to during his active career as the "dean of American playwrights." It is therefore somewhat surprising to realize that his permanent fame rests with only three successful plays, all completed before 1930. Within those three, however, lie some of his most important contributions. He regarded the assilmilation by the movies of the vapid romantic and melodramatic themes of the nineteenth- and early-twentieth-century stage as an opportunity for the stage to turn to more serious, mature work, and his fearless dramatic and theatrical experimentation was directed at audiences he felt were increasingly receptive to such innovations. Meeting with only limited success with most of his plays, he still was able, even in comparative commercial failure, to move American drama into new ways of conveying life on stage, into a "new language," which illustrated how the realistic drama could actually absorb a variety of experimental devices.

Despite a childhood spent in near poverty, Rice, born Elmer Reizenstein in New York, was able to study law and even to practice it briefly. He always identified himself with the working people, especially those in grinding, low-paying white-collar jobs, whose displacement by modern technology and exploitation by callous employers created the basis of his greatest successes. In 1914, when Rice was 21, his first play, *On Trial*, was an explosive sensation. His knowledge of courtroom procedure and his inborn theatrical sense guided him along the path that has always made trial scenes, those displays of the essence of the Greek dramatic *agon*, so suspenseful and gripping to theater audiences. The play's importance lies not in its melodramatic and somewhat mundane plot, with its stock characters reminiscent of any good nineteenth-century potboiler—the innocent young woman abused by a rich, already married hypocrite and the heroic husband who will kill to defend his wife's honor—but rather in the original technique of placing onstage the scenic methods of cinematic flashbacks.

The play's murder trial offers little out of the ordinary, but Rice's choice of two sets on the stage at the same time does. On one side is the courtroom itself, on the other side a space in which scenes from the past are played out, each one occurring earlier than the one before it. The effect of the reverse flashbacks during the trial's progress is a tour de force that rises considerably above the gimmick it might have been in lesser hands.

Although he had so quickly established his reputation at a young age, Rice would not achieve another success anything like his first for almost a full decade. He tried a couple of antimilitaristic plays during the first war, neither of which is worth remembering. Then he attempted to capitalize on his legal background with *For the Defense* (1919) and in *It Is the Law* (1922), a collaborative effort with Hayden Talbot. Nothing happened in either play to enhance his standing, and neither was ever published. His sudden venture into full-fledged expressionism, sprung on the unsuspecting audience with almost the same impact as *On Trial*, returned him to a prominence he never lost thereafter.

The Adding Machine (1923), a grim picture of modern technological society consuming and destroying the individuals who make it work, made no pretense of any literal reality. Its protagonist was put through experiences in life and after death that followed the best of European expressionism. The play's universality of theme remains as pertinent today as when it was written.

In *The Adding Machine* Rice moved beyond mere stylized portrayal of the deadly outward effects of the monotony of work in a mechanized society in order to go into the subconscious conditioning of his nonhero driven by fear, guilt, and envy. Thus he was able to consider not only the debilitating effects of exploitation, low wages, and depressing working conditions, favorite subjects of many leftish-slanted expressionistic plays, but also the more insidious inner destructiveness and the undermining of personal initiative.

From the opening monologue we are graphically introduced into the protagonist's distorted universe. We enter the bedroom of Mr. Zero and his wife, he a man who is no more than a cipher in his existence, she an equal nonentity. The room is lit by a single glaring hanging light bulb, and its walls are papered with foolscap covered with figures. Mrs. Zero pours out a long invective of disconnected sentences as she prepares to retire, while her husband, "thin, sallow, and undersized" silently awaits her in bed. She deplores her life, centered on household drudgery broken mainly by trashy movies, and berates Zero for having worked 25 years to gain nothing except an unrewarding bookkeeper's job. She is also well aware that his thoughts and eyes wander to the windows of the neighboring flat and its painted, whorish occupant. As the curtain descends on this first scene, Mrs. Zero is still talking to her unmoving, passive spouse, who is plainly used to and unaffected by this tirade.

The suffocating routine of Zero's dead-end job and its sensational ending are played out in the department-store accounting office where he works, perched on a high stool, endlessly writing figures in a ledger as directed by his coworker, a middle-aged, somewhat frumpish female, Daisy Diana Dorothea Devore. She is desperate for an affair with him and dreams of receiving the kind of luscious kisses she sees on the screen; he fantasizes about his quick advancement up the ladder once the Boss comes to realize the worth of his quarter-century of service. The explosion within his mind and his utter loss of control at the news from the Boss that, for the sake of efficiency and economy, he is to be replaced by an adding machine is a superb expressionistic sequence. Totally unbelieving, Zero begins, along with the audience, to hear distant merry-go-round music as the floor on which both figures stand starts to revolve. As the reality of his situation sinks in, the music swells, the floor turns more quickly, and eventually, as the Boss's mouth moves with unheard words drowned out by increasing noise of every kind of offstage effect of wind, galloping horses, whistles, bells, and crashing glass, the maddening din ends in a crack of thunder and a flash of red at the moment when Zero, unseen in the sudden blackout, stabs the Boss with a bill file. No realistically staged killing could be as effective as this enactment of what takes place in a human mind driven beyond sanity by a brutal turn of events.

The most explosive scene has come early, but Rice continues unabated in his exploration of what goes on within the psyche not only of Zero himself but of others who function along with him in this enervating society. Before he is arrested at his home, Zero and his wife entertain their equally undistinguished friends, Mr. and Mrs. One, Two, Three, and so on, in all shapes and sizes but, except for variations in color, dressed identically. Gossip among the women, politics and dirty jokes

The Adding Machine (Elmer Rice, 1923). The trial of Mr. Zero for the murder of his boss. Lee Simonson's expressionistic sets caught the sensation of the hapless Zero's confused and failing mind. Here Zero pleads his case in a long, wildly disjointed soliloquy before a less-than-human judge in a crazily tilted courtroom.

among the men, climax with a burst of outrage against "foreign agitators" who are ruining the country—"dagoes, Catholics, sheenies, niggers" who should be shot, hanged, lynched, and burned—culminating in a few bars of "America."

The pitiful Zero is tried before his peers, One through Six and their wives. His reason is now gone; his long defensive statement reviews the unconscious drives that have kept him going—his sexual frustration, his hatred of Jews and blacks (he wishes he could attend a lynching)— interspersed with pointless recitation of meaningless numbers as his mind drifts back atop the office stool. This laying forth of a man's uncontrolled inner hates and helplessness is terrifying to behold.

Rice pursues the exposure of the Zeros of the world as he sends this one to an afterlife of glorious beauty and heavenly music that is simultaneously revealed to be hell; his companion, the matricide Shrdlu, cannot understand why he is *not* in a literal hell for what he did. Ironically, in heaven Shrdlu suffers the tortures of hell as effectively as if subject to fire and brimstone. Here, too, is the suicide Diana Devore, who could not live without Zero; she is now available to him without restraint. But Rice knows the mentality of his Zeros. At first succumbing to Diana's middle-aged sexual charms, Zero suddenly realizes that a lot of nasty people have been let into heaven, and he flees these elysian fields that so offend him. His puritanical prejudices cannot tolerate the presence here of Rabelais, Swift, and others of such nature. He will, in fact, never learn.

There is no future, on earth or elsewhere, for the Zeros in Rice's devastating picture. The figure in later years of the sad, beaten Willy Loman, Arthur Miller's "low man" on the social totem pole, may have had the wrong dream, though for all his mistaken ideals, "attention must be paid." But there is no sympathy for Zero, and none need be extended. He has always been a cipher, and as we learn, reconditioned and rebuilt, his soul is to be sent back to earth to be even less significant than ever, for he will operate the new super adding machines with only the energy of his right big toe. There is no real future ahead, only increased oblivion for this creature whom the powers in heaven find useless, a waste product, a slave, indeed, a "poor spineless brainless boob." Rice offers one glimmering bit of salvation—the blonde, blue-eyed, red-lipped illusion of Hope, who seductively leads Zero back to his dead-end reincarnation. Nobody sees her, but she is, Zero is told, right there in front of him, and he rushes joyfully after her.

The tale of Mr. Zero, it seems, is not a tragedy of the fates, of disinterested gods, but, in the best expressionistic tradition, a revelation of what man has done to himself. The tedium of Zero's job is man-made. His callous, unthinking dismissal is an act of another human being in the name of progress. The pap fed to the Zeros and their friends in endless movies, the prejudices against outsiders, the frustrating inability of the Zeros of the world to express themselves sexually or otherwise, are all the end products of mankind's basic shortsighted stupidity. Unlike the elements of tragedy, however, all this *is* man-made; thus, there is the sense of hope. It must be there if we are to survive, and the solution lies not in the hands of the gods but in the human ability to change, even in the face of doubt that any change will ever be made. As Samuel Beckett's Vladimir and Estragon know, Godot, eventually, somehow, sometime, must appear. Otherwise, existence has no point.

The Adding Machine, uniformly accepted as an outstanding expressionistic play by any measurement, was Rice's only full-scale attempt at this specialized style. He understood its principles well, but he also knew that, even during its short-lived period of greatest acceptance in Europe and in America, it was never able to receive widespread public approval. His book *The Living Theater* includes a concise explanation of expressionism that acknowledges its limited audience appeal in its attempt "to go beyond mere representation and to arrive at interpretation" through "symbols, condensation, and a dozen devices which to the conservative seem arbitrarily fantastic."[16]

Rice failed with several other plays after *The Adding Machine*. Another with a legal plot, *It Is the Law* (1922), and two collaborations, one with Dorothy Parker and the other with Philip Barry, had little merit. *See Naples and Die* (1929) was not successful. *The Subway* in the same year tried to be a combination of expressionism and realism, but this story of a working girl who ends her life under a subway train was melodramatic and soon closed. The appearance of *Street Scene*, then, was a welcome reinstatement of Rice's leadership.

The Pulitzer Prize–winning *Street Scene* (1929) is one of those plays that make drawing clear lines between realism and naturalism so difficult, raising the legitimate question of whether any distinction should be made at all. Rice made use of a striking and structurally complex stage setting, which he himself had described as "by all odds the most experimental I have ever attempted" (Rice, *Minority*, 237). The significant factor in his experiment is that by creating the near-total illusion of a New York tenement building, the street in front of it, and the atmosphere of the city around it, Rice tried to convey with realistic detail the authentic-

Street Scene *(Elmer Rice, 1929). Jo Mielziner's tenement setting created a remarkable illusion of the building's indefinite height. Though intently realistic, the setting did not intrude and became an effective backdrop for the action, all of which takes place in the conveniently blockaded street.*

ity of life among a widely diverse assortment of individuals inhabiting the building during a sweltering New York summer.

The setting was a startling photographic reproduction; its multi-level exterior presented some challenging design and structural problems for the stage architect who built it, since it was conceived not as a mere backdrop but as the very center of the action. The basement and first two floors of the facade of the building showed the windows and steps down into the janitor's apartment below ground, the main entrance with the familiar fanlight over the door, together with first-floor windows, and the full windows of the second floor above them. The sense of the building's height continuing out of audience sight lines was provided by third-floor window sills, disembodied voices, and references to the tenants of the fourth floor, soon to be evicted. All doors and windows were practical to permit characters to enter and leave the building and to lean far out in a futile effort to escape the heat. City noises recurred frequently—cars, streetcars, police and fire sirens in the background, rattling garbage cans, and human voices near and distant. The problem of vehicular traffic, which could break the illusion, was solved by blocking the street for construction work, a common enough urban hazard.

This impressive and almost overpowering setting was, in a way, merely a contemporary extension of nineteenth-century attempts at literal representation of rushing locomotives or burning steamboats, or, more recently, Belasco's detailed "reality" in tenement interior or western cabin. To avoid turning the setting into nothing more than a sensational visual device depends on what is done with the characters who function within it. Once the audience takes in the illusion, the setting must cease to command attention and permit the play to proceed on its own, serving its purpose as the visible but unobtrusive milieu of the action. The characters of *Street Scene* are not products of the environment represented by the building itself, for they act apart from it as individuals who happen to be living there. It is not a slum by any means; its tenants are driven outside by the heat, which, in pre-air-conditioning days, would drive anyone in the steaming city to find similar relief. The building, other than becoming an intolerable oven at this time of year, has had little to do with what the characters are. The action develops far more from *who* they are than *where* they are. True, privacy can be a problem in any crowded block of flats, but it is apparent that there is considerable personal inconvenience in living here, quite apart from overpowering environmental forces in the naturalistic sense.

This is not a Depression society; it may have its oppressive elements, but the great crash has not yet occurred, and society as a whole is prospering. The Hildebrands' eviction is not a result of a collapsing economy but a matter of law: they haven't paid the rent. Everyone else in the building is in one way or another gainfully employed. Maurrant is a theater stagehand, and his daughter Rose has a steady office job. Shirley Kaplan teaches school, Kaplan is the building's custodian, and Fiorentino teaches music. There is a lot of talk about social conditions, with interplay among the characters in the many accents of their gossipy dialogue, but their complains against the "system," their condemnation of the carryings-on of some of the tenants, and so on, are what would be found in almost any lower-middle-class urban environment. The most consistent observations of what is wrong with everything come from Abraham Kaplan, the left-wing sympathizer and reader of radical papers. "Eets da folt of our economic system," he says, regarding the eviction. "As long as de institution of priwate property exists, de verkers vill be at da moicy of de property-owning klesses." But Kaplan only talks; nobody bothers to listen, and he himself does not act, becoming more of a comic figure than one to be taken seriously.

Then what does prompt the action in this drama of daily existence, with its several story lines? The most central, of course, is the violent triangle of Frank Maurrant, Anna, his wife, and Stankey the milkman. The murder of Stankey and Anna is a crime of passion, and the subsequent chase of the fleeing Frank a natural sequel to his violent act. Family pressures—a husband's jealousy and brutality and a wife's desperation for some form of kindness and sympathy—not social conditions, drive the action. Rose repeatedly urges her father to move somewhere else to ease family problems, but it is Maurrant's stubborn refusal, even though he could easily afford the change, that fuels the catastrophe.

Rose Maurrant's story of personal frustration and fear for her family follows closely in dramatic interest. Her low-paying job has a limited future, but there are possibilities for escape. Her hot-handed employer, Harry Easter, offers relief, unattractive but immediately available, and Sam Kaplan's hopeless love for her provides another, if also limited, avenue. Rose cannot abandon her mother, and she is intent on keeping her brother Willy from becoming a street bum. Her decision to stay is a matter of her own free will, little affected by naturalistic determinism.

In *Minority Report* Rice explains his attempt to blend this large cast of diverse individuals in what he had hoped was a seemingly natural way, actually making use of the play's structure along symphonic lines, with statement, restatement, and interplay of the contrasting human instruments. Overall, he succeeded amazingly well. His combination of believable and convincing *dramatic realism* in character and action with the *theatrically naturalistic* detail of the entire mise-en-scène in lighting, sound, and structure carries *Street Scene* far beyond the pattern of earlier Belascoesque naturalism, which may have been visually sensational but always fell back on romantic clichés and sentimentalities. Further, he was able to form within his microcosm a metaphor of life from birth through death, from the agonizing difficulties of Mrs. Buchanan's delivery to the violent deaths of Anna Maurrant and her lover. Still, it is not difficult to recognize the problem involved in labeling the play stylistically, as the qualities of realism and naturalism overlap and blend, forcing the realization that any hard-and-fast distinction may not always be possible. Nevertheless, the cumulative effect of what was in many ways a risky theatrical experiment was powerful and remains so; the play still succeeds in revival. In 1947 *Street Scene* was made into a successful musical with music by Kurt Weill and lyrics by Langston Hughes.

Aside from the popular hit *Dream Girl* (1945), a lightweight, well-crafted comedy combining the real-life experiences of an overly imaginative young woman and her romantic dream fantasies, no other Rice play gained the heights of *The Adding Machine* and *Street Scene*. Rice did have modest runs with *The Left Bank* (1931), a critical portrayal of irresponsible Americans abroad that he produced himself, and with *Counsellor-at-Law* the same year, in which he once more made use of his legal training. This realistic picture of prejudices against blacks and immigrants, the cold inhumanity of the legal system, the snobbery of the wealthy, and the ruthlessness of business practices gained Rice a new place of importance as both director and producer. As the Depression deepened and war tensions arose in Europe, Rice responded emotionally with three unsuccessful dramas, all purporting to show the state in which America found herself and to suggest some solutions: *We the People* (1933), *Judgment Day* (1934), and *Between Two Worlds* (1934).

Ironically, Rice's lack of overt partisanship in his social thinking brought criticism from both superpatriots on the Right and Marxists on the Left. To neither way of thinking did he demonstrate sufficient fervor. His portrayal of the evils of business (which was, as expressed by President Coolidge himself, "the business of America"), as in *The Adding Machine*, offended those on the Right, and his social comments in *Street Scene* did not go far enough for those on the Left.

After a short, tempestuous relationship in 1935 with the Federal Theatre Project, which he helped to establish, Rice turned away from the theater world, which to him seemed to serve the cause of commerce rather than art. Refreshed from a trip abroad, however, he joined with Anderson and Sherwood to found the Playwrights' Company. His *American Landscape* (1938), a plea for racial tolerance and peace between capital and labor, was a failure, but he was redeemed somewhat by his boy-meets-girl comedy, *Two on an Island* (1940), which proved his ability to see humor in common characters and familiar situations on the Manhattan island he knew so well. With the coming of World War II, Rice reflected the immediate concerns of his country in *Flight to the West* (1941), but this artificially melodramatic play set on a transatlantic clipper full of European refugees was too polemical to be good drama.

Of four postwar plays, the only one to achieve any success was *Cue for Passion* (1958), based on a modern Freudian interpretation of *Hamlet*. This one-sided portrayal of characters in a plot even more melodramatic than Shakespeare's was Rice's last professionally produced play.

Rice's later scripts were never the equal of his early works, but throughout his four decades of promoting the art of the drama in his wide variety of dramatic styles and social topics, as a proponent of tolerance and understanding, and as an opponent of the cold impersonality of business and the law, Rice spoke his new language and opened the theater to new ideas. Although most of his plays have not been revived, his artistic integrity substantially raised the aesthetic standards of American drama and theater during the unsettling post- and prewar years.

□   □   □

The Playwrights' Company never quite achieved the stature of the The-atre Guild and, of course, never had the same kind of resources. Nonethe-less, the members who composed it, hoping, as so many such groups had before them, to improve the standards of American drama, were certainly among the most important contributors who did succeed in raising Ameri-can drama to new levels of excellence; some of the most enduring and important plays in American dramatic literature came from their pens. Without them, the modern American drama would have missed a great portion of its growing world reputation.

6

Imitation, Mimicry, and Modification

Variations on a Realistic Theme

Whether it be called religious ritual in the Middle ages or show business in the twentieth century, observes Gerald Weales, "the theater at any moment provides an intellectual and artistic milieu . . . in which the dramatists work and by which most of them are defined."[1] From ancient Greece to modern Broadway, the theater has demanded a drama in form and style that limited, indeed defined, the dramatists working within it.[2] On this basis we can state with reasonable accuracy that the predominant style of American drama between the wars was *realistic*. At once, however, the flag of caution is raised, for generous allowances must be made for the nonrealistic experiments in style and dramaturgy taking place simultaneously. Well aware of this, Weales goes on to warn against any attempt to erect a "critical barrier" around a particular time, because playwrights will quickly be "scrambling over the wall" with scripts that refuse to be arbitrarily confined (Weales, 398). The Playwrights' Company, as already noted, proved the validity of this caveat through some very important "scramblers" who varied the underlying realistic tradition with verse, expressionism, and some downright old-fashioned romanticism.

Whatever the milieu or the era, the psychology of dramatic art, from the viewpoint of the practicing dramatist, the serious critic, or the attendant audience, should acknowledge, as Eric Bentley notes, "the impulse toward sheer imitation." Paradoxical as it appears, this imitation permits the drama to reproduce, often with minute fidelity, objects that in reality would be viewed with pain but onstage can be contemplated with "delight." Bentley's assertion is not as perverse as it might appear. Delight comes not through the pleasure of observing pain and suffering as such, but in the unique quality of all successful dramatic art: audience recognition and subsequent acceptance of the dramatic imitation—the *artistic interpretation*—of a familiar, if not always directly encountered, reality. The aesthetic distance of the audience must always be properly maintained, however. It must be commensurate with the entertainment value, the delight, of a vicarious experience, however unpleasant. If the pain becomes so literal, so real, as to turn the audience away, the imitation has failed, and the aesthetic distance has been shattered. In Bentley's terms, the *realist*, though sufficiently imitative to turn the pain into delight, must also recognize that the possibilities of "faithful mimicry" are "extremely limited in practice."[3] There are always the restrictive conventions that must be imposed on character, plot, and setting, forcing the realistic play as an art form into a *modification* rather than a direct imitation of reality.

The five playwrights to be considered below practiced their profession as dramatic realists within a society and an age in which anxiety concerning the human condition had long supplanted any belief in the intrinsic heroism of mankind or the existence of a divine providence. Tragedy, that demonstration of human worth and noble stature, had been replaced by the depiction of twentieth-century life as too often controlled by materialistic forces that determined the destiny of characters who lacked any aspiration toward the high ideals demanded by tragedy. The central theme, as seen by Bigsby, had become *alienation*, brought about by "a largely urban and industrial environment" denying the "animating myths that drew their strength and credibility from a predominantly rural world in which the individual's responsibility for his own fate and identity was an article of national no less than individual faith" (Bigsby, vii).

If one holds to Bigsby's tenet, one might at first seriously question Bentley's further view that "as modern persons we are willy-nilly under the spell of Naturalism" (Bentley, 215). The apparent contradiction immediately complicates the issue, recalling the persistent difficulty in establishing clear-cut stylistic differences. Bentley seems to imply that modern man, in experiencing Bigsby's alienation, is alone and helpless in an indifferent and godless universe and functions in this abject position, with little control over his own destiny, affected as he is by the deterministic forces surrounding him and by his lack of free will. This implication, of course, is counter to the concept of realism, with its assumption of man's free will to act independently within the society around him, and Bigsby's and Bentley's positions can be reconciled if one recalls that man has created that society in the first place. The gods, fate, or nature have had nothing to do with its creation; man has alienated himself, and this, then, becomes the basis of the principle of realism, supporting the generalized view of the American dramatist's fundamental position within this era as realistic.

The semantic problem—is this or that play realistic or naturalistic, or something of both—recurs frequently in the plays of the five dramatists now to be considered. Each of them develops theme and character along traditional realistic lines. Actions arise from situations readily accepted by the audience as stemming from a society they recognize. Speech patterns for the most part are contemporary and colloquial. At the same time there is frequent intense concern for mankind's position within a modern society that has spun out of control. The social and economic patterns, created as they may have been by human actions, have taken on lives of their own and have imposed upon the lives of the individuals who exist within them an almost deterministic force that can fit Bentley's statement. And in keeping with Bigsby's assertion, there is little doubt of the alienation as well.

Reality, stark and immutable, is the subject matter of these plays. The playwrights' attempts to reproduce it through "faithful mimicry" are limited by the artistic necessity of its modification, but the minute detail of imitation in character and plot development, often combined with strikingly illusionistic, that is, naturalistic, stage settings, gives added legitimacy to Bentley's observation. Furthermore, these playwrights could set down the pain with exceptional effect, shocking, or, if you wish, delighting their audiences.

Clifford Odets: Imitation on the Left

With the Great Depression at its worst, the voice of the Group Theatre's most radical young member, Clifford Odets, unabashedly speaking the Communist party line, was able to make itself heard not on street corners or in converted warehouses in the often disorganized and slapdash style of crude and propagandistic agitprop ventures, but within the sophisticated (and capitalistic!) enterprise of the New York commercial theater. The floundering Group, having been saved by the success of the Pulitzer-winning and very unproletarian *Men in White* in 1933, was able, with the support of the New Theatre League, to undertake Odets's first play, *Waiting for Lefty*, in once-a-week Sunday benefit performances at the Civic Repertory Theatre, beginning in January 1935. The more radical groups too often did more to turn off their limited audiences than to stimulate them; *Lefty* gained its enthusiastic support not in preaching to the converted but in speaking to those against whom the message of the play was targeted. By March it had gathered sufficient public support to appear daily, paired with Odets's *'Til the Day I Die*.

   Waiting for Lefty is a fine example of how imitation, even mimicry, can succeed without any of the trappings of conventional illusionistic staging. Appearing on a bare stage (not by necessity, as with *The Cradle Will Rock*, but by choice), the casual semicircle of labor leaders seated on ordinary hiring-hall chairs and facing the audience creates an immediate feeling of literal reality, all the more so as the audience, addressed directly and upon occasion responding to those onstage, becomes the rank-and-file union membership. The viewer cannot remain separated from the action in the usual theatrical sense but is drawn into the situation as a participant. The climactic call to action openly plays on mob psychology; the cry to strike is meant to be irresistible. Imitation now becomes very close to life itself. It is more than good mimicry; for the moment, aesthetic distance is forgotten. Caught up in the authenticity of what is going on, the audience should now be prompted to rush into the streets and man the barricades.

   But this is, after all, theater, and Odets, knowing very well the limits of the reality he protrays, makes excellent use of theatrical conventions while holding his grip on the closely involved audience. First of all, the initial speaker, the "porcine . . . well-fed and confident" head of the cab drivers' union, who is trying to head off a strike, is named, appropriately, Harry Fatt. He smokes big cigars and calls anybody opposing his view a damn Red, and yellow as well. It is soon apparent that he represents the archetypal, bloated, exploiting capitalist, a clear symbol of the enemy, protected from the union rabble out front by a toothpick-chewing, gun-toting thug. Then, as a constant refrain throughout, the question is raised and remains unanswered: where is the committee's duly elected chairman, named, again appropriately, Lefty?

Waiting for Lefty *(Clifford Odets, 1935). The sparse furniture on a bare stage was meant to resemble a labor union hall. Here Fatt is accosted from the audience by a union member. The various short scenes frequently made use of the furniture and were performed downstage, while Fatt, puffing his cigar, and others remained in the background.*

Within the semicircle Odets spotlights a series of emotional vignettes exploring one by one the committee members' reasons for demanding a strike, while the others, in semidarkness, comment choruslike on the action in front of them, and Fatt contemptuously blows smoke into the scene. Aided only by minimal props—a table, a stenographic desk— each man enacts with wife, sweetheart, or coworkers the debilitating, dehumanizing impositions of the workplace that are destroying all of them. Wages at the starvation level of $6 or $7 a week, spying on fellow workers, anti-Semitism and political favoritism, joblessness, and so on, lead those onstage and the audience out front to one frightening conclusion: society is tearing itself apart. Workers must unite, and who can guide them? Buy and read *The Communist Manifesto;* go to Russia where racial discrimination is outlawed; join those who call you "Comrade" and lift you from the gutter.[4]

When, finally, those at the meeting learn that Lefty is dead behind the car barn, a bullet through his head, there is one course of action left: Fatt and his henchmen are overwhelmed in the shouts to strike. If ever sheer theatricality could play upon the emotions of an audience for calculated, and in this case ideological, effect, *Waiting for Lefty* did so. Overnight Odets shot into prominence as the writer of a truly radical play that, at the time it appeared and ever since, has driven nearly all others of its ilk permanently into the background.

Waiting for Lefty raises some serious problems as a work of art. The subjectivity of its oversimplified bad guy / good guy propagandizing limits its appeal, and brilliant as its theatricality may be, the pertinence of its plea for worldwide labor cohesion is of *one* time more than of *all* time. It is a one-shot effort; repetition by others or by Odets himself could not inspire the same reaction. Odets recognized that if his message were to be heard, he would have to develop his radical consciousness-raising views more fully. There would have to be more work below the surface in longer and less emotional pieces.

'Til the Day I Die, *Lefty's* companion in its extended run, has been all but forgotten. Its theme of the anti-Nazi underground in Berlin is filled with ardor for the cause of justice, but its picture of the agonies of the central figures, while supposedly based on a true account, is too politicized along narrow Communist party lines. Its emphasis upon resistance to tyranny is praiseworthy enough, but the action descends into overdone melodramatics, while a lack of character depth does little to promote more than surface interest in the young cell members as sacrificial, if noble, victims in a hopeless cause.

Odets's most productive year was 1935; *Awake and Sing* appeared in February and *Paradise Lost* in December. These two plays, the first arguably Odets's best and most popular work, earned him a reputation as the "American Chekhov." One hardly need point to the obvious differences. Chekhov's decaying upper class, indolent and emotionally distant from reality, has little in common with Odets's lower-middle-class Jewish families in the midst of the Great Depression. Two factors, however, support a broad general comparison. Both groups of characters find themselves frustrated and helpless, suffocating within a world that is closing in on them, while, ironically, simultaneously disintegrating. They quibble and quarrel among themselves as they make the semblance of a fight for human dignity, upholding as best they can the eroding social standards that are relentlessly slipping out of their control. The second factor is the low-key dramatic style of each playwright. Individual characters are isolated, preoccupied with their own private concerns; unheard and ignored, they constantly talk past each other. Very little happens, as in the reality of day-to-day life, and the denouement, while suggesting possibilities of ultimate change, leaves a lot of things unresolved. After the curtain falls, life will proceed much as it was long before the curtain rose.

Odets, like Chekhov, designed a virtually plotless drama, with the forward movement of the action all but nonexistent. To describe what goes on is to consider the characters one by one. Self-centered, hardly aware of the surrounding bigger picture, they form a cumulative group portrait in which everyone receives equal emphasis and no one stands apart. The ups and downs of events onstage never reach the emotional pitch of a dramatic climax as such, but the underlying tensions and individual inner struggles are constantly evident. These plays fit perfectly the aims and purposes of the Group Theatre's concept of ensemble acting, providing nothing for a single star to grasp but rather offering the entire company, as Chekhov did for the Moscow Art Theatre, an opportunity for a moving collective performance. As a result, dialogue becomes singularly important. Odets's ear for the peculiarities of the New York Bronx idiom brings a reality to the play's speech that eschews any sense of staginess or theatricality; the language is so revealing of personalities that the plays readily come alive.

Odets's underwritten dramatic style in the portrayal of the Berger family in *Awake and Sing* is a remarkable achievement in realistic imitation. As the audience becomes involved with each member's private frustrations, there is a growing sense of sympathy and understanding in spite of some unthinking and unnecessarily spiteful cruelties. We cannot help but reach out emotionally to Ralph, the 22-year-old "boy with a clean spirit"; ardent, romantic, sensitive, and naive, as Odets describes him, he must sleep on a daybed in the front room, despite his young adulthood, cannot buy a pair of black-and-white shoes, and has to see his girlfriend clandestinely to avoid his disapproving mother's interference. Nor can we really disapprove of Hennie, 26, physically attractive and strong of will, whose self-assertion has taken her to the point where the family's name must be protected by a marriage she does not want to a man she does not love; she abandons husband and child for the one whose own strong will equals hers and who loves her for it. Can one condemn Hennie's lover, the war-maimed Moe Axelrod, cynical about the society that nearly destroyed him, leaving him to hobble through life abandoned by those he served? Everybody else, in one way or another, calls up an understanding audience reaction: Sam Feinschreiber, helpless, insecure, lonely, and hypersensitive, who marries Hennie and does not know her child is not his; Myron Berger, the mild, inept father of the family, unable on his own to support them, henpecked and submissive, accepting life as it is; old Jacob, the grandfather, a permanent boarder and dignified idealist who plays ancient Caruso records and sees salvation in

Marxism; even rich Uncle Morty, playboy businessman, conscious of his wealth, intolerant, yet likable; and above all, Bessie, the family matriarch, who keeps Ralph away from his girl, forces Hennie into her marriage, browbeats Myron, and in a fit of petulance smashes old Jake's precious records. Unsupported by Myron, the supposed head of household, the family would drift aimlessly, so Bessie, determined to maintain a modicum of dignified respectability, steps in, wielding her verbal assaults indiscriminately. The family cannot exist without Ralph's pittance in the household treasury, so he must be kept from leaving to pursue his own life. Hennie must be brought to heel. Old Jacob, driving others frantic with his endless record playing, must be made aware of who is boss. But there is something more to Bessie than mere surface vindictiveness. Can we fully blame her? Did she bring the family to its present position? Is she wholly wrong in trying to hold a collapsing world together? Not entirely. She does some monstrous things, but she is no monster. She becomes the seriocomic heroine in a seriocomic effort at survival.

"Awake and sing, ye that dwell in dust," says Isaiah. How does one do so? One hopes, as Ralph must, to achieve a life that is not "printed on dollar bills." One flees defiantly, as Hennie does. One reads Marx and preaches the free life of Russia, as old Jacob does. (In an apparent capitalistic denial of his faith, Jacob maintains a life insurance policy that will give Ralph a future when Jacob "falls" from the apartment house roof while walking the dog.) The outlook is not totally fatalistic; there *is* hope that the Ralphs and Hennies of this depressed society can eventually do more than just survive. It may or may not take a Marxist solution. After all, old Jacob is ridiculed and scoffed at, but he does offer some good advice to Ralph: "Look on this failure and see for seventy years he talked with good ideas, but only in the head. It's enough for me now I should see your happiness. This is why I tell you—DO! Do what is in your heart and you carry in yourself a revolution. But you should act. Not like me. A man who had golden opportunities but drank instead a glass of tea."

The play's slant, in true Odets fashion, is to the left, but only marginally. If the force expended against the Bergers is a naturalistic determinism from which escape seems impossible, it is man-made. At the end, after Bessie has grabbed for the insurance money, and as Moe and Hennie prepare to depart, Ralph does awake and can, we assume, transcend that force. Gazing after the figure of his father, retiring for the night, Ralph becomes aware of what he, in his own way, can do:

RALPH: When I look at him, I'm sad. Let me die like a dog, if I can't get more from life.

HENNIE: Where?

RALPH: Right here in the house! My days won't be for nothing. Let Mom have the dough. I'm twenty-two and kickin'! I'll get along. Did Jake die for us to fight about nickles? No! "Awake and sing," he said. Right here he stood and said it. The night he died, I saw it like a thunderbolt! I saw he was dead and I was born! I swear to God, I'm one week old! I want the whole city to hear it—fresh blood, arms. We got 'em. We're glad we're living.

MOE: I wouldn't trade you for two pitchers and an outfielder. Hold the fort!

RALPH: So long.

MOE: So long.

(They go and RALPH stands full and strong in the doorway seeing them off as the curtain slowly falls.)

Although it is sudden and a bit stagy, this outburst is probably not all that much out of character, and it does provide Odets with a brief opportunity to have his say.

Odets seems to have preferred *Paradise Lost* to *Awake and Sing,* but it never caught on with nearly the same poignant appeal. And yet, in its treatment of the homeless, of underhanded business proposals, and of politics, except for the mildly revolutionary sentiments uttered by Mr. Pike, the furnace man, it is more relevant to the society of half a century later than are the Depression-era problems of *Awake and Sing.*

Unlike the Berger's Bronx flat, the Gordon's home is an urban house in an unidentified American city. The living room is a focal point for a larger cast involved not only in immediate family problems but in broader social issues as well. They are quickly recognizable as an Odets family, moving and speaking in a disarmingly natural manner very similar to that of the earlier play's characters, with close mimicry of actual conversation.

Clara Gordon is personally more attractive and less domineering than Bessie Berger, with interests lying more in card games than in the needs of the family. Her most frequent advice, regardless of the circumstances, is "Have a piece of fruit." Leo Gordon, a stronger, more active head of family than Myron Berger, is put through trials considerably more overwhelming than Myron could ever handle. Their total effect wreaks havoc within the family, and the compounding disasters are heaped up by a dramatist-God throwing down gratuitous challenges more for effect than for credibility: the older son, Ben, a champion runner, dies while committing a crime with his mobster friend Kewpie; the younger son, Julie, who has dreamed of making it big on the stock market, is dying slowly of a debilitating disease; the talented daughter, Pearl, who hopes to be a great musician, loses her piano when the family is dispossessed of home and furniture in an eviction that results from the longtime embezzlement of company funds by Sam Katz, Leo's partner in a now-ruined leather business.

There is a temptation to classify both *Awake and Sing* and *Paradise Lost* as dramas of naturalistic determinism, given the crushing and inescapable disruption of the Depression society that constantly thwarts both families' attempts to maintain a decent level of human dignity. Hennie's flight, Ralph's upbeat assertion of what he is going to do, however modest, and Leo's curtain speech make clear that Odets does not wholly accept the premise that the nature of society will be the final controlling factor. The Depression is beyond the understanding, much less the control, of either the Bergers or the Gordons, and it is relentless in its debilitating pressures; but what happens within each family does not follow any deterministic pattern. Myron Berger may be, by nature, mild, indecisive, and sweet-tempered, "a born follower," according to Odets, but his ineffectiveness within the household is a result of long browbeating under the strong-willed domination of Bessie. Leo Gordon, in his innocence, has been hoodwinked by Sam Katz, who pleads that his ledger-juggling was necessary and therefore acceptable for survival in the face of economic conditions; but an alert partner should have suspected something long before disaster struck. Ben Gordon, driven to fatal crime, may be able to rationalize his decision to break the law and take the risks by blaming society, but his own poor judgment in associating with Kewpie is more responsible for what happens than anything else. Julie is doomed by the disease that is beyond his control, a natural calamity that cannot be attributed to any deprivation the Depression may have caused. Moreover, there are those who prosper, Depression or not, like Uncle Morty, and those like Moe, who will continue to defy the cold indifference of society with cynicism and independent courage (the collapse of Moe's artifical leg and his refusal of help to right himself are grimly comic but also highly symbolic), which will, together with Hennie, see him through.

Harold Clurman, who directed both plays, sees considerably more than a naturalistic study of middle-class life in *Paradise Lost*. He recognizes what both plays accomplish, writing that *Paradise Lost* is "a poetic play in the sense that the author's point of view creates real characters that are virtually symbols in the formal meaning of the word" (Clurman, 425). There is, in truth, a strong poetic sense in Odets's serious, but gently comic, realistic dialogue, with its distinctive urban Jewish speech pattern. Gerald Weales, writing 50 years later, makes the point that the play was ahead of its time, that it advanced beyond the purely naturalistic and was therefore able to communicate to later generations who, less concerned with realistic causes and effects, can appreciate the "comedy and pain with which the family scenes are so rich" (Weales, 100). Not unlike Clurman, Margaret Brennan-Gibson, in her long psychological study of the life and works of Odets, views the play as "uncertainly poised between psychological naturalism and allegory."[5] There is no question that the symbol of resurrection at the end of *Awake and Sing* compares favorably to the symbol of paradise regained at the end of the later play, when Leo Gordon comes to recognize that human sympathy can create a new world, even while his lost middle-class paradise sits out on the sidewalk with the evicted furniture.

Paradise Lost poses a real problem in the final speech by the "born-again" Leo. It almost wrecks the hitherto well-established believability in Leo as a character and in the play's action. The Gordons find themselves in a many-cornered quandary. While they prefer that their furniture remain outside as a symbol of the plight of themselves and others, they are being forced to bring it back in so a long-planned "prosperity block party" may proceed with "no dampers." Furthermore, the neighbors have accumulated a purse, which Leo and Clara refuse to accept. Money from Ben's abortive venture into crime is thrown at them by the hood Kewpie, and their good friend Gus, through personal sacrifice, presents them with an amount substantial enough to see them through their present financial crisis. It is a tremendously emotional moment; neither Leo nor Clara is quite sure what will come next. Leo appeals to his wife, "Everything is my fault. Clara, tell me what to do," but she can only turn her back and shrug her shoulders while Leo puts his face in his hands.

Shaking off this momentary lapse into helplessness, Leo determines that Kewpie's "gift" belongs not to them but to the homeless men down at the corner. When two of these men enter, summoned by news that Leo has something for them, their skepticism at this offer of cash is understandable. Leo, suddenly taking unto himself the sins of the world, tells them, "People like me are responsible for your condition," but he receives a strong jolt from the resentful response:

> You think you're better off. . . . You're worse. . . . The slight dif-
> ference in our social standing is you got a whole pair of pants. . . .
> Why, you're sleeping! All over the country people are sleep-
> ing. . . . All over millions dreaming of democracy and liberty
> which don't exist. . . . This kind of dream paralyzes the will—
> confuses the mind. Courage goes. Daring goes. You had a sorta
> little paradise here. Now you lost the paradise. That should teach
> you something. But no! You ain't awake yet. . . . But don't be
> fooled by the good old days. That's through for ever. You been
> took like a bulldog takes a pussy cat. Finished! They left you the
> dust of the road.

If Odets had only stopped there! This unexpected attack, politically contrived as it is, would make a dramatically emphatic curtain and would leave Leo and Clara, and the audience, to ponder the very clear message. Unfortunately, Odets succumbs to the "Ralph syndrome" and contrives an ending that stretches audience credulity considerably beyond Ralph's fairly mild optimism. It is as jarringly unconvincing as if it were coming straight at the audience from a soapbox podium. As the two homeless men leave, Clara asserts the rightness of what they said and is near tears. But Leo suddenly stops his pacing across the room, shouts "No!" and pours it all out:

> No! There is more to life than this! Everything he said is true, but
> there is more. That was the past, but there is a future. Now we
> know. We dare to understand. Truly, truly, the past was a dream.
> But this is real! To know from this that something must be done.
> That is real. We searched; we were confused! But we searched,
> and now the search is ended. For the truth has found us. For the
> first time in our lives—for the first time our house has a real founda-
> tion. Clara, those people outside are afraid. Those people at the
> block party whisper and point. They're afraid. Let them look in our
> house. We're not ashamed. Let them look in. Clara, my darling,
> *listen to me.* Everywhere now men are rising from their sleep.
> Men, men are understanding the bitter black total of their lives.
> Their whispers are growing to shouts! They become an ocean of

understanding! *No man fights alone.* Oh, if you could only see
with me the greatness of men. I tremble like a bride to see the time
when they'll use it. My darling, we must have only one regret—
that life is so short. That we must die so soon. (CLARA *slowly has
turned from* JULIE *and is listening now to her husband.*) Yes, I want
to see the new world. I want to kiss all those future men and
women. What is this talk of bankrupts, failures, hatred . . . they
won't know what that means. Oh, yes, I tell you the whole world
is for men to possess. Heartbreak and terror are not the heritage of
mankind! The world is beautiful. No fruit tree wears a lock and
key. Men will sing at their work, men will love. Ohhh, darling, the
world is in its morning . . . and *no man fights alone.* (CLARA *slowly
comes down to her husband and kisses him. With real feeling.
Every one in the room,* LEO *included, is deeply moved by this
vision of the future. . . .*) Let us have air. . . . Open the windows.
(*As he crosses to the windows a short fanfare is heard without.*)

The only thing that Odets omits as the curtain slowly falls is a nineteenth-
century-style tableau in which all on stage freeze and look admiringly at
the hero, who has paid the mortgage, defied the villain, rescued the
heroine, and needs only to have the flag descend to the bars of "America
the Beautiful" to bring the audience to its feet, tossing hats in the air in
cheering exaltation. Intended to be stirring and inspirational, the speech
instead throws sand in the cogs, and the gears don't mesh. Odet's wonderfully smooth machine grinds to a shuddering halt.

In his next two plays, *Golden Boy* (1937) and *Rocket to the Moon*
(1938), Odets does not entirely abandon his leftish sociological views, but
they have become sublimated to the extent that little remains of the
playwright's one-time radical convictions. No longer a revolutionary but
now a social liberal, in a day when that term held none of the pejorative
connotations of later years, Odets still moves his characters through a
society that offers its substantial rewards not for sensitive artistic or professional talents but for brute strength or the sacrifice of honor and decent
principles.

Golden Boy shifts from the Jewish families Odets knows so well to
the Italian Bonapartes, but it loses none of the casual intimacy in dialogue and movement that marks the Odets style. The limits on the
action, however, are not the same. *Awake and Sing* and *Paradise Lost* are
confined to a single domestic setting, the living areas of the Bergers and
Gordons. The outside world is talked about at length; various friends,
neighbors, and relatives enter and discuss its problems, but the action of

both plays is inward, encompassing a limited and confining space. *Golden Boy*, on the other hand, expands to provide a direct look into society's complexities; the many scenes shift from the boxing manager's office to the Bonaparte home, to the gym and the arena dressing room, and back again. The world outside the family's living room is no longer something to talk about; it becomes an important part of the action, and it is inhabited by members of a culture unfamiliar to and never fully understood by the Bonapartes. This important added dimension combines with the carefully plotted sequence of Joe Bonaparte's gradual seduction by the allure of the boxing ring, with its promise of a fortune and the fast cars that have always fascinated him. He becomes the central figure around whom everyone revolves, both at home and among the slick, fast-talking players in the fight game. The outside forces Joe must combat and come to terms with are placed in full view, concrete evidence of what destroys him beyond the abstractions of an unseen Depression society. On the one hand, this expanded world, into which Joe moves in depths obviously over his head, succeeds in developing his talents as a skilled fighter, something he has to be taught in order to please the crowds who watch and cheer. On the other hand, the inner world of home and family fails to hold him to the deep personal rewards that could be achieved through his natural gift as an accomplished violinist.

Joe is as frustrated as Ralph Berger by his limited prospects of attaining society's full benefits. The economics of the depressed society keep Ralph in a dead-end job with no apparent means of bettering himself. His talents are limited, and his immediate prospects for improvement lie mostly within his optimism as the play ends. Joe is caught in the same trap; he may have talent as a musician, but given the existing conditions, the likelihood of material gain is about as elusive as it is for Ralph. Ralph's dilemma keeps him suspended between two evils: if he strikes out on his own, he will be damned for deserting his family; if he remains where he is, he is damned in his own sight for not asserting his independence. The result is an indefinite extension of the status quo. Joe's dilemma involves a more sinister option. He can sacrifice immediate personal gain by remaining faithful to his artistic self, a clear moral choice, or he can attain the rewards of becoming "somebody" if he is willing to surrender to those who prosper by exploiting him and to ignore, or at least to passively accept, the personal corruption and degradation in being owned by a mercenary manager and his sycophants. Ralph's choices, neither of them acceptable, keep him where he is. Joe momentarily battles within himself, but he makes his own choice, resulting in his moral and physical destruction. Step by step, egged on by those who profit from him, he brings disaster on himself. Many of those around him know Joe's true nature; none, from his broken-hearted father to his sympathetic trainer, can keep him from pursuing the dream. "Your heart ain't in fighting," says Tokio, the trainer, "your hate is." Tokio articulates the central theme of the play, that one's decisions should accord with one's inner nature, but how can that inner nature succeed when all around lies evidence that such accord can offer very little of the tangible goods of a successful life? Why starve as an artist when unlimited prosperity is there for the taking?

Golden Boy's allegorical indictment of the society that liberally rewards cunning, strength, and power as manifested in the brutalities of prizefighting, while withholding encouragement from the aesthetic endeavors of music and art, is subdued, but its implications are obvious. Joe Bonaparte, as his trainer knows, is not really a fighter. The killer instinct of the slugger is missing; Joe is a skilled *boxer*, his techniques often ridiculed in his reliance on deftness of movement and strong defense rather than frontal attack. It is when the *fighter* takes over that Joe is doomed. The allure of hard cash and fast cars is too much, and Joe finally shows the crowds what they want. Joe has had imposed upon him a persona entirely contrary to his inner nature. Joe the fighter is, of course, a fraud, for he is now an angry, driven man, hating the brute he has become. His murderous assault on the Chocolate Drop is a thing of rage; he has become, in the words of gambler Eddie Fuseli, "a bum." With broken hands, never again able to play the thousand-dollar violin that was a gift from his father, a killer who knows he has killed himself as well, Joe acknowledges the fact in his own words: "I was a real sparrow, and I wanted to be a fake eagle." He races off after the fatal fight with sweetheart Lorna to die in his speeding car, probably happier than when he lived.

More allegorical but less successful, *Rocket to the Moon* chooses as its central figure struggling under many of the same pressures not the artist but the professional, this time a dentist whose roster of late-Depression patients is barely enough to provide a subsistence living. The names are obvious: Ben Stark, the dentist, now 40, is face-to-face with the stark economic and personal realities of a world that keeps him down. Belle, his wife in a dreary failing marriage, has lost the one-time happy qualities implied in her name. The inefficient, good-hearted young assistant and innocent seductress, Cleopatra Singer, many years Ben's junior, is the joyous object of his infatuation. Belle's father, Mr. Prince, lives up to the generous connotations of his surname.

Gentler and lacking nearly all the hallmarks of Odets's more vivid attacks on the system, *Rocket to the Moon* ("A Romance in Three Acts") carries a certain downbeat sadness. Set entirely in Ben Stark's office, stifling in the city's summer heat because Ben can't afford an air conditioner, the play uses the weather itself as an effective symbol of the oppressiveness of Stark's personal life, of his desperate need to reach out and become something as a human being. The brief rocket ride of Ben and Cleo's attraction to each other is an impossible effort to shoot the moon. It is an unlikely but believable interlude of romance between two lonely, misunderstood people.

The realistic patterns of speech remain, amusing, poignant, but less self-centered, less "Chekhovian," than in Odets's earliest plays. The exchanges between Cleo and the pragmatic Mr. Prince, who would happily seduce her but knows he can't, are touching. The awakening of Cleo and Ben to their mutual love, impossible to consummate, is developed with a natural simplicity. The play has no plot to speak of, but Odets sustains interest in these ordinary people through their appealing three-dimensional quality, enhanced by the unsentimental and uncontrived dialogue.

The happy ending of such a romance might imply the departure into a happier tomorrow of Ben and Cleo together, but their affection, too much involved with mutual pity and the atmospheric and emotional heat of the occasion, has no depth to sustain a long relationship. Ben cannot leave Belle, herself frantically grasping to salvage something with Ben, and Cleo knows the gap is unbridgeable. She is sensible enough to recognize Belle's prior claim, and through a few weeks' intense affair, she has become a stronger person who can now strike off on her own. Ben must and does accept the reality of the situation; as he returns to Belle he can conclude, in speaking to his father-in-law, who has all along been aware of Ben's brief flight, "For the first time in years I looked out on the world and saw things as they really are."

In his last prewar plays, *Night Music* (1940) and *Clash by Night* (1941), Odets failed to hold his erstwhile public appeal. In the former, less reassuring on the theme of love than *Rocket to the Moon*, he was unable to combine the elements of well-planned Ibsenesque construction with the Chekhovian quality of character and dialogue. In the latter, a pessimistic portrayal of a melancholy love affair culminating in a murder, Odets seemed to have lost the drive and the attractive style of his earlier successes. Not until after the war, when he returned with the psychological study of an alcoholic one-time matinee idol in *The Country Girl* (1950), did he regain a portion of his former reputation.[6]

Clifford Odets was the Group Theatre's most important play-wright in the troubled thirties, and his contributions between wars made him one of the most important American dramatists as well. The impressive authenticity of his imitation of Depression-era life in *Waiting for Lefty, Awake and Sing,* and *Golden Boy,* left-leaning as it is (a problem for Odets in the later days of HUAC and McCarthy witch-hunts), has maintained remarkable power. As the twenty-first century looms, these plays still speak to a middle class questioning the myths of American life that love conquers all and that success is there for any who diligently apply themselves. Odets's sensitive manner in exploring and exposing these fantasies is as relevant to the torn fabric of American society at century's end as it was in the days when that very fabric seemed ripped into irretrievable shreds.

George Kelly's Portrayal of Painful Delights

George Kelly's contribution to the American drama prior to the second war was limited to only eight plays. In the manner of others such as Rice and Howard and, to some degree, Odets, Kelly had his greatest success with his earliest efforts, which have retained an appeal strong enough to keep his name among the important dramatists of his era. Relying in structure on the framework of the well-made play, with its curve of action rising and falling with predictable regularity, and making good use of the familiar interior box set, he seemed to be a practitioner of all the aspects of unembellished realism. Unlike Odets, for whom the social environment was a controlling factor in the lives of his characters, Kelly preferred to limit his realism by stressing personal characteristics as the primary motivations for their actions. He was not above turning his protagonists into object lessons, making his point with some fairly obvious moral preachments that were only marginally relevant to the conditions of the social environment. Throughout his career it was difficult to ascertain if Kelly was writing a satire, a morality play, a modern melodrama, or simply a contemporary romantic comedy.[7]

One thing is certain, especially in the three early plays that established his importance: Kelly was able to handle topics fundamentally painful in reality but quickly comprehended by audiences able to recognize familiar human idiosyncracies with the delight of which Bentley speaks. Kelly may have bordered on caricature in exposing certain human weaknesses, and he may even have seemed narrowly didactic at times, but he never strayed from the painful reality of what he was attempting to portray.

Like Eugene O'Neill, George Kelly was born to an Irish Catholic family not unfamiliar with the stage (an older brother, Walter, was a well-known vaudeville monologist), but there the resemblance abruptly ends. The O'Neills could never quite shed their shanty-Irish image and remained outside the polite society of New London. The Kellys were wealthy Main Line Philadelphians whose most famous family product was George's niece Grace, a major screen star and the fairy-tale princess of Monaco. Respectable, almost puritanical in their morals and devotion to excellence, they were accepted and admired both in the theater and in the community. George's dislike of pretension and narrow-minded arrogance, derived from his family background, is plainly evident in his three best plays.

The Torchbearers (1922), the first of the trio, is the least sure of where it is going, but the pain it reveals is the foundation of all comedy, embarrassing to those who experience it, amusing to those who watch. The play drives its satiric barbs at the amateurs who attempt to create "art" but who succeed in merely making fools of themselves. The painful disasters are well known by any who have aspired to "putting on a show." At the same time, from a distance, they can become hilarious, as is the case with Kelly's display of bumbling nonprofessionals. The first-act rehearsal in the Ritters' living room, exposing the pretensions of Mrs. Pampinelli as an utterly incompetent director way over her head, is good comedy in its own right, but the second-act backstage view of the performance at a local hall completely disintegrates into pure farce. Performers trip on carpets, miss their entrances, and forget their lines, while stage effects malfunction to compound the consternation. In the third act, however, Kelly abruptly turns around to become an unexpected and severe critic of amateur productions by having Mr. Ritter castigate his wife, Mrs. Pampinelli, and the cast as a whole for attempting something so far beyond their capacities. Suddenly the onstage pain is real, leaving the audience wondering if perhaps they shouldn't have laughed so much at the sorry mishaps.

The turnaround raises the question of Kelly's point. If laughter at the expense of human pomposity is invited in the first two acts, the abrupt switch to an unpleasantly critical condemnation seems an unnecessarily gratuitous action that turns unexpectedly, and a bit unfairly, on an unwary audience. Kelly considered the play to be a serious comedy, with a third-act message that theatrical productions should be left to professionals, a somewhat narrow view that tends to cancel out what at first had appeared to be pure fun. Is it a spoof, a takeoff, or a painful lesson to be learned? Whatever Kelly really had in mind, in spite of Ritter's biting last-act remarks, the play was popular, possibly because so many civic and community groups doing the little-theater bit at the time offered many an aspiring producer or actor, no matter how untrained, a chance to bear the torch for drama.

In *The Show-Off* (1924) and *Craig's Wife* (1925), both well made in the traditional sense, Kelly continues to grind the axe wielded in *The Torchbearers*, but in each the sardonic atmosphere of the last act becomes more relevant to the entire play. The farcical action and minimal plot structure now give way to a more serious and orderly development of theme.

There is, to be sure, considerable comedy in *The Show-Off*, mainly at the expense of its title figure, Aubrey Piper. It creates the laughter of recognition, with scorn and ridicule directed at a character whom everyone at one time or another has encountered: the boring, self-centered blowhard. Kelly's skilled mimicry of this aspect of human behavior was so successful that for many years thereafter to refer to a person as an Aubrey Piper was an instant put-down.

Almost everything socially and personally repellent about this kind of misfit, who loudly pipes his own tune, is present in Kelly's creation. Raucous, attention-getting laughter that grates the nerves, plus glad-handing, backslapping behavior, succeed in annoying almost everybody in sight, while the perpetrator proceeds, blindly unaware of his unpleasant impact on others. Always optimistic, always with a carnation in his lapel, bragging about his big business deals (he is acutally a low-paid railway clerk) and real estate possessions (he and his wife, Amy, occupy a single room in his mother-in-law's home), Aubrey Piper blusters his way through life. Inept, unreconstructed, surviving on the braggadocio that covers a very insecure individual, the self-styled "pride of old West Philly" suffers the delusions of the Willy Loman syndrome, so well articulated by Arthur Miller some 25 years later: success is measured in the perception of being well liked. Unimaginative in the extreme, he spouts platitudes such as "Rome wasn't built in a day" to his chiding mother-in-law, or an unthinking, offhanded "We're here today, and gone tomorrow" upon the death of his father-in-law. Egotistical and empty-headed in his ever-buoyant spirit, he still manages to elicit sympathy, or perhaps more accurately, sympathetic pity; he is a person who, even in caricature, is not entirely unrealistic.

The surprising triumph of Aubrey Piper appears at first to be a tacked-on happy ending designed to redeem a not very attractive protagonist. This apparent undermining of all that has been said is Kelly's method of satirizing the boisterous era of the twenties. He permits the least promising member of the clan to save the family fortune through sheer bluff and bluster as he persuades the steel barons to double their $50,000 offer to his brother-in-law for a rust-preventive process. Vacuous exhibitionism apparently pays off. That, however, is not really Kelly's point. It is, rather, his expression of the profound irony and his ultimate disapproval of Aubrey's success, which parallels the behavior pattern of Americans who have forgotten the work ethic of their forebears and have relied on questionable schemes to make millions at the expense of human decency. With the postwar recession over and the future unlimited, it was a time of "anything goes." Kelly may not have anticipated the social and economic catastrophe of the thirties, but he was clearly offended by the unscrupulousness of practitioners out to get the fast buck. One may deplore the Aubrey Pipers, but one has to admire some of their gall. Kelly may thus trick us into a certain admiration of Aubrey, but he is saying at the same time, "For shame!" even while he grants his antagonistic protagonist the rewards.

More serious in its condemnation of its central figure is *Craig's Wife*, Pulitzer Prize winner for 1925–26 and Kelly's best play by far. It is almost classical in its adherence to the "unities" of time, place, and action. Its carefully planned plot moves within a time span of one evening and the next morning, with action confined to the single interior of the Craigs' living room while the fates close in. Every word and action leads to the finality of the isolation of a lying, conniving woman. No sudden last-act moralizing or unexpected rewards of fortune interfere with the inexorable approach of the fate the title figure has brought upon herself. Harriet Craig runs very close to, perhaps even passes, Sidney Howard's Mrs. Phelps in the race for sheer bitchiness. Her name, like Aubrey Piper's, entered the language as a pejorative cognomen for the impossibly demanding housewife protecting her meticulous home to the total exclusion of any and all who would intrude upon it. Unlike Mrs. Phelps, who envelops her helpless son, Harriet Craig is left abandoned, the only victim of her own unbending nature, evoking no audience sympathy in the sterility of her immaculate but now useless domestic kingdom.

The strength of Kelly's characterization of Harriet Craig, which makes her more believable than Mrs. Phelps, is the playwright's ability to represent a character type through strikingly realistic dramatization. Mrs.

Phelps's outrageous insults to her sons' wife and fiancée, and the momentary lapse of both sons in their acquiescence to her, can stretch credulity. Harriet Craig is more convincing in her single-minded obsession, amounting to a psychotic phobia. Mrs. Phelps's frightening incestuous leanings are disgustingly repellent; Mrs. Craig's possessiveness for the artifacts that surround her and her complete alienation of everybody who touches her life, while repugnant and not inspiring audience sympathy, draw audience attention to her as a more acceptable and rounded character.

Kelly steadily mounts the evidence against Harriet from the moment she enters, upon her return from a visit to her seriously ailing sister. She spots a bouquet of roses left by a friendly neighbor, whom Harriet sees only as a nosy intruder who sneaked in during her absence. The flowers must be removed at once so she won't have "to be picking up petals every two minutes." She advises her niece, Ethel, not to marry the young professor she loves but to seek a man of wealth who can provide her with the world's goods. (Only two years earlier, having married her middle-aged husband for that very purpose, she has been able to maintain her security by domination over him.) She confronts her spouse with the barefaced admission that she will lie to protect herself and that she had married him only for his money. Left alone, Walter Craig, seething with humiliation and rage, deliberately removes his wife's most prized ornament from the mantelpiece and smashes it to bits on the hearth, to the inward, if not vocal, cheers of the audience.

Leaving the Craigs' house, Walter's aunt, Miss Austin, who had been living there, warns Harriet that "People who live to themselves are generally left to themselves." The prophecy is soon fulfilled. Relatives, servants, friends, and finally Walter himself leave Mrs. Craig alone in her now meaningless home. With a telegram announcing her sister's death, Harriet wanders desolately across the room, "her eyes wide and despairing," as the curtain falls. The impact is devastating, and Kelly redeems himself for all the dramatic flaws of his two earlier productions. The universality of the play's theme has made it consistently playable, with a dramatically attractive, if personally unpleasant, protagonist who remains recognizable in any era.

George Kelly was never again able to rise to the level of either *Craig's Wife* or the lesser *Show-Off*. Sanctimonious and moralizing, his plays became less popular. *Daisy Mayme* (1926) contrasts the good-hearted and self-sustaining Daisy against the conniving Mrs. Fenner, whose schemes are thwarted by her brother, who marries Daisy. *Behold the Bridegroom* (1927) involves Spencer Train and his badly tainted love,

Antoinette Lyle, whose "lamp was not trimmed and burning" properly enough to attend the sterling prospective bridegroom. A Camille-like ending, with Spencer recognizing at her death that a love like Antoinette's is rare, does nothing to enhance a fairly routine plot. In *Maggie the Magnificent* (1929) the ambitious Maggie rises above her family to leave her dispirited mother with high-handed disdain. Whatever convincing dialogue or character may have been present in these three plays, it was lost in Kelly's firm moral tone and the artificial poetic justice of their endings.

Kelly turned again to the world of theater in *Philip Goes Forth* (1931) and *Reflected Glory* (1936). His attempt to convey a message of great social consequence in the former (that hometown business life is best for those grossly incompetent in the arts—no change of view since *The Torchbearers*) and in the latter (that being honest to one's professional career, in this case that of a talented actress, is better than opting for marriage) failed to attract. Neither these nor the two postwar plays, *The Deep Mrs. Sykes* (1945) and *The Fatal Weakness* (1946), both of which depended more on brilliant dialogue than meaningful plot, proved of lasting interest.

Kelly's reputation rests, therefore, with his first three plays, fortunately less pedagogic, less focused on people's concern with material things, than his others. His strongly held opinions and his didacticism too often interfered with his good theatrical sense, but the pain he felt over unprofessionalism or, as with Harriet Craig, overweening dominance, was well conveyed and understood, or (back to our original premise) delighted in, by those who could recognize the validity of his characters and the situations into which they got themselves. Often directing his own plays, Kelly was as meticulous in staging as he was in his careful plotting, but too often he provided his characters with repetitious and sometimes platitudinous dialogue. A less important or lasting figure than many of his contemporaries, he must still be regarded as a leading, if limited contributor.

Beyond Belasco: Sidney Kingsley and the Ultimate in Stage Mimicry

The arch-practitioner of theatrical naturalism, David Belasco, who was always determined to make his mise-en-scène into a venue of literal reality, attempted the impossible task of transcending the restrictive conventions that force the realistic play into the modification of reality demanded by good dramatic art. Placing onstage an actual slum tenement room, wallpaper and all, or a genuine oaken saloon bar, or a New York restaurant kitchen with real chefs cooking real food, is of course a travesty of the art and does nothing to further the dramatic points in theme, action, or character. Belasco's exaggerations deny the ability of scene designer or stage technician to have a part in the creation of the one thing that makes the theater what it is: illusion.

In their romantic sentiments and their sensations of contrived melodrama, Belasco's original and adapted scripts only further underlined the essential foolishness of his attempts to portray rather than to imitate reality behind the proscenium arch, with the result that his naturalistic stagecraft did little to further the development of native American drama. But within a decade after Belasco's last New York production in 1928 appeared three plays by a writer whose "latter-day Belascoism," as Brooks Atkinson once remarked in the *New York Times*, would seem to be a throwback to a discredited technique. Sidney Kingsley, however, was a different matter entirely; his close mimicry and detailed imitation in both the written drama and the ultimate theatrical product combined in the creation of stunning artistic illusion.

Sidney Kingsley was already a successful actor in regional theater when his first production, *Men in White* (1933), not only saved the floundering Group Theatre but also took the Pulitzer Prize for 1933–34. Although its quick commercial prosperity ran counter to the Group's original artistic premises, it meant more than just their survival. It introduced a strong, socially conscious voice not all that far removed from the Group's vision, one that reinforced their belief in the viability of what they were attempting. *Men in White's* large cast and diverse nonstarring roles were in keeping with the Group's emphasis on ensemble acting, but its further importance to the Group lay in its timely and convincingly developed exploration of the social and personal implications inherent in the functioning of a large city hospital. Viewed half a century later, even though the intervening years have seen astonishing developments in medical and surgical techniques that the play's doctors could hardly have imagined, Kingsley's detailed recreation of the inner workings of a hospital and the professionals whose lives are almost wholly preoccupied with it remains impressively gripping and remarkably contemporary.[8]

Men in White was criticized for the weakness of its script, its simplistic conclusion, its emphasis on production over the development of a strong dramatic line, and its tendency to emphasize the heroics of the dedicated physician over the more mundane reality of a doctor's life, but criticism of Kingsley's supposedly romanticized portrayal of his doctors is largely irrelevant. In the same manner that plays about lawyers, for valid dramatic reasons, tend to center on courtroom excitement while ignoring the many tedious, even plodding, aspects of the reality of a lawyer's life in and out of court, Kingsley's play restricts and condenses so that the audience witnesses only those aspects of the doctors' lives inside the hospital, where romantic idealism is replaced by physical and emotional pressures that can tax one almost beyond endurance. When a life is saved, the doctor may understandably appear to be a hero to those affected; but Kingsley balances any temptation to emphasize only the miracles of modern healing by making it obvious that patients do die, all efforts notwithstanding, and that all the answers simply aren't there. Far from being gods, the doctors are shown as only too human. They can be stupid and incompetent; they suffer from professional rivalries as well as misunderstanding and resentment by those who love them but cannot comprehend what drives them; they can be pushed into personal indiscretions as a release from the incessant demands placed upon them 24 hours a day. Underlining all is Kingsley's naturally flowing dialogue, in which patients are spoken of by room number or affliction, interlaced with hospital jargon, including the casual use of "passing out" for dying. This is no early-day *M*A*S*H*, with macabre humor practiced to maintain sanity in the midst of surrounding horror, but it does employ a manner of speaking and behavior that helps these doctors to keep their personal emotions as far removed as possible from their professional lives.

What proved most effective, and prompted some of the negative criticism that the play was too production-oriented, was Kingsley's meticulous presentation of the physical surroundings within the hospital and the intricate choreography in the operating room during major surgery. Every one of the play's many scenes, from the opening in the hospital library lounge, through the emergency procedures of saving a young child's life, to the climactic surgical operation, with the nurses and orderlies constantly moving about and the PA system relentlessly paging, showed just how Belasco's kind of naturalism was outdated and appallingly unimaginative. Kingsley's hospital settings are designed for integral, intimate use by the characters; they appear to be real but at the same time are unintrusive. The ultranaturalistic surgery scene, the most riveting in the play, stands out not so much for its sensational quality—the elaborately coordinated effort to save a human life, with everything modern medicine can assem-

Men in White *(Sidney Kingsley, 1933). Mordecai Gorelik's design combined with Kingley's insistence on meticulously authentic detail in action made this portrayal of surgical preparation into a vividly realistic stage picture.*

ble to do so laid out step by step—as for the scene's appropriateness to the entire play. It is beautifully assimilated into the overall action of the play as all the medical personnel, galvanized by the emergency, play their roles with professional perfection. And the tremendous irony of it all is failure. No miracles here; the girl dies.

Perhaps Kingsley gives in to a certain artificiality in the play's resolution. Dr. Ferguson is saved from a forced marriage by the death of the unfortunate Barbara, whom he has, in his weakness, impregnated and who in desperation has suffered a botched abortion.[9] Laura, his offended fiancée, recognizes at last that he has done the right thing in his decision to study many years in Vienna, placing his professional development and possible future greatness above his chance to marry and have a posh hospital post secured by Laura's father. The ending does not, however, actually detract. The whole affair of the struggle between love and duty, important for its demonstration of the significant sacrifices of life's pleasures that must be made if one is to believe in and practice the ideals of the doctors' Hippocratic oath, is entirely plausible. Ferguson's decision is not out of line, nor is it a sudden last-act conversion; it is an acceptable step, in keeping with his development as a character.

If any decision were to be made as to which is the best naturalistic American play, both in writing and staging, the choice could easily be Kingsley's next production, *Dead End* (1935). This portrayal of the literally dead-end existence of those trapped in the East River slums of New York was the season's sensation and has remained Kingsley's finest and best-remembered play. Though set in the depths of the Depression, its message has not perceptibly altered. Like *Men in White*, given the change of a few outdated references and perhaps a character or two—the introduction of minorities comes immediately to mind—*Dead End* is timeless in its social and moral implications.

The stage setting of *Dead End*, by Norman Bel Geddes, was almost overwhelming; its illusion of reality created the unnerving sensation that the whole back wall of the stage had been removed to reveal the city outside the theater. The perspective of the tenements, with their rickety fire escapes, crowded laundry lines, and filthy streets extending into an indefinite distance with vague glimpses of the towers of Radio City and the Empire State Building, has been compared with the apartment-house facade of *Street Scene*. In form and purpose, however, they were very different. The *Street Scene* tenement was not a slum. More important, it served primarily as the backdrop for the play's action; except for the heat, which forces the action outside, the setting does not play a direct part in what goes on. The characters live there, but they are not its product, and escape is possible. Not so in *Dead End*. The characters *are* a product of this man-made urban hell. They emerge from it and return to it. Its forces have created them, and their lives are driven by it; the unrelenting grip it holds on its desperate inhabitants denies them any hope of escape. The setting becomes an active participant, not a passive one. Except for the requirement of a tank of water in the orchestra pit, all has been accomplished by imaginative design instead of real and ultimately unconvincing artifacts.

The action of the play, centering entirely on the open space where the street dead-ends at the water's edge, is dominated by the gang of five teenage boys, rowdy, obscene creatures of their tenement homes, whose lives during this summer moment are concentrated on pitching pennies or swimming illegally in the slimy filth of the polluted sewer known as the East River. Totally uninhibited in their earthy street language and behavior, raucous and crude, they lead an animal existence, ill-nourished in mind and body, the end products of the hopeless environment in which they live. As a group, on the screen as well as on the stage, they gave the language a new phrase to describe their kind everywhere: Dead End Kids.

The horrors of this urban jungle extend beyond just this group of unfortunate adolescents. The adult product is equally stunted, making Kingsley's point about the impossibility of escape even stronger and more terrifying. Foremost is Gimpty, the rickets-crippled, degree-holding architect whose education and skills cannot in this depressed economy secure him any meaningful employment. As a graduate of these very slums, still residing in them, he does his best to help this hopeless gang to achieve some decency and meaning in their lives. His ally is Drina, the older sister of the gang's leader, Tommy; her frantic efforts to keep her brother clean and respectable are constantly thwarted not only by the conditions but also by her own loss of income after walking a strike picket line and getting beaten up for her pains. Their adversary, the successful fugitive mobster, Baby Face Martin, who returns to see his girlfriend and mother, instructs the boys in how to win a fight outside the rules. His abundance of money and flashy clothes make him the idol for the boys to emulate. The two women in his life who stayed behind have become human wrecks. His mother is now a gaunt, unkempt survivor, decayed almost beyond recognition but with fire enough remaining to slap his face and call him the murdering punk he has become. Francy, his girlfriend, has become a diseased and hardened prostitute.

The other side of Kingsley's coin is the towering apartment building whose back entrance abuts the street, inhabited by the powerful rich who would rid the earth of these vermin-children by sending them off to prison. When the gang administers the savage "cockalizing" initiation ritual to the chauffeur-driven, French maid–attended Philip Griswold and steals his watch, the livid father can only call down the wrath of the law to teach the proper lesson. The irony of all this rests in the fact that the rich are as much prisoners of their own shortsighted prejudices as are the urchins against whom Griswold and his kind feel so helpless.

Kingsley makes clear that any escape must involve surrender of ideals and abandonment of human decency. Kay, whom Gimpty loves but cannot keep, departs with her unloved suitor on his yacht, resolving to provide herself with more than Gimpty could offer in the stench-ridden, slimy-walled tenement he has shown her. Baby Face does receive his ultimate reward in an ambush by the law, but he dies a much-admired martyr in the eyes of those who will grow up to replace him. Young Tommy, the only gang member with promise, despite the best legal defense he can be provided by Gimpty's reward money for fingering Baby Face, will no doubt end up in "refawm school," envied by his followers, who instruct him on whom to meet in order to learn even better street behavior during his incarceration.

It is easy to look at *Dead End* as polemical social propaganda, but Kingsley's ultranaturalistic display of an appalling reality is in no way on the same level as Odets's indictment of society and his appeal to the specifics of, say, *The Communist Manifesto*. Without taking a stand by suggesting a political solution, revolutionary or otherwise, or by despairing of the social inequalities, Kingsley presents a social nightmare for what it is, backed not by personal views but by the undeniable evidence itself. The pain exhibited is in no way a "delight"; the audience is attracted by the frightfulness, repulsed but gripped by something it cannot ignore. Without personal comment, the dramatist has created a work of theater art that can speak for itself and vividly reveal to its privileged audiences what goes on outside their world, something they most likely would never view on their own. The medicine is bitter, but it can be effective.

Kingsley's *Ten Million Ghosts* (1936) was squarely in the deep-Depression, antiwar tradition common among intellectuals and artists. Its documentary style, exposing and condemning their favorite target, munitions makers, as the real culprits in fomenting and supporting war, was more along the lines of left-wing agitprop than it was a legitimate commercial production. Such exposés had never really worked, and they were growing tiresome. The greater humanitarian themes, such as those of Odets or even the unsubtle, consciously designed shocks of *Dead End*, are consistently more effective than soapbox oratory. *Ten Million Ghosts* quickly failed and became forgotten in the wake of the public's increased awareness that the idiocies and downright criminality of governmental shortsightedness are more responsible for war than weapons manufacturers have ever been.

In 1939 Kingsley wrote his third "superrealistic" play, *The World We Make*, adapted from Millen Brand's *The Outward Room*. The original novel had been mainly a portrait of recovery from mental illness through loving and being loved, but Kingsley used it as the basis for a more fully developed character study that Brooks Atkinson found "infinitely more sensitive" than *Dead End*, in which the characters embody broader sociological implications. Nevertheless, the story of a mentally disturbed heroine who finds a man to love was not enough to carry *The World We Make* beyond the theatricality of Kingsley's production, which he staged himself. The battered room and dark hallways of a New York tenement, known only by reference in *Dead End*, were here set out for all to see. A strikingly real steam laundry, where the woman works, was stage illusion at its best, but it became an unfortunate throwback to ultra-Belascoism and drowned the play and its message.

In the midst of the war, while serving as an army NCO, Kingsley wrote *The Patriots* in 1943. The Playwrights' Company took it on as a kind of sequel to *Abe Lincoln in Illinois*, which it had produced two years earlier. Compared to Sherwood's popular prizewinner, this story of Thomas Jeffrson's struggle between his duty and his desire to leave public life for comfortable peace in Monticello found limited public response. In the closing scene, Kingsley's use of Jefferson's inaugural address, which expresses his belief that "this government is the world's best hope," had its positive effect, but the play's allegory of Jefferson's struggles in the early Republic against Hamilton's wish for a monarchy and Burr's dictatorial leanings, supposedly designed to draw parallels with the fight against Nazism, did not come across. Still, the play won the New York Drama Critics' Award, almost as prestigious as the Pulitzer, and there was praise for Kingsley's characterization of Jefferson as a believable dramatic extension of documented history.

Although Kingsley was to continue his prizewinning ways after the war with some of the best of his social and political realism, to mention his name and his contribution to the dominance of American drama between wars is to recall *Men in White* and *Dead End*. If there was any one playwright who practiced the best of realistic drama and theater with the least modification—one who intimately knew, for instance, the thinking and behavior patterns of the slums, imitating them in the best theatrical tradition—it would have to have been Kingsley. Some may have found him too melodramatic, but his style can be defended, as it was by Eric Bentley, who refused to downgrade good melodrama as "eccentric or decadent." "It is," he wrote, "drama in its elemental form; it is the quintessence of drama" (Bentley, 216).

The Well-Made Morality of Lillian Hellman

For half a century, from her first play in 1934 at the age of 29 until her death in 1984, Lillian Hellman was one of the most visible participants in twentieth-century American arts and letters. Vigorously independent, a strong advocate of women's social rights without becoming a "radical feminist" in the later limited and pejorative sense of the term, she was in many ways a personification of the "free" woman pursuing her personal and professional lives as she wished. Through extensive memoirs widely read and honored during the 1970s, she provided considerable insight into her private and public behavior.[10] These revelations, as well as her long open relationship with novelist Dashiell Hammett and her defiant stand against the congressional witch-hunts of the 1950s, combine with her prewar success as a leading American dramatist to make her a fascinating and sometimes controversial American figure.

Hellman's theatrical versatility was shown in her eight original plays, four adaptations of stories and other plays, and several original or collaborative screenplays; but her permanent fame as America's best-known woman playwright was gained through three widely different prewar dramas. Tightly constructed in the best well-made tradition, they exhibit more than mere facility in plot maneuvering; they prove that the well-made play is not unworthy of modern use.

The intensity of feeling that Hellman puts into her work can bring it perilously close to old-fashioned melodrama. All of her stage pieces carry her strong moral convictions in the constant struggle between good and evil, and the obvious dichotomy between the villainous and the virtuous can run counter to the complexities of reality, but fortunately, in Hellman's best plays, the characters talk and move in a believably realistic fashion, so that the danger of drawing simplistic lines between the bad and the good is avoided. Her sublimation and integration of the elements of melodrama into the plot lines of her plays are executed in a manner that Bentley would approve. The illusion of real life on stage is well maintained.

In her introduction to *Six Plays* (1942), Hellman discusses the whole matter of well-made realism and the necessary pretenses of attempting to carry conviction within the limitations of the theater:

> Obviously, I can have no argument with those whom my plays do not convince. Something does not convince you. Very well, and that is all. But if they convince you, or partly convince you, then the dislike of their being well-made makes little sense. The theatre has limitations: it is a tight, unbending, unfluid, meager form in which to write. And for these reasons, compared to the novel, it is a second-rate form. . . . What the author has to say is unhampered; his means of saying it are not. He may do without scenery . . . and he still must *pretend* the empty stage is a garden or an arena. . . . He has three walls of a theatre and he has begun his pretense with the always rather comic notion that the audience is the fourth wall.[11]

Recognizing that "there is something vaguely awry, for me, about the pretense of representation," she still concludes that "the realistic form has interested me most."

Hellman's first play, *The Children's Hour* (1934), gained her the best form of instant recognition: it was banned in Boston. For its time the play was unquestionably sensational, not only in its treatment of pathological lying by a malicious child but more so in its subject of possible lesbianism. Discreetly handled as it was, the mere suggestion of any sexual deviation was enough to shock society's firm guardians of public morality into action.[12]

Evil children have always seemed more sinister, more deadly, than their adult counterparts. However vicious an adult may be, this quality can be assigned to any number of life experiences, but the assumed innocence and the natural attractiveness of children compound the frightfulness. It is very difficult to accept the twisted machinations of one so unschooled in the ways of the world, who is able, nontheless, to terrify and even to destroy others of far greater wisdom and sophistication. These little monsters have a shuddering fascination about them that can hold an audience with ease.[13]

Sardonically using Longfellow's tender poem about his three little children, Hellman turns her "hour" into a nightmare of major proportions. At the center is Mary Tilford, spoiled and vindictive, willing to impugn her schoolmates and schoolmistresses at the expensive private school run by Karen Wright and Martha Dobie. For the play to rise above the simplistic portrayal of a nasty preadolescent, the character of Mary must be more than just a wicked little conniver. She must carry credibility, and she must be able to deceive with a craftiness that is acceptable for her age level. If she acts beyond her years, she risks audience rejection; she cannot appear too farfetched and must do her worst within a play that maintains the realistic illusion. Hellman succeeds in her characterization of Mary, both as a tyrannizing bully, a type not at all unknown among students in any school, and as the sweet, maligned thing she appears to her grandmother. Fortunately for all concerned, both onstage and off, Mary does get her comeuppance when Mrs. Tilford finally realizes the damage her granddaughter has done and resolves to keep her under strict control in the future.

The exposure and punishment of this wicked little villain were considered acceptable, but what bestirred the censors was the lesbian question and Hellman's use of it. The immediate audience reaction is to deny Mary's suggestion to her grandmother that Karen and Martha have an unnatural relationship. There is nothing whatever in the course of the play to support her accusations, and it is clear that Mary has latched onto something more by accident than intent. Her immediate sensing of the power of her suggestion enables her to pursue the point and get her vengeance against those who would discipline her. Confident that her blackmailing of a schoolmate keeps her power unchallenged, Mary's innuendos succeed in ruining the school. Hellman does, however, somewhat dull the evil-child theme by having Martha admit to Karen that she may have loved her "the way they said" before killing herself. The question then arises as to whether or not Mary spoke sublimated truth. Does this increase the horror of the situation, or does it become too obvious a twist? Although the two teachers are innocent of any demonstrated lesbian relationship, Martha's admission undercuts the whole thesis that a malicious child can wreck innocent lives.

This unexpected turn raises serious criticism about the ambivalence of Hellman's purpose. Is her thesis that two women, unaware of any sexual content to their friendship, can become aware of it through this personal catastrophe? Martha is not completely sure about her feelings, and there is nothing to indicate any reciprocation on Karen's part.

And is this enough motivation for the drastic act of suicide? Or is the play about the gullibility of those who believe and act precipitously upon a child's unfounded rumor, as do the grandmother, Mrs. Tilford, and the parents who withdraw their children from the school? Is it a play about trust, shown in Karen's "loyal" fiancé, Joe, who vows to stand by her no matter what, but then ruins everything by asking if the charge is true? It is, as a matter of fact, a little of each. It may keep the focus blurred, but that is not entirely outside the province of dramatic realism. Reality seldom explains anything with orderly cohesion; catastrophe such as befalls the women in *The Children's Hour* cannot be the result of a single factor, nor does it necessarily add up to the neat sum of all the parts.

Since the play first appeared, society has become more tolerant of what the majority may regard as sexual aberration, so that the possibility of a lesbian relationship does not raise the violent objections it once did. This does not, however, alter the play's dramatic impact. The central moral point, that rational adults can be taken in by wicked children, is still pertinent.

Hellman's second play, *Days to Come* (1936), was a bifurcated melodrama about strikes and strikebreakers, with a confusing plot involving the unfaithful wife of the factory owner and his spinster sister. The play's failure apparently taught Hellman that characters who represent merely a political or moral stance lack the reality she sought, a lesson that may have guided her in the dramatic control exhibited in her next.

The Little Foxes (1939) is one of the best examples of how a well-made play can be dramatically convincing and continuously absorbing. With no wasted steps or superfluous words, no loose ends to distract or mislead, everything that happens onstage is a direct contribution to the development of character, plot, and theme. The entire first act, given wholly to exposition, reveals the past naturally and unobtrusively throughout the opening dialogue. In front of their guest, the outsider Marshall, the vicious Hubbard clan display their ignorance, hypocrisy, and greed; Marshall serves as a credible catalyst, bringing out details the audience must know.

As the theme of social degradation and moral decay unfolds in sordid plans and conspiracies, the depth of each character is simultaneously revealed. Unattractive and repugnant, mesmerizing in their behavior as snarling beasts, Oscar and Ben Hubbard and their sister, Regina Giddens, are in complete control of their own destinies. They proceed as opportunists without conscience; the drama of their ugly lives is forcefully real. All emerge in logical fashion as characters with more qualities than just surface evil to define them. Regina, for instance, is more than a mere vixen in this den of predators. She carries understandable human qualities as a woman—beautiful, a gracious and dignified hostess, seeking elegance, social position, and public respect. Even the pitiful Birdie has well-expounded reasons for what she has become, and her ineffectual attempts to stem this irresistible machine of evil, which threatens to make Alexandra's life a duplicate of her own, together with her one revealing outburst, make her sympathetic and dramatically important. Once the background is established, the ruthless infighting of Ben and Oscar and their blackmailing of Oscar's son, Leo, evolve from realistically credible premises.

The acceptability of the characters and the logical plot development, from the opening overtures to Marshall, through the badgering of the dying Horace, to the triumph, temporary as it may be, of Regina over her brothers, save *The Little Foxes* from becoming a Grand Guignol of horrors, or simply a melodrama of good and evil in the nineteenth-century sense. In the first place, the justice implied in traditional melodrama does not occur. The greatest force of good is Horace Giddens, but in order to achieve any kind of justice he must play by the same vicious rules, and he dies before all the injustices can be corrected Alexandra may possibly escape, and then she may not.

None of this prevents Hellman's use of some vivid and not inappropriate melodramatic scenes. The first begins in Act 2 with the tense exchange between Regina and Horace and ends in the violent upstairs exchange of shouts while the other jungle beasts plan to divide the spoils. The second is the heart attack, a harrowing event of pure melodrama from the start of the argument on to the broken bottle as Horace collapses on the stairs. But Hellman avoids pulling everything together in traditional melodramatic fashion. The play has no definitive ending. There is triumph and defeat on both sides; nobody emerges on top. The conclusion affirms, if anything, that there will always be Reginas, Oscars, and Bens in some form among us, and nobody, playwright or audience, knows how it will all come out. The last line in the play, Alexandra's response to her mother's invitation to sleep in her room, "Are you afraid, Mama?" is more foreboding to Regina than she can admit. The curtain comes down in a fitting, if indeterminate, conclusion.

The concentrated evil of Hellman's central characters, whose lack of any saving grace of human compassion makes the sordidness virtually unrelieved, could be taken as evidence of the writer's direct intercession without regard to logical probability. This interference is not as direct as it might seem. These people exist in a historical period when material fortunes are based on merciless capitalizing on the opportunity at hand, regardless of consequences. They live in a geographical locale where polite society is still torn apart by a desire to cling to old beliefs and by an inability to recognize the kind of change that must come. It would be foolish to regard *The Little Foxes* as any kind of document of social reform, but it does represent the fate of all human beings deprived of self-respect, unable to regain the strength of confidence to oppose the evil that rushes into the vacuum. Hellman herself claimed that she "might be a moral writer," but she wanted "no truck with moralistic types."[14] Addie and Alexandra, neither of whom can be considered mere moralizers, provide very good evidence of her claim.

Still, confusion does exist as to the play's social importance. Though it was widely admired, some critics found the Hubbards too specialized to represent a norm. To Joseph Wood Krutch, "The wickedness of the central characters is somehow connected with the social system. . . . Plainly the play is directed against contemporary society which is assumed to have acquisitiveness as its mainspring, and yet the action seems almost too extraordinary as well as too artificially contrived to serve as a very effective indictment, and one is again driven back upon whatever satisfaction can be obtained from the contemplation of unadulterated meanness and villainy wholly triumphant" (Krutch, 132). If the Hubbards did not exactly represent the larger world, which Hellman perhaps intended, she created a realistic, mercenary southern family, as well as one of the most outstanding parts for an actress in all of American drama. Tallulah Bankhead was only the first of a series of famous actresses to triumph in the role of Regina.

Hellman's two most important postwar plays, *The Autumn Garden* (1951) and *Toys in the Attic* (1960) will not be discussed here, but a between-wars consideration cannot close without the inclusion of her wartime dramas. The second of two, *The Searching Wind* (1944), focused on left-wing politics, international intrigue, and the causes of World War II. The all-too-familiar triangle of two women in love with the same man added little of value. The other play, however, is worthy of more than passing reference.

Opening eight months before Pearl Harbor, *Watch on the Rhine* (1941) provided American audiences with timely documentation of the dangers faced in Europe. The citation of the New York Drama Critics' Circle Award described it as "a vital eloquent and compassionate play about an American family suddenly awakened to the danger threatening its liberty." Hellman's quiet revelation of the horrors of Nazism through a demonstration of what it could do to individuals of honesty and integrity who chose to stand against it compares favorably with Sherwood's Finnish-Greek family's determination in *There Shall Be No Night* a year earlier.

The underground nature of the particularly nasty kind of war involving Kurt Müller and his family makes the complacent isolationism of America's myopic view of the conflict all the more shameful. The refugee family, always just a step ahead of the Nazis, are decent people, themselves repelled by violence but coldly determined to wage their part of the battle vigorously, inviting death or worse all along the way as they help their compatriots in Germany in the cause of freedom.

Hellman's sense of dramatic construction enables her to underplay the situation of the Müllers by contrasting their constant danger and defensive wariness with the comfort and luxurious safety of the Washington home of Fanny Farrelly, Sara Müller's mother. This familiar dowager-matriarch is often painfully close to the archetypal stage mother-in-law, spoiled, rich, and always in the way, but fortunately she is kept more or less on the sidelines. The refugee villain, Teck de Brancovis, could be accused of being too sinister, but within the framework of the plot, he fits.

In conceiving the Müllers, Hellman exhibits some of her best style. The family forces others onstage, and in the audience as well, to recognize that there is a war on and that this is a war play. The adults, Kurt and Sara, are three-dimensional; possessing no desire to become heroes, they nevertheless practice genuine heroism without stance-taking or propagandizing for a cause. The three charming children, whose sometimes wondrous wise behavior might be held against them, are products of a refugee life that has made them grow far beyond their years. Their mature attitude toward what they have been through and what is still bound to happen is balanced by their amazement at the abundance of food and the availability of toilets that actually work. Avoiding any temptation toward a sentimental, tearstained exposé of their predicament, the play shows this family, children and all, as the combatants in a battlefield that follows them wherever they are, fighting a constant and deadly enemy with quarter neither given nor asked. Because the whole situation is underplayed at first, the realization that the tolerant, honest, and respectable father is, when necessary, a coolly efficient killer who acts so that his kind of honesty and respectability can endure, comes as a devastating shock.

With Kurt threatened by the Nazi sympathizer Teck, who would reveal Kurt's aliases as well as names of escapees he has helped, the killing is necessary. The act, of course, changes everything within the Farrelly household. Not only must Kurt now flee, but the murder has placed everybody else at severe risk. The lesson learned by Fanny and David, Sara's brother, has awakened them abruptly to reality ("shaken out the magnolias"). They are determined to face questions about Teck's death with a heroism of their own, something they know they can do after experiencing the Müller family's quiet heroics. "I'm not put together with flour paste," Mrs. Farrelly asserts. Her conversion, which might at first be seen as a bit too pat, is brought about in her jolting realization of what is going on around her. Her amusing, detached flightiness is checked in its path by the inescapable realities.

Kurt Müller's farewell to his family is no maudlin departure, for it is evident to all that this sort of thing is not new but is accepted by the family; there is no other choice. In Kurt's reiteration that lying, stealing, and killing are not civilized manners of behavior, he tells his children that such actions are necessary if there is going to be a "childhood for every child," of which his own children have been so cruelly deprived. Urged by David to remain safe in America for the sake of the children, Kurt responds, "My children are not the only children in the world, even to me." Kurt Müller may feel, as does Hamlet, the cursed spite that ever he was born to set things right, but act he must in a time and world badly out of joint.

Doris Falk's critical biography makes an interesting division of Hellman's plays into those in which "despoilers" dominate and those emphasizing the "bystanders," something on the order of Addie's statement in *The Little Foxes:* "Well, there are people who eat the earth and eat all the people on it like in the Bible with the locusts. Then there are people who stand around and watch them eat it." Falk further claims that "Hellman clearly differentiates between evil as a positive, rapacious force, and evil as the negative failure of good."[15] Hellman's moral vision does seem to bear out Falk's assertion. The evils of *The Little Foxes* are the acts of conscious despoilers ("Take us the foxes, the little foxes, that spoil the vines"), and the bystanders, Horace, Alexandra, and Birdie, are helpless against them. Only Alexandra, who asserts her determination not to stand by and watch, has the possibility of escape. The bystanders in *The Children's Hour*, their negative failure of good plainly evident, are destroyed. Kurt Müller and his family, however, refuse to sit around and watch the predator consume the earth, and they provide a positive resistance to the overwhelming positive evil of Teck and the Nazi world.

Hellman's ability to create tightly constructed plays that reflect reality is an exceptional accomplishment. Her modification is only enough to meet some absolutes of theater art—limits of time, space, and the like—while her morality is strong enough to reveal her feelings without preachment, and her control enough to avoid the shortcomings of mere propaganda.

John Steinbeck and the Staged Novel

The attempt to imitate and to mimic is more easily accomplished in the novel than on the stage. With no time limits or other theatrical restrictions, modification is hardly necessary. The novelist who aspires to the theater, however, must learn the rules of modification, lest he or she meet the same fate as Henry James. In his attempts at playwriting, this greatest of American novelists failed dismally for lack of a true sense of theater, although his novels, when adapted by others, have frequently become successful plays. For John Steinbeck the transfer of relatively short and economically written novels to the theater was not a serious problem, mainly because the novels themselves, consisting mainly of dialogue, were dramatic in their basic structure in the first place.

Steinbeck's novel *Of Mice and Men* and its stage adaptation both appeared in 1937. The play was critically welcomed for its realistic portrayal of the country's rural dispossessed. It was the kind of subject that would have readily fit into the dynamics of the Federal Theatre and its technique of the Living Newspaper. The novelist-momentarily-turned-playwright chose a quieter style, however, letting his underwritten picture of California migrant farm workers, caught in the Depression as much as their urban counterparts, stand on its own without emphasizing a social or political point. The play won the Critics' Circle Award for 1937–38, an unusual recognition of a writer with such limited theatrical experience. George F. Kaufman, well known as a "play doctor," lent his assistance in the adaptation, but the play was Steinbeck's creation.

The familiar story of George and his companion Lennie, the hulking childlike giant, has entered the mythical lore of American literature, acknowledged and accepted as an allegory of mankind's "difficult conscious rejection of his dreams of greatness and acceptance of his own mediocrity."[16] It takes place between Friday and Sunday, and it has about it the suggestion of the fall of man and possible redemption. (George's last name is Milton, which may or may not mean anything.) These outcasts, fugitive vagabonds who are cursed and avoided, suggest the trials of the solitary wanderer Cain. Those who work on ranches, says George, "are the loneliest guys in the world," and these two, each in his way his brother's keeper, may stand in a larger sense for all mankind.[17]

The play is so carefully plotted as to become, at times, simplistically obvious. The opening scene by the riverbank, where George tells Lennie to hide if he gets in trouble, telegraphs the closing scene when Lennie returns, knowing he has done "a bad thing." Aware of Lennie's problems in touching and invariably destroying soft things, everyone knows full well what will happen when Curley's enticing, sluttish, but desperately lonely wife appears in the bunkhouse. Putting Candy's decrepit old dog out of its misery is an unsubtle warning of George's final act in saving Lennie from a violent lynch mob.

The relationship of these two grossly dissimilar characters raises questions about the psychological basis for their friendship. Is George merely a "mother figure" in his care of this lumbering creature whose brain works no better than a very small child's? Does George actually delight in Lennie's presence, his protestations to the contrary notwithstanding, because he takes equal pleasure in the endless reciting of their dream of an Edenic place of their own, rabbits and all? Does George realize that he cannot survive without Lennie any more than Lennie can without him?

Allegory aside, taken as a straight play, *Of Mice and Men* presents its naturalistic picture mainly through Steinbeck's impressive character studies drawn from his acute observation of California ranch life. The lonely isolation of the ranch hands, collectively and individually, is shown in highly graphic terms: the precarious economic situation of all, homeless, without family, lacking any close ties with each other as they blow their money on alcohol and prostitutes; the black man set apart, living alone with no involvement in bunkhouse life; the old hand who has outlived his usefulness; Curley, the boss's son, isolated because of his position; and his doomed wife, ignored and alone, the only woman on the ranch.

Steinbeck sees the battle of life as ending disastrously, or at best dubiously, if George is assumed to survive for a better future after Lennie. Like Burns's destroyed "wee beastie" of the poem that gives the play its title, well-laid plans do indeed "gang aft-agley," and man is like the mouse "in proving foresight may be vain." Just as the Depression prevented the individual from controlling his political, social, and personal lives, so Steinbeck's work illustrated how thoroughly even those of strong body and will must succumb, unaided by divine providence, to what life may bring.

In the midst of the war Steinbeck's second play, *The Moon Is Down* (1942), also appeared as a novel. Set in an unidentified occupied town, presumably in Norway, the play's message of hope for the underground resistance is personified in the mayor's heroic refusal to save his own life by compromise with the Nazis. The play's strongest criticism decried Steinbeck's humane portrayal of the occupiers, specifically the colonel who is sensitive to the intense hatred he must face each day and the lonely young soldier, desperate for affection, who succumbs to the enticements of the girl who willingly kills him. In light of the fervid heat of warfare and the widespread public attitude toward the Germans, the strong antipathy toward them was reasonable enough, but Steinbeck recognizes a very important fact: most members of the Wehrmacht were not bloody brutes. He succeeds in making the horror of the situation even more evident by showing occupiers and occupied alike as compassionate human beings who equally dread what they have to do. Like the best of war plays, *The Moon Is Down* keeps the action out of the trenches and off the firing line as it focuses not on grim battlefield conditions but on the hideous destruction in decent human souls that war can cause. *The Moon Is Down* survived only two months in New York but was more favorably received in Europe, where the realities of occupation made a substantial difference in public appreciation.[18]

So much for Steinbeck's dramatic career. He did, however, prove that a well-constructed naturalistic "slice of life" could convey not only a specific social situation but also an outlook on life reflecting the thirties in particular as well as mankind's plight in general, insights that undoubtedly helped him win the Nobel Prize for Literature in 1962.

□   □   □

Realism-Naturalism. Is it worth the effort to keep them apart? Those playwrights who chose the middle ground of straight, nontragic drama in all likelihood cared little whether or not their art would receive one label or another. Neither they nor the critics who tried to apply the labels could satisfactorily determine precisely what they were. All, however, attempted to reflect reality in terms as close as the theater would allow; their best efforts, however near the "real thing" the writers may have wished them to be, were perforce imitations, mimicking and modifying while convincing the audience of their authenticity. The variations, as these writers have shown, can be infinite. Natural determinism and lack of free will may make these plays *naturalistic*; independence of fate and exertion of free choice may make them *realistic*; but in their final analysis as successes or failures, it probably doesn't really matter at all. From Odets to Steinbeck, these dramatists were often able to thwart the critics' insistence on sticking on labels, and they created a body of serious drama with memorable characters and action. The universality of their best efforts makes those works relevant to any era—call them what you will.

7

Seeing Ourselves as Less than We Are

The Great Age of American Comedy

Aristotle wrote very little about comedy, or if he did write more, it has not survived. In the *Poetics* he briefly noted the fundamental difference between comedy and serious drama in his statement that tragedy shows men as greater than they are and comedy shows men as less than they are. This differentiation still holds; in the eyes of the comic writer, we are all considerably less than we would like to be, or even believe ourselves to be. At all levels comedy takes us down a peg or two and mocks, satirizes, and ridicules our noble aspirations. From the pratfall to the most brilliant witty retort, the result is the same: our dignity is subject to the whims of gravity or the well-aimed barbs of sophisticated language, which can physically and emotionally expose us for the second-rate creatures we are.

All this can hurt. To the object of ridicule, the butt of the jibe, being laughed at is most unfunny, and a certain broadness of mind is needed to take a joke. If extended far enough, every comic situation has a potential for disaster, based as it is on human faults and often compromising circumstances. Fortunately, in good comedy the point of view of both creator and viewer is never permitted to cross that line. Audience awareness of the infliction of actual suffering in mind or body cannot be the source of laughter, which derives from audience recognition of the same shortcomings in all of us, however painful. This aspect of aesthetic distance, vital in experiencing Bentley's "delight" in all drama, becomes doubly important in comedy.

Truly good comedy, therefore, is difficult to write not only because of the need to keep that required distance in point of view but also because of constantly changing tastes. The basis of serious drama remains essentially the same from generation to generation, but what is funny in one age can be strictly taboo in another; a situation once seen as hilarious can later fall embarrassingly flat. Sex and the dirty joke, together with their frank language or double entendres—common sources of comedy from ancient Greece to this week's Broadway opening—are always held in check by the permissiveness of the time; peculiarities of race or national origin, handicap, or personal deformity, once considered fair comic game, are no longer amusing. But the war between men and women, equally well known by Aristophanes and James Thurber, social pretense, and all human stupidities will always provide the comic writer with endless amounts of material.

In a period of little more than two decades, as American drama between the wars became the world's leader in the development of serious realistic / naturalistic plays and experimented with modern tragedy, verse, and stylization, it also produced some of the best comedies in modern theater. Many of them, even with relatively dated topics and dialogue, have remained as attractive in revival as they were when they first appeared.

George S. Kaufman: Collaborative Master of Action and the Quick Quip

The most remarkable aspect of the between-wars comedies is the fact that a great many of them were collaborative efforts. S. N. Behrman and Philip Barry, with their respectable bodies of individual work, stand out as exceptions; but others, save for perhaps Clare Boothe, remain mostly in the shadows of the major collaborators and their many successes.[1]

The name George S. Kaufman is synonymous with American comedy. He wrote only one well-known play entirely on his own, but as a frequent collaborator he became as familiar as any who practiced the profession alone. Considered by those who knew him well as a curmudgeon of irascible temper, he was nevertheless able to combine his talents with others to produce a long string of outstanding hits. Sometimes accused of being merely a "play doctor" who rescued dying scripts, Kaufman was often actually the originator, if not of the scripts themselves, at least of their ingenious ideas. Furthermore, his contribution was so welcomed by his collaborators, whose own fame often came about because of this cooperation, that they never seem to have questioned his name being listed first in theater billings and published plays. In the Burns Mantle *Best Plays* series, for instance, up to 1940 his name appears 18 times, always as "Kaufman and ————."

Kaufman's magic touch as both a writer and one of Broadway's best directors (he also acted on occasion in his own plays) is evident in the phenomenal number of his successes between 1922 and 1957. Over the course of 35 years he directed 45 productions, 27 of which were hits, and an astonishing 24 of which he coauthored. Although he scorned the frequently satirical bent of comedy—"Satire is what closes Saturday night," he once said—his wit nevertheless skewered Hollywood, corporate business, the theater itself, national politics, the mores of the rich, and the foibles of privileged individuals. He may have regarded all of what he did as something else, but by any other name, it's still satire.

Furthermore, to Kaufman's permanent credit, his barbs were never cruel. Those at whom he aimed, though they could feel the sting, were just as likely as anyone to laugh; it was very difficult to feel offended. Howard Teichman, his friend and collaborator, summarizing a number of the best critics of the day, points to the great versatility that Kaufman could display. His extraordinary wit flashes through nearly all of his work, and he could use it to mix together in a single play the best of slapstick farce and the best of high comedy. His technical skill was one of his greatest assets, derived from a sharply creative mind thoroughly oriented toward the theater. He had, says Teichman, the "greatest track record in the American theater."[2]

Themes of the great "American dream"—rags to riches, poor boy to millionaire, and the like—appear with regularity in a number of Kaufman's plays, but his treatment of sympathetic characters who gain their rewards, often by hit-or-miss tactics, is considerably different from the methods of George Kelly in *The Show-Off,* whose irritating and unattractive Aubrey Piper gains the last laugh in an undeserved and unanticipated switch in fortune. Neither does Kaufman introduce early hilarity only to kick the audience in the shins, as Kelly did in *The Torch-bearers*. Kaufman's solo performance, *The Butter and Egg Man* (1925), illustrates his more gentle approach. In a routine portrayal of a popular daydream, the play takes the innocent country boy with a sizable legacy through the darker alleys of shady promoters who dupe him into spending his fortune as the butter and egg man, or "angel," for a losing Broadway production that of course turns into a hit. Displaying little more than the kind of fluff that always delights audiences, *The Butter and Egg Man* has remained ever since a standard piece for stock companies and community theaters.[3]

Kaufman's earliest collaborator was Marc Connelly, with whom he created five plays between 1921 and 1924. Three of them go down the line in their version of the success story; all were commercially profitable, none worth revival. The heroine of *Dulcy* (1921) is a scatterbrain who, somewhat like Aubrey Piper, brings about her husband's advancement in the business world through luck rather than intellect. A reversal occurs in *To the Ladies* (1922). The husband gets his promotion all right, but this time it's the intelligent, quick-thinking opposite of Dulcy who does the trick. In spite of a supposedly complimentary view of the "liberated" women of the twenties, the wives remain behind the scene, loyally furthering their spouses, properly keeping their place as the menfolk gain the benefits. It is difficult for later generations of women to look kindly at this attitude, which may explain why both plays are now seldom seen. *Merton of the Movies* (1922) is one more up-the-success-ladder stereotype; the small-town boy makes his fortune in Hollywood. An unsuccessful musical, *Be Yourself* (1924), can be ignored.

The exceptional play among these five is *Beggar on Horseback* (1924), based loosely on an earlier German play adapted to American life. A hilarious satire on the efficient inefficiencies of big business, it has never lost the impact of its attack on the crassness of millionaires and the whole get-rich-quick syndrome of the early 1920s. In the atmosphere of leveraged buy-outs and corporate greediness so prevalent in the twentieth century's last two decades, the play still works and has remained the best remembered and playable of the Kaufman-Connelly collaborations.

Beggar on Horseback (the title is derived from the old saying, "If wishes were horses, beggars would ride") is a "framework" play, with the brief realistic beginning and ending bracketing the expressionistic main body of the drama, the dream of the central figure, Neil. It is a nightmare world with frequent parallels to Rice's expressionistic condemnation of materialism in *The Adding Machine*, or even to O'Neill's *The Hairy Ape*.

Neil, the struggling artist who composes classical music, has considerably more humanity than Mr. Zero, but he is equally frustrated in his inability to succeed in a money-mad world that refuses to reward his talents. He belongs best in his world of genteel poverty, but like O'Neill's Yank, he moves in his dream into the outside world of business, which has the capacity to destroy him and reduce him to nothingness. Torn between Cynthia, the faithful girl next door who genuinely appreciates him, and the filthy-rich Gladys Cady, Neil falls into a deep sleep and dreams his life as Gladys's husband.

The expressionistic world that Neil encounters is terrifying, but Kaufman and Connelly turn it into a wildly exaggerated travesty of life at the top. In a sequence of action played entirely for laughs, the play stresses the impossible situation of the little guy in an overpowering industrial culture, at the same time avoiding the grimness of Rice or O'Neill. It does, however, make its point equally well. Neil's attempt to work in his father-in-law's business is thwarted, for example, by his inability to secure the basic tool of a pencil, for which endless forms are needed. Gladys destroys his manuscript, and, surpassing Zero, Neil stabs her and her entire family. His trial becomes a bizarre parade of his victims testifying against him (Cady himself is the judge), resulting in the guilty verdict that sends Neil to work in the Cady factory, where art is produced as mechanically as machines on an assembly line. Upon awakening, the chastened Neil welcomes the embrace of Cynthia in a happy ending far removed from Yank's crushing death in the gorilla's cage or Zero's return to earth as an even greater nonentity.

The comic condemnation of mercenary exploitation and human shortsightedness in *Beggar on Horseback* is as stinging and effective as any more serious attempt, harking back as far as Strindberg's own nightmare portrayal of existence in his *Dream Play* (1902). While Strindberg's Daughter of Indra finds that to be a man is a terrible thing, and Rice and O'Neill condemn their protagonists to destruction, *Beggar's* upbeat happy ending does not lessen the impact. And there is no reason to abandon hope; Neil's look into the future, like Scrooge's, does make him a better man. Unlike Dickens's romanticized ending, however, Kaufman and Connelly's makes it clear that Neil will have a struggle.

In 1929 Moss Hart, a young aspiring playwright who had spent a good part of his youth attending productions of Kaufman's plays, approached the great man with a script that needed a lot of work. In his autobiography of his early life, *Act One* (1959), Hart reports his surprised delight that Kaufman not only liked the play, called *Once in a Lifetime*, but wanted to begin work on it at once. Hart's detailed account of their collaboration provides what is probably the fullest description available anywhere of the creation process of a Broadway play. Kaufman is shown to have had almost superhuman stamina, putting in long hours, day after day, from December to June, with little or no time for rest or food, renovating dialogue and action, sometimes spending hours on a single line or a day on a single exit.[4] In his preface to *Six Plays by Kaufman and Hart*, Hart tells of the lesson he soon learned, that the old saying "Plays are not written, but rewritten" was no mere aphorism: "The rewriting process under the guidance of the eagle-eyed Mr. Kaufman slowly formulated itself in my mind as a combination of the Spanish Inquisition and the bloodiest portions of the First World War."[5]

Once in a Lifetime, directed by Kaufman, opened in New York in September 1930. It was an immediate hit. Set in the early days of talking pictures, when Hollywood was being turned topsy-turvy in the discovery that a new film dimension, voice, was making new careers as fast as it was destroying old ones, it involves the lives of three down-at-the-heel New York vaudevillians who grab at a once-in-a-lifetime chance to strike it rich. The play touches on just about every cliché of the mad world of movie-making. Everyone involved seems just a little bit crazy or, like the New York playwright (acted by Kaufman) who sits endlessly in an office, getting his fat weekly check for doing absolutely nothing, is driven into a breakdown from underwork. Disaster looms when it is discovered that a mixup in scenarios had resulted in the production of the wrong picture, which in good comic fashion promptly becomes a rousing critical success and makes a star of the lamebrained floozy who has replaced the big-name actress. Even the continual snapping on the soundtrack, made by one character cracking Indian nuts off-camera, is hailed as an artistic equal to Eugene O'Neill's tom-toms in *The Emperor Jones*.

It is difficult to consider *Once in a Lifetime* a hard-line satire. Its target, true, is Hollywood's inanities, but it smacks far more of a spoof than of anything with a message, however hidden. The lines crackle and snap, the action never flags, and the situations are always funny without becoming absurd. The play's basis is farcical, of course, but it never descends into mere sight gags or wisecracks for their own sake. It creates a feeling that things could almost have been this way as characters, action, and dialogue blend beautifully into a comedy of Hollywood manners without the biting edge of satire.

Four other plays between 1934 and 1940, all less broadly comic than *Once in a Lifetime*, cannot be termed failures by any means, but they never quite displayed the unity of Kaufman and Hart's best combined efforts. Two involved the theater and its people: *Merrily We Roll Along* (1934) and *The Fabulous Invalid* (1938). The former, an exposure of a failing playwright, employed the not so new device of working backward in time from 1934 to 1916. The latter was a historic reprise of highlights of the American theater. *I'd Rather Be Right* (1937)—the title was taken from Henry Clay's famous statement, "I would rather be right than be President"—was a musical satire of Franklin Roosevelt's presidency, redeemed by George M. Cohan's lively performance of a singing and dancing FDR. *George Washington Slept Here* (1940), the story of a couple from Manhattan who try to renovate a Bucks County farmhouse, sported the usual Kaufman-Hart pungent lines and lively action but achieved no lasting fame.

The collaboration did result in two plays that have become comic classics of the American theater, on both stage and screen. The first, *You Can't Take It with You* (1936), won the Pulitzer Prize. Its hilarious putdown of the sacrosanct puritan work ethic centers on the eccentric and individualistic Vanderhof family. Thirty-five years before the play opens, the 75-year-old patriarch of the clan, Grandpa Vanderhof, had decided that going to the office every day was not worth the effort. Ever since, he has enjoyed himself doing precisely what he pleases, surrounded by family members and off-the-street hangers-on who do exactly the same. His fiftyish daughter writes endless plays because a typewriter was delivered to the house by mistake years ago. A granddaughter takes ballet from a mad Russian dancemaster, while her husband, when he is not playing the xylophone for his wife's dancing, makes and distributes candy with quotations he prints for the fun of it, currently taken for no known reason from Leon Trotsky. A son-in-law makes fireworks in the basement. It is a frenetic and happy world into which the serious outsiders, such as the IRS man desperately explaining why Grandpa owes 22 years' back taxes, or the FBI men tracking down the source of the seditious candy-box quotes, enter at their peril.

The real world, the world wherein one earns money, is that of the very rich Kirbys, parents of Tony, the boyfriend of Alice, the only "sane" working member of the Vanderhof household. Their disastrous dinner engagement at the Vanderhof mansion, when fireworks explode and the law descends to arrest everyone in sight, is the climactic event in a series of purely farcical scenes, but the events that lead up to and follow the debacle make the authors' point that accumulating the fortune you can't take with you is not worth the deadly-dull marriage relationship and the ulcers that can accompany it. Mr. Kirby's conversion to Grandpa's philosophy brings everything happily together as Tony and Alice receive the needed blessing from both sides.

You Can't Take It with You is a wonderful fairy tale and, to a degree, is valid. Certainly, life is not worth living if the supposed pursuit of happiness leads only to the piling up of riches and kills one off in the process. There must be some sort of middle ground, but very few can afford to practice the Vanderhof philosophy. Some sort of financial security must provide the necessary resources, and fortunately Grandpa's riches, accumulated earlier by hard work, do just that. The anarchy of this wacky household provides marvelous scenes of pure comedy, but the play is the kind that only a privileged class can find relevant. Woe to a society that would pay no taxes and live the life of total freedom. Yet it is delightful to think how it might be, and Kaufman and Hart, in their zestful enthusiasm, have designed in this never-never land an appealing dream world that asks us to not take ourselves too seriously, to seize the moment and enjoy the brevity of existence. Few writers have said it better.

Of Kaufman and Hart's top three plays, *The Man Who Came to Dinner* (1939) wears the label of satire the most easily. This madcap farce, "a comedy of bad manners," as it was once called, was meant to place a specific person on the rack and roast him unmercifully on the coals of the authors' unrelenting wit. The object of the often outrageous slings and arrows was the irascible writer, lecturer, critic, and radio personality Alexander Woollcott. In fact, the play was dedicated to him, "for reasons that are nobody's business," but to anyone acquainted with the man himself there could be no uncertainty about those reasons.

A member of the Algonquin Round Table, the "portly Falstaffian" Woollcott, as his alter ego in the play, Sheridan Whiteside, is described, was a dominating, self-centered, and dogmatic individual of acid tongue and searing wit who was a perfect figure for the Kaufman and Hart scalpel to dissect. The result was one of the most enduringly successful satiric comedies in contemporary American drama. Like Aubrey Piper and Harriet Craig, Whiteside, as interpreted on stage and screen by Monty Woolley, entered the language as the archetype of the curmudgeonly egotist. Nailed to the wall as he was, incapable of denying the portrait, Woollcott made no apologies and brazened the whole thing out by successfully playing Whiteside in the touring company.

The Man Who Came to Dinner, in addition to its well-aimed satire on the eccentric world of national celebrities, is also an outstanding example of what rousing farce can achieve in the hands of writers of more than ordinary intellect. The plot is based on the unlikely premise that this reluctant dinner guest in a small Ohio city, an international celebrity at that, would be confined for weeks in the house of his hosts with a broken hip suffered from a fall on an icy front step rather than being whisked off to a hospital, where all the best care would be available. The farcical insanity rises steadily as the hapless, helpless Stanley family attempts the impossible task of coping. From Whiteside's built-up entrance in his wheelchair, whereupon he surveys the gaping, beaming figures that surround him as he quietly utters "I may vomit," to the wild conclusion in which an interfering actress-vamp is removed in an Egyptian mummy case and the screams of the departing guest are heard as Whiteside slips on the step once more and is born back onstage in a towering rage, the pace never lets up. Whiteside tyrannizes the family in word and deed, commandeering rooms, kitchen, telephone, and all else for his own use, bullying his secretary and his nurse, sticking his nose into family affairs where he is not wanted. Meanwhile, with Christmas greetings and gifts arriving for Whiteside from around the world, including a shipment of live penguins, and Whiteside's own slushy, sentimental Christmas-eve message airing worldwide from the Stanley home, the farce keeps up its frantic and at times fantastic pace; but it is polished and, above all, tasteful. No double entendres, no multiple slamming doors and bedroom shenanigans, only action and words proceeding pell-mell, but always consistent with character and such plot line as there is. In the end, the other side of Whiteside, his softer if limited humanity, prevails long enough to enable him to straighten out the love life of his secretary and set himself reasonably straight with his host family. But not for long; the curtain catastrophe starts the disastrous circle over again.

Just before World War II, Kaufman and Hart, like others, felt the threat from Hitler's Germany and responded with *The American Way* (1939), a serious condemnation of the American Nazi Bund in a peaceful Ohio town. Thereafter, they never collaborated again. Hart went on to further success on his own in *Lady in the Dark* (1941), with music by Kurt Weill, but he remains best remembered for his work with his more famous partner. It is unfortunate that Hart's untimely death prevented his writing the projected *Act Two* as a sequel to his best-selling *Act One*, which dealt mainly with *Once in a Lifetime*. How the relationship developed as seen from Hart's vantage point would have been good to know. We do know that both generously acknowledged their debts to each other, and Kaufman is said to have preferred Hart to any of the others with whom he worked.

Between 1924 and 1948, a period overlapping the Moss Hart era by some years at both ends, Kaufman collaborated on six plays with the popular novelist Edna Ferber. It was, on the surface, an unlikely pairing. Ferber, the writer of such melodramatic novels as *Show Boat*, was a sharp contrast to the misanthropic critic of life whose strength lay so clearly in fast-paced action and witty retort. It was a combination that on occasion worked surprisingly well; Ferber provided the dialogue for the love scenes and the more serious passages, along with several aspects of the basic plot, while Kaufman contributed the witty lines. It did not always succeed, however, as they discovered in *Minick* (1924), adapted from a folksy Ferber story of a self-sacrificing old man. Kaufman's wisecracking was out of place and fell flat in this low-key, less rambunctious comedy. Their talents were happily blended in *The Royal Family* (1927), based loosely on the lives of America's stage royalty, Lionel, John, and Ethel Barrymore. The theatrical setting was intimately familiar to Kaufman, offering him a more sophisticated situation, which he could better handle. The balance between the two writers kept the play from being either too sentimental or too cynical. The result was greater depth of characterization and more humanity, creating a level of high comedy better suited to the subjects themselves and maintaining respect for the original models, the Barrymore family, at the same time.

In 1932 *Dinner at Eight*, one of Kaufman's more telling satires, provided the partnership with an even better venue for their skills. The vacuous troubled lives of the rich presented a perfect opportunity for Kaufman's particular kind of barbed humor to strike the targets unmercifully. Ferber's ability to assimilate Kaufman's style into a natural-sounding dialogue kept the play believable throughout its revelation of the events in the lives of a series of guests invited to a lavish dinner party. As the scenes progress, the audience learns more about the unhappy, sordid, and intertwined lives of the partygoers than they know about each other; the truth of their sadly troubled existence cannot entirely be concealed under the slick party conversation. The harsh treatment of these empty characters would have fit easily into one of the agitprop dramas of the same period. But better than any propagandizing social agitation, the more intellectual and remorseless Kaufman-Ferber attack, with its constant witty repartee and the satiric laughter at the expense of these poor little rich people, was more effective with those who watched, many of whom, more's the pity, could be identified with those onstage.

Ferber's sentimentality won out over Kaufman's iconoclasm in the morality tale *Stage Door* (1936). Once more the lure of quick fame and fortune in Hollywood provides the central theme. This time, however, the serious aspects of responsible professionalism take precedence. The girl who sees only the glitter of the film capital takes the fatal step of abandoning the stage, in the end ruining herself as a promising legitimate performer. Predictably, for this is at heart a romance, the one who chooses the less immediately rewarding and much harsher road by remaining true to her talents attains a name for herself on the stage. The play's setting in a New York hotel for young actresses provides an authentic behind-the-scenes look at the painful struggles, deep frustrations, and disappointments, including a suicide, as well as the joyous moments of promise, in the world of dreams that draws these disparate individuals together.

Kaufman's ability to fit into a variety of comic styles kept him simultaneously occupied with musical productions as well. With Morrie Ryskind he helped propel the Marx Brothers to stage and screen immortality in *The Cocoanuts* (1925) and *Animal Crackers* (1928). Special recognition must be given to the effective satire of the American election process, *Of Thee I Sing*, produced with Ryskind in 1931. With music and lyrics by George and Ira Gershwin, this perennial favorite won the 1931–32 Pulitzer Prize, the first ever awarded to a musical play. Its ridicule of political mores moved the Pulitzer committee to bypass such legitimate pieces as O'Neill's monumental *Mourning Becomes Electra*.

There were to be other plays with the familiar Kaufman imprimatur. Two more with Ferber, *The Land Is Bright* (1941) and *Bravo* (1948), have long since disappeared. With John P. Marquand, author of the original novel, he wrote *The Late George Apley* in 1944, and with Howard Taubman *The Solid Gold Cadillac* in 1955, but nothing ever quite equaled the earlier accomplishments. While often addressing a particular time, his best plays have retained their universal attraction in their awareness of the basic comic nature of all men and women. The appealing fantasy of the Vanderhof way of life never grows old; the outrageous insolence of the selfish, oafish Sheridan Whiteside remains as explosively funny as ever. Frequent revivals from Broadway to the most obscure regional theaters have kept the rousing action and the fast-flying wisecracks of George S. Kaufman a continuing part of American theatrical tradition. His fondness for the American people, of whom he was so thoroughly a part, is plain enough, enabling us to recognize our lesser, second-rate nature while laughing uproariously at it.

Philip Barry's Sophisticated Morality

Philip Barry and S. N. Behrman were both students in George Pierce Baker's 47 Workshop, but it was Barry who profited most immediately from the association. The first of the Workshop plays to be published, Barry's *You and I* (1923), was also the playwright's first Broadway production, and a success as well. Baker wrote the introduction to the printed version, praising Barry's light, sure touch in revealing the husband's conflict between business success and artistic longings. Two modestly successful romantic comedies followed quickly. *The Youngest* (1924) made further use of the theme of family relationships in which artistic, creative, or spiritual members battle those who are traditional or materialistic. *In a Garden* (1925), the story of the Ibsenesque rebellion of the wife of a playwright, enhanced Barry's reputation for graceful dialogue and intellectual challenge. Establishing Barry as a welcome voice in the development of American comedy, these three plays remain journeyman efforts, overshadowed by the succeeding works for which he continues to be remembered.[6]

Barry's own life, spent among the rich, enabled him to write with a satiric edge as pointed as Kaufman's, but his best talents lay in the polished artificialities of his rapidly flowing dialogue. It may have lacked the epigrammatic intellectualism of Shaw or Wilde, or the crackling wit of Kaufman or even Behrman, but in his next four comedies it firmly and permanently established him as a leading comic playwright.

In *Paris Bound* (1927) Barry began to hit his stride. It is the first of his comedies that can properly be labeled "high," and it immediately placed him alongside the developing Behrman. The first notable aspect is the language, improved in its brilliance and wittiness over the earlier pieces, fitting the more sophisticated quality of the subject. These are civilized people, treating the problems of real or suggested infidelity in typical high comic, that is, civilized, fashion. The wronged young wife considers fleeing to Paris, where seeking divorce seemed at that time to be a popular method of handling such things. Gaining redress in this manner ultimately becomes pointless, as does dissolving an otherwise successful union because of a sin she had long been unaware of anyway. Her own impulsive act in kissing an attractive young man reveals human susceptibility on both sides, so why all the fuss? No tearful sentimental forgiveness, just practical recognition of reality, with nobody hurt in the end.

The success of *Holiday* (1928) firmly established Barry's reputation for high comedy. As high comedy, it is properly set in the spacious home of the very rich financier Edward Seton, with plenty of servants gliding about and money no object. Its plot is miniscule, a not unknown aspect of American high comedy, but its character emphasis, primarily on poor but honest Johnny Case, is just a bit different from what might be expected. Introduced by Julia, his fiancée, to her millionaire father, Johnny creates consternation for both when he announces his scorn for the immediate accumulation of wealth, an incomprehensible attitude to father and daughter. He prefers to "find himself" and, in simple terms, to see the world before he settles down to the grubby business of earning money. George Bernard Shaw had once bemoaned the fact that youth is wasted on the young, and Johnny is the perfect example of one who refuses to let that waste occur. He sincerely means to live his life while he can enjoy it and to worry about any practical means of earning a living after that. The engagement's breakup is inevitable under these circumstances, but the independent-minded Johnny has a convenient and much more human choice in the equally independent family rebel, Linda, who prefers fun and games in the old nursery at the top of the house over the pompous hollowness of the abortive engagement party downstairs. In the end, recognizing the smallness and the essential immorality of the glittering but insincere world of wealth, Johnny takes the strong moral step of departing on his before-the-fact holiday from life with Linda, who races joyously to join him on the ship headed for Europe.

Delightfully polished and sophisticated as *Paris Bound* and *Holiday* may be, Barry's permanent reputation as a high comic writer must rest with *The Animal Kingdom* (1932) and *The Philadelphia Story* (1939). The title of *The Animal Kingdom* was intentionally ironic; Barry looked into the mating habits of the higher biological species and found that marriage must be based on more than animal appetites. Although he could be accused of condoning adultery in *Paris Bound*, elopement without benefit of clergy in *Holiday*, and extramarital love in this play, Barry always held the thesis that spiritual values outweigh the bonds of social and legal ceremonies, an attitude well within the amoral tradition of good high comedy. Hence, his triangle plot can send Tom back to his ever-loving mistress, Daisy, even while suffering a disastrous marriage into which he has been led by the seductive Cecilia. There is more than a little sentimentality in *The Animal Kingdom*, a bothersome quality if one is to assume that Barry was writing traditional high comedy. But Barry's touch, like Behrman's, was being applied to a society of a different age, temperament, and background from that ridiculed by the more famous British high comic counterparts. His characters may have had a basic decency that makes them lack the brittleness and hard edge of characters in, say, a Restoration comedy of manners, but American audiences loved them for it.

Barry's writing about upper-class American manners did show a culture that still held middle-class values, and all the infidelities and elopements succeeded in retaining those decencies despite the appearance of moral indiscretion. His most famous play, *The Philadelphia Story,* is no exception. The setting is the mandatory drawing room in the home of the wealthy Lord family, whose verbal banter among themselves and their houseguests provides the slick but still realistic-sounding dialogue that Barry executed so well. The Barry trademark of pointed, if mild, moral condemnation of the rich is plainly evident, but it is without rancor. Having the privilege of being one of them himself, Barry could at the same time express his admiration for their best qualities.

Plot, again, remains unimportant; the play emphasizes the character development of the Main Line heiress Tracy Lord, a prudish snob, into an acceptable and attractive human being. Her inhibitions and her repressed nature have made a failure of her marriage, but after excessively imbibing at a social gathering she shocks all, including herself, by taking a totally uninhibited nude swim with a radical newspaper reporter. Awareness of what she has done succeeds in releasing all the confining prudery, and she happily remarries her former husband. The moral seems to be that a virginal moon-goddess like Tracy fares poorly in the normal world, but the seeming loss of that haughty virginity can make an acceptable human individual. As in all the other adventures through which Barry sends his leading characters, the basic morality remains, and the indiscreet frolic in the pool proves a positive act that still fits the light tone of the play. Not unimportant in the comedy's long run was the appearance of an actress of uniquely angular features and distinctive voice named Katharine Hepburn. The play has been a perennial favorite on screen as well, featuring Hepburn in the original version and Grace Kelly with Bing Crosby and Frank Sinatra in a musical variation called *High Society.*

The Hit Singles: Comedy beyond the Big Three

Each of the "big three" comic writers—Behrman, Barry, and Kaufman—gave Americans a very good look at themselves; the public laughed at the exposure of their pretensions as the fast-paced zaniness of high comic wit and wisdom revealed them as far less than they would have liked to consider themselves. By virtue of the quality and quantity of their plays, the three remain the dominant figures in American comedy between the wars, helping to provide substantial balance against the more serious dramas of O'Neill, Odets, Rice, and others.

But there were comic writers of equal if not greater popularity whose fame rests primarily on a single big hit. Of the half-dozen or so most memorable, only one or two of their plays can be assigned any literary merit, but all of the other important writers deserve recognition for the high quality of the entertainment they provided. Many of the plays have maintained lasting audience appeal. Moreover, their contribution to the great age of American comedy during the 1930s was substantial. In comparison with comedies of the post–second war period, most of the comedies of the thirties, no matter who wrote them, seem almost naively innocent. In language and action they rely on surefire fun that has no use or need for the rougher and darker images, sometimes termed "sick," that comedy in later years seemed to require in a world rapidly becoming disillusioned by the polarization of the globe after the "good war" of the 1940s. The scattered *goddamns, Christs,* and *hells,* along with compromising situations, may have provided the earlier comedies with a sense of sophistication and reality, but these elements did not alter the often romantic sentiments and upbeat endings.

Ben Hecht and Charles MacArthur, both successful newsmen, may not have regarded *The Front Page* (1928) as a farce, but their racy, rowdy revelation of what supposedly goes on in a big-city courthouse pressroom has all the ingredients. Irreverent it certainly is in its broad mocking of city government, criminal justice, and the press itself. With its riotous pace, full of jangling phones, drinking and gambling reporters who will do anything for a story even if it has to be invented, personal rivalries, thwarted romance, and a condemned convict locked up in a rolltop desk, it is a play in which sanity has very little place. It is in no sense a realistic transcription onto the stage of the daily routines of such individuals—none of the characters is more than a cardboard stereotype—but audiences who have accepted the wild fun of the play on screen and in revival ever since have undoubtedly taken the entire fracas as a representation of what the pursuit of news at least *seems* like.

George Abbott, another product of Baker's 47 Workshop, has often been compared to Kaufman for his success as producer, writer, and play doctor over a long career beginning with various acting roles as early as 1913. Somewhat less prolific and far less a serious satirist than Kaufman was, he nonetheless left his mark in a series of farce-comedies and musicals extending well past the Second World War.

Abbott's collaboration began with James Gleason in something called *The Fall Guy* (1925), long and deservedly forgotten. The same applies to *Love 'em and Leave 'em*, written with John V. A. Weaver in 1926. In the same year he joined with Philip Dunning to write *Broadway*. Its 603 performances made it the longest-running play in the New York theater up to that time and placed Abbott permanently among the American theater's all-time all-around participants. To treat *Broadway* as anything of serious dramatic importance is, of course, foolish, but its fast-paced backstage comedy and melodrama set a precedent often copied but never excelled.

The strong audience appeal of *Broadway* is not difficult to understand. There is a little bit of everything to please an audience seeking fast-moving dramatic entertainment with no pretenses. Set in a room just offstage in a New York cabaret, the play is filled with beautiful chorus girls, lovely to look at in their wide assortment of costumes and delightful to watch as they form their precise dance line to move out before the unseen audience. The action takes place during the years of Prohibition; there are ruthless bootleggers surrounded by various thugs and goons, whose argument over respective turfs ends in a cowardly onstage murder. The melodramatic undercurrent of suspense builds; everybody in the audience knows who did it, but justice must wait until very near the end, when the murderer himself gets his from the pistol of a grief-stricken chorister. The crafty cop enters and leaves from time to time, and finally departs when his prime suspect dies; it's a suicide, says the cop, who knows full well it isn't. And there is sentimental romance: the innocent star dancer, in over her head in her involvement with the murderer, is finally won over by her devoted, hard-working dancing partner. What more could one ask?

To list all of the plays with which George Abbott was associated either as writer or director would be an exercise in redundancy, especially when it comes to the many successful formula-based farces. One of the best-remembered is *Room Service* (1937), involving the entanglements of a producer unable to pay his hotel bill and the running gag of a mounted moose head, all well suited to the Marx Brothers, who made their usual shambles of reason and rationality in their screen adaptation.

Two other plays, both produced in 1935, arguably remain Abbott's best, although he was involved in writing only one of them. The first, *Three Men on a Horse*, was a collaboraton with John Cecil Holm. It is a fine example of the use of a preposterous premise to build the best elements of farce. Its central figure, Erwin, a mild, wimpish writer of abominable but successful greeting-card verses, lives with little wife Audrey in a cozy tract cottage in Ozone Heights, New Jersey. He is the answer to a racetrack tout's prayer: he has an infallible knack for picking winning horses. Once he encounters three diehard bettors down to their last few dollars and reveals his talent, the play takes off into sheer fun having no relationship to plausibility. Whisked away by the gamblers, held captive in a hotel room where he is guarded for the gold mine he is, Erwin reveals two catches in his skill that bring endless complications: he can pick the winners only on a certain bus going to a certain destination, and he breaks the spell if he himself does any betting. Everything is readily predictable, and Erwin eventually returns to his peaceful pursuits of verse writing and making a happy home with Audrey. The play hasn't a single redeeming quality outside of being a well-paced farcical exploration of a fantasy; for that quality alone it deserves respect as one of the best of its kind.

Abbott's production of *Boy Meets Girl*, written by Bella and Samuel Spewack, was the second of the year's best comedies. Its picture of Hollywood writers, producers, and stars, like the pressroom madness in *The Front Page*, is a consistently frenzied portrayal of the imaginative shenanigans that the authors would like us to believe are the typical birthpains of a successful film. We know they are not; nothing in *Boy Meets Girl* can remotely be taken seriously. The birth of a baby to Susie, the naive, unmarried commissary waitress, provides the instant solution to all the story problems the writers have been struggling with. Happy, the baby ("The most precious thing in life. The cutest, goddam little bastard you ever saw," as described by one writer, the visionary Law), becomes the film's star attraction. The old formula of boy meets girl, boy loses girl, boy gets girl, with Happy at its center, works its magic. The money rolls in, and prosperity reigns. *Boy Meets Girl*, in its broad parody of everything Hollywood and its high energy and masterful exaggeration, easily surpasses Kaufman's earlier *Once in a Lifetime*.

Three of the best comedies of the era, each the single most important work of its author, appeared between 1936 and 1940. Only one of them can justifiably be called important dramatic literature, but each was a popular success, and each did an excellent job of exposing the lesser aspects of human nature.

Opening in December 1936 and closing a year and a half later was Clare Boothe's savaging of her own sex, *The Women*. With a cast of 35 characters, every one of them female, Boothe's play caused a furor. It was regarded as either a brilliant exposé of the narrow and meaningless lives of bridge-playing, backbiting Park Avenue socialites, many of them eventually Reno-bound, or a brutally vulgar, even crude attempt at satire. Both viewpoints have a certain legitimacy. In the ensuing 50 years, however, with the growth of militant feminism and the schism over the Equal Rights Amendment, *The Women* appears less attractive than it once did.

On the positive side is Boothe's insight into the vacuities of a class of privileged women who have nothing of significance to contribute beyond beauty-parlor gossip and the destruction of each other's lives by innuendo or direct assault. They are idle and unproductive members of an upper level of society who regard their sex lives, licit and illicit, as the most immediately important item of discussion. There is genuine comedy in the wittiness of the dialogue and the unfolding revelation of the appalling shallowness of a gaggle of predatory, bare-clawed females. If one wishes to enjoy a fast-paced, unrelenting put-down of these creatures by one clearly knowledgeable about their habits, then *The Women* is an unqualified triumph. No man could have written it or would have dared even to try. The playwright's credentials are beyond question.

A closer look reveals very little of substance beneath the superficialities of this pack of unscrupulous bitches who are hardly more than caricatures. None of them, not even the one "good" woman trapped in their midst, is appealing; if they appear at first to possess any depth of character, this hope is soon dissipated. And if any man were to conclude that they resembled reality, his outlook would be distressing indeed. They are not "liberated" women; they have no sense of any female "freedoms." They are apolitical social parasites without ambition, of no visible assistance to their husbands, and they are not particularly effective mothers. *The Women* did give the female of the species something of a day in court, exposing the offstage males as irresponsible, fickle, faithless, and inconsiderate beasts, but Boothe's indictment of her flock, whose riches have spoiled and ruined their mates and paramours, suggests a verdict of guilty—in the first degree.

In November 1939 Howard Lindsay and Russell Crouse adapted Clarence Day's *New Yorker* sketches about his family into *Life with Father*. This wonderfully charming look into a well-to-do New York family of father, mother, and four redheaded sons remains the all-time long-running legitimate play in New York history, lasting through the war into its eighth year for a total run of 3,224 performances. Coming as it did just at the war's beginning, as Brooks Atkinson observed, it "restored the era of good feeling to the stage."[7]

The gentle comedy of *Life with Father* provides that good feeling in its marked contrast to most of the other successful comedies of the thirties. In the prosperous comfort of a Madison Avenue home in the late 1800s, the domestic problems have little to do with the sophisticated complexities of a Behrman or Barry play set in similar surroundings. *Life with Father* makes no pretense at satire, has no social or political bone to pick. The family's deepest concerns are with rotating maids, children's prepubescent and adolescent antics, a decision as to whether or not to sponsor a musicale with a performing whistler, and how much to contribute toward the new church. The comedy's important running gag is the determination of Vinnie, the very proper Victorian wife, to get her recalcitrant and occasionally bombastic husband Clare baptized. The lack of this rite in his background is a frightening discovery to the devout spouse, who suddenly sees her marriage invalid in the eyes of the church and her sons as, horror to contemplate, perhaps illegitimate.

Throughout the action the loud roars of Clare, the dominating male, who sees himself put upon from all sides by the commerce of the outside world and his conviction that his family is extravagantly costly, do not hide the loving, compassionate nature of this head of household. He would be lord of the manor were it not for the natural ability of his wife to work around and undermine his surface tyranny to achieve her own goals, including the baptism, against which he cries the loudest. Clare may frighten away one maid after another, cow his son into eating his oatmeal, and insist that his wife can never understand the intricacies of household finances, but Vinnie's soft answers always turn away the foot-stomping wrath. As Atkinson observes, while Clare lacks humor and imagination, he has the enduring virtues of fondness for his sons and devotion to his wife; he is a man ultimately to be respected, "the backbone of America."

Comedies in the Behrman-Berry tradition, presenting characters of intelligence and sophistication speaking their polished language, represent the most literate aspect of the comic genre. Generally developed as three-dimensional individuals who are well aware of the comic nature of their world, the characters take their own behavior seriously in their attempt to be accepted as far better than they really are, but they are seldom funny in themselves. Laughter derives from their pretentions and their not infrequently surprising behavior, together with the witty repartee. The often slashing edge of satire or the preposterous complexities of farce, when practiced by a Kaufman or Abbott, can make superb theatrical entertainment, but at the sacrifice of the special qualities of good dramatic literature, which can carry beyond the onstage antics.

It is the rare comedy that can combine all of the elements of high comedy, satire, and farce and still retain a serious enough nature to be called good dramatic literature. The play that does accomplish all of this, one of the greatest all-around comedies in American drama, is *The Male Animal*, which opened in January 1940 as the European war settled into its prolonged stalemate and the United States yawned and looked to its own devices before the overwhelming disaster of the following summer changed everything.

James Thurber and Elliot Nugent's dissection of the sacred American college rite of the homecoming weekend is a combination of admirably pointed satire and truly uproarious comedy. Its fundamental quality is high comedy in the conflict of wits that will never end: the War Between Men and Women, of which James Thurber was the past master in his knowledge of its tactics and its strategies. This is an uneven battle for the quiet little man, the absent-minded, inoffensive English professor Tommy Turner, who is ill equipped to counter the onrushing giant creatures who rumble and roar and play football while sweeping the women off their feet in their invasion of the hitherto comfortable privacy of a modest college-town home. It is the age-old brains / brawn combat, and when driven to fight for his mate, Tommy does his utmost.

The intrusion of physical combat into Tommy's life carries the play into the farther reaches of simple farce, but the reliance on sight gags and broad action develops logically and convincingly from the initial premise, highly improbable as it may be. The whole circus of loosened beasts is well within the realm of farce as Tommy attempts to make sense of what goes on around him in this world of irrational lunatics.

But *The Male Animal* is not just farce, nor is it quite pure high comedy. It is a play with a deliberate message, made forcefully and tellingly in the midst of enormous fun. It is comedy with a genuine, even literary, purpose, namely, to make a strong plea for tolerance and understanding within the academic community, where both should be practiced without question or interference. Sadly, these qualities are all too often obscured or obliterated by homage paid to the gridiron greats and by the support of good old "Americanism," which everybody understands but nobody can define, as practiced by trustees and alumni of limited mentality, who measure success not in the brilliance of a badly underpaid faculty but in the size of the new stadium. Tommy's victory in his reading of Vanzetti's letter shoots down Keller, the obstinate trustee, but even as Keller sinks, he refuses to strike his flag and departs amid the audience's derisive laughter.

The Male Animal is never trite; it is honest, and it tells the truth.

Because of its appeal both to the intellect and to the emotions, it is wrong to view it as predominantly satiric. The follies of the Ed Kellers and Joe Fergusons, the kind who see any show of liberal tendencies as "red," are ridiculed as faults that can frequently occur within society, but the emotional needs of all the Tommy Turners who desire sympathetic understanding within their own homes and their professions are also made clear, and they are not the elements of satire. This is a world that is unquestionably comic, but the overtones are intensely serious. The play asks for laughter on nearly every occasion; yet when the human animal must take the form of the enraged tiger, particularly a tipsy, glasses-wearing, English-teaching tiger, the play becomes more than fun. Its strong and bitter purpose may be sugar-coated, but it has its desired effect.

□   □   □

S. N. Behrman's emotionally depressed playwright may have felt that there was "no time for comedy" in the age of war and rebellion, but insofar as the greatest of American comedy is concerned, he was seriously misled. From the first cracks in the optimistic fabric of American society, suggesting that the chicken-in-every-pot, car-in-every-garage spiral of prosperity might be flawed, through the economic collapse of the Great Depression, the natural disaster of the Dust Bowl, and the terrifying rise of dictatorial madness, genocide, and total war, American comedy of the 1930s and early 1940s seemed to function as a social paradox. But just as the flickering screen magic of Astaire and Rogers kept up the nation's morale in one tuneful fairy tale after another, so, it seems, did American stage comedy thrive as seldom before and never afterward.

We have treated here but a portion of the farces, comedies, and musical fare that dominated the stage. These were the best; the others were often no less successful with the public. There was Preston Sturges's *Strictly Dishonorable* (1929), an instantly popular comedy set in a speakeasy; Howard Lindsay's *She Loves Me Not* (1933), about a Princeton undergraduate and a nightclub performer; Abbott's production of *Brother Rat* (1936), set in a military school where the cadets manage to get mixed up in all manner of misbehavior; Mark Reed's *Yes, My Darling Daughter* (1937), concerning a supposedly emancipated mother of the last century faced with her own daughter's liberated rebellion against social formalities such as marriage; Arthur Kober's *Having Wonderful Time* (1937), offering vacationing office workers fun and romance in a brief interlude in a Catskills summer camp; Clare Boothe's *Kiss the Boys Goodbye* (1938), almost as successful as *The Women*, satirizing the long Hollywood search for Scarlett O'Hara.

All of them, the best and the less than best, helped to make a long and frightening decade a time when we could look at ourselves, see that we weren't all that smart and brilliant, but have a good time doing it.

8

The Fanciful Flights of Fantasy

High-quality dramatic fantasy is a rare thing on the modern stage. It does exist, to be sure, and can on occasion be very successful, but there are dangers. Among its greatest weaknesses are a lack of substance to go along with the whimsy and, by virtue of its overrefined and often capricious nature, a constant tendency to become affected and precious. The classic example is J. M. Barrie's *Peter Pan*, with its flying hero who never grows up, always played by a woman; the Darling family, a name sufficient in itself to give pause; the nursemaid dog; and the Never-Never Land of lost children.[1]

Furthermore, *fantasy* can metamorphose into the *fantastic*, considerably different in focus. The pleasant associations of fantasy, with its play of imagination and its lack of exaggeration and distortion, can disappear if the emphasis shifts toward images of the strange, the weird, and the grotesque, often involving fear. Both fantasy and the fantastic have their places, so long as their creators remain aware of their respective aims and purposes. Fantasy is well illustrated in the low-key eeriness of the late Rod Serling's "Twilight Zone," always set within contemporary society;

the fantastic is perfectly displayed in the wild excitement of *Star Wars* and its gallery of androids and robots projected into a future centuries away.

Dangers or not, stage fantasy has been around ever since Aristophanes sent his frogs into Hades. Reaction to fantasy or its extension into the fantastic has always been a factor of the existing social climate. The fourth-century B.C. Athenian audiences, surrounded by their myths and legends, had no problem accepting chanting amphibians and talking birds. The flames of Hellmouth and the fork-tailed demons of medieval religious drama were projections of a place that directly concerned the faith of those who watched. The Elizabethan citizen who attended Shakespeare's *A Midsummer Night's Dream* or *The Tempest* was quite aware that spirits, fairies, and elves interfered in human affairs. The ultrasophistication of the Restoration and the sentimentalities of the eighteenth century were poor ground for the development of such fanciful drama, but in the late eighteenth and early nineteenth century, fascination with the sinister and ghostly, particularly in Germany, started a revival of interest that culminated in the heights of Goethe's *Faust*. Most of these fantasies, however, were wild melodramas of Gothic horror in the style of the German dramatist August von Kotzebue, whose adaptations by William Dunlap were so popular in the early American theater.

Before the First World War American writers had found a receptive market for fantasy. Augustus Thomas's *The Witching Hour* (1907) and William Vaughn Moody's *The Faith Healer* (1909) made considerable use of the supernatural, and Percy MacKaye's *The Scarecrow* (1908), adapted from Nathaniel Hawthorne's witchcraft tale "Feathertop," was a successful and full-fledged fantasy satirizing the foppish foolishness of a society that accepts into its midst the well-dressed, elegant-mannered Ravensbane, who is merely a scarecrow transformed by Goody Rickby, the local witch. Josephine Preston Peabody's *The Piper* (1910), a happy-ending version of Browning's "The Pied Piper of Hamelin" (the children return home), was a prizewinner as the best original play to open the new theater in Stratford-on-Avon, England. The postwar decade of the 1920s, however, the time of flappers, sexual freedom, social emancipation, and "normalcy," held little patience for the charms of fantasy. Millay's *Aria da Capo* (1920) did well, and Glaspell explored the edges of fantasy in *The Verge* (1921), but nothing very serious developed until the end of the decade, which had just collapsed with the stock market when one of the more popular plays was John Balderston's *Berkeley Square* in November 1929.

Adapted from Henry James's unfinished novel, "A Sense of the

Past," Balderston's play raises a familiar question in fantasy: can one travel in time? The protagonist, Peter Standish, residing in the ancestral London mansion in fashionable Berkeley Square, is convinced it can be done. By some mental power not made entirely clear, he returns to the late eighteenth century. There in the same house, among his now living forebears, he hopes for the beautifully uncluttered and pure life of a better day. He discovers only ugliness in dirt, disease, smells, and the religious ignorance that brands him as a witch. Unable by dint of historical fact to marry the girl with whom he falls in love, he forces himself back into the present with the realization that the romance of the past is just that— romantic fiction. The play's quiet nature held considerable audience attraction amidst the existing realism of Rice's *Street Scene* or the marathon extravagance of O'Neill's *Strange Interlude*.[2] Balderston's message is not very substantial, but it does make a good, if obvious, point of the need to accept the present, grim as it may appear, and to let the past rest. The greener grass on the other side of the time fence is mostly weeds and nettles.

It might seem that the floundering Depression era regarded the otherworldliness of fantasy to be as out of place in the thirties as it had been in the twenties, out of touch with the social and economic crises that drew the attention of Odets, Kingsley, the Federal Theatre, or the agitating propagandists. It was, however, the age of great escapist comedy from Kaufman and the rest, so that fantasy fit remarkably well into the theater scene. It was practiced by few, but some memorable plays resulted.

The Mystic Psychodramas of Philip Barry

Interspersed with the comedies of high society on which Philip Barry's reputation rests are the four plays in which he used mythical and allegorical symbols to underline his mystic exploration of a variety of psychological problems. These psychodramas retained Barry's hallmarks, sprightly dialogue and attractive characters, but they involved the serious struggle of those afflicted to return to balanced mental health and, presumably, happiness.

The first and best known was *Hotel Universe* (1930). Nine assorted characters, who could easily have populated any one of Barry's high comedies, all suffer torment within themselves and in their relationships with others. They have assembled in an old chateau on the shores of the

Mediterranean, hosted by an eccentric physicist who seems acquainted with each of his guests' afflictions. He sends them one by one, group by group, into the chateau's magic grounds where, by some power of enchantment, they relive their painful memories, projecting themselves into the past to become adult children compelled to face the traumas that have ruined them. To some it is a shattering experience, but as each returns to present-day reality, the glimpse into eternity proves to have resolved the disparate problems. The old man's unique form of psychotherapy has worked a permanent cure.

The time travel and psychic aspects of *Hotel Universe* are more complex than those of *Berkeley Square*. The adventures of Peter Standish are out-and-out fantasy, their point readily accessible. Barry's play proceeds through a mélange of Freud and Einstein as it crosses into a kind of fourth dimension, all mixed up with allegorical symbolism. The result becomes consciously fey, whimsical in the least complimentary sense. If some of the obvious flaws in the characters' obscure discussions of life and death and the herafter can be overlooked, *Hotel Universe* does remind us that facing up to what we are, were, and have become can lead to a psychic balance, all to the good. But then, that is Freud at his simplest, with no significant embellishment in Barry's hands.

The mysticism of the moral allegory *Tomorrow and Tomorrow* (1931), a modern adaptation of the Old Testament story of the childless Shumanite woman promised a son by the prophet Elisha, has very few of the elements of fantasy. With some striking echoes of *Strange Interlude*, the lonely, disturbed Eve bears a child by a noted doctor, but Eve's night of love, instead of destroying her, makes her whole. The doctor, after restoring the child, Christian, to life following an almost fatal injury, departs to leave Eve's marriage intact. The play did not gain the positive response of *Hotel Universe*; its symbolism and its transparent use of characters names were too simplistic for audience support. Even less successful was *The Joyous Season* (1934), involving the return at Christmas of a nun, significantly bearing the name of Christina, to her unhappy family. She succeeds, Barry-fashion, in restoring their faith and happiness, but the parable was too obvious.

In the fourth of Barry's allegorical plays, *Here Come the Clowns* (1938), an ex-stagehand returns to a theater appropriately called the Globe to look for the manager, clearly God, who is missing. Things seem to be run instead by an illusionist with an aura of the unholy who makes all of the wretched and unhappy human beings of the play reveal the pain of their innermost experiences. Very close in concept to *Hotel Universe*, the play is more expressionism than fantasy; its symbolism supports rather than dominates the action, and its basic realism keeps it from becoming entirely stylized. *Here Come the Clowns* is creative in its melding of forms, but its hybrid nature failed to win an audience.

Like his contemporary in fiction, F. Scott Fitzgerald, who also admired the rich and lived among them and who, as a Catholic, was also something of a pariah, Barry died before living out a full life. His work in comedy and fantasy, most of it resting unrevived, nonetheless enriched the drama of its time.

Thornton Wilder's Individualistic Experiments: The World in Micro- and Macrocosm

Thornton Wilder became known first as a novelist with his Pulitzer Prize–winner, *The Bridge of San Luis Rey*, in 1927. Unlike Steinbeck, who remained primarily a novelist, Wilder earned his greatest reputation in the drama as the creator of two highly unconventional plays in which the universe seems contained in one rural New England town, and the history of the world in the fantastic adventures of a New Jersey family. Although his total output was relatively small, the unique imagination that Wilder displayed in both one-act and full-length form brought something distinctively new to the American theater. An urbane traveler, conversant in several languages, and a friend of leading figures in the arts at home and abroad, Wilder had a broad vision of American life and history, yet always seemed to marvel at the endurance of little people through private sorrow and universal catastrophe.

Wilder's career as a dramatist began with a series of 16 moralistic, three-minute one-acts, published under the title *The Angel That Troubled the Waters* (1928). These plotless little interludes bear strong resemblances to medieval morality plays in their introduction of a series of allegorical characters who argue the case for such ideals as humility, religious faith, responsibility, and love. In 1931 the six longer pieces published as *The Long Christmas Dinner and Other Plays*, still intensely moralistic, were beginning to show the writer's skill in combining realism and a modified expressionism with less abstract characters and the semblance of a plot.

Three of them have remained popular. *The Happy Journey to*

Trenton and Camden and *Pullman Car Hiawatha* forecast the simple, unadorned staging of *Our Town* in their use of plain kitchen chairs to represent the two seats of a car or the face-to-face seating of a Pullman section. In *The Long Christmas Dinner* a dining table and chairs suffice to provide the seating for a family that, in the course of a single holiday meal, progresses through 90 years as characters enter and leave, grow up, age, and die in the span of about 20 minutes. In *Pullman Car Hiawatha* Wilder brings in the planets to enunciate philosophical thoughts as the train speeds through the night, while in the Pullman berth the young bride quietly dies. Wilder always maintained that he attempted not to capture verisimilitude but to show reality. The images he created in his simplified settings are surprisingly good; the suggestion of the family car or train compartment creates a remarkable illusion as Wilder *expresses* reality rather than literally *demonstrating* it. He recognizes very well that the theatrical world is one of pretense, and he pointedly avoids any attempt at literal representation. It is a style that demands a considerable amount of audience imagination and participation beyond a mere suspension of disbelief.

Wilder's first full-length play struck a daring new note that provided the sophisticated Broadway audience with its first sustained encounter with the Wilder style. It was a stunning surprise in the midst of a commercial theater dominated by the tenets of representational realism. Since its opening in February 1938, soon after which it won the season's Pulitzer Prize, *Our Town* has become what is probably the most familiar American play of all time. It has been translated into every major language and is continually revived by amateurs and professionals everywhere. As recently as 1988 it won the Antoinette Perry Award (the Tony) for the best New York revival of the season.[3]

Our Town is a curious mixture of dramatic realism in its characters and dialogue and a unique form of theatrical expressionism in Wilder's world of pretense, but it is not really expressionism in the usual sense. Except for tables and a few chairs and two stepladders to represent upper stories of next-door houses, there are no stage properties at all; the performers must be trained in expert pantomime to handle what is not there. The play is unabashed fantasy in its last act, with the talking dead and Emily's momentary return to past life. Imposed upon the play is a pseudo-Oriental interlocutor, a one-man Greek chorus, the Stage Manager, who enters the bare stage, the curtain of which has been raised before the audience enters, to set the scene, inform the viewers about what is going on, and participate as needed in the action itself.

Our Town *(Thornton Wilder, 1938). Wilder made no attempt at verisimilitude, using as properties objects to be found around any theater. The backstage walls were left fully exposed. Here George and Emily, supposedly doing their homework, talk from the second-story windows of their neighboring homes on a bright moonlit night.*

The play lacks any semblance of a conventional plot, carrying its two neighboring families, the Gibbses and the Webbs, through three particular days over the course of twelve years in a small New Hampshire town at the turn of the century. Daily life, love and marriage, and death provide the themes for the three acts as George Gibbs and Emily Webb fall in love, marry, and face Emily's death in childbirth. The play is designed to flow like the life of the town, opening on a bright morning when Dr. Gibbs returns home after presiding over a birth, and closing with Emily's burial in the hilltop graveyard amidst a dismal downpour of rain. Throughout, the play speaks with simple directness in the dialogue of ordinary people, illuminating human emotion with simple sentimentality, unmarred by bathos. The poignancy of deep sorrow at Emily's death is suggested without words, except for the singing of "Blest Be the Tie That Binds" by the umbrella-covered mourners as Emily herself moves out from among them to join the villagers who inhabit the cemetery, sitting immobile on chairs facing full front. Warned not to look back, Emily is granted one day of her past life, her twelfth birthday, only to discover the heartbreak of knowing what is to come, and to face the final realization that the living simply "don't understand."

The perennial appeal of *Our Town* is not difficult to explain. Its small-town American heritage, its recognition of the value of family devotion, hard work, and high moral standards, inspire a deep emotional reaction in spite of attempts by the Stage Manager to keep emotion at bay by his frequent direct addresses to the audience and sometimes to the performers as well. This is the way it once was, or should have been, and the down-to-earth human appeal is undeniable. This is the New England that has provided the nation with a solid stock, making us what we nostalgically believe we are. Its conclusion tells us what we already know but like to hear repeated: we must appreciate the fleeting moments of life and must overcome our tendencies toward insensibility and preoccupation.

There remain some bothersome aspects about *Our Town*. It is easy to be carried away by the play's appeal, but the fact remains that this is a Norman Rockwell world, pleasant and attractive, but, alas, a world that has existed only in our most sentimental recollections. It is a WASP world; if accepted as a representation of the American small-town norm, *Our Town* is painfully misleading in its avoidance of certain realities. The Catholic church and Polish Town, plus a few "Canuck" families, are "over beyond the tracks" and can be comfortably ignored. It is a provincial, inbred town concerned with very little beyond its borders. As explained to the audience by Editor Webb, it is a town whose limited cultural and social interests lie almost entirely within itself. When asked if there is no one in town aware of social injustice and inequality, he replies, "Oh yes, everybody is,—something terrible. Seems like they spend most of their time talking about who's rich and who's poor." When pushed further as to why they don't do something about it, he can only offer this nonanswer: "Well, we're ready to listen to everybody's suggestion as to how you can see that the diligent and sensible 'll rise to the top and the lazy and quarrelsome sink to the bottom. We'll listen to anybody. Meantime until that's settled, we try to take care of those that can't help themselves, and those that can we leave alone."

In response to a question from a lady in the audience, "Is there any culture or love of beauty in Grover's Corners?" Editor Webb admits to very little. The girls who play the piano at high school commencement "ain't happy about it" (presumably no self-respecting boy would do so), and the Shakespeare that the kids read in school "seems all pretty remote to 'em." The elements of nature and the change of seasons provide a lot of pleasure, and he concludes: "But those other things—you're right, ma'am—these ain't much—'Robinson Crusoe' and the Bible; and Handel's 'Largo,' we all know that; and Whistler's 'Mother'—those are just about as far as we go." The lady's reaction, "So I thought," speaks volumes.

Wilder attempts to make his Grover's Corners into a tiny spot within the universe, somewhat holding within itself a microcosm of all existence. Introducing the pedantic university professor to explain the town's geographic and geological position, Wilder lets us know all the data of latitude and longitude, of anthropology, and the details of the Pleistocene granite on which it rests. In his own particular fashion, he seeks to place the action within a kind of cosmos, to make it all seem part of a drama that began millions of years ago, with intimations of the distant past as well as the eternal rhythm that has enabled the human race to survive. If, however, human survival has been predicated on the Grover's Corners syndrome, it has been limited and narrow; making the town a microcosm of existence remains alarmingly pretentious.

Our Town is fundamentally a fantasy, not just in terms of the talking graveyard and Emily's return to her birthday but also in terms of its whole concept of the nation's past. No argument—it *is* a pleasing fantasy, and it strikes chords of human response that enable audiences to view the play in its most attractive light. To condemn it for its flaws is preposterous, but to praise it unconditionally should prompt some earnest pondering of its ultimate meaning.

If Wilder had limited success in placing the world in microcosm in *Our Town*, he turned fully in the opposite direction with *The Skin of Our Teeth* (1942), his second Pulitzer winner. Here the macrocosm, the world in all its history, crosses the stage with the Antrobus family of Excelsior, New Jersey, who exist in all time from the age of dinosaurs to the present. It uses elaborate stylized scenery and costumes in a complex series of scenes full of anachronisms and historical convolutions in its attempt to squeeze millennia into a few short hours.

The familiar Wilder techniques are still present. A disembodied Announcer replaces the Stage Manager in setting the scene. Sabina (a Sabine woman?), the rouged and scantily dressed housemaid, from time to time plays the eternal seductress, the other woman, who sometimes confuses the issue by addressing the audience as a real actress playing the stage actress playing the part. The whole mystic nature of existence is once more considered as the planets of the solar system intrude to offer their philosophical observations.

At first encounter *The Skin of Our Teeth* can be baffling. The Announcer, assisted by front projections of satirical newsreel-style images, describes the advancing Ice Age while the Antrobus pet dinosaur suffers. In the first act, Mr. Antrobus, who is reported to have once been a gardener but "has left the situation under circumstances that have been variously reported," returns home after having invented the wheel. By the second act, when a powerful storm threatens the Atlantic City convention attended by Mr. Antrobus, the family escapes, barely, with pairs of animals in a gigantic boat. At the end, a devastating war has destroyed much of civilization, creating violent animosity between the father and son while the mother and daughter cower in the cellar subsisting on grass soup. Sabina continues to inform the audience that they should not take the play seriously.

The Skin of Our Teeth is a fascinating and not infrequently intriguing comment upon the precarious nature of mankind, demonstrating that human resilience has kept things going and probably always will, enabling us to avoid permanent destruction by "the skin of our teeth." Its fantasy, its expressionistic scenes, and its often very funny observations on mankind's inability to learn anything from the past keep the play moving at a fast clip, forcing audiences to abandon any rational analysis of it but to recognize the appalling reality on which it is based. For best comprehension, the play demands viewing more than once, a quality that goes against good theater practice and has its obvious limits.

Writing before the threat of atomic annihilation and holding his eternal faith in the positive nature of humanity, Wilder was still warning

that the apocalypse is always frighteningly close. He never became dogmatic, and even as he visualized the doom ahead, he showed a continuing
strong belief that there is something in all of us that is eternal. He admitted
to a bit of uncertainty in his own thinking by acknowledging that "I'm
optimist and pessimist and religious and non-religious. I try 'em on for size.
I'm tossed from pole to pole. I'm an awful wobbler."[4] This outlook led to
the paradoxes that are evident in both *The Skin of Our Teeth* and *Our
Town*, but perhaps the wobbling was what made the former speak so well of
our uncertainty about our place and time in the universe.

Wilder continued as a novelist throughout his life, but he always
admired the theater for its dependence on the skills of many kinds of
artists, so different from the fiction writer's mere "storytelling." The further necessity that the audience support the ritual and pretense of the play
convinced him that conventional realistic plays, trying to assert "that the
personages in the action really are . . . loses rather than gains credibility."
Wilder held that huge Greek theatrical masks or Elizabethan women
characters played by men were conventions that, like the demands placed
on the audience in *Our Town* and *The Skin of Our Teeth*, never interfered
with credibility, and that a play was better for making use of "the collaborative activity of the spectator's imagination" (Harrison, 359). That he was
able to master nonrealistic theatricalism in these two plays and succeeded
in forcing the audience to admit that the stage is not and cannot be real
life yet still can portray life's truth was a substantial accomplishment and
a tribute to his genius.[5]

William Saroyan: The Fanciful at Its Best

William Saroyan's fame was gained initially by *The Daring Young Man
on the Flying Trapeze* (1934), a collection of short stories characterizing
the people among whom he lived in the Armenian colony of southern
California. In a literary sense, especially in his plays, he was considered
the embodiment of that daring young man. The trapeze artist, of course,
must rely on perfection in timing and absolute trust in his or her partner,
something of a contradiction to the often formless and confused nature of
Saroyan's dramatic work. But there is an optimism among his cheerful
characters, in spite of precarious and stressful times, that brings them
fulfillment in the simplest pleasures and hence safety in the wide swings
of the trapeze carrying them along through life.

My Heart's in the Highlands, expanded from his earlier "The Man with His Heart in the Highlands," in turn adapted from a short story, was produced by the Group Theatre in 1939. Its suggestive setting, with an open-sided view of a small house and porch and a surrealistic tree in front, fit the play's form and substance, but it was a considerable departure from the Group's usual reliance on realistic representational staging. Although it often left audiences and critics bewildered, the play was accepted by enough of those who saw it to receive the Critics' Circle Award.

Nine-year-old Johnny, surrounded by an impecunious father who writes poetry instead of earning a living, his grandmother, and an old self-proclaimed actor, Jasper MacGregor, who plays the title song on a bugle, is keenly aware that all of this is somehow not a particularly gainful method of existence. When the family is evicted and MacGregor is carted off to the old people's home while playing the death scene from *King Lear*, Johnny exclaims to his father that something is wrong. Saroyan prefers, however, not to emphasize the "something wrong" but to imply it. The audience, along with Johnny, is left to define it on its own. With a lack of clear direction, the play assumes that the spiritual can overcome the material in the irresolute lives of the characters. Although Johnny's father shows bitterness toward those who do not appreciate his poetry and who pollute people's dreams by promoting hatred, he is a kind and generous parent. Johnny takes courage from his father's optimism, and even with his stomach empty at times, he knows that whatever is wrong, it is not his father.

In his preface to his first full-length play, entitled, not surprisingly, *The Time of Your Life* (1939), Saroyan offers the following admonition, a concise statement of his general philosophy: "In the time of your life, live—so that in that good time there shall be no ugliness for yourself or for any life your life touches. . . . In the time of your life, live—so that in that wondrous time you shall not add to the misery and sorrow of the world, but shall smile to the infinite delight and mystery of it." Produced by the Theatre Guild, *The Time of Your Life* won the 1939–40 Pulitzer Prize and has remained Saroyan's best remembered drama. It is set within a world of its own that is mostly oblivious to the trials and evils of what goes on outside, in a San Francisco waterfront bar where Nick, the proprietor, liberally dispenses his liquid cheer. Center stage is Joe, rich and expensively dressed, who drinks champagne and philosophizes that money is only useful for helping people, but hazardous if it gets in the way of the relaxed life he enjoys. Where he comes from and the source of his income remain mysteries, except for the implication that like all rich men, he derives his money from those who can ill afford to lose it. Happy in spirit, generous in his benevolence, Joe is also severely crippled, remaining seated at one of the bar's tables.

Joe, some sort of wounded saint, "born again" in his recognition of what his past has been, makes recompense by using his wealth for the down-and-outs who find their way into Nick's haven (heaven?). Dispensing financial largesse and good advice to all, Joe offers hope in this fantasy world of wish fulfillment, buying up all the newsboy's papers, convincing others that they can play the piano, sing, or dance, and making the prostitute Kitty believe that she has indeed been in burlesque. He promotes the love affair between Kitty and Tom, who waits on him and carries out his various orders; in some mysterious way, we believe, he induces the pinball machine to flash its lights, ring its bells, and pop up an American flag for young Willie, who has been feeding it his limited wealth in nickels for most of the play. Finally, old Kit Carson, teller of tall tales, gets rid of the cruel Detective Blick, who has haunted the place. Thus, all can live in the good time of their lives, ignoring the constant complaint of a character called the Arab that there is "no foundation . . . all the way down the line."[6]

Saroyan's later plays, likewise concerned with offbeat characters in loosely structured, optimistic plots, never equaled the popularity of his first two. *Love's Old Sweet Song* (1940) involves an improbable romance between a well-to-do spinster and a con man, and a family of 14 intruding Okies, and concludes with a happy ending appropriate to vaudeville. *The Beautiful People* (1941) features an even-tempered protagonist who believes that all life is miraculous. Saroyan's originality seemed less striking in these plays, which have been seen only rarely since their first appearance. Saroyan complained that while the audience enjoyed his high jinks, as in *Love's Old Sweet Song*, his message of the redemptive power of love was never understood. Either Saroyan did not sense the despair that others felt in American life during the Depression years and the approach of war, or he covered his feelings of doubt through capricious characters, plots, and settings that on the surface convey a hopeful view of life. But in spite of the ebullience of his characters and their fanciful lives, beneath the surface lie the joys and sorrows of the real world, creating a struggle between faith and doubt, with undertones of pessimism. That the human spirit can rise above the realities of what happens to and around it is Saroyan's persistent hope. Whatever they are, parables, fables, or allegories, Saroyan's plays usually opt in favor of faith, but almost never without the unsettling awareness articulated by Johnny and the Arab that doubt presses hard upon a large part of humanity.

Mary Chases's Magic Bunny

It isn't really a between-wars play, yet it doesn't belong in the postwar category either. It opened when the European conflict was winding down, and its run extended years after hostilities had ended. As one of the most successful plays in American stage history, however, Mary Chase's *Harvey* (1944) must be considered in any discussion of the make-believe world of dramatic fantasy. And unlike some of Wilder's simplistic moralizing and Saroyan's mystic obscurities, it conveys a fundamental and easily comprehensible lesson about human behavior.

By most standards of effective dramaturgy—a consistent style, careful construction, and orderly progression of events, together with uniformly developed characters—*Harvey* should soon have collapsed. It mixes realism with whimsical fantasy, interspersed with farce, plus more than a little satire. Its lopsided, hysterical first act is overweighted with wild improbabilities; thereafter the play proceeds at a moderate walking pace, abandoning along the way an incipient and uninteresting love affair. Some characters are wonderfully rounded, while others are sketchily outlined. The play explores a single situation: does or does not a six-foot one-and-a-half-inch white rabbit exist? Dramaturgical violations can mean very little to the average audience, and *Harvey* proved the point by winning the Pulitzer Prize for the season and by enjoying a run of 1,775 performances, the fifth-longest for an American legitimate play.

Elwood Dowd's introducing Harvey into the horrors of a musical afternoon at the Wednesday Forum is precisely the kind of thing most of us would relish doing, including bringing Miss Greenawalt's quart of gin into the midst of these hypocritical, social-climbing, gossiping dowagers. It is remarkably easy to accept Harvey's existence, but we all would no doubt be as confused as Vita Louise in her desperate attempt to explain him to the young psychiatrist who sees her as a dangerous mental case. By the time the doctor has discovered the punctured hat, and Wilson the orderly has read the cheerfully mocking greeting in the encyclopedia, Chase leaves us with no doubt at all.

The balance of the play is a clever satire on "normal" life, with the totally unperturbed Elwood displaying more common sense and offering sounder psychiatric advice than any professional. Elwood has long practiced what few of us can ever do: he has overcome reality in order to make life bearable. The weary Dr. Chumley's frantic effort to capture Harvey by fair means or foul attests to Elwood's deep wisdom, but the doctor is never sure if he should fear or embrace this creature. Still, there must always remain the question of Harvey's existence, regardless of every viewer's private conviction that he is present. The hat, the spontaneously opening and closing doors, and Elwood's accurate predicitions of the future are fair proofs, but nobody will admit it in public. After all, the power of suggestion is strong. Or maybe, as Dr. Chumley comes to recognize, there are facts of life that his training can never tell him. Harvey cannot be explained away either in medical jargon or as a carryover from delirium tremens, and any attempt by Dr. Sanderson to discredit him is lost in Elwood's rational explanation. Chase realized the necessity of the doubt / acceptance aspect and quickly abandoned the tryout experiment of an actor in a giant rabbit suit.

The gentle Elwood Dowd and his unseen long-eared friend have carried a plea for tolerance of human individuality, however eccentric, into the world's major languages. *Harvey*'s message about deadening conformity and its spoof of scientific efforts to eliminate social deviation have won sympathetic understanding in every type of civilized community. At the heart of things, messages or not, *Harvey* has probably succeeded because, if nothing else, it is a superb example of modern theatrical escapism. It is wacky, cockeyed, zany—name your term. Its fundamental wisdom lies in its lesson that there is much to be gained from those whose grip on reality is not as deathlike as that of most of us. Being crazy, it seems, can be great fun.

□   □   □

Fantasy has its place in drama; there is absolutely nothing wrong in seeking theatrical entertainment in unbridled make-believe. After all, it is the promise of the theater that it will always be a place where ideas, fears, and joys will receive their graphic interpretation without restriction. So why not in fantasy, as a counter to the heavy dosage of grim reality surrounding us? Indeed, why not.

9

Drama in the Folk Tradition

The United States, this new world forged by hand in relatively recent history by a population entirely of European old-world origins, has been almost completely lacking in the development of any genuinely indigenous folk tradition. The reasons are not difficult to discern. A native "folk," often semiliterate at best, are those who have developed and preserved through several generations a body of knowledge, beliefs, and customs passed on by oral tradition. Furthermore, they have remained over time removed from the main body of society by geographical or socioeconomic conditions that tend to prevent intrustion from the outside world. Thus, the accumulated myth, legend, and superstition evolving from the imagination and often naive minds of these folk develop into the collective body of folklore. America's rapid growth and headlong western expansion provided little opportunity for the establishment of the isolated pockets of culture from which a folk tradition can arise.

Only our native American Indian culture has created anything resembling truly indigenous folklore passed on by myth and legend, but it is still devoid of drama as we are defining it here. Much of what we call

American folk tradition was acquired from European immigrants, especially those who settled in the mountains of the Upper South. Many of the songs, ballads, and tales of these mountaineers are readily traceable to their origins in the British Isles or the European continent, although the peculiarities of American social conditions have created a distinctly American pattern. Furthermore, the very nature of what is considered true folk denies the possibility of establishing a body of dramatic literature. Whatever may be tagged "folk drama" is more *in* the tradition and does not spring forth as part *of* the tradition.

Genuine American folk drama is therefore a rare thing, if indeed it exists at all. The United States has nothing to compare with, say, the highly complex symbolic dramas of the Far East, surviving today in the form of the religiously stylized shadow plays of India and Java, or the elaborate puppet performances of Japan's Bunraku, all having descended from a remote past. The numbers of English holiday celebrations and the "George and Dragon" plays, once common but now rarely encountered, are fully native in their medieval origins. So are the ceremonial dances and sacred rituals of African or even American Indian tribes. Therefore, to establish ground rules in a discussion of what is commonly regarded as American folk drama, we must accept the fact that nearly all of this drama, written by professionals for an audience culturally distant from the source, is a *derived* art. But if the writer is honest, knowledgeable about the subject, and accurately represents it without caricature or comment, the result can be accepted as *folk drama*.

There are three indigenous areas out of which such folk tradition as America can offer has evolved. First, and probably the most well known, is the Upper South of Appalachia, in Tennessee, Kentucky, and the Carolinas. Second is the Deep South, with its plantation tradition and its frequent emphasis on the enslaved or freed black. Third is the Great Plains and the mountain West. One might insist on the inclusion of the Yankee tradition of New England or the more sophisticated legends of upstate New York as told, or invented by, Washington Irving, but these differ from the truly "folk" in their origin within the society as a whole, often provincial, to be sure, but hardly isolated from the social mainstream.

The popularity of nineteenth-century Indian and frontier plays would seem to justify their presence in a discussion of American dramatic folk tradition, but these works, characterized by often preposterous melodramatic romanticizing, have little to do with folk culture. The plethora of "noble savage" creations—endless variations on the Pocahontas–John Smith theme, for instance—were sheer invention. John Augustus Stone's

Metamora (1829) makes an impossibly dignified hero out of the leader of King Philip's War. Frank Murdoch's *Davy Crockett* (1872), equally outrageous, was widely favored. There was a spate of gold-mining plays and others of similar nature set in California and the Southwest, with Mexican and half-breed heavies and with comedy often supplied by gross racist caricatures of quaint queue-wearing Chinese. These plays appeared almost entirely in mining camps and Far West "opera houses," without which no boomtown could be considered respectable. They were replete with hero-heroine-villain skullduggery and rescue in impossible melodramatic plots. The most notable exceptions were *The Girl of the Golden West* (1905) by David Belasco and *The Great Divide* (1906) by William Vaughn Moody. The latter has some literary merit in its character development and its contrast of the "code of the West," not always entirely moral, with the "higher" standards of the sophisticated East. Belasco's play explores the code through the behavior of his rough but tenderhearted Girl (whose name, Minnie, is seldom mentioned), keeper of a California frontier bar, and the "road agent," Johnson, whom she loves. Its derring-do and constant melodramatics—the drip, drip of the wounded Johnson's blood from the loft above onto his pursuer, Rance, for instance—keep *The Girl* on a level inferior to Moody's play, but it was famous in its day and attracted Puccini sufficiently to transcribe it with considerable fidelity and success into his opera.

The American public's interest in the "Wild West" has, as we all know, never died away, as motion picture and television have kept its myths alive. The lonely song of the night-riding cowboy or the raucous saloon ballad, both developed and abandoned within little more than a quarter-century, are genuinely native and in the finest folk tradition. Staged dramatization of the cowpuncher's hard life, however, is all but nonexistent. The most familiar tradition of the primitively beautiful Negro spiritual, a combination of what the white man taught his captive blacks and the temperament and emotions of the African past, is equally authentic as true folk. The "Ole Black Joe" tradition of Stephen Foster and James A. Bland's "Carry Me Back to Old Virginny" is strictly derivative.

Serious interest in the authentic dramatization of American folk culture began in 1910 with the foundation of the Dakota Playmakers by Prof. Frederick Koch at the University of North Dakota. In 1918 Koch moved to the University of North Carolina, where he organized the Carolina Playmakers. At first limited to the lore of North Carolina, the Playmakers expanded to include all regions of the South, bringing American audiences an awareness of the tragedy, comedy, and melodrama inherent in the honest presentation of the simple folk of the backwoods and hills.

Before the full impact of Koch's Carolina group was made manifest, there had been some brief attempts at folk dramatization, mostly in one-act form. Lewis Beach's *The Clod* was produced by the Harvard Dramatic Club in 1914, and Susan Glaspell's *Trifles* by the Provincetown in 1916. Glaspell's vignette was not specifically localized as "folk," but its rural atmosphere and suppressed suffering gave it a definite folk quality. Beach's play, also set in a farmhouse kitchen, this time on the North–South border, was closer. Its emaciated, exhausted drudge, Mary Trask, absorbs all she can take from two brutal Confederates tracking a Union soldier she is hiding. After they force her to feed them from her meager provisions, repeatedly insult her as if she were a brainless hag, use her best towel to clean their guns, and smash her precious china teacup, she grabs a gun from the wall and kills them both. In a dazed tone she says plaintively that she must now drink out of a tin cup.

The years 1923 and 1924 were notable for several plays dealing with Carolina and Kentucky mountaineers. *The Shame Woman* by Lula Vollmer and *This Fine Pretty World* by Percy MacKaye can be disregarded. Vollmer's *Sun-Up*, however, staged at the Provincetown in May 1923, remains one of the best. Vollmer, an officer in the Theatre Guild, was a North Carolina native whose contacts and interviews with hill people as a newspaper reporter qualified her for writing this touching story of the Widow Cagle and her son. Set at the time of the First World War, the play creates an unforgettable portrait of the hardworking, pious mountain woman who finds it incomprehensible that her only son, Rufe, must go to a war neither he nor she has anything to do with, when harvesting the "craps" is far more important. In total ignorance of world affairs beyond her farm and the local town, which she cannot even name, she assumes that Rufe has to go fight the Yankees again in some place called France, just beyond the mountains. Rufe, almost equally ignorant, knows his obligation to register for the draft and leaves behind Emmy, his bride of a few hours, only to die in a conflict his mother thought had been settled once and for all. Vollmer succeeds admirably in the characterization of each of her varied mountain figures, but none is better than the Widow Cagle. The wife of a murdered moonshiner, she cannot understand why the law, in the person of Sheriff Weeks, her good friend, has to be enforced to the detriment of her family, particularly when bending and breaking the law in feuding and making illicit whiskey have been natural parts of living. Her faith in religion and in the code of the mountains is shaken when she realizes that the army deserter she has sheltered is the son of the man who killed her husband, but the voice of Rufe tells her to let him go. Vollmer permits no ridicule or comment of any sort, and the Widow Cagle, who could so easily become a L'il Abner caricature, remains one of the most believable and memorable characters in the American folk tradition.

In January 1924 Hatcher Hughes's Pulitzer Prize–winning *Hell-Bent fer Heaven* followed a similar path. Once more set in the Carolina mountains (Hughes, like Vollmer, was a North Carolina native), the play dwells not so much on native innocence and ignorance as on the latent hatreds contained in mountain feuding and the hypocrisy of superstitious evangelism. The First World War has ended, and Sid Hunt returns to his home as a legitimate war hero, ready to resume his life, marry Jude Lowry, and maintain his friendship with her brother, Andy. But the ashes of the Hunt-Lowry feud, long assumed to be cold, are fanned by the Bible-quoting, table-thumping Rufe Pryor, who, directed by the Lord, sets Sid and Andy against each other in his determination to have Jude for himself. He blows up the unfinished local dam on the twisted assumption that the deed will somehow change the social order of things. Denying his crimes, blaming all on God, Rufe is finally left behind in the rising flood waters, cursing God and screaming for help while all the others, having forgotten the feud, escape.

Hughes is in greater danger with the portrayal of Rufe Pryor than Vollmer is with her Widow Cagle. Rufe's obvious villainy, combined with his never-ending biblical injunctions, reduces the character's believability and heightens what is almost a parody of the ignorant self-made preacher, a not uncommon figure in southern mountain tales. Mag has some of the qualities of Widow Cagle, and her Civil War–veteran husband, David, is an amusing foil to Sid when the two men bicker about whose war experience was more significant, while Jude, caught between her love for Sid and loyalty to her family when David momentarily renews the feud, has more opportunity to develop than has Vollmer's Emmy. The extended melodramatics of raging storm, rising waters, near-fatal conflict between Sid and David, and Rufe's appeal to the Lord, which mesmerizes the women into a brief religious ecstasy, mount steadily into an exciting climax. *Hell-Bent fer Heaven* lacks, however, the more subdued and deeply affecting aspects of Vollmer's insight into the minds and behavior of her mountain folk.

Eugene O'Neill had dealt with a black character atavistically returning to the ancient past of race in *The Emperor Jones*, and his *All God's*

Chillun Got Wings treated blacks and whites in an urban setting. The use of blacks as protagonists and as actors in these plays was, as we have seen, of considerable significance in the maturing of the American theater. As a northerner with no experience in the mixed society of the South, O'Neill had small acquaintance with the black psyche and the deeper conflicts of racial antagonism and southern segregation. He made no attempt to write in any folk tradition at all. The first play to create a realistic black family in the rural South was the Pulitzer winner for 1926–27, *In Abraham's Bosom* by Paul Green. Produced in December 1926 at the Provincetown, it was a genuine breakthrough for folk drama involving the Negro.

Green was a product of the Carolina Playmakers and lived most of his life in North Carolina, where his poet's ear and sympathy for the blacks enabled him to catch the melody of their speech while picturing the life he saw around him. *In Abraham's Bosom* concerns the unfulfilled aspirations of southern blacks, particularly those of mixed parentage, living in a depressed world forced upon them by their "tainted" blood, but always hoping for some way out. Thus, the tragic situation of Abraham McCranie, the half-black son of a plantation owner, aspiring to teach the grossly deprived children of the area, becomes a sad and poignant reminder of the absolute station of his race. Even though his father has deeded him a farm, Abe is so set on improving his people that he permits his crops to go to ruin. The pupils don't want to learn, and all his efforts are ridiculed by other blacks. Betrayed by his no-good son, he accidentally kills his white half-brother, who was bent on helping him, and he is gunned down by vigilantes. His death, a sad and painful loss, is the result of his own confusion of ideals, his neglect of his land and faithful wife, and, in great part, his violent and uncompromising nature. The play does suggest that in spite of the evils of his environment and the irreconcilable conflicts of the miscegenation that gave him life, Abe could have come to a recognition of his own shortcomings and survived relatively securely within the system. But perhaps his insistence that "color hadn't ought to count," a line that bespeaks Green's own insistence on the dignity of blacks, would have inevitably brought his downfall. Pulitzer Prize and critical success notwithstanding, *In Abraham's Bosom* was not popular, even uptown. Sympathy for Green's ideals and his expression of hatred for the blatant practices of a dominant and fearful white society attracted only limited audiences. The episodic nature of the play (which was made up of a series of one-acts and lacked steady forward movement) could not carry it for long.

Green's next play, *The Field God* (1927), echoed both Edith Wharton's novel *Ethan Frome* and O'Neill's *Desire under the Elms*. The unhappy marriage of a farm couple is interrupted by the arrival of the wife's niece, with easily anticipated consequences. The first version permits the husband and young woman to survive the wife's dying curse to face a new life together, but the second version emphasizes the overwhelming suffering of the husband, who finally kills himself. The play is not among Green's best, but its emphasis upon the hard farm life and the question of whether God is in the church, in the fields, or only in the heart creates some good drama.

The *House of Connelly*, the Group Theatre's first production in 1931, is less episodic than *In Abraham's Bosom* and is only marginally folk, but its treatment of the decaying plantation tradition and its emphasis on rehabilitation through the soil-loving and devoted tenants who take over give it a considerable aura of the southern folk atmosphere. Its mixture of black and white cultures, especially as personified in the threatening, superstitious nature of the sinister old mulatto retainers Big Sis and Big Sue, with their often lewd and suggestive choruslike comments and their hatred for what they regard as the usurping tenant farmer's daughter, Patsy, is convincingly authentic. The optimistic ending, in which the marriage of Patsy to Will, the last male Connelly heir, is a sign of eventual family recovery, was insisted upon by the Group over strong objections by both Green and the Guild. The Group's avoidance of the original ending, in which Patsy dies at the hands of Big Sis and Big Sue, was probably a miscalculation. While still wishing to convey the ancient evils that had brought the family to such a pass that Will, his superficial spinster sister, his dying mother, and his lecherous and cynical Uncle Bob are all crumbling like the pillars of the house, the Group was so attuned to their belief in the possibility of the improvement of humanity that they demanded Patsy's survival and marriage in a happy ending out of keeping with the overall tragedy. Whether the ending is happy or tragic, Green does not despair, and his suggestion of the possibility of a new life, once all the old evils are recognized, still comes through.

Green wrote and published a series of one-act plays about the lives of southern rural folk, black and white. *Hymn to the Rising Sun* remains the best known. This sordid drama focuses on the horrifying conditions of a southern prison camp where the depraved warden puts an adolescent black into a hot box to die of suffocation for the sin of masturbation and flogs a young white prisoner nauseated by the cruelty. As the sun rises on the Fourth of July, the whipped prisoner is forced to sing "America" while the sadistic warden delivers an Independence Day speech.

Two other works, differing from Green's earlier plays, were *Johnny Johnson* (1936) and *Native Son* (1941). The latter, written in cooperation with Richard Wright, author of the original novel, was another expression of Green's concern for blacks, this time in the North. In Wright's novel, Bigger Thomas, the Chicago slum youth, perishes as he lived, lost in the city that disregarded him. Green sought, less successfully, to characterize Bigger as a young man who could come to some understanding of his own nature. *Johnny Johnson* was atypical of Green in its partly expressionistic depiction of the dehumanizing effects of war and in its use of Kurt Weill's music for the first time on the American stage. The innocent southern tomb carver's attempt to end the war by spraying the High Command with laughing gas sends him to an asylum as one deranged by "peace monomania."

DuBose Heyward, a dignified but impoverished member of Charleston's blue-blooded white aristocracy, wrote a short novel, *Porgy*, in 1925. No social reformer, he was still able to recognize the situation under which the blacks of Charleston had to live, subjected to the white man's orders and patronizing condescension. After Heyward's marriage to the playwright Dorothy Kuhns, the couple moved into an old renovated tenement across from the courtyard he had portrayed as Catfish Row, where they observed the life of this closely contained black community. In 1927 they redid the novel into a full-length play in which the speech and action of the Row's dwellers are presented without sentimentality or derision, a powerful dramatization of the shifting pattern of color and sound within the tight-knit group.

Porgy is in every instance the best play of its kind from the period of revived folk interest, remaining true to the spirit of the society it portrays. One of its most striking effects comes from the authenticity of its speech, a close transcription of the heavy, almost unintelligible Gullah dialect of the Charleston black. Next in importance is the setting itself, which the Heywards explain in the opening stage direction. The one-time elegant colonial courtyard "*reechoes with African laughter and friendly banter. . . . The audience understands none of* [the language.] *Like the laughter and movement, the twanging of a guitar from an upper window, the dancing of an urchin with a loose, shuffling step, it is part of the picture of Catfish Row as it really is—an alien scene, a people as little known to most Americans as the people of the Congo.*"

As the play moves through its comedy and its tragedy, through the violence of a hurricane and the more subtle but equally destructive human forces that intrude from outside, there is swift recognition that this is

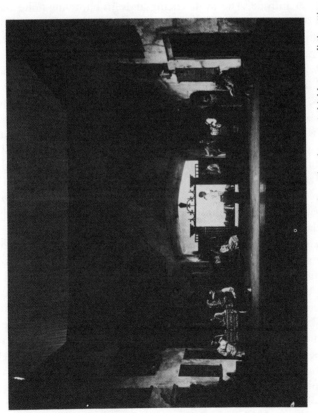

Porgy (DuBose and Dorothy Heyward, 1927). Cleon Throckmorton's highly naturalistic setting of Charleston's Catfish Row. The re-creation of a crumbling mansion converted into a ghetto tenement is meant to underline the inhabitants' isolation from the white man's outside world. In a manner beyond the realistic background of Street Scene, this setting becomes a kind of continuing participant in the actions and relationships of the characters.

no romanticized glossing, no picture of the happy-go-lucky, childlike indolence or naïveté of comic black figures who pleasantly divert white audiences with their capers. The men and women of Catfish Row are deadly earnest about their lives. The most impressive overall effect is the demonstration of the wide separation of the Row from the "civilization" beyond its walls. The white man is the intruder; his system has little meaning within the Row. No matter how vicious the crime within the circle, the white policeman is the enemy; his threats are useless. When justice is done and Porgy, the crippled beggar, kills the menacing Crown and triumphantly tells Bess, "Yo' gots a *man* now," the community's silence and professed ignorance are impenetrable when the representatives of the law intrude. The white enemy finds his blustering noise and legal social supremacy to be of little effect. Leaderless, without organization, all within the Row react without prompting when the outer gates are breached; the inner defenses invariably hold.

The Heywards, not forgetting the importance of character and plot, avoid the usual flat-dimensioned stereotypes. They give full life to Porgy, Bess, Crown, Sporting Life, and all who enter and leave the sagging gates. Porgy's great capacity for love equals Bess's desperate need for it. She is a wicked woman, even by the standards of Catfish Row, but she arouses pity and a hope that she can win her struggle for respectability. Her fight is successful until, in Porgy's momentary absence, she yields to the evil of the "happy dust" dispensed by the "high yaller" Sporting Life, himself a victim of a system in which a young black could only go North to make more than a subsistence living, unfortunately on the shady side of the law.

The continued melodramatics of the action and the interplay of the Row's inhabitants provide a constant feeling throughout that violence is something these people have learned to expect and to endure. The plot never departs beyond probability; plot and character combine with absolute conviction. Furthermore, the violence has no relationship to the inhabitants' plight vis-a-vis the white man's attitude. The play never descends into a social document, nowhere preaches or extols. Instead, it becomes the drama of a vibrant people's collective life, and we can meet it on no other terms.

While the musical stage of the period is of little concern here, consideration of *Porgy* must take note of its greatest source of world fame, George Gershwin's 1935 musical *Porgy and Bess*. Backed by Ira Gershwin's lyrics and DuBose Heyward's faithfully adapted libretto, Gershwin's score turned the original play into a genuinely American opera of magnificent proportions. To call it a folk opera is not completely accurate, since it is, of course, derived and not original in the true folk sense; the music is in many ways pure Broadway. But Gershwin made a very carefully detailed background study in a serious attempt to capture the tones, rhythms, and cadences of the southern black tradition. The result was a major historical event for the American musical stage. Whether in its light opera form with spoken dialogue, or in the less frequently performed full operatic version complete with arias and recitatives, *Porgy and Bess* has been enthusiastically welcomed from Moscow to Paris, Belgrade, and London, and in Milan's La Scala. It has had no equals and stands as its composer's greatest achievement, arguably the finest contribution to American musical theater. [1]

In 1939, a dozen years after *Porgy*, the Heywards dramatized another of DuBose's novels, *Mamba's Daughters*. Also set in Catfish Row, the emphasis of this play is considerably different from that of *Porgy*. Its story concerns the attempt of Lissa, with a voice of operatic potential, to escape North, where her talents have a real chance of recognition. Filled with melodramatic contrivance, the play lacks the quality of the folk life so beautifully created in *Porgy*. The singing of Ethel Waters in the starring role made the play and its incidental music a moderate success.

Marc Connelly, the successful Kaufman collaborator, is probably best known as the creator of *The Green Pastures* (1929), based loosely on Roark Bradford's southern Negro sketches, "Ol' Man Adam and His Chillun." If he had written nothing else, his name would be famous for this one work alone.

This dramatization of events from the Old Testament is set within the framework of a black Sunday School teacher's attempt to explain the mysteries of the Bible to his curious young charges. To make everything comprehensible, the events and the characters are all shown in the simplified terms of the rural black experience in the Deep South. From the joys of the opening Heavenly Fish Fry and the grand buildup of the entrance of De Lawd—"Gangway! Gangway for de Lawd God Jehovah!" shouts the Archangel Gabriel—the episodes depict creation (the earth is made from the excess firmament needed to flavor the boiled custard), the Garden of Eden, and the stories of Cain and Abel, the Flood, the Exodus, and so on in delightful comedy and serious drama. God comes to realize that he has created an imperfect world that defies his ability to correct; as the problems mount he sighs, "Even bein' God ain't a bed of roses." De Lawd discovers a basic principle of all existence, heavenly or otherwise: that one learns and grows only through suffering. He sends down his son to be a part of life on earth and to bear the cross and die.

The Green Pastures has been criticized for its condescending view

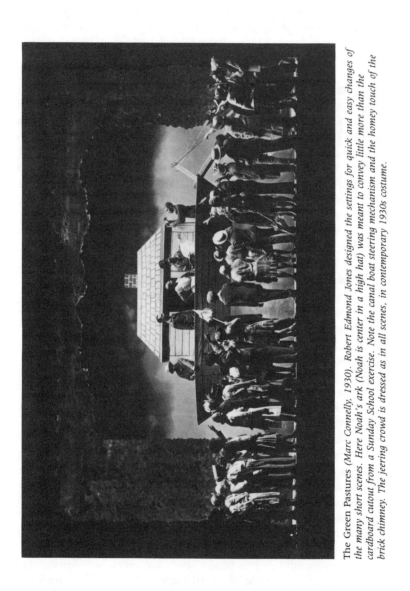

The Green Pastures *(Marc Connelly, 1930). Robert Edmond Jones designed the settings for quick and easy changes of the many short scenes. Here Noah's ark (Noah is center in a high hat) was meant to convey little more than the cardboard cutout from a Sunday School exercise. Note the canal boat steering mechanism and the homey touch of the brick chimney. The jeering crowd is dressed as in all scenes, in contemporary 1930s costume.*

of ignorant folk who visualize a fish fry with God as the height of happiness or who see whorish Babylon in a Negro nightclub. This criticism ignores the sincerely religious atmosphere, which Connelly explains in his note to the published version:

> "The Green Pastures" is an attempt to present certain aspects of a living religion in the terms of its believers. . . . Unburdened by the differences of more educated theologians they accept the Old Testament as a chronicle of wonders which happened to people like themselves in vague but actual places, and rules of conduct, true acceptance of which will lead them to a tangible, three-dimensional Heaven. . . . The Lord may look like the Reverend Mr. Dubois as our Sunday School teacher speculates in the play, or he may resemble another believer's own grandfather. In any event, His face will be familiar to the one who has come for his reward.

The acceptance of the play by both black and white audiences is proof of its inoffensive and positive nature. When it was first proposed there was considerable fear that it would indeed offend as some kind of racial slur. When Richard B. Harrison, the original Lawd, was offered the part, he is reported to have declined, but fortunately for all concerned, he reconsidered and ultimately became convinced of its merits. His dignified, frock-coated appearance and his benevolent yet frequently angry concern for his people brought the God figure to life in one of the most outstanding performances in American theater history. Backed by a huge cast of experienced black actors and the magnificent Hall Johnson choir, *The Green Pastures* was an instant sensation, won the Pulitzer Prize for 1929–30, and ran for six years. Its film version with Rex Ingram as De Lawd was equally impressive. It remains an important drama, although as shown by a failed revival as late as 1951, a changing and more enlightened view of American blacks has possibly made the play's tone less acceptable. This is a regrettable attitude, for *The Green Pastures*, a play about all mankind, still retains its universal value. When the black God is driven to renounce his people, he speaks directly and equally against all of whatever race.[2]

One might try to dismiss the second-longest-running play in American theater history (3,182 performances) as a sensational and sordid attempt to capitalize on human misery and degradation and refuse to acknowledge any "redeeming social value," but it can't be done. *Tobacco*

Road, adapted in 1933 by Jack Kirkland from Erskine Caldwell's novel, aimlessly repulsive as it seems, remains a unique classic. Having faced total condemnation by nearly every opening-night critic, the play could not have held the stage for nearly eight years merely on the basis of its shock value.

Compared to the dignity of the Widow Cagle of *Sun-Up* or the decency of the Hunts and Lowrys in *Hell-Bent fer Heaven*, the degeneracy of the Lesters can be difficult to place in any legitimate folk tradition. Their salaciousness and the shiftlessness of Jeeter would appear to be a crude parody of the red-dirt Georgia farm family of hillbilly jokes. Caldwell's success (the Kirkland adaptation is so close to the original that for all intents and purposes it is Caldwell's play) is achieved by making the horror of white-trash existence into a genuine comedy. The macabre outhouse humor permits the characters to become credible, if grotesque, and conveys an underlying sense of outrage at a society that permits all of this to occur. What makes the comedy succeed is Caldwell's full recognition of the need for absolute audience detachment, quite easy for the audience to achieve as it witnesses the grossness enacted on stage. And a thoroughly naturalistic comedy it is, unrestrained in its literal earthiness of speech, its physical and sexual brutalities, and its utterly callous lack of human compassion. Joseph Wood Krutch, never one to be taken in by stage fraud or chicanery, found that for all the lack of ordinary humanity in the hideous nature of things, "one is bound to regard these crimes almost as one regards the deeds of that traditional embodiment of moral imbecility, Mr. Punch." Krutch saw *Tobacco Road* as a funny play, which, "though perhaps ambiguously so—it was, I believe, intended to be" (Krutch, 123). In the later years of the twentieth century, characterized by strong interest in ecology and rural preservation, Jeeter Lester's insistence on staying on the land, no matter how impoverished his family is, arouses a certain admiration.

□   □   □

From *Sun-Up* to *Tobacco Road*, the American drama between the wars treated a variety of native folk groups in manners unique to the period and never since emulated. Sympathy with the mountain whites was clear and was generally attractive to the sophisticated New York audience. But in retrospect, it was the picture of the blacks that made the drama that grew out of folk tradition so significant. Long gone were the stereotypical characters, played by whites in blackface, that had fostered the picture of Uncle Tom as faithful, loyal, and trusting, even in the face of brutal abuse, and of Topsy, who "just growed," as the carefree pickaninny. From Emperor Brutus Jones to the crippled Porgy, black American characters, played by black performers, came to life in a way that helped to reshape America's aesthetic and social view of the race.

epilogue

It has been said that America came of age through the disillusionment of
World War I. Nowhere is that process of maturation more apparent than
in the theater and the drama written for it. To audiences becoming
attuned to the fresh ideas of artistic expression fostered by the "new spirit,"
the nineteenth century seemed archaic and simplistic. The playwrights
who had earlier made careers of patching together formulaic patterns in
melodrama, farce, or sentimental romance now discovered that their
picture of human nature and society would be expected to convey an
essential accuracy and relevance to the time and to give serious consideration to American mores and economic conditions.

The award of the Pulitzer Prize during the period between the
wars provides evidence of the break with the past. The prize was originally
conceived in 1918 as a reward for an American play "which shall best
represent the educational value and power of the stage in raising the
standard of good morals, good taste, and good manners." By 1928, happily, the Pulitzer committee omitted the morals, taste, and manners
stipulation. The choices for the first award, Jesse Lynch Williams's *Why*

Marry? (1917–18), and for the third, Zona Gale's *Miss Lulu Bett* (1920–21), were comedy romances from the past. The second Pulitzer Prize, for O'Neill's *Beyond the Horizon* (1919–20) (none was awarded for 1918–19), and nearly all subsequent awards, went to plays showing genuine originality and an escape from the nineteenth century's grip. Winning dramas such as *They Knew What They Wanted*, *Craig's Wife*, *In Abraham's Bosom*, and *Street Scene* would have found no audience at all in the previous century. The so-called psychological (and roaring) twenties and the fervently political thirties provided energy that opened the stage to stimulating new ideas.

Another indication of the break is in the history of long runs on Broadway. In the early 1920s a run of 600 consecutive performances, like that enjoyed by *Broadway*, was the great exception. The artistic throwback of Anne Nichols's stereotyped Irish and Jewish families in *Abie's Irish Rose* (1927) started the long-run tradition with 2,327 appearances. Surpassed only by *Life with Father* and *Tobacco Road*, and closely followed by *Harvey*, it now stands as a quaint museum piece, copied in TV sitcoms but almost never on Broadway. Long runs and Pulitzer Prizes do not always identify the significant work of art. Shorter and even aborted runs of such radical creations as *The Cradle Will Rock*, or the dramatic social commentaries of Anderson, Sherwood, and Hellman and the tragedies of O'Neill, prove the point.

The depressed 1930s were, paradoxically, the greatest era of legitimate American drama. The continued thriving of Broadway, where hundreds of new productions were mounted in some 70 theatres, was augmented by the unprecedented efforts of the Federal Theatre Project in bringing dramatic art literally to the masses and in speeding the long-delayed recognition of blacks as artists, first encouraged by the Harlem Renaissance. Unfortunately, the period did little for the women playwrights who at the beginning of the century seemed so promising. Glaspell, Crothers, Vollmer, and others were not leaders of any school or trend. Clare Boothe's pride of bitches and Hellman's leader of the despoiling foxes, Regina Giddens, were but momentary glitches in the general rule of male domination both in writing and in characterization.

Certain themes of the twenties and thirties consistently reappeared. A particular kind of loneliness, an integral part of the era, was a recurring motif. Some of it led to self-recognition, some to tragedy and death. Mrs. Maurrant of *Street Scene*, Mio of *Winterset*, Mrs. Phelps of *The Silver Cord*, Lavinia Mannon of *Mourning Becomes Electra*, Nina Leeds of *Strange Interlude*, and Joe Bonaparte of *Golden Boy* all strove to overcome their loneliness and inability to find an environment in which to confirm their identities. The plea of O'Neill's Yank in *The Hairy Ape*, "Where do I fit in?" was ever-present.

A second and consistent central theme was that of the American family caught between the security of home and the need to assert a social individuality. It was present in Hellman's warring Hubbards, in Odets's mom-dominated Bergers, in O'Neill's mismatched Cabots and Mannons, and even in the Millers of *Ah, Wilderness!*

Then there was a third, the adaptation of certain archetypal patterns to American culture. O'Neill's unabashed use of Greek tragic forms and assorted Dionysian and Apollonian themes of man and nature stands foremost. But in *Winterset* Anderson conveyed the Christian descent into hell, and in his historical plays there were archetypes of kings and queens.

In spite of the perilous times, playwrights voiced a new enthusiasm for the future of America. There was a sense of history, of the background against which America had been formed. Washington and Lincoln had their day as well. Politics was not without its followers, and society's ills were not uncomon subjects in Odets, Lawson, Sherwood, and Anderson. Allegory held its own in O'Neill's *The Emperor Jones* and *The Great God Brown*, in Rice's *The Adding Machine*, and Barry's *Hotel Universe*. Thornton Wilder perfected it in *Our Town* and in *The Skin of Our Teeth*. The era of the twenties and thirties was an exhilarating time for audiences and playwrights alike. The theater was diverse and stimulating; it provided a forum for many new voices and for a variety of stagings. Broadway dominated the theater scene, but it was an open Broadway, with great possibilities for originality. It was a playful theater, which, in accord with American pragmatism, proposed no ideological solutions but generally maintained hope for human individuals and for America as a country. Even the agitprop dramas visualized better days if the capitalistic system could be adjusted. Although harrowed by the war just past and the war to come, with the Great Depression in between, the American theater reflected an energetic, forward-moving land, to which it enthusiastically contributed its very lively art.

chronology

Date	Drama, Literature, Art*	World and National Events
1913	New York Armory Exhibition opens 17 February. Eugene O'Neill copyrights his first play, *A Wife for a Life*.	United States blockades Mexico to help support revolution. Federal Reserve System established.
1914	O'Neill enters George Pierce Baker's 47 Workshop at Harvard.	World War I begins in August; United States declares neutrality. Henry Ford establishes basic wage of $5 a day.
1915	Neighborhood Playhouse opens. Provincetown Players and Washington Square Players established.	First continential telephone hookup. *Lusitania* is sunk 7 May.
1916	First production of an O'Neill play, *Bound East for Cardiff*, 28	General Pershing enters Mexico. First woman elected to Congress,

*Dates indicate production of plays.

266

July. Susan Glaspell's *Trifles*. Carl Sandburg's *Chicago Poems* published. The Cleveland Playhouse and Pasadena Community Playhouse founded.

Jeanette Rankin, Montana. Woodrow Wilson reelected: "He kept us out of war."

1917   Strike by Actors' Equity closes down New York theaters. O'Neill's *The Long Voyage Home*.

United States enters World War I in April; Russian Revolution begins.

1918   First Pulitzer Prize for drama awarded to Jesse Lynch Williams's *Why Marry?* Theatre Guild organized 19 December.

First World war ends 11 November. Influenza epidemic kills an estimated 20 million worldwide.

1919   Edna St. Vincent Millay's *Aria da Capo*. First Guild production, Jacinto Benavente's *Bonds of Interest*, 14 April. Sherwood Anderson's story collection *Winesburg, Ohio* published.

First transatlantic flight is made, with many stops. Boston police strike brings national attention to Calvin Coolidge. Eighteenth amendment establishes prohibition.

1920   O'Neill's *Beyond the Horizon* wins his first Pulitzer Prize. O'Neill's *The Emperor Jones*. Sinclair Lewis's *Main Street* and F. Scott Fitzgerald's *This Side of Paradise* published.

Sacco and Vanzetti convicted. Nineteenth amendment gives vote to women. First licensed radio broadcast is made. Warren G. Harding elected; return to "normalcy." United States rejects League of Nations.

1921   O'Neill's *Anna Christie* wins his second Pulitzer.

United States signs peace treaty with Germany.

1922   Jig Cook goes to Greece. O'Neill's *The Hairy Ape*.

Labor strife in Herrin, Illinois, coal mines leaves 36 dead. Mussolini marches on Rome, establishes dictatorship.

1923   Formation of the Provincetown Players "triumvirate" of Eugene O'Neill, Kenneth Magowan, and Robert Edmond Jones. Elmer Rice's *The Adding Machine*.

Death of Harding; Calvin Coolidge becomes president.

1924   Cook dies in Greece. Maxwell Anderson and Laurence Stalling's *What Price Glory?*; George S.

Election of Coolidge. Nellie Ross first woman elected governor, Wyoming. Lenin dies.

Kaufman and Marc Connelly's
Beggar on Horseback; O'Neill's
Desire under the Elms; George
Kelly's *The Show-Off*.

1925	Kelly's *Craig's Wife*. George Pierce Baker moves from Harvard to Yale to found what will become Yale School of Drama.	Scopes "monkey trial" in Tennessee.
1926	Sidney Howard's *The Silver Cord*; George Abbott's *Broadway*; O'Neill's *The Great God Brown*.	
1927	Neighborhood Playhouse closes. New Playwrights' Theatre begins. S. N. Behrman's *The Second Man*; DuBose and Dorothy Heyward's *Porgy*. Al Jolson's *The Jazz Singer*, first sound motion picture, opens in New York.	Charles Lindbergh flies across Atlantic nonstop.
1928	Guild produces its first O'Neill play, *Marco Millions*. Ben Hecht and Charles MacArthur's *The Front Page*. *Strange Interlude* wins O'Neill's third Pulitzer.	Herbert Hoover elected. Stalin has absolute power in the Soviet Union. Kellogg-Briand Peace Pact signed.
1929	Marc Connelly's *The Green Pastures*; John Balderston's *Berkeley Square*.	Stock market crashes 29 October. Albert Fall convicted in Teapot Dome scandal.
1930	Maxwell Anderson's *Elizabeth the Queen*; Barry's *Hotel Universe*; Glaspell's *Alison's House*.	Al Capone and bootlegging gangsters flourish in Chicago and other cities.
1931	Group Theatre established. Paul Green's *The House of Connelly*; Behrman's *Brief Moment*; Crothers's *As Husband's Go*; Robert Sherwood's *Reunion in Vienna*.	Empire State Building opens.
1932	Behrman's *Biography*; O'Neill's *Mourning Becomes Electra*.	Lindbergh baby kidnapping and murder leads to "Lindbergh Law," making kidnapping a federal offense. Veterans' Bonus March on Washington, D.C. Franklin Roosevelt elected.

1933   Left-wing Theatre Union formed. Sidney Kingsley's *Men in White*; Erskine Caldwell and Jack Kirkland's *Tobacco Road*; O'Neill's *Ah, Wilderness!*

Depression deepens. Roosevelt declares bank holiday to stabilize nation's collapsing financial structure. Eighteenth amendment repealed. Hitler becomes chancellor of Germany.

1934   O'Neill begins 12-year hiatus from the theater. Lillian Hellman's *The Children's Hour*.

1935   Gershwin's *Porgy and Bess*; Clifford Odets's *Waiting for Lefty*; Kingsley's *Dead End*; Maxwell Anderson's *Winterset*; Odets's *Awake and Sing*; Sherwood's *The Petrified Forest*. Federal Theatre Project begins.

Social Security Act enacted. Mussolini invades Ethiopia.

1936   Federal Theatre Project's "voodoo" *Macbeth*; Sherwood's *Idiot's Delight*; George S. Kaufman and Moss Hart's *You Can't Take It with You*; Clare Boothe's *The Women*. International Ladies' Garment Workers Union presents *Pins and Needles*.

Boulder Dam completed. Roosevelt reelected; wins 46-state landslide. Hitler occupies Rhineland. Spanish Civil War begins.

1937   Marc Blitzstein's *The Cradle Will Rock*; John Steinbeck's *Of Mice and Men*; Odets's *Golden Boy*. Orson Welles establishes Mercury Theatre. Playwrights' Company established.

Roosevelt fails to pack the Supreme Court. First big steel and auto labor contracts signed.

1938   Welles's Halloween radio broadcast of "The War of the Worlds" terrifies the country. Mercury Theatre collapses. Thornton Wilder's *Our Town*; Sherwood's *Abe Lincoln in Illinois*; Odets's *Rocket to the Moon*.

Britain and France appease Germany at Munich.

1939   Federal Theatre Project killed by Congress. Hellman's *The Little Foxes*; Barry's *The Philadelphia Story*; Willian Saroyan's *The*

New York World's Fair opens. Hitler invades Poland to begin World War II. United States declares neutrality. Hitler and Stalin

Time of Your Life; Howard Lind-
say and Russell Crouse's *Life with
Father*. Steinbeck's *The Grapes of
Wrath* published.

sign 10-year peace pact. Spanish
Civil War ends.

1940   Sherwood's *There Shall Be No
        Night*; James Thurber and Elliott
        Nugent's *The Male Animal*.

Fall of France and Battle of Britain. United States begins peace-
time draft. Roosevelt elected to
third term.

1941   Hellman's *Watch on the Rhine*;
        Paul Green and Richard Wright's
        Native Son.

Lend-Lease program to aid Britain begins. Japanese attack Pearl
Harbor 7 December.

1942   Maxwell Anderson's *The Eve of
        St. Mark*; Steinbeck's *The Moon
        Is Down*.

Battle of Midway. Allies invade
North Africa.

1943

Allies invade Italy.

1944   Mary Chase's *Harvey*.

D-Day, 6 June. Allies invade the
Continent. Roosevelt elected to
fourth term.

1945

Roosevelt dies 12 April; Harry
Truman becomes president. Germany surrenders 7 May. United
States drops atom bomb on Hiro-
shima 6 August. Japan surrenders
9 August.

notes and references

Many of the plays discussed in this volume are available in a number of different editions and anthologies. Therefore, quotations from plays are not accompanied by page references. Please refer to the Bibliography for a complete list of primary sources used.

Prologue

1. Floyd Dell, *Homecoming: An Autobiography* (Port Washington, N.Y.: Kennikat, 1969), 218.

2. See the brief discussion by Beaumont Newhall, "Stieglitz and '291,' " in *Art in America* 51 (February 1963): 48–50.

3. Goldman was an early acquaintance of Eugene O'Neill and is widely considered to be the model for the offstage Rosa Parritt in *The Iceman Cometh*. See Winifred Frazer, *E. G. and E. G. O.: Emma Goldman and "The Iceman Cometh"* (Gainesville: University Presses of Florida, 1974).

Chapter 1

1. Alice Lewisohn Crowley, *The Neighborhood Playhouse: Leaves from a Theatre Scrapbook* (New York: Theatre Arts, 1959), 237. Hereafter cited in the text as Crowley.

2. Susan Glaspell, *The Road to the Temple* (New York: Stokes, 1927); Helen Deutsch and Stella Hanau, *The Provincetown: A Story of the Theatre* (New York: Farrar & Rinehart, 1931).

3. C. W. E. Bigsby, *A Critical Introduction to Twentieth-Century American Drama*, vol. 1 (Cambridge: Cambridge University Press, 1982), 6. Hereafter cited in the text as Bigsby.

4. By 1929 O'Neill and his colleagues were firmly committed to Broadway, and the Greenwich Village Theatre was also unable to continue. An attempt to establish itself as the Irish Theatre failed, and in 1930 the building was demolished.

5. It may be skewing things a bit to include Stowe in this discussion of drama, but her name was uniformly associated with the play, despite her strong objections. Gaudy posters advertising this "sterling historical drama," this "great and moral play . . . with all the grandeur and magnitude that the mind of man ever conceived," almost never mentioned any playwright, stating only that it was "by H. B. Stowe."

6. Revealing something about the contemporary attitude toward Akins as a writer and a prizewinner, members of the New York Drama Critics' Circle were so incensed at her receipt of the Pulitzer for what they saw as an unoriginal melodrama that they decided to make their own awards thereafter.

Chapter 2

1. Quoted in Jordan Y. Miller, *American Dramatic Literature* (New York: McGraw-Hill, 1961), 37. Howard "proved" his theme in his two most famous plays, *The Henrietta* (1887), a satire on financial life, and *Shenandoah* (1888), the first important Civil War melodrama. In the latter play his "laws" are especially apparent: all the proper rewards and punishments are meted out to spotless heroes and heroines and skulking villains.

2. The original version did not permit a reunion of Margaret and Philip Fleming, but it was clear that the husband was at fault and would be made to suffer for his infidelity (as women do). Herne could not permit the "other woman," the sister of the Flemings' housemaid, whom Philip had seduced, to live (Howard would approve). Furthermore, he drives Margaret into blindness at the shocking discovery of it all, a result amply telegraphed by earlier references to

an affliction of her eyes. The revised conclusion, in which Margaret not only allows Philip to return on *her* conditions but, at the curtain, prepares to suckle Philip's bastard infant, was a bit beyond what audiences of the day would accept.

3. George Bernard Shaw was one of the first and strongest supporters of Ibsen. His *The Quintessence of Ibsenism* (1891, revised 1913) remains one of the best critical analyses of the Norwegian and includes samplings from some of the vituperative public assaults upon him. Plays by both authors were often subject to censorship, police reprisals, and other indignities during the early years of their careers.

4. Gas and electricity vied with each other in the theater for some years; actors and producers were reluctant to abandon what they felt were the softer tones of gas. But the constant risks of gas were obvious, and by 1887, when two disastrous fires occurred in Europe and England, electricity was installed in nearly all of the important theaters in Europe, England, and America.

5. Eric Bentley, in some of his criticism, uses *drame* to identify the nontragic, noncomic realistic play, but the term has not found wide use. It is sometimes a convenient substitute, however, for the more comprehensive *drama*.

6. Strindberg is one of the best examples of a playwright who went both directions. His violent sex battles in *The Father* (1887) and other plays are in the best tradition of stage naturalism.

7. At the same time other disciplines were developing expressionistic techniques. On the screen the image of a mind deranged within an irrational society was portrayed in Eric Pommer's classic horror film *The Cabinet of Dr. Caligari* (1919). Paintings by Munch and Picasso cannot be discounted.

8. The Guild took its historic, if tenuous, initial steps by opening a theater that had housed two other historical events. First was the appearance of William Gillette's tremendous success, *Secret Service* (1895), the best of the Civil War melodramas. Second was the sensational American premiere of Shaw's *Mrs. Warren's Profession* (1905), which had been banned in New Haven and so shocked the New York police that producer Augustin Daly and his star were arrested for putting on an immoral play.

9. Walter Prichard Eaton, *The Theatre Guild: The First Ten Years* (New York: Brentano's, 1929), 36–37. Hereafter cited in the text as Eaton.

10. One of the most noteworthy was *Heartbreak House*, which appeared on 10 November 1920. Shaw had been denied production in Britain because of his unpopular antiwar stance.

11. Nancy L. Roberts and Arthur W. Roberts, *As Ever, Gene: The Letters of Eugene O'Neill to George Jean Nathan* (Rutherford, N.J.: Fairleigh Dickinson University Press, 1987), 34. Hereafter cited in the text as Roberts.

12. The abundance of material in the several biographies and other studies of O'Neill makes redundant here any background discussion of his life. Knowl-

edge of his family traumas from childhood through his three marriages, his unsettled and derelict youth, including his sanitorium confinement for what was diagnosed as incipient tuberculosis, and his ambivalence, with so much attendant guilt, toward women provides considerable information about the thematic origins of his plays and the rationale behind his major characters. The plays, however, must stand on their own; what we know of their origins may enlighten us about the artist as a person and why he did what he did, but that knowledge has nothing to do with the final critical reaction, and very little to do with the public acceptance of the plays.

13. At least one critic called O'Neill the "Conrad of Playwrights." The first title of the play almost certainly was inspired by Joseph Conrad (1857–1924), whose sea stories had influenced O'Neill before he ever went to Provincetown. *Thirst, Fog,* and *Warnings* each involve the sea, as does *The Personal Equation* (also known as *The Second Engineer*), which O'Neill wrote in Baker's class in 1915. The later plays of the *Glencairn* series further demonstrate the writer's Conrad-like affinities. The original "Children" was first published in a volume of the same name, edited by Jennifer McCabe Atkinson (Washington, D.C.: NCR Microcard Editions, 1972), together with *Bread and Butter* (1914), *Now I Ask You* ((1917), and *Shell Shock* (1918), none of which was produced.

14. O'Neill's acting career, such as it was, had begun with his role as the mulatto sailor in the single appearance of *Thirst* in Provincetown during the summer of 1916, but it ended abruptly with his role as the First Mate in *Bound East for Cardiff*. His paralyzing stage fright was too strong for subsequent performances. In *Before Breakfast* his hand appeared from offstage and he emitted a required groan, but he did not walk onto the stage itself.

15. This reference by Mantle is not surprising since the name O'Neill was still associated with the now hoary melodrama *The Count of Monte Cristo*, played endlessly throughout the country by James O'Neill. *In The Zone* subsequently proved popular enough on a 34-week tour of the Orpheum vaudeville circuit to bring the 28-year-old O'Neill his first substantial income.

16. Jordan Y. Miller, *Eugene O'Neill and the American Critic* (Hamden, Conn.: Shoe String Press, 1962; rev. ed., 1973) and Margaret Loftus Ranald, *The Eugene O'Neill Companion* (Westport, Conn.: Greenwood Press, 1984) contain complete lists of all surviving and destroyed O'Neill plays before 1920.

17. Barrett H. Clark, *Eugene O'Neill: The Man and His Plays* (New York: McBride, 1926, 1929; rev. ed., New York: Dover, 1947), 56, 59.

18. William L. Sipple. "From Stage to Screen: Long Voyage Home and Long Day's Journey into Night." *Eugene O'Neill Newsletter* 7 (Spring 1983): 10–14.

19. *The Dreamy Kid* will be discussed later in conjunction with the more famous black play, *The Emperor Jones*. The only other short play of any note was O'Neill's attempt at a pantomimic dramatization of Coleridge's *The Rime of the*

Ancient Mariner, which the Provincetown staged on 6 April 1924. It was a total failure, and most critics, by that time regularly reviewing O'Neill's plays, felt he was far out of his element.

Chapter 3

1. One of the most interesting aspects of Eugene O'Neill's career is the evidence of his steady artistic growth, culminating in the plays that have permanently established him as a world figure: *The Iceman Cometh* and *Long Day's Journey Into Night,* and the increasingly important *A Moon for the Misbegotten,* all written at the end of his productive life. The high point of O'Neill's artistry remains with these last plays; there is no disillusioning anticlimax, and the memory of his many catastrophes is gratefully obliterated.

Speculation can be made, however, regarding what direction his career might have taken had his creative life not been cut short by progressive physical disability. The remarkable scholarship of Virginia Floyd, whose search through the O'Neill archives at Yale has provided revealing details of the scope of O'Neill's last abandoned efforts, shows the still experimental, sometimes mystic playwright outlining works that might well have been his crowning achievements, or might equally well have been the greatest debacles of his career. See Floyd's *Eugene O'Neill at Work* (New York: Ungar, 1981) and *Eugene O'Neill: The Unfinished Plays* (New York: Ungar, 1988). The latter volume reproduces the substantial surviving fragments of scenarios and scenes from "The Last Conquest," "The Visit of Malatesta," and "Blind Alley Guy," all works in progress during the early 1940s, and all abandoned as O'Neill's health rapidly deteriorated.

2. O'Neill never reacted publicly with indignation, but he was not above expressing some strong personal feelings in letters to his friends and professional associates. Though never aired in public, O'Neill's disagreement with such close acquaintances as George Jean Nathan, who never hesitated to lambaste O'Neill in the press for his frequent sins, could be quite pointed; see Roberts, passim. The exchanges with long-time friend and producer Kenneth Macgowan are also revealing; see Jackson Bryer, *The Theatre We Worked For: The Letters of Eugene O'Neill to Kenneth Macgowan* (New Haven: Yale University Press, 1987).

3. See Jordan Y. Miller, *Playwright's Progress: O'Neill and the Critics* (Chicago: Scott, Foresman, 1975), for a collection of favorable and unfavorable reviews of each major play, Hereafter cited in the text as Miller, *Progress.*

4. Arthur and Barbara Gelb, *O'Neill* (New York: Harper & Row, 1960), 413. Hereafter cited in the text as Gelb.

5. *Thirst,* presented in 1916 at the Wharf Theatre in Provincetown, featured a mulatto sailor, but the part was played by O'Neill himself.

6. The black dialect that O'Neill used in *The Dreamy Kid* and in *Jones* at first glance seems to be a rather crude form associated mainly with vaudeville and other comic black characters. This may be somewhat true in the shorter play, but in *Jones* the speech pattern has been shown to be remarkably akin to the Gullah dialect of southern blacks, particularly in South Carolina.

7. Oliver M. Sayler, "Delving into the Sub-conscious," *Freeman* 24 (November 1920).

8. Hubert H. Harrison, "The Emperor Jones," *Negro World*, 4 June 1921.

9. John Shand, "The Emperor Jones," *New Statesman* 25 (19 September 1925): 628–29.

10. The play soon found its way into other media, namely, an expanded film version in 1933 starring Paul Robeson, who succeeded Gilpin in the role uptown and in London, and an opera by Louis Gruenberg, also in 1933, sung by the great American baritone Lawrence Tibbett in blackface. Robeson's film version was adapted by Dubose Heyward, and about half of it was devoted to a detailed coverage of Jones's background, creating a considerable change in emphasis by the time the O'Neill portion took over.

11. Travis Bogard, *Contour in Time: The Plays of Eugene O'Neill* (New York: Oxford, 1972), 134.

12. See L. E. Levick, "*The Hairy Ape* and the IWW: Marine Transport Workers Turn Dramatic Critics and Praise O'Neill," *New York Call*, 14 May 1922; R. Robbins, "The IWW on the Stage," *Industrial Solidarity*, 8 April 1922; and R. Robbins, "The Emperor O'Neill." *Industrial Pioneer* 2 (January 1925): 26–27. The Industrial Workers of the World (IWW) was a far-left union organization that was generally perceived to be a group of bomb-throwing terrorists, an opinion voiced by Yank in his visit to the union hall.

13. See Patterson James, "Off the Record," *Billboard* 34 (15 April 1922): 18, for a wild and vitriolic attack against the play, in which the critic is not only grossly offended by action and language but cannot distinguish between what he assumes is a naturalistic portrayal of life in the stokehold and O'Neill's intended stylization.

14. Quoted in Oscar Cargill, N. Bryllion Fagin, and William J. Fisher, *O'Neill and His Plays* (New York: New York University Press, 1961), 110. Hereafter cited in the text as Cargill.

15. O'Neill subtitled *The Hairy Ape* "A Comedy of Ancient and Modern Life." Perhaps he felt this would provide a universality lacking in the "animalistic" main title, but he made no attempt to clarify his meaning. The best one can do is to make the broad assumption of a rough Dante-esque parallel in Yank's progress from hell, the stokehold, through a variety of purgatorial experiences in his vengeful pursuit of the offending Mildred, to the "heaven" of a gorilla's cage,

where he at last "belongs" and finds peace in death. "Comedy" in this case would be defined in the medieval sense of a narrative with a happy ending, including its metaphysical theme of mankind as ever subjected to the depths of hell but striving for the heights of heaven. There could also be a twisted application of "comedy" to Yank's harrowing physical and psychical experiences, a turnabout on the common expression of the "human comedy" of mankind's experience. Yank also attains the symbolic stature of a universal character of no particular time who encounters the scorn and degradation that might be visited upon such a creature in any era, ancient or modern.

16. Among the most outraged was New York's Mayor John Hylan. Learning that a white woman was to kiss the hand of a black man, he made a blundering attempt to keep the play from opening by refusing to permit children to appear in the first scene, even though children were appearing nightly elsewhere on Broadway without hindrance. The opening scene was read to the audience, after which the play proceeded without incident throughout its run.

17. Given the names of the leading characters, there has been speculation that O'Neill had in mind his own mismatched parents; James and Ella, a union in which a popular star actor and a much younger, convent-educated girl were ill suited through differences not of race but of social background.

18. *Anna Christie* did provide the great silent screen star, Greta Garbo, with her first talking role in a successful and faithful adaptation in 1930. The play was the basis for a moderately successful stage musical, *New Girl in Town*, in 1956.

19. The biblical names of the characters carry additional significance. Ephraim, "the fruitful," was progenitor of the tribes of Israel, but O'Neill's Ephraim is ironically left without the heir he hoped for, his fierce God of vengeance having destroyed rather than supported life. Of the older sons, Peter, meaning "the rock," does indeed talk about "stone atop o' the stones—makin' stone walls," and with his brother throws stones at the house as they depart. Simeon, "an instrument of cruelty," whose Old Testament namesake killed a man and "digged down a wall" in anger, tears off the yard gate. Eben reflects Ebenezer, "the stone of help," which the Israelites set up as a moment to their victory over the Philistines, and the beautiful Abigail was one of King David's wives who bore him a son.

20. In Los Angeles the play was closed by the police as obscene because the heroine dared appear in her nightgown. And, of course, the British Lord Chamberlain took a very dim view of it, all in all. But *Desire Under the Elms* has remained moderately active in revival. Karl Malden's Cabot won praise in 1952, despite a lack of public support and a run of only 46 performances. José Quintero and the Circle in the Square Theater succeeded much better in 1963 with 164 performances; Rip Torn played Eben, George C. Scott was Ephraim, and Colleen Dewhurst was Abbie. An all-star motion picture with Burl Ives, Tony Perkins, and Sophia Loren as a very Italianate Abbie was released to limited success in 1958.

21. Gilbert Gabriel, "DeLeon in Search of His Spring," *New York Sun*, 1 December 1925.

22. O'Neill's planned cycle of some 11 plays entitled collectively "A Tale of Possessors Self-Dispossessed" was to demonstrate how the members of a single American family, from the eighteenth century to the present, acquired and dissipated great fortunes in their drive to possess goods and power and to thus dominate their society. Greedy and corrupt, they became "self-dispossessed," their souls forever lost. *A Touch of the Poet* was completed and successfully produced in New York in 1958. *More Stately Mansions*, adapted by Donald Gallup from a completed draft, was produced in 1967. (Both had been done earlier in Sweden.) *The Calms of Capricorn*, surviving only in a long scenario, was given an experimental production at the University of Wisconsin in 1981 in a version again adapted by Gallup. The rest of the cycle was destroyed.

23. James A. Robinson, *Eugene O'Neill and Oriental Thought: A Divided Vision* (Carbondale: Southern Illinois University Press, 1982), 110.

24. Ruby Cohn, *Dialogue in American Drama* (Bloomington: Indiana University Press, 1971), chap. 2, 8–67.

25. The play was given in two parts in the afternoon and evening, with a dinner break in between. In those days one often "dressed" for an evening in the theater but not for matinées. Patrons who followed protocol were unsure what to do, and some were known to miss dinner so they could rush home and change into proper attire. Not surprisingly, considering its frank subject matter and dialogue, the play was banned in Boston, so the touring company appeared in nearby Quincy. Because there were limited dining facilities in the vicinity, one restaurant in particular propsered from the intermission crowds; this helped, it is reported, to make the fortune of the young owner. His name was Howard Johnson.

26. Frederick I. Carpenter, *Eugene O'Neill* (Boston: Twayne, 1979), 119–21.

27. Edwin Engel, *The Haunted Heroes of Eugene O'Neill* (Cambridge: Harvard University Press, 1953). Hereafter cited in the text as Engel. Engel's discussion of *Strange Interlude* is contained in his section entitled "Everywoman."

28. Such a larger-than-life mythic character would be expected to attract performers eager to try their own interpretations, but unlike many a modern dramatic figure—a Nora, a Hedda, a Candida, played over and over again by virtually every modern actress—Nina Leeds has experienced only two major revivals. Aside from the sheer exhausting length of the role and some of the problems with the play itself, the role is perhaps just too overwhelming, or possibly too forbidding and unattractive. It is true that at least four of the best have tackled the part with fairly reasonable success—Nina's creator, Lynn Fontanne followed by Judith Anderson, then Geraldine Page and Glenda Jackson on stage and television—but it is a rare occasion when one can view a full-length produc-

tion of this formidable drama. A widely heralded screen version in 1932 starred one of the loveliest and most popular film actresses, Norma Shearer. The picture was an artistic flop, with Miss Shearer badly miscast in a heavily bowdlerized version of the story. The support of the rising matinée idol Clark Gable as Darrell could do little to save the situation.

29. Doris M. Alexander, "*Strange Interlude* and Schopenhauer," *American Literature* 25 (May 1953): 213–28; Robinson, *O'Neill and Oriental Thought*, 157.

30. Michael Manheim, *Eugene O'Neill's New Language of Kinship* (Syracuse, N.Y.: Syracuse University Press, 1982), 61. Hereafter cited in the text as Manheim.

31. Krutch's and Anderson's reviews from the *New York Herald-Tribune*, 11 March 1928, and *New York Evening Journal*, 31 January 1928, respectively, are reprinted in Miller, *Progress*.

32. *Lazarus Laughed* could easily bankrupt a commercial producing company, with its requirements of some 400 costumes, 300 masks and wigs, a chorus of 150, and some dozen important speaking characters. The following are O'Neill's directions for the opening scene. Each succeeding scene demanded further changes to indicate Greek, Roman, or Jewish types.

All of these people are masked in accordance with the following scheme: There are seven periods of life shown: Boyhood (or Girlhood), Youth, Young Manhood (or Womanhood), Manhood (or Womanhood), Middle Age, Maturity and Old Age; and each of these periods is represented by seven different masks of general types of character as follows: The Simple, Ignorant; the Happy, Eager; the Self-tortured, Introspective; the Proud, Self-reliant; the Servile, Hypocritical; the Revengeful, Cruel; the Sorrowful, Resigned. Thus in each crowd (this includes among the men the Seven Guests who are composed of one male of each period-type as period one—type one, period two—type two, and so one up to period seven— type seven) there are forty-nine different combinations of period and type. Each type has a distinct predominant color for its costumes which varies in kind according to its period. The masks of the Chorus of Old Men are double the size of the others. They are all seven in the Sorrowful, Resigned type of Old Age.)

Through the volunteer help it was able to call on, the Pasadena Playhouse did everything O'Neill requested.

33. Cyrus Day, "Amor Fati: O'Neill's Lazarus as Superman and Savior," *Modern Drama* 3 (December 1960): 297–305.

34. O'Neill intended to follow up *Dynamo* with two more plays, "Without Ending of Days" and "It Cannot Be Mad." The first eventually became the

failed religious tract *Days without End*. The content of the second remains unknown.

35. O'Neill had always been interested in the Greek classics, but his son, Eugene, Jr., made them a career. A brilliant classical scholar at Yale, he co-edited an edition of the complete Greek drama, published in 1938. His death by suicide in 1950 was a major trauma to O'Neill, who had become quite close to him, far more than to either of his other children.

36. Quoted in Virginia Floyd, *Eugene O'Neill at Work* (New York: Ungar, 1981), 185.

37. George Steiner, *The Death of Tragedy* (New York: Knopf, 1961), chap. 1, passim.

38. Roger Asselineau, "*Mourning Becomes Electra* as a Tragedy," *Modern Drama* 1 (December 1958): 43–150.

39. Philip Weissman, "*Mourning Becomes Electra* and the Prodigal: Electra and Orestes," *Modern Drama* 3 (December 1960): 257–59.

40. The first major attempt at showing the relationship between the two plays was undertaken in 1977 by the Milwaukee Repertory Theatre, which staged them back to back. In 1988, during O'Neill's centenary, with José Quintero as director and Jason Robards and Colleen Dewhurst in leading roles, the two were once again performed in tandem, first at the Yale Repertory Theatre and then on Broadway. They were only moderately successful.

41. Thomas F. Van Lamm, "Singing in the Wilderness: The Dark Vision of Eugene O'Neill's Only Comedy," *Modern Drama* 22 (March 1979): 9–18.

42. John Gassner, *O'Neill* (Englewood Cliffs, N.J: Prentice-Hall, 1964), 166.

Chapter 4

1. According to the Burns Mantle *Best Plays* yearbooks, 150 plays and musicals opened in New York during the 1919–20 season. In the middle of the decade, before talking pictures, the total for 1924–25 was 230. By the end of the 1920s, with movies all-talking and radio shows increasing in popularity, 235 shows opened during the 1929–30 season before the full impact of the market crash. At the height of the Depression, the 1934–35 season total had dropped sharply to 137. By the time the war began in Europe (the 1939–40 season), the total of all productions, legitimate, musical, new, and revival, was 94.

2. Except for the still-pertinent *Theory and Technique*, Lawson remains mainly of historical interest, although some years before his association with the New Playwrights' Theatre he had made a substantial contribution in *Processional*,

a lively expressionistic portrayal of a West Virginia coal town during a strike, staged successfully by the Guild in 1925. His much earlier *Souls* (1915) may have inspired O'Neill in *Strange Interlude,* and *Nirvana* (1926) may have given O'Neill the idea for *Dynamo.* See Leroy Robinson, "John Howard Lawson's Unpublished Nirvana," *Eugene O'Neill Newsletter* 3 (May 1979): 15; and "John Howard Lawson's Souls: A Harbinger of *Strange Interlude,*" *Eugene O'Neill Newsletter* 4 (Winter 1980): 12–13.

3. Howard Clurman, *The Fervent Years: The Story of the Group Theatre and the Thirties* (New York: Hill & Wang, 1945, 1957), 21. Herafter cited in the text as Clurman.

4. The Actors' Studio, founded in 1947 by Cheryl Crawford, Elia Kazan, and Bobby Lewis, became best known under the direction of Lee Strasberg, who took over the following year. The Studio's continued strong advocacy of Method acting has always been controversial. Its detractors, who are many, regard it as not acting at all but merely just "being." A good illustration of differences of opinion within the profession is an anecdote about an encounter between the veteran Laurence Olivier and the much-younger Dustin Hoffman, who worked together in the film *Marathon Man.* Hoffman, a devoted Method actor, spent days getting himself physically worn out in order to convey the exhaustion needed in a particular sequence. Olivier, bemused by it all, is reported to have said, "Young man, if you would learn how to *act* you wouldn't need to do all that."

5. The WPA provided work for hundreds of artists who enlivened many a public building with often controversial murals and other decorations. The series of Guides to the States, though now seriously outdated, still remains a valuable reference. The WPA should not be confused with the PWA (Public Works Administration), which undertook major construction projects. Many post offices and other public buildings stand as impressive legacies of the time.

6. Hallie Flanagan may be listed in library catalogues under her married name, Davis. Her book *Arena,* published in 1940, is her personal history of the Project and reveals the details of her ongoing contests not only with bureaucrats and self-appointed congressional censors but also with the participants themselves, as well as with rival commercial theater managers.

7. The conservative Supreme Court had only recently declared the AAA (Agriculture Adjustment Act) unconstitutional. Its rejection of the NRA (National Recovery Act) and other emergency measures pushed President Roosevelt into his abortive attempt to pack the court with additional liberal members.

8. Hallie Flanagan, *Arena* (New York: Duell, Sloan & Pearce, 1940), 347. Hereafter cited in the text as Flanagan.

9. Republican Representative (later Senator) Everett Dirksen of Illinois praised the demise of these works of "salacious tripe." Ironically, one of the Federal Theatre's original productions, criticized by congressional witnesses en-

dorsing the withdrawal of support, was *Sing for Your Supper,* whose finale, "Ballad for Americans," became the theme song of the 1940 Republican national convention (Flanagan, 434). Government support for the arts has always been suspect to many a politician and made the subject of some very narrow scrutiny. As recently as 1988 the National Endowment for the Arts (NEA), a longtime government-funded support group, was vociferously criticized in Congress for its grant to an art exhibit deemed offensive, obscene, and pornographic. Legislation was passed placing certain limits on government money for displays deemed questionable.

10. Quoted in John Houseman, *Run-Through* (New York: Simon & Schuster, 1980), 202. Hereafter cited in the text as Houseman.

11. Houseman revived *The Cradle Will Rock* on Broadway in 1983 to only moderate success, but its relevance was still felt beyond the nostalgia for an exciting if frightening past.

12. See Houseman's extended and nearly unbelievable account of the national pandemonium that started even before the show was off the air (Houseman, 392–405).

13. It is one of the ironies of politics that the worst persecution of American citizens by HUAC and by the McCarthy hearings occurred *after* the United States had fought as an ally of the Soviet Union during World War II.

14. One could argue that O'Neill had broken the ground of social awareness in drama, but his mysticism and not always clearly expressed social philosophy were never intended as agitation or propaganda.

Chapter 5

1. No play created in O'Neill's final retreat to his California home was produced until after World War II.

2. George Bernard Shaw's *Back to Methuselah* (1921) was initially conceived as a multinight production. French playwright Jean Genet used masks in his highly stylized postwar plays. Jean Anouilh's *Antigone* (1944) turned the classical myth of Oedipus's daughter into an allegory of the French resistance against German occupation. No American playwright attempted anything similar to O'Neill's experiments during his lifetime.

3. Elmer Rice, *Minority Report: An Autobiography* (New York: Simon & Schuster, 1963), 133. Herafter cited in the text as Rice.

4. The dialogue that gives the appearance of accurate transliteration of soldiers' language was, of course, considerably watered down. Not until much later, particularly in David Rabe's Vietnam plays, *The Basic Training of Pavlo*

Hummel (1971) and *Sticks and Bones* (1972), did the constant stream of barracks-room obscenities appear. With the 1980s films, notably *Platoon* and *Full Metal Jacket*, among others, all restraints were dropped and the reality of the language, uttered in context, became accepted as an integral and powerful part of the production.

5. Louis Wolheim, the original Yank of *The Hairy Ape*, and William Boyd (not to be confused with the later screen actor, William Boyd, who became Hopalong Cassidy of screen and television), created the roles of Flagg and Quirt. In the first screen version (1926) Wolheim repeated his role opposite a powerful antagonist in Victor McLaglen. In the much later film version (1952) James Cagney was a somewhat different Flagg, less brutish and physical in demeanor, played in Cagney's well-known lighter, staccato style. Moreover, Cagney's Flagg was reduced to weeping at the death of Aldrich, something difficult to imagine as the writer's intention and certainly not what Wolheim's Flagg would have done.

6. Friedrich Schiller, the great German romantic, probably best known in America as the author of *Wilhelm Tell* (1904), took many liberties with history in addition to those he took in *Maria Stuart*. Another of his most famous was *Die Jungfrau von Orleans* (1801), in which he could not permit the martyrdom of Joan of Arc; instead, he had her die gallantly in battle. Anderson's *Joan of Lorraine* (1946) at least avoided that historical blooper.

7. *The Eve of St. Mark* was presented in 1943 in London by a cast of soldiers and Red Cross personnel chosen under Anderson's personal supervision. Running for 50 performances before Allied forces in the old Scala Theatre, now demolished, its reception was overwhelmingly enthusiastic. At one point in the run, because of the illness of a leading actor and a lack of understudies, the back-home scenes were eliminated to no ill effect. When those scenes were included, audiences, which often responded to some of the more "intimate" domestic scenes with unappreciative laughter, made very clear the superiority and authenticity of the army sequences.

8. Anderson's fantasy-comedy *The Star Wagon* (1937), featuring a miraculous time machine, was one of his longest-running successes, with more than 200 performances. His postwar plays had widely varied success. *Joan of Lorraine* (1946) explored Joan of Arc's psychology, and *Barefoot in Athens* (1951) examined the relationship of Socrates with his shrewish wife. Anderson adapted Alan Paton's poignant *Cry, the Beloved Country* as *Lost in the Stars* (1949), with music by Kurt Weill. *Truckline Cafe* (1946) failed miserably, prompting Anderson's strong rebuttal to the critics in a paid newspaper response. *Bad Seed* (1954), a chilling melodrama about a genetically evil child, did well.

9. Walter J. Meserve, *An Outline History of American Drama* (Totawa, N.J.: Littlefield, Adams, 1969), 258.

10. Sidney Howard White, *Sidney Howard* (Boston: Twayne, 1977), 39.

11. *They Knew What They Wanted* was made into no less than three film versions, the most famous starring Carole Lombard and Charles Laughton in 1940. Frank Loesser's adaptation, *The Most Happy Fella*, was a successful musical in 1956.

12. The character of Duke Mantee was played by an impressive new actor, Humphrey Bogart. The role made him a star. Leslie Howard, the fine British actor who created Alan Squier, when approached for the 1936 film version accepted only on the condition that Bogart appear with him. With Bette Davis as Gabby, the picture has become something of a classic, and it guaranteed Bogart's place as one of Hollywood's most famous and talented performers.

13. Sherwood's postwar dramas, *The Rugged Path* (1945) and *Small War on Murray Hill* (1957), were unsuccessful. But after long service under Franklin Roosevelt, he demonstrated his creative ability outside the theater in *Roosevelt and Hopkins* (1948); this factual, well-written biography of these very different but very close friends brought him a fourth Pulitzer Prize.

14. John Gassner, ed., *Twenty-five Best Plays of the Modern American Theatre*, early ser. (New York: Crown, 1949), 334.

15. Joseph Wood Krutch, *The American Drama since 1918* (New York: Braziller, 1939; rev. ed., 1957), 189–90. Hereafter cited in the text as Krutch.

16. Elmer Rice, *The Living Theatre* (New York: Harper's, 1950), 124.

17. Bigsby, *Critical Introduction*, 39.

Chapter 6

1. Gerald Weales, *The Group Theatre and Its Plays* (New York: St. Martin's, 1967), 396. Hereafter cited in the text as Weales.

2. Without knowing the contents of a play or who composed it, one can readily describe its form and style simply by identifying it with the era in which it appeared. A "classic Greek tragedy" is at once associated with a particular style and a particular theatrical structure; its subject matter and its form can be outlined in considerable detail. Likewise, to mark a play as "Elizabethan" or "Shakespearean," whether comedy, tragedy, or pastoral, places it within a theater of known shape and size, and within a well-established chronological period. And so with "Restoration/eighteenth-century comedy of manners," "neoclassic tragedy," or "nineteenth-century romantic melodrama." The theater building, the audience that came, and the general concept of the play are easily identified.

3. Eric Bentley, *In Search of Theatre* (New York: Knopf, 1953; Vintage, 1954), 10. Hereafter cited in the text as Bentley.

4. In the 1930s ignorance of what was really going on in Russia under the iron dictatorship of the near-maniacal Stalin was widespread. John Reed's

best-selling account of the Bolshevik Revolution, *Ten Days That Shook the World*, and his blind praise for the Soviet system were widely influential. The brutalities of forced collectivization of agriculture and the death of tens of thousands of the prosperous peasants known as *culaks* were unknown or ignored, as were the horrors of the Siberian concentration camps exposed much later by Aleksandr Solzhenitsyn (it has been estimated that some 20 million Soviet citizens died at the hands of the state). But in the turbulence of America's Depression society, the admiration for Russian stability, the "progressiveness" of the Stalin methods, the illusion of social equality, and the apparent absence of class differences was understandable. (As these words are being written, the naive views of the 1930s become doubly ironic as the fate of the Russian Revolution, after 70 years of failure, seems to be complete disintegration in the face of truly revolutionary changes in both the Soviet Union and Eastern Europe that point, in the symbol of the fallen Berlin Wall, to the collapse of the whole Communist dream.)

5. Margaret Brennan-Gibson, *Clifford Odets, American Playwright: The Years from 1906–1940* (New York: Atheneum, 1981), 290.

6. *The Country Girl* may not have been the result of Odets's flight to Hollywood in the 1940s, but it was good enough in its screen version to win Grace Kelly the Academy Award for best actress in 1954 and Bing Crosby a nomination for best actor.

7. We are making no attempt here to establish precisely where Kelly falls as a dramatist, simply because even the most erudite of his critics have been unable to do so. Krutch saw him as a straightfoward realist (Krutch, 60). John Mason Brown said that Kelly's "conscientious" realism might "also make him pass as a naturalist," but that when he becomes tragic, he "not only ceases to be a modern realist but becomes a Nineteenth Century romanticist" (*Upstage: The American Theatre in Performance* [New York: Norton, 1930], 31, 38). Eleanor Flexner saw him as a writer of comedy (*American Playwrights, 1918–1938* [New York: Simon & Schuster, 1938], 198) who was skilled in amusing dialogue and humorous situation. Foster Hirsch, noting "realistic" foundations, said that Kelly's themes and character types and his distinctive dialogue and unfailing rhythm are "too much of the theater to fit comfortably into a Realistic tradition" (*George Kelly* [Boston: Twayne, 1975], 7). In direct contrast is Arthur Wills, who believed Kelly "never once . . . ventured beyond [realism's] narrow confines" ("The Kelly Play," *Modern Drama* 6 [December 1963]: 245–55).

8. A line by Hochberg, the hospital's top surgeon, provides an example of how much distance has been covered in that half-century. Speaking to the grumbling rich trustee who is a cardiac patient and who refuses to follow orders, Hochberg says, "I don't understand people like you, John. Whitman is the best cardiac man in the country, but he can't give you a new heart!"

Another aspect that can date the play is the relegation of women to nursing and support roles to the exclusion of any suggestion of a female physician, a flaw that could easily be corrected in a contemporary production by changing the sex of any of a number of the exclusive male club represented in the play without altering a word of dialogue.

9. In a prolonged footnote to the published version, Kingsley was decades ahead of his time in raising the question of abortion and the law. As a socially conscious artist, he was unable in 1933 to say what he would have liked to onstage and thus only hinted at the evils of the prevailing attitudes toward abortion. In print he is far more blunt. Recognizing that it is a social problem that legislation cannot solve, he makes the point of the later "pro-choice" advocates in the debate that has raged ever since Roe v. Wade. He attacks "the lash of the law," which instead of correcting an evil, "only whips it into dark corners, creating a vicious class of criminal practitioners, bootleg doctors and ignorant midwives who work in dark, back-room apartments" (Kathryn Coe and William H. Cordell, eds., *The Pulitzer Prize Plays* [New York: Random House, 1935], 836; hereafter cited in text as Coe and Cordell). In *Detective Story* (1949) Kingsley develops his point further in centering his story on a zealous police officer determined to get rid of these "butchers," only to discover that his wife has been driven to engage the services of one of them.

10. Hellman's *An Unfinished Woman* (1969) won the National Book Award. The Book-of-the-Month Club chose *Pentimento* (1973) as a major club choice; *Julia*, a sensitive film released in 1977, starring Jane Fonda as Hellman and Jason Robards as Dashiell Hammett, was based on it. Hellman received the Edward McDowell Medal for *Scoundrel Time* in 1976.

11. *Six Plays by Lillian Hellman* (New York: Random House, 1942), x–xi.

12. As is invariably the case, a point never learned by those highly "moral" censors, such bluenosed stupidities only call increased attention to the condemned work and, in the case of *The Children's Hour*, may very likely have contributed to its long run of 700 performances. The irony is all the more obvious because *The Children's House* is a very moral play. But even the Pulitzer Prize committee frowned on it, and one of its members refused to view it. For a later and more frank look at suggested homosexuality, this time in a boys' school, see Robert Anderson's *Tea and Sympathy* (1953). In the first loosely adapted motion-picture version of *The Children's Hour*, titled *These Three* (1936), all suggestions of lesbianism were omitted. The 1962 remake followed the original play more closely and included the objectionable passages.

13. Henry James's suggestion of evil in children in *The Turn of the Screw* (1891) was adapted by William Archibald into a gripping play, *The Innocents* (1950), as well as a fine motion picture. Maxwell Anderson's *Bad Seed* (1954) and Arthur Miller's *The Crucible* (1953) are further excellent examples of works about children's devastating power in wrecking adult lives.

14. Quoted in Richard Moody, *Lillian Hellman, Playwright* (New York, Pegasus, 1972), 16.

15. Doris V. Falk, *Lillian Hellman* (New York: Ungar, 1978), 30. Falk's division of the plays includes the postwar dramas as well, none of them under discussion here. *The Children's Hour*, *The Little Foxes*, *Watch on the Rhine*, and *Another Part of the Forest* are "despoiler" plays. *The Searching Wind*, *The Autumn Garden*, and *Toys in the Attic* belong to the "bystanders."

16. Warren French, *John Steinbeck* (New York: Twayne, 1961), 76.

17. See William Goldhurst, "*Of Mice and Men*: John Steinbeck's Parable of the Curse of Cain," *Western American Literature* 8 (Summer 1971): 123–35.

18. The possibility of the humaneness of occupying German army units was demonstrated during the war in the long occupation of the channel islands of Jersey and Guernsey, the only conquered parts of Britain. Through his basic decency, the commanding officer was able to create a livable, if always precarious, balance between occupier and occupied, to the degree that upon his surrender after the invasion of France and his subsequent removal to a POW camp on the Continent, the grateful islanders actually sent him Red Cross packages. A fine British television production in 1977, *Enemy at the Door*, dramatized the event.

Chapter 7

1. S. N. Behrman, discussed in detail in chapter 5 as a member of the Playwrights' Company, will not be considered further here.

2. Howard Teichman, *George S. Kaufman: An Intimate Portrait* (New York: Dell, 1973), 105–6. Like George Bernard Shaw in England, Kaufman was widely touted for his personal, pungent comments on people and affairs in the news. Of the so-called Algonquin Wits who met for food, drink, and the trading of humorous quips at the Algonquin Hotel Round Table in the theater district, Kaufman was among the most quotable. Testifying to his wit and unique character are four books extolling his life as a theater personality through more than three decades. A collection of his prose and poetic pieces, *By George*, ed. Donald Oliver (New York, St. Martin's, 1979), provides several excellent illustrations of his sense of humor. Another large volume, *George S. Kaufman and His Friends* by Scott Meredith (New York: Doubleday, 1978), reviews his association with his many collaborators. Teichman's book details Kaufman's early life as a *New York Times* drama critic through his later theatrical successes. *George S. Kaufman: His Life, His Theatre* by Malcolm Goldstein (New York: Oxford, 1979; hereafter cited in the text as Goldstein) documents his importance for his era and his creation of an Americana on the stage that has not been forgotten and that in some instances has been revived with great success.

3. Kaufman did write other pieces on his own in variety-show sketches and screenplays. His one-act parody of ladies' bridge clubs, "If Men Played Cards

as Women Do," has never faded away and remains a steady favorite wherever high school and college theater groups perform.

4. Moss Hart, *Act One* (New York: Random House, 1959), passim.

5. *Six Plays by Kaufman and Hart* (New York: Modern Library, 1942), xxii–xxiii.

6. Two other failures, a whimsical comedy called *White Wings* (1926) and *John* (1927), a re-creation of the story of John the Baptist, did nothing to further Barry's status.

7. Brooks Atkinson, introduction to Bennett A. Cerf and Van H. Cartmell, eds., *Sixteen Famous American Plays* (New York: Random House, 1941), unpaginated.

Chapter 8

1. This childhood fantasy has never lost its appeal to either audiences or actors. The beautiful Maude Adams brought the first performances to America in 1905. Two very successful revivals in 1954 and 1979 were undertaken by America's top musical comedy star, Mary Martin, and by the popular light comic actress Sandy Duncan. "Never-never-land" has become a standard label for any impractical or utopian scheme. Sir Thomas More's *Utopia*, from which the adjective is taken, is as much a never-never land as Barrie's.

2. The exaggeration and distortion of the expressionism of O'Neill and Rice during this period are essentially fantastic, but their purposes are very different from those of the fantasy writer. The expressionist is interpreting reality in a world that *does* exist; the writer of fantasy creates a world that *might* exist or, more likely, that exists only in the free flow of imagination.

3. When *Our Town* was first produced in London in 1944 by the U.S. Army's Special Services, primarily for Allied forces, the response, contrary to some predictions, was instantly and overwhelmingly favorable; the show filled the small Playhouse Theatre for nearly a month. Its homey nostalgia appealed at once to troops on the verge of the Continental invasion; in barracks and mess-hall chow lines the word was passed on that here was something worth seeing. The few professional London newspaper critics who saw it for the first time were equally enthusiastic.

4. Quoted in Gilbert A. Harrison, *The Enthusiast: A Life of Thornton Wilder* (New Haven: Ticknor & Fields, 1973), 359. Hereafter cited in the text as Harrison.

5. *Our Town* and *The Skin of Our Teeth* remain Wilder's permanent legacy to the American theater, but his other major contribution cannot be

ignored. His 1955 farce, *The Matchmaker*, adapted from the earlier *The Merchant of Yonkers* (1938), became the source for *Hello, Dolly* (1964), whose 2,844 performances make it the sixth-longest-running musical in American stage history.

6. Comparisons have been made between *The Time of Your Life* and O'Neill's *The Iceman Cometh*. O'Neill is reported to have sought Eddie Dowling, who created Joe, for the part of Hickey, but instead he became the director of the original production in 1946, and the role of Hickey went to James Barton. Although the plays have similar settings, the derelicts in Harry Hope's bar have nothing in common with Nick's patrons, and their hopes are never realized. The benevolent Joe is, as well, a far cry from the wife-murdering Hickey, who bears a false message unrelated to Joe's upbeat goodness. (One can regard Joe as a redeeming Jesus figure, but such parallels are dangerous to pursue very far.)

Chapter 9

1. As is often the case with great stage classics, the first performance of *Porgy and Bess* was not especially well received. Critics could not categorize it, and the seeming hybrid of folk tradition and modern music was confusing.

If we are to acknowledge *Porgy and Bess*, we cannot ignore that other musical sensation, based on Lynn Riggs's unsuccessful *Green Grow the Lilacs* (1931). When Richard Rodgers and Oscar Hammerstein adapted the play in 1943 as a musical called *Away We Go*, its initial reception in tryout performances threatened a fate worse than that of its source. Given the more catchy title *Oklahoma!* from its rousing title song, it permanently changed the modern musical theater with its full integration of song and dance into the plot. Though in many ways further removed from being a folk musical than Gershwin's, it has run ever since a very close race with *Porgy and Bess* as the unchallenged best in modern American musical theater.

2. An indication of changed attitudes can be seen in the difference between the treatment of the cast of *The Green Pastures* then and now. Unproducible in the South, the play made a triumphant tour elsewhere in the country, with cast virtually unchanged. No matter where the play appeared, no hotel would accept the performers, and arrangements always had to be made with local homeowners to take them in at night.

selected bibliography

PRIMARY WORKS

When consulting primary sources, the reader must remember that playwrights frequently prepared manuscripts specifically for publication, making changes and adding embellishments that did not always reflect the promptbook of the original production. Plays were often published singly soon after their appearance on stage, and although issued by major houses, they went out of print relatively quickly. Moreover, many of the plays mentioned in the text did not appear in single editions.

Fortunately, a large number of plays written between the wars, including those never published singly, have been printed in a variety of play collections and anthologies. Another source of publication is the Burns Mantle *Best Plays* series, annual volumes originally edited by the late critic of the *New York Daily News*. They are an invaluable source of general information about each New York theater season, listing every play produced, together with cast lists, directors and technicians, the theaters in which the plays appeared, opening and closing dates, and total number of performances. Each volume contains the ten best plays of the season as selected by the editor, but because of copyright and other restrictions, the plays appear only as synopses with frequent extended portions of dialogue. Nevertheless, the abridgments provide an excellent sense of the plays.

Major Anthologies of Drama, 1914–1945

Block, Haskell M., and Robert G. Shedd, eds. *Masters of Modern Drama.* New York: Random House, 1962.

Bloomfield, Morton W., and Robert C. Elliott, eds., *Ten Plays.* New York: Rinehart, 1951.

———. *Great Plays, Sophocles to Brecht.* New York: Holt, Rinehart & Winston, 1965.

———. *Great Plays, Sophocles to Albee.* New York: Holt, 1975.

Cerf, Bennett A., and Van H. Cartmell, eds. *Sixteen Famous American Plays.* New York: Random House, 1941.

———. *SRO: The Most Successful Plays of the American Stage.* Garden City, N.Y.: Doubleday, 1944.

Chandler, Frank W., and Richard A. Cordell, eds. *Twentieth Century Plays.* New York: Nelson, 1934 (revised 1939).

———. *Twentieth Century Plays,* American ed. New York: Nelson, 1939.

Clark, Barrett H., and William Davenport, eds. *Nine Modern Plays.* New York: Appleton-Century-Crofts, 1951.

Clurman, Harold, ed. *Famous American Plays of the 1930s.* New York: Dell, 1959.

Coe, Kathryn, and William H. Cordell, eds. *The Pulitzer Prize Plays.* New York: Random House, 1940. (Two earlier editions were published in 1935 and 1938.)

Corbin, Richard K., and Miriam Balf, eds. *Twelve American Plays 1920–1960.* New York: Scribner's, 1969.

Cordell, Richard A., ed. *Representative Modern Plays.* New York: Nelson, 1929.

———. *Twentieth Century Plays, American.* New York: Ronald, 1947.

The Critics' Prize Plays. Intro. by George Jean Nathan. Cleveland: World, 1945.

Dickinson, Thomas H., ed. *Chief Contemporary Dramatists.* Boston: Houghton Mifflin, 1915.

———. *Chief Contemporary Dramatists,* 2d ser. Boston: Houghton Mifflin, 1921.

———. *Chief Contemporary Dramatists,* 3d ser. Boston: Houghton Mifflin, 1930.

Durham, Willard H., and John W. Dodds, eds. *British and American Plays, 1830–1945*. New York: Oxford, 1947.

Gassner, John, ed. *Best American Plays*, 3d ser. New York: Crown, 1952.

———. *Best American Plays*, 4th ser. New York: Crown, 1958.

———. *Best American Plays*, suppl. vol., 1918–1958. New York: Crown, 1968.

———. *Best Plays of the Early American Theatre, Beginnings to 1916*. New York: Crown, 1967.

———. *Best Plays of the Modern American Theatre*, 2d ser. New York: Crown, 1947.

———. *Twenty Best Plays of the Modern American Theatre*. New York: Crown, 1947.

———. *Twenty-five Best Plays of the Modern American Theatre*, early ser. New York: Crown, 1949.

———, and Burns Mantle, eds. *A Treasury of the Theatre, Aeschylus to O'Neill*. New York: Simon & Schuster, 1935.

———. *A Treasury of the Theatre*, 2 vols., rev. by Philo Buck, Jr. and H. S. Alberson. New York: Simon & Schuster, 1940.

———. *A Treasury of the Theatre*, 3 vols., rev. ed. New York: Simon & Schuster, 1951.

———. *A Treasury of the Theatre*, 2 vols., rev. for colleges. New York: Simon & Schuster, 1950–51.

———. *A Treasury of the Theatre, Ibsen to Ionesco*, 3d ed. New York: Simon & Schuster, 1960.

———. *A Treasury of the Theatre*, 3 vols., New York: Simon & Schuster, 1963.

———, and Bernard F. Dukore, eds. *A Treasury of the Theatre*, 4th ed. New York: Simon & Schuster, 1970.

———, and Clive Barnes, eds. *Fifty Best Plays of the Modern American Theatre*, 4 vols. New York, Crown, 1969.

Gaver, Jack, ed. *Critics' Choice: New York Drama Critics' Circle Prize Plays 1935–1955*. New York: Hawthorn, 1955.

Hatcher, Harlan H., ed. *Modern American Dramas*. New York: Harcourt Brace, 1941.

———. *Modern American Dramas* new ed. New York: Harcourt Brace, 1949.

———. *Modern Dramas*, shorter ed. New York: Harcourt Brace, 1944.

———. *Modern Dramas*, new shorter ed. New York: Harcourt Brace, 1948.

Leverton, Garrett H., ed. *Plays for the College Theatre*. New York: Samuel French, 1932.

————. *Plays for the College Theatre.* New York: Samuel French, 1934.

Macgowan, Kenneth, ed. *Famous American Plays of the 1920s.* New York: Dell, 1959.

Miller, Jordan Y., ed. *American Dramatic Literature.* New York: McGraw-Hill, 1961.

Moses, Montrose, ed. *American Dramas, National and Local.* Boston: Little, Brown, 1926.

————. *American Dramas, National and Local,* rev. ed. Boston: Little, Brown, 1933.

————, and Joseph Wood Krutch. *American Dramas, National and Local,* rev. ed. Boston: Little, Brown, 1941.

————. *Dramas of Modernism and Their Forerunners.* Boston: Little, Brown, 1931.

————, and Oscar James Campbell. *Dramas of Modernism and Their Forerunners,* rev. ed. Boston: Little, Brown, 1941.

Quinn, Arthur Hobson, ed. *Contemporary American Plays.* New York: Scribner's, 1923.

————. *Representative American Plays.* New York: Century, 1917.

————. *Representative American Plays 1767–1923.* New York: Century, 1925.

————. *Representative American Plays from 1880 to the Present Day.* New York: Century, 1928.

————. *Representative American Plays from 1767 to the Present Day.* New York: Century, 1930.

————. *Representative American Plays.* New York: Appleton-Century, 1938.

————. *Representative American Plays.* New York: Appleton-Century-Crofts, 1953.

The Theatre Guild Anthology. New York: Random House, 1936.

Tucker, Samuel M., ed. *Modern American and British Plays.* New York: Harper's, 1931.

————. *Modern Plays.* New York: Macmillan, 1932.

————. *Twenty-five Modern Plays.* New York: Harper's, 1943.

————, and Alan S. Downer, eds. *Twenty-five Modern Plays,* rev. ed. New York: Harper's, 1948.

————. *Twenty-five Modern Plays,* 3d ed. New York: Harper's, 1953.

Warnock, Robert, ed. *Representative Modern Plays, American.* Chicago: Scott Foresman, 1952.

Watson, Ernest, and B. Pressey. *American Plays,* 2 vols. New York: Scribner's, 1931–38.

———. *Contemporary Dramas: European, English, Irish, American.* New York: Scribner's, 1941.

———. *Contemporary Dramas: American, English, Irish, European.* New York: Scribner's, 1959.

———. *Contemporary Dramas, Nine Plays.* New York: Scribner's, 1941.

———. *Contemporary Dramas, Eleven Plays.* New York: Scribner's, 1956.

Whitman, Charles H., ed. *Representative Modern Dramas.* New York: Macmillan, 1936.

Works by Individual Playwrights

Noted first under each playwright are volumes of the dramatist's collected plays with their contents. Plays not included in these collections are noted next, together with their sources in the several anthologies listed above, indicated by editor(s) or appropriate short titles. Anthologies not listed above receive full bibliographic information. The final reference is to the Burns Mantle series, noted as *Best Plays* with the season's date. No individual editions of the plays are included.

Abbott, George (b. 1888)

Broadway (with Philip Dunning [1891–1968]) (1926). In Bennett Cerf and Van H. Cartmell, eds., *Famous Plays of Crime and Detection* (Philadelphia: Blakiston, 1946); Gassner, *25 Best*; *Best Plays* 1926–27.

The Fall Guy (with James Gleason [1885–1959]) (1925). In *Best Plays* 1924–25.

Three Men on a Horse (with John Cecil Holm [1906–1981]) (1935). In Gassner, *20 Best*.

Akins, Zoë (1886–1958)

Declassé (1919); *Daddy's Gone a-Hunting* (1921); *Greatness* (1922) (New York: Boni & Liveright, 1924). *Declassé* also in *Best Plays* 1919–20.

The Old Maid (1935). In *Best Plays* 1934–35.

Anderson, Maxwell (1888–1959)

Eleven Verse Plays by Maxwell Anderson 1929–1939 (New York: Harcourt Brace, 1940). Includes *Elizabeth the Queen* (1930); *Night over Taos* (1932); *Mary of Scotland* (1933); *Valley Forge* (1934); *Winterset* (1935); *The Wingless Victory* (1936); *High Tor* (1936); *The Masque of Kings* (1937); *Key Largo* (1939).

Anne of the Thousand Days (1948). In Gassner, *Best Plays*, 3d ser.; *Best Plays* 1948–49.

Bad Seed (1954). In Stanley Richards, *Best Mystery and Suspense Plays of the Modern Theatre* (New York: Dodd, Mead, 1971); *Best Plays* 1954–55.

Barefoot in Athens (1951). In Marjorie W. Barrows, et al., eds., *The American Experience: Drama* (New York: Macmillan, 1968); *Best Plays* 1951–52.

Both Your Houses (1933). In Coe and Cordell, *Pulitzer Plays; Best Plays* 1932–33.

Candle in the Wind (1941). In *Best Plays* 1941–42.

The Eve of St. Mark (1942). In *Best Plays* 1942–43.

Gods of the Lightning (with Harold Hickerson) (1928). In Gassner, *25 Best.*

Gypsy (1929). In *Best Plays* 1928–29.

Joan of Lorraine (1946). In *Best Plays* 1946–47.

Saturday's Children (1927). In Gassner, *25 Best;* Tucker, *Modern American and British; Best Plays* 1926–27.

The Star Wagon (1937). In *Best Plays* 1937–38.

Storm Operation (1944). In *Best Plays* 1943–44.

What Price Glory? (with Laurence Stallings [1894–1965]) (1924). In Chandler and Cordell, *20th Century* (1934); Gassner, *25 Best;* Gassner, *Treasury* (1951, 1960, 1963); Gassner, *Treasury* (1940); Gassner and Mantle, *Treasury* (1935); Macgowan, *Famous American; Best Plays* 1924–25.

Ardrey, Robert (1904–1972)

Thunder Rock (1939). In Ardrey, *Plays of Three Decades* (New York: Atheneum, 1978).

Balderston, John L. (1889–1954)

Berkeley Square (1929). In Gassner, *25 Best; Best Plays* 1929–30.

Barry, Philip (1896–1949)

States of Grace: Eight Plays by Philip Barry, ed. Brendan Gill (New York: Harcourt Brace Jovanovich, 1975). Contains: *You and I* (1923); *Holiday* (1928); *Hotel Universe* (1930); *The Animal Kingdom* (1932); *Here Come the Clowns* (1938); *The Philadelphia Story* (1939); *White Wings* (1926).

In a Garden (1925). In Tucker, *Modern American and British;* Tucker, *25 Modern.*

The Joyous Season (1934). In Catholic University of America, *Catholic High School Literature Series* (New York: Sadler, 1944); Sister Mary Agnes David, *Modern American Drama* (New York: Macmillan, 1961).

Paris Bound (1927). In Gassner, *25 Best;* Quinn, *Representative* (1930, 1938, 1953); *Best Plays* 1927–28.

Tomorrow and Tomorrow (1931). In *Best Plays* 1930–31.

The Youngest (1924). In *Best Plays* 1924–25.

Beach, Lewis (b. 1891)

The Clod (1914). In Charles O. Burgess, ed. *Drama: Literature on Stage* (Philadelphia: Lippincott, 1969); Gassner, *25 Best; Washington Square Plays* (Garden City, N.Y.: Doubleday, Page, 1916).

Behrman, S. N. (1893–1973)

Four Plays (New York: Random House, n.d.). Contains: *The Second Man* (1927); *Biography* (1932); *Rain from Heaven* (1934); *End of Summer* (1936).

Brief Moment (1931). In *Best Plays* 1931–32.

No Time for Comedy (1939). In Bennett Cerf, ed., *Tne Pocket Book of Modern American Plays* (New York: Pocket Books, 1942); *Best Plays* 1938–39.

Belasco, David (1859–1941)

The Girl of the Golden West (1905); In Daniel C. Gerould, *American Melodrama* (New York: Performing Arts Journal, 1983); Moses, *American Dramas* (1926, 1933, 1941).

Madame Butterfly (with John Luther Long [1861–1927]) (1900). In Quinn, *Representative* (all editions).

Blitzstein, Marc (1905–1964)

The Cradle Will Rock (1937). In William Kozlenko, *Best Short Plays of the Social Theatre* (New York: Random House, 1939).

Boothe, Clare (1903–1987)

Kiss the Boys Goodbye (1938). In *Best Plays* 1938–39.

The Women (1936). In Cerf and Cartmell, *16 Famous*; Gassner, *20 Best*; Victoria Sullivan and James V. Hatch, eds., *Plays by and about Women* (New York: Random House, 1973); *Best Plays* 1936–37.

Caldwell, Erskine (1903–1987)

Tobacco Road (1933) (closely adapted by Jack Kirkland [1904–1969] from the novel). In Cerf and Cartmell, *SRO*; Gassner, *20 Best*; Gassner and Barnes; *50 Best*; Stanley Richards, *The Most Popular Plays of the American Theatre* (New York: Stein & Day, 1979).

Chase, Mary (1907–1981)

Harvey (1944). In Gassner, *Best Plays* (suppl.); Gassner and Barnes, *50 Best*; Miller, *American Dramatic*; Stanley Richards, *The Most Popular Plays of the American Theatre* (New York: Stein & Day, 1979); *Best Plays* 1944–45.

Connelly, Marc (1890–1980)

The Green Pastures (1929). In Cerf and Cartmell, *16 Famous*; Gassner, *20 Best*; Gassner, *Treasury* (1935, 1940, 1950, 1951, 1960, 1963); Coe and Cordell, *Pulitzer Plays*; *Best Plays* 1929–30.

Crothers, Rachel (1878–1958)

Three Plays (New York: Brentano's, 1924). Contains *Nice People* (1921); *Expressing Willie* (1924).

As Husbands Go (1931). In Chandler and Cordell, *20th Century* (1934); *Best Plays* 1930–31.

He and She (1911); In Quinn, *Representative* (all editions).

Let Us Be Gay (1929). In *Best Plays* 1928–29.

Mary the Third (1923). In Tucker (all editions); Thomas H. Dickinson and Jack R. Crawford, eds., *Contemporary Plays* (Boston: Houghton Mifflin, 1925); *Best Plays* 1922–23.

Susan and God (1937). In *Best Plays* 1937–38.

When Ladies Meet (1932). In *Best Plays* 1932–33.

Crouse, Russell (See Howard Lindsay)

Federal Theatre Project: Living Newspapers

Federal Theatre Plays. New York: Random House, 1938. Reprint ed. New York: Da Capo Press, 1973. Issued in two volumes. Contains *Triple-A Plowed Under* (1936); *Power* (1937); *Spirochete* (1938); *Haiti* (1938); *One-third of a Nation* (1938).

Fitch, Clyde (1865–1909)

The City (1909). In Richard Moody, ed., *Dramas from the American Theatre 1762–1909* (Cleveland: World, 1965); Moses, *American Dramas* (1926, 1933, 1941).

The Climbers (1901); In Cordell, *Representative Modern*; *Best Plays* 1899–1909.

Gale, Zona (1874–1938)

Miss Lulu Bett (1920). In Judith Barlow, ed., *Plays by American Women* (New York: Avon, 1981); Coe and Cordell, *Pulitzer Plays*.

Gerstenberg, Alice (1885–1972)

Overtones (1915). In Jay B. Hubbell and John O. Beatty, eds., *An Introduction to Drama* (New York: Macmillan, 1927); Sullivan and Hatch, *Plays by and about Women*.

Gillette, William (1855–1937)

Secret Service (1895). In Gassner, *Best Plays Early American*; Quinn, *Representative* (all editions); *Best Plays* 1894–99.

Glaspell, Susan (1882–1948)

Plays by Susan Glaspell, ed. C. W. E. Bigsby (New York: Cambridge, 1987). Contains *Trifles* (1916); *Outside Looking in* (1917); *The Inheritors* (1921); *The Verge* (1921).

Alison's House (1930). In Coe and Cordell, *Pulitzer Plays*; *Best Plays* 1930–31.

Suppressed Desires (with George Cram Cook [1873–1924]) (1915). In Lee A. Jacobus, ed., *The Longman Anthology of American Drama* (New York: Longman, 1982).

Goodman, Edward (1888–1962)

Eugenically Speaking (1915). In *Washington Square Plays.*

Green, Paul (1894–1981)

Five Plays of the South (New York: Hill & Wang, 1963). Contains *In Abraham's Bosom* (1926); *The House of Connelly* (1931); *Johnny Johnson* (1936); *Hymn to the Rising Sun* (1936).

The Field God (1927). In Tucker, *Modern American and British*; Tucker, *25 Modern* (1948, 1953); Allan Gates Halline, *American Plays* (New York: American Book, 1935).

Native Son (with Richard Wright [1908–1960]) (1941). In James V. Hatch, ed., *Forty-Five Plays by Black Americans* (New York: Free Press, 1974); *Best Plays* 1940–41.

Hecht, Ben (1893–1964)

The Front Page (with Charles MacArthur [1895–1956]) (1928). In Cerf and Cartmell, *16 Famous*; Gassner, *25 Best*; Gassner and Barnes, *50 Best*; *Best Plays* 1928–29.

Hellman, Lillian (1905–1984)

Collected Plays (Boston: Little, Brown, 1972). Contains *The Children's Hour* (1934); *Days to Come* (1936); *The Little Foxes* (1939); *Watch on the Rhine* (1941); *The Searching Wind* (1944); *Another Part of the Forest* (1946); *The Autumn Garden* (1951); *Toys in the Attic* (1960).

Six Plays (New York: Random House, 1942). Contains *The Children's Hour; Days to Come; The Little Foxes; Watch on the Rhine; The Autumn Garden; Another Part of the Forest.*

Herne, James A. (1839–1901)

Margaret Fleming (1890). In William Coyle and H. E. Damaser, eds., *Six Early American Plays, 1798–1890* (Columbus, Ohio: Merrill, 1968); Myron Matlow, ed., *The Black Crook and Other Nineteenth Century American Plays* (New York: Dutton, 1967); Myron Matlow, ed., *Nineteenth Century American Plays* (New York: Applause Theatre Book, 1985); Quinn, *Representative* (1930, 1938, 1963).

Heyward, DuBose (1885–1940)

Porgy (with Dorothy Heyward [1890–1961]) (1927). In Gassner, *25 Best*; Gassner and Barnes, *50 Best*; Macgowan, *Famous American*; Miller, *American Dramatic*; *Theatre Guild*; *Best Plays* 1927–28.

Howard, Bronson (1842–1908)

The Henrietta (1887). In Allan Gates Halline, ed., *American Plays* (New York: American Book, 1935).

Shenandoah (1888). In Myron Matlow, ed., *The Black Crook and Other Nineteenth Century Plays* (New York: Dutton, 1967); Quinn, *Representative* (all editions).

Howard, Sidney (1891–1939)

Alien Corn (1933). In *Best Plays* 1932–33.

Dodsworth (1934). In Hatcher, *Modern American* (1941); *Best Plays* 1933–34.

The Late Christopher Bean (1934). In John Gassner and Morris Sweetkind, eds., *Introducing the Drama* (New York: Holt, Rinehart & Winston, 1963); Warnock, *Representative Modern American*; *Best Plays* 1932–33.

Lucky Sam McCarver (1925). In Alvin S. Kaufman and Franklin D. Case, eds., *Modern Drama in America*, vol. 1 (New York: Washington Square, 1982); Moses, *American Dramas* (1933, 1941).

Ned McCobb's Daughter (1926). In Fred B. Millett and Gerald E. Bentley, eds., *The Play's the Thing* (New York: Appleton-Century, 1936).

The Silver Cord (1926). In Cordell, *20th Century Plays*; Quinn, *Representative* (1930, 1938, 1953); Moses, *Dramas of Modernism* (1931, 1941); Tucker, *Modern American and British*; Tucker, *25 Modern* (1948); Watson and Pressey, *American Plays*; Watson & Pressey, *Contemporary Drama* (1941); *Best Plays* 1926–27.

They Knew What They Wanted (1924); In Cerf and Cartmell, *16 Famous*; Gassner, *25 Best*; Macgowan, *Famous American*; *Best Plays* 1924–25.

Yellow Jack (1934). In Gassner, *Best Plays* (suppl.); Joseph Mersand, ed., *Three Plays about Doctors* (New York: Washington Square, 1961); Munjou M. Nagelberg, ed., *Drama in Our Time* (New York: Harcourt Brace, 1948).

Hughes, Hatcher (1881?–1945)

Hell-Bent fer Heaven (1924). In Cordell, *Representative Modern*; Coe and Cordell, *Pulitzer Plays*; Tucker, *Modern Plays*; *Best Plays* 1923–24.

Kaufman, George S. (1889–1961)

Six Plays by Kaufman and Hart (New York: Modern Library, 1942). Contains *Once in a Lifetime* (1930); *Merrily We Roll Along* (1934); *You Can't Take It with You* (1936); *The American Way* (1939); *The Man Who Came to Dinner* (1939); *George Washington Slept Here* (1940).

Beggar on Horseback (with Marc Connelly [1890–1980]). (1924). In Chandler and Cordell, *20th Century* (1939); Cordell, *Representative Modern*; Gassner, *25 Best*; Warnock, *Representative Modern American*; Watson and Pressey, *American Plays*; Watson and Pressey, eds., *Contemporary Drama* (1941); *Best Plays* 1923–24.

Bravo (with Edna Ferber [1887–1968]) (1948). In *George S. Kaufman and His Collaborators* (New York: Performing Arts Journal, 1984).

The Butter and Egg Man (1925). In Leverton, *College Theatre* (1932, 1934); *Best Plays* 1925–26.

Dinner at Eight (with Edna Ferber) (1932). In *Best Plays* 1932–33.

Dulcy (with Marc Connelly) (1921). In Helen Louise Cohen, ed., *Longer Plays by Modern Authors (American)* (New York: Harcourt Brace, 1922); S. Perry Congdon, ed., *The Drama Reader* (New York: Odyssey, 1962); Moses, *American Dramas* (1926, 1941); *Best Plays* 1921–22.

First Lady (with Katharine Dayton [d. 1945]) (1935). In *Best Plays* 1935–36.

Merton of the Movies (with Marc Connelly) (1922). In Raymond W. Pence, ed., *Drama by Present-Day Writers* (New York: Scribner's, 1927).

Minick (with Edna Ferber) (1924). In *Best Plays* 1924–25.

Of Thee I Sing (with Morrie Ryskind [1895–1985]) (1931). In Durham and Dodds, *British and American*; Gassner, *Treasury* (1935); Coe and Cordell, *Pulitzer Plays*; Stanley Richards, ed., *Ten Great Musicals of the American Theatre* (Radnor, Pa.: Chilton, 1973); *Best Plays* 1931–32.

The Royal Family (with Edna Ferber) (1927). In *Best Plays* 1927–28.

To the Ladies (with Marc Connelly) (1922). In Quinn, *Contemporary*; Tucker, *Modern American and British*.

The Solid Gold Cadillac (with Howard Teichmann [1916–1987]) (1953). In Gassner, *Best Plays* 4th ser.

Stage Door (with Edna Ferber) (1936). In Clark and Davenport, *Nine Modern Plays*; Gassner, *20 Best*; *Best Plays* 1936–37.

Kelly, George (1887–1974)

Behold the Bridegroom (1927). In *Best Plays* 1927–28.

Craig's Wife (1925). In Gassner, *25 Best*; Lodwick C. Hartley and Arthur Ladu, eds., *Patterns in Modern Drama* (New York: Prentice-Hall, 1948); Moses, *Dramas of Modernism* (1931, 1941); Coe and Cordell, *Pulitzer Plays*; *Best Plays* 1925–26.

Daisy Mayme (1926). In *Best Plays* 1926–27.

The Fatal Weakness (1946). In *Best Plays* 1946–47.

Poor Aubrey (1929). In Gassner, *25 Best*; Russell B. Thomas, ed., *Plays and the Theatre* (Boston: Little, Brown, 1937).

The Show-Off (1924). In Moses, *American Dramas* (1926, 1933, 1941); *Best Plays* 1923–24.

Kingsley, Sidney (b. 1906)

Dead End (1935). In Cerf and Cartmell, *16 Famous*; Gassner, *20 Best*; *Best Plays* 1935–36.

Detective Story (1949). In George Freedley, ed., *Three Plays About Crime and Criminals* (New York: Washington Square, 1962); Gassner, *Best Plays* 3d ser.; Adrian H. Jaffe and H. Weisinger, eds., *The Laureate Fraternity* (Evanston, Ill.: Row, Peterson, 1960); *Best Plays* 1948–49.

Men in White (1933). In Gassner, *Best Plays* (suppl.); Gassner and Barnes, *50 Best*; Mersand, *Three Plays About Doctors*; Coe and Cordell, *Pulitzer Plays*; *Best Plays* 1933–34.

The Patriots (1943). In *Critics' Prize*; Gassner, *Best Plays*, 2d ser.; Gaver, *Critics' Choice*; *Best Plays* 1942–43.

The World We Make (1939). In *Best Plays* 1939–40.

Kober, Arthur (1900–1975)

Having Wonderful Time (1937). In Cerf and Cartmell, *16 Famous*.

Kummer, Clare (1889–1958)

Good Gracious Annabelle (1916). In *Best Plays* 1909–19.

Her Master's Voice (1933). In *Best Plays* 1933–34.

Lawson, John Howard (1895–1977)

Processional (1925). In Watson and Pressey, *American Plays*; Watson and Pressey, *Contemporary Dramas* (1941).

Roger Bloomer (1923). In Albert R. Fulton, ed., *Drama and Theatre* (New York: Holt, 1946).

Lindsay, Howard (1889–1968)

Life with Father (with Russell Crouse [1893–1966]) (1939). In Cerf and Cartmell, *16 Famous*; Cerf and Cartmell, *SRO*; Gassner, *Best Plays*, 2d ser.; Gassner and Barnes, *50 Best*; Stanley Richards, *The Most Popular Plays of the American Theatre* (New York: Stein & Day, 1979); *Best Plays* 1939–40.

Mackaye, Percy (1875–1956)

The Scarecrow (1908). In Gassner, *Best Plays Early American*; John Gassner and Morin Sweetkind, *Introducing the Drama* (New York: Holt, Rinehart & Winston, 1963); Moses, *American Dramas* (1926, 1933, 1941); Quinn, *Representative* (1917, 1925, 1928, 1938, 1953).

Millay, Edna St. Vincent (1892–1950)

Three Plays (New York: Harper's, 1926). Contains *Aria da Capo* (1919); *The Lamp and the Bell* (1921); *Two Slatterns and a King* (1918).

Moody, William Vaughn (1869–1910)

The Faith Healer (1909). In Quinn, *Representative* (all editions).

The Great Divide (1906). In Dickinson, *Chief Contemporary* (1915); Alan S. Downer, ed., *American Drama* (New York: Crowell, 1960); Gassner, *Best Plays Early American*; Richard Moody, ed., *Dramas from the American Theatre 1762–1909* (Cleveland: World, 1966); *Best Plays 1899–1909*.

Odets, Clifford (1906–1963)

Six Plays (New York: Modern Library, 1939). Contains *Awake and Sing* (1935); *Paradise Lost* (1935); *'Til the Day I Die* (1935); *Waiting for Lefty* (1935); *Golden Boy* (1937); *Rocket to the Moon* (1938).

Three Plays (New York: Random House, 1935). Contains *Awake and Sing; 'Til the Day I Die; Waiting for Lefty.*

The Country Girl (1950). In Stanley A. Clayes and David Spencer, eds., *Contemporary Drama* (New York: Scribner's, 1962); Stanley A. Clayes and David Spencer, eds., *Thirteen Plays*, 2d ed. (New York: Scribner's, 1970).

O'Neill, Eugene (1888–1953)

NOTE: Dates of the one-act plays and the unproduced plays are dates of composition (or, in limited cases, first publication); all others are dates of first production.

The Ancient Mariner (1923), ed. Donald Gallup, *Yale University Library Gazette* 35 (October 1960): 61–86.

Children of the Sea and Three Other Unpublished Plays by Eugene O'Neill, ed. Jennifer McCabe Atkinson (Washington, D.C.: NCR Microcard Editions, 1972). Contains *Bread and Butter* (1914); "Children of the Sea" (1914) (the first version of *Bound East for Cardiff*); *Now I Ask You* (1917); *Shell Shock* (1918).

Complete Plays of Eugene O'Neill, gen. ed. Travis Bogard (New York: Library of America [distributed by Viking], 1988).

Later Plays of Eugene O'Neill, ed. Travis Bogard (New York: Modern Library, 1967). Contains *Ah, Wilderness!* (1933); *Hughie* (published 1959); *A Moon for the Misbegotten* (1942); *A Touch of the Poet* (1942; published 1957).

The Long Voyage Home: Seven Plays of the Sea (New York: Modern Library, 1946). Contains *Bound East for Cardiff* (1916); *The Long Voyage Home* (1917); *The Moon of the Caribbees* (1918); *In the Zone* (1919); *Ile* (1917); *Where the Cross Is Made* (1919); *The Rope* (1919).

Lost Plays of Eugene O'Neill (New York: Citadel, 1963) (the original and unauthorized edition was published by New Fathoms Press [1950]). Contains *Abortion* (1914); *The Movie Man* (1914); *Servitude* (1914); *The Sniper* (1915); *A Wife for a Life* (1913).

Nine Plays by Eugene O'Neill (New York: Modern Library, 1959) (originally published by Liveright [1932]). Contains *All God's Chillun Got Wings* (1924); *Desire under the Elms* (1924); *The Emperor Jones* (1920); *The Great God Brown* (1926); *The Hairy Ape* (1922); *Lazarus Laughed* (1928); *Marco Millions* (1928); *Mourning Becomes Electra* (1932); *Strange Interlude* (1928).

Plays of Eugene O'Neill, 3 vols., (New York: Random House, n.d.) (unpaginated) (published as part of the Random House Lifetime Library). Contains all of O'Neill's produced one-act and full-length plays through *The Iceman Cometh* (1946), excluding *The Ancient Mariner*.

Selected Plays of Eugene O'Neill (New York: Random House, 1969). Contains *Anna Christie* (1921); *Desire under the Elms*; *The Emperor Jones*; *The Great God Brown*; *The Hairy Ape*; *The Iceman Cometh*; *Mourning Becomes Electra*; *Strange Interlude*.

Six Short Plays of Eugene O'Neill (New York: Vintage, 1965). Contains *Before Breakfast* (1916); *Diff'rent* (1920); *The Dreamy Kid* (1920); *Gold* (1921); *The Straw* (1921); *Welded* (1924).

Ten Lost Plays of Eugene O'Neill (New York: Random House, 1964). Contains *Abortion*; *Fog* (1914); *The Movie Man*; *Recklessness* (1914); *Servitude*; *The Sniper*; *Thirst* (1914); *Warnings* (1914); *The Web* (1914); *A Wife for a Life*.

Thirst and Other One-Act Plays (Boston: Gorham Press, 1914). (published at the expense of James O'Neill; except for a single review by family friend Clayton Hamilton in *Bookman* [April 1915], the volume went completely unnoticed; now extremely rare). Contains *Fog*; *Recklessness*; *Thirst*; *The Web*; *Warnings*.

Three Plays by Eugene O'Neill (New York: Modern Library, 1937). Contains *Anna Christie*; *The Emperor Jones*; *The Hairy Ape*.

Three Plays of Eugene O'Neill (New York: Vintage, n.d.). Contains *Desire under the Elms*; *Mourning Becomes Electra*; *Strange Interlude*.

Peabody, Josephine Preston (1874–1922)

The Piper (1910). In Moses, *American Dramas* (1926, 1933, 1941).

Rice, Elmer (1892–1967)

Three Plays (New York: Hill & Wang, 1965). Contains *The Adding Machine* (1923); *Street Scene* (1929); *Dream Girl* (1945).

Counselor-at-Law (1931). In *Famous Plays of 1932–1933* (London: Gollancz, 1933).

Flight to the West (1941). In *Best Plays 1940–41*.

Judgment Day (1934). In *Famous Plays of 1937* (London: Gollancz, 1937).

The Left Bank (1931). In *Best Plays* 1931–32.

See Naples and Die (1929). In *Famous Plays of 1932* (London: Gollancz, 1932).

We the People (1933). In *Best Plays* 1932–33.

Riggs, Lynn (1899–1954)

Green Grow the Lilacs (1931). In Clark and Davenport, *Nine Modern Plays*; Gassner, *Best Plays* (suppl.); Leverton (1932, 1934); *Best Plays* 1930–31.

Saroyan, William (1908–1981)

Three Plays (New York: Harcourt Brace, 1940). Contains *My Heart's in the Highlands* (1939); *The Time of Your Life* (1939); *Love's Old Sweet Song* (1940).

Three Plays (New York: Harcourt Brace, 1941). Includes *The Beautiful People* (1941).

Shaw, Irwin (1913–1984)

Bury the Dead (1936). In Gassner, *20 Best*; Stanley Richards, ed., *America on Stage* (Garden City, N.Y.: Doubleday, 1976).

Sherwood, Robert E. (1896–1955)

Abe Lincoln in Illinois (1938). In Clark and Davenport *Nine Modern Plays*; Cordell, *20th Century Plays*, American ed.; Gassner, *Best Plays*, 2d ser.; Gassner and Barnes, *50 Best*; Hatcher (1941, 1944, 1948, 1949); Watson and Pressey, *Contemporary Dramas* (1941); Watson and Pressey, *Nine Plays*; *Best Plays* 1938–39.

Idiot's Delight (1936). In Clurman, *Famous American Plays*; Gassner, *20 Best*; William Hildreth and Wilson Dumble, eds., *Five Contemporary American Plays* (New York: Harper's, 1939); Joseph E. Mersand, ed., *Three Dramas of American Realism* (New York: Washington Square, 1961); Moses, *Dramas of Modernism* (1941); *Best Plays* 1935–36.

The Petrified Forest (1935). In Cerf and Cartmell, *16 Famous*; Alan S. Downer, ed., *American Drama* (New York: Crowell, 1960); Moses, *American Dramas* (1941); Watson and Pressey, *American Plays*; *Best Plays* 1934–35.

Reunion in Vienna (1931). In *Theatre Guild*; *Best Plays* 1931–32.

The Road to Rome (1927). In Gassner, *25 Best*; *Best Plays* 1926–27.

There Shall Be No Night (1940). In John Mason Brown, *The Ordeal of a Playwright: Robert E. Sherwood and the Challenge of War* (New York: Harper & Row, 1970); Corbin and Balf, *Twelve American Plays*; Durham and Dodds, *British and American*; *Best Plays* 1939–40.

Spewack, Bella (b. 1899) and Samuel (1899–1971)

Boy Meets Girl (1935). In Cerf and Cartmell, *16 Famous*; Gassner, *20 Best*; Robert Saffron, ed., *Great Farces* (New York: Collier, 1966); *Best Plays* 1935–36.

Steinbeck, John (1902–1968)

The Moon Is Down (1942). In *Best Plays* 1941–42.

Of Mice and Men (1937). In *Critics' Prize*; Clurman, *Famous American Plays*; Gassner, *20 Best*; Gaver, *Critics' Choice*; *Best Plays* 1937–38.

Thomas, Augustus (1857–1934)

The Witching Hour (1907). In Dickinson, *Chief Contemporary* (1915); Gassner, *25 Best*; Moses, *American Dramas* (1926; 1933); Quinn, *Representative* (all editions); *Best Plays* 1899–1909.

Thurber, James (1894–1965)

The Male Animal (with Elliott Nugent [1900–1965]) (1940). In Bloomfield and Elliott, *10 Plays*; Bloomfield and Elliott, *Great Plays* (1965, 1975); Gassner, *Best Plays*, 2d ser.; Lodwick C. Hartley and Arthur Ladu, eds., *Patterns in Modern Drama* (New York: Prentice-Hall, 1948); Louis Kronenberger, ed., *Cavalcade of Comedy* (New York: Simon & Schuster, 1953); Miller *American Dramatic*; *Best Plays* 1939–40.

Treadwell, Sophie (1891–1970)

Machinal (1928). In Judith Barlow, *Plays by American Women* (New York: Avon, 1981); Gassner, 25 Best; *Best Plays* 1928–29.

Vollmer, Lula (1898–1955)

Sun-Up (1923). In Quinn, *Representative* (1925, 1928, 1930, 1938, 1953); Tucker, *Modern American and British*; Tucker, *25 Modern*; *Best Plays* 1923–24.

Walter, Eugene (1874–1941)

The Easiest Way (1909). In Dickinson, *Chief Contemporary* (1921); Gassner, *25 Best*; *Best Plays* 1909–19.

Wilder, Thornton (1897–1975)

The Long Christmas Dinner and Other Plays (New Haven: Yale University Press, 1931). Contains *The Long Christmas Dinner* (1931); *The Happy Journey to Trenton and Camden* (1931); *Pullman Car Hiawatha* (1931).

Three Plays (New York: Bantam, 1957). Contains *The Matchmaker* (1935); *Our Town* (1938); *The Skin of Our Teeth* (1942).

Our Town is also available in the following collections, most of which are more readily available than the small Bantam paperback: Cerf and Cartmell, *16 Famous*; Corbin and Balf, *12 American Plays*; Gassner, *Treasury* (1951, 1950–1951, 1960, 1963, 1970); *Best Plays* 1937–38.

The Skin of Our Teeth is also available in the following collections, most of which are more readily available than the small Bantam paperback: Robert W. Corrigan, ed., *The Modern Theatre* (New York: Macmillan, 1964); Paul M. Cubeta, ed., *Modern Drama for Analysis* (New York: Sloane, 1950); Paul M. Cubeta, ed., *Modern Drama for Analysis*, rev. ed. (New York: Dryden, 1955); Paul M. Cubeta, ed., *Modern Drama for Analysis*, 3d ed. (New York: Holt, Rinehart & Winston, 1962); Lee A. Jacobus, ed., *The Longman Anthology of American Drama* (New York: Longman, 1982); *Best Plays* 1942–43.

Williams, Jesse Lynch (1871–1929)

Why Marry? (1917). In Coe and Cordell, *Pulitzer Plays*; Quinn, *Contemporary*; *Best Plays* 1909–19.

SECONDARY WORKS

General References

Because critical and historical material in periodicals, histories, textbooks, and anthologies is abundant and easily available, no attempt has been made here to compile a complete reference bibliography. General histories of world drama and theater, such as those by John Gassner, George Freedley, Allardyce Nicoll, and others, have been omitted. Their discussions of the American theater are mostly noncritical historical reviews, and they often contain extensive bibliographies of their own. Periodical references are limited to a few that hold special interest. Newspaper and periodical critics such as John Mason Brown, Eric Bentley, George Jean Nathan, and others frequently published collections of their own essays covering the period between the wars, but because of space limitations only those pertinent to the contents of this volume have been listed. Titles that do not clearly indicate contents or those of special value have been annotated.

Anderson, John. *The American Theatre and the Motion Picture in America.* New York: Dial, 1938.

Anderson, Maxwell. *The Essence of Tragedy.* Washington, D.C.: Anderson House, 1939.

——— *Off Broadway: Essays about the Theatre.* New York: Sloane, 1947.

Baker, George Pierce. *Dramatic Technique.* Boston: Houghton Mifflin, 1919. Written by the man behind the Harvard 47 Workshop, this remains important in the history of dramatic criticism.

Bentley, Eric. *In Search of Theatre.* New York: Knopf, 1953; Vintage, 1954. Bentley ranks as one of the foremost American critics, editors, translators, and teachers of the drama. His enthusiasm for American drama, however, is limited, and he has many difficulties with O'Neill, demonstrated in "Trying to Like O'Neill," reprinted in this volume from the *Kenyon Review* of 14 July 1952.

———. *The Life of the Drama.* New York: Atheneum, 1964.

———. *The Playwright as Thinker.* New York: Renal & Hitchcock, 1946; Harcourt Brace, 1949.

Bigsby, C. W. E. *A Critical Introduction to Twentieth-Century American Drama,* 3 vols. Cambridge: Cambridge University Press, 1982–85.

Blake, Ben. *The Awakening of the American Theatre.* New York: Tomorrow Publishers, 1935. An account of the left-wing theater of the 1930s.

Block, Anita. *The Changing World in Plays and Theatre.* Boston: Little, Brown, 1939.

Broussard, Louis. *American Drama: Contemporary Allegory from Eugene O'Neill to Tennessee Williams.* Norman: University of Oklahoma Press, 1962.

Brown, John Mason. *Upstage: The American Theatre in Performance.* New York: Norton, 1930. Consult a library catalogue for other titles by Brown that incorporate collected criticism from his *Saturday Review* column, "Seeing Things."

Buttita, Tony, and Barry Witham. *Uncle Sam Presents: A Memoir of the Federal Theatre 1935–1939.* Philadelphia: University of Pennsylvania Press, 1982.

Cheney, Sheldon. *The Art Theatre.* New York: Knopf, 1925.

Clurman, Harold. *The Fervent Years: The Story of the Group Theatre and the Thirties.* New York: Hill & Wang, 1945, 1957.

Cohn, Ruby. *Dialogue in American Drama.* Bloomington: Indiana University Press, 1971.

Crowley, Alice Lewisohn. *The Neighborhood Playhouse: Leaves from a Theatre Scrapbook.* New York: Theatre Arts, 1959.

Deutsch, Helen, and Stella Hanau. *The Provincetown: A Story of the Theatre.* New York: Farrar & Rinehart, 1931.

Downer, Alan. *Fifty Years of American Drama, 1900–1950.* Chicago: Regnery, 1951.

Dusenbury, Winifred L. *The Theme of Loneliness in Modern American Drama.* Gainesville: University Presses of Florida, 1960.

Eaton, Walter Prichard. *The Theatre Guild: The First Ten Years.* New York: Brentano's, 1929.

Flanagan, Hallie. *Arena.* New York: Duell, Sloan & Pearce, 1940.

Flexner, Elizabeth. *American Playwrights, 1918–1938.* New York: Simon & Schuster, 1938.

Freedman, Morris. *American Drama in Social Context.* Carbondale: Southern Illinois University Press, 1971.

Gagey, Edmond. *Revolution in the American Drama.* New York: Columbia University Press, 1947.

Gilder, Rosamund. "The Federal Theatre: A Record." *Theatre Arts* 20 (June 1936): 430–38.

Glaspell, Susan. *The Road to the Temple.* New York: Stokes, 1927.

Goldberg, Isaac. *The Drama of Transition.* Cincinnati: Stewart, Kidd, 1922. One of the first books to discuss the new American realism of O'Neill and others.

Goldstein, Malcolm. *American Drama and the Theatre of the Great Depression.* New York: Oxford, 1974.

Gorelik, Mordecai. *New Theatres for Old.* New York: Samuel French, 1940. Thorough treatment of twentieth-century stage techniques by one of America's greatest scene designers.

Hamilton, Clayton. *The Theory of the Theatre.* New York: Holt, 1939.

Hartman, John Geoffrey. *The Development of American Social Comedy, 1787–1936.* Philadelphia: University of Pennsylvania Press, 1939.

Hewitt, Barnard. *Theatre USA, 1668–1957.* New York: McGraw-Hill, 1959.

Himelstein, Morgan Y. *Drama Was a Weapon: The Left-Wing Theatre in New York 1929–1941.* New Brunswick, N.J.: Rutgers University Press, 1963. Important discussionn of agitprop and other Depression plays.

Houseman, John. *Run-Through.* New York: Simon & Schuster, 1980. First of a three-volume autobiography by one of the most important figures in modern American drama, radio, screen, and television. The second and third volumes, less relevant to the between-the-wars theater but of equal interest, are *Front and Center* (1980) and *Final Dress* (1983) (also published by Simon & Schuster).

Isaacs, Edith J. R. *The Negro in the American Theatre.* New York: Theatre Arts, 1935.

Jones, Robert Edmond. *The Dramatic Imagination.* New York: Duell, Sloan & Pearce, 1941.

Kinne, Wisner Payne. *George Pierce Baker and the American Theatre*. Cambridge: Harvard University Press, 1954.

Kronenberger, Louis. *The Threat of Laughter: Chapters on English Comedy from Jonson to Somerset Maugham*. New York: Knopf, 1953. Discusses British rather than American playwrights, but a valuable study of all aspects of stage comedy.

Krutch, Joseph Wood. *The American Drama since 1918*. New York: Braziller, 1939; rev. ed., 1957. Outstanding general survey of American playwriting between the wars, written by one of America's leading critics and academic scholars.

————. *Modernism in Modern Drama*. Ithaca: Cornell University Press, 1953.

Langner, Lawrence. *The Magic Curtain*. New York: Dutton, 1951. Personal recollections by a founder of the Theatre Guild.

Lawson, John Howard. *Theory and Technique of Playwriting*. New York: Putnam's, 1936.

McCarthy, Mary. *Theatre Chronicles 1937–1962*. New York: Farrar, Straus, 1961.

Macgowan, Kenneth, and Robert Edmond Jones. *The Theatre of Tomorrow*. New York: Liveright, 1921.

Mathews, Jane DeHart. *The Federal Theatre, 1935–1939: Plays, Relief, and Politics*. Princeton: Princeton University Press, 1967.

Meserve, Walter J. *An Outline History of American Drama*. Totawa, N.J.: Littlefield Adams, 1969.

Nannes, Caspar H. *Politics in the American Drama*. Washington, D.C.: Catholic University of America Press, 1960.

Nathan, George Jean. *Art of the Night*. New York: Knopf, 1928. Consult a library catalogue for Nathan's many other books of reviews and criticism.

Nicoll, Allardyce. *The Theory of Drama*. London: Harrap, 1931. Excellent discussions of tragedy and comedy by one of the world's leading drama and theater scholars.

O'Connor, John, and Lorraine Brown. *Free, Adult, Uncensored: The Living History of the Federal Theatre Project*. Washington, D.C.: New Republic Books, 1978.

Orr, John. *Tragic Drama and Modern Society: Studies in the Social and Literary Theory of Drama from 1870 to the Present*. New York: Macmillan, 1981.

Porter, Thomas E. *Myth and Modern American Drama*. Detroit: Wayne State University Press, 1969.

Quinn, Arthur Hobson. *A History of American Drama from the Civil War to the Present Day*. New York: Appleton-Century-Crofts, 1937. The standard history of the period; somewhat overbalanced toward nineteenth- and early twentieth–century drama.

Rabkin, Gerald. *Drama and Commitment: Politics in the American Theatre of the Thirties*. Bloomington: Indiana University Press, 1964.

Scanlan, Tom. *Family, Drama, and American Dreams*. Westport, Conn.: Greenwood Press, 1978.

Sievers, W. David. *Freud on Broadway*. New York: Hermitage House, 1955.

Simonson, Lee. *Part of a Lifetime*. New York: Duell, Sloan & Pearce, 1943. Report of the famous designer's life with the Theatre Guild.

———. *The Stage Is Set*. New York: Harcourt Brace, 1932. Theatrical and dramatic techniques from the designer's viewpoint.

Smith, Wendy. *Real Life Drama: The Group Theatre and America, 1931–1940*. New York: Knopf, 1990.

Stanislavsky, Konstantin. *An Actor Prepares*. New York: Theatre Arts, 1939. Provides much of the basis for the Group Theatre's development of Method acting.

Sypher, Wylie, ed. *Comedy*. New York: Doubleday, 1956. Excellent study for all types of comedy, on stage and off.

Valgemae, Mardi. *Accelerated Grimace: Expressionism in the American Drama of the 1920s*. Carbondale: Southern Illinois University Press, 1972. One of the few extended studies of expressionism.

Waldau, Roy S. *Vintage Years of the Theatre Guild 1928–1939*. Cleveland: Western Reserve University Press, 1972.

Weales, Gerald. *The Group Theatre and Its Plays*. New York: St. Martin's, 1967.

Weisman, Philip. *Creativity in the Theatre: A Psychoanalytic Study*. New York: Basic Books, 1965.

Whitman, Willson. *Bread and Circuses: A Study of the Federal Theatre*. New York: Oxford, 1937.

Zeigler, Joseph Wesley. *Regional Theatre*. Minneapolis: University of Minnesota Press, 1973.

Books and Articles on Individual Playwrights

Anderson, Maxwell

Bailey, Mabel. *Maxwell Anderson: The Playwright as Prophet*. New York: Abelard-Schuman, 1957.

Clark, Barrett H. *Maxwell Anderson: The Man and His Plays*. New York: Samuel French, 1933.

Mason, Jeffrey D. "Maxwell Anderson's Dramatic Theory and Key Largo." *North Dakota Quarterly* 48 (Summer 1980): 38–52.

Miller, Jordan Y. "Maxwell Anderson: Gifted Technician." In *The Thirties: Fiction, Poetry, Drama*, ed. Warren French. Deland, Fla.: Everett / Edwards, 1967.

Shivers, Alfred S. *The Life of Maxwell Anderson*. New York: Stein & Day, 1983.

———. *Maxwell Anderson*. Boston: Twayne, 1976.

———. *Maxwell Anderson: An Annotated Bibliography of Primary and Secondary Works*. Metuchen, N.J.: Scarecrow, 1985.

Barry, Philip

Parker, H. T. "Off the Deep End Plunges Philip Barry." In *American Drama and Its Critics*, ed. Alan S. Downer. Chicago: University of Chicago Press, 1965.

Roppolo, Joseph P. *Philip Barry*. New York: Twayne, 1965.

Weales, Gerald. "The Very High Comedy of Philip Barry." *Commonweal* 103 (17 August 1976): 564–66.

Behrman, S. N.

Reed, Kenneth T. *S. N. Behrman*. Boston: Twayne, 1975.

Belasco, David

Marker, Lise-Lone. *David Belasco: Naturalism in the American Theatre*. Princeton: Princeton University Press, 1974.

Timberlake, Craig. *The Bishop of Broadway*. New York: Library Publishers, 1954.

Winter, William. *The Life of David Belasco*. New York: Moffat Yard & Co., 1918.

Boothe, Clare

Carlson, Susan L. "Comic Textures and Female Communities 1937 and 1977: Clare Boothe and Wendy Wasserstein." *Modern Drama* 17 (December 1984): 564–73.

Connelly, Marc

Nolan, Paul T. *Marc Connelly*. New York: Twayne, 1969.

Crothers, Rachel

Gottlieb, Lois C. *Rachel Crothers*. Boston: Twayne, 1979.

Gale, Zona

Derleth, August W. *Still Small Voice: The Biography of Zona Gale.* New York: Appleton-Century, 1940.

Glaspell, Susan

Sarlós, Robert K. *Jig Cook and the Provincetown Players: Theatre in Ferment.* Amherst: University of Massachusetts Press, 1982.

Waterman, Arthur. *Susan Glaspell.* New York: Twayne, 1966.

Green, Paul

Kenny, Vincent S. *Paul Green.* New York: Twayne, 1971.

Hecht, Ben

Fetherling, Doug. *The Five Lives of Ben Hecht.* New York: New York Zoetrope, 1977.

Hellman, Lillian

Falk, Doris V. *Lillian Hellman.* New York: Ungar, 1978.

Feibleman, Peter S. *Lilly: Reminiscences of Lillian Hellman.* New York: Morrow, 1988.

Lederer, Katherine. *Lillian Hellman.* Boston: Twayne, 1979.

Moody, Richard. *Lillian Hellman, Playwright.* New York: Pegasus, 1972.

Rollyson, Carl E. *Lillian Hellman: Her Legend and Her Legacy.* New York: St. Martin's, 1978.

Wright, William. *Lillian Hellman: The Image, the Woman.* New York: Simon & Schuster, 1986.

Herne, James A.

Edwards, Herbert J., and Julia R. Herne. *James A. Herne: The Rise of Realism in the American Drama.* Orono: University of Maine Press, 1964.

Perry, John. *James A. Herne, the American Ibsen.* Chicago: Nelson-Hall, 1978.

Heyward, DuBose

Durham, Frank. *DuBose Heyward: The Man Who Wrote Porgy.* Port Washington, N.Y.: Kennikat Press, 1954, 1975.

Slaavik, William H. *DuBose Heyward.* Boston: Twayne, 1981.

Howard, Sidney

Meserve, Walter J. "Sidney Howard and the Social Drama of the Twenties." *Modern Drama* 6 (December 1963): 256–66.

White, Sidney Howard. *Sidney Howard.* Boston: Twayne, 1977.

Kaufman, George S.

Goldstein, Malcolm. *George S. Kaufman: His Life, His Theater.* New York: Oxford, 1979.

Hart, Moss. *Act One.* New York: Random House, 1959.

Mason, Jeffrey D. *Wisecracks: The Farces of George S. Kaufman.* Ann Arbor: University of Michigan Research Press, 1988.

Meredith, Scott. *George S. Kaufman and His Friends.* New York: Doubleday, 1978.

Oliver, Donald, ed. *By George: A Kaufman Collection.* New York: St. Martin's, 1979.

Pollack, Rhoda-Gale. *George S. Kaufman.* Boston: Twayne, 1988.

Teichman, Howard. *George S. Kaufman: An Intimate Portrait.* New York: Dell, 1973.

Kelly, George

Hirsch, Foster. *George Kelly.* Boston: Twayne, 1975.

Wills, Arthur. "The Kelly Play." *Modern Drama* 6 (December 1963): 245–55.

Lindsay, Howard

Skinner, Cornelia Otis. *Life with Lindsay and Crouse.* Boston: Houghton Mifflin, 1976.

Millay, Edna St. Vincent

Atkins, Elizabeth. *Edna St. Vincent Millay and Her Times.* New York: Russell & Russell, 1936.

Brittin, Norman A. *Edna St. Vincent Millay.* New York: Twayne, 1967.

Brown, Maurice. *Estranging Dawn: The Life and Works of Edna St. Vincent Millay.* Carbondale: Southern Illinois University Press, 1973.

Cheney, Anne. *Millay in Greenwich Village.* Tuscaloosa: University of Alabama Press, 1975.

Gould, Jean. *The Poet and Her Book: A Biography of Edna St. Vincent Millay.* New York: Dodd, Mead, 1969.

Gurko, Miriam. *Restless Spirit: The Life of Edna St. Vincent Millay.* New York: Crowell, 1962.

Moody, William Vaughn

Halpern, Martin. *William Vaughn Moody.* New York: Twayne, 1967.

Odets, Clifford

Brennan-Gibson, Margaret. *Clifford Odets, American Playwright: The Years from 1906 to 1940.* New York: Atheneum, 1981.

Cantor, Harold. *Clifford Odets: Playwright-Poet.* Metuchen, N.J.: Scarecrow, 1978.

Mendelsohn, Michael J. *Clifford Odets, Humane Dramatist.* DeLand, Fla.: Everett / Edwards, 1969.

Murray, Edward. *Clifford Odets: The Thirties and After.* New York: Ungar, 1968.

Shuman, Robert B. *Clifford Odets.* New York: Twayne, 1962.

Weales, Gerald. *Clifford Odets: Playwright.* New York: Pegasus, 1971.

O'Neill, Eugene

Alexander, Doris. *The Tempering of Eugene O'Neill.* New York: Harcourt, Brace & World, 1962.

Asselineau, Roger. "Mourning Becomes Electra as a Tragedy." *Modern Drama* 1 (December 1958): 143–50.

Atkinson, Jennifer McCabe. *Eugene O'Neill: A Descriptive Bibliography.* Pittsburgh: University of Pittsburgh Press, 1974.

Barlow, Judith E. *Final Acts: The Creation of Three Late O'Neill Plays.* Athens: University of Georgia Press, 1985.

Berlin, Normand. *Eugene O'Neill.* New York: Grove, 1982.

Bogard, Travis. *Contour in Time: The Plays of Eugene O'Neill.* New York: Oxford, 1972.

Boulton, Agnes. *Part of a Long Story.* New York: Doubleday, 1958.

Bowen, Croswell, with the assistance of Shane O'Neill. *The Curse of the Misbegotten.* New York: McGraw-Hill, 1959.

Bryer, Jackson R., ed. *The Theatre We Worked For: The Letters of Eugene O'Neill to Kenneth Macgowan.* New Haven: Yale University Press, 1987.

Cargill, Oscar, N. Bryllion Fagan, and William J. Fishner. *O'Neill and His Plays.* New York: New York University Press, 1961.

Carpenter, Frederic I. *Eugene O'Neill.* Boston: Twayne, 1979.

Charbrowe, Leonard. *Ritual and Pathos: The Theatre of O'Neill.* Lewisburg, Pa.: Bucknell University Press, 1976.

Chothia, Jean. *Forging a Language: A Study of the Plays of Eugene O'Neill.* Cambridge: Cambridge University Press, 1979.

Clark, Barrett H. *Eugene O'Neill: The Man and His Plays.* New York: McBride, 1926, 1929; rev. ed., New York: Dover, 1947.

Engel, Edwin. *The Haunted Heroes of Eugene O'Neill.* Cambridge: Harvard University Press, 1953.

Falk, Doris. *Eugene O'Neill and the Tragic Tension.* New Brunswick, N.J.: Rutgers University Press, 1958.

Floyd, Virginia. *Eugene O'Neill: A World View.* New York: Ungar, 1979.

―――. *Eugene O'Neill at Work.* New York: Ungar, 1981.

―――. *Eugene O'Neill: The Unfinished Plays.* New York: Ungar, 1988.

―――. *The Plays of Eugene O'Neill: A New Perspective.* New York: Ungar, 1985.

Frazer, Winifred L. *E. G. and E. G. O.: Emma Goldman and "The Iceman Cometh."* Gainesville: University Presses of Florida, 1947.

Frenz, Horst. *Eugene O'Neill.* New York: Ungar, 1971.

―――, and Susan Tuck, eds. *Eugene O'Neill's Critics: Voices from Abroad.* Carbondale: University of Southern Illinois Press, 1984.

Gallup, Donald, ed. *Eugene O'Neill Work Diary, 1924–1943,* 2 vols. New Haven: Yale University Library, 1981.

Gassner, John. *O'Neill.* Englewood Cliffs, N.J.: Prentice-Hall, 1964.

Gelb, Arthur, and Barbara Gelb. *O'Neill.* New York: Harper & Row, 1960.

Long, Chester Clayton. *The Role of Nemesis in the Structure of Selected Plays by Eugene O'Neill.* The Hague: Mouton, 1968.

Lucow, Ben. "O'Neill's Use of Realism in *Ah, Wilderness!*" *Notes in Modern American Literature* 1 (1977): item 10.

Manheim, Michael. *Eugene O'Neill's New Language of Kinship.* Syracuse, N.Y.: Syracuse University Press, 1982.

Martine, James J. *Critical Essays on Eugene O'Neill.* Boston: G. K. Hall, 1984.

Miller, Jordan Y. *Eugene O'Neill and the American Critic.* Hamden, Conn.: Shoe String Press, 1962; rev. ed., 1973.

―――. *Playwright's Progress: O'Neill and the Critics.* Chicago: Scott Foresman, 1975.

Orlandello, John. *O'Neill on Film,* Rutherford, N.J.: Fairleigh Dickinson University Press, 1982.

Raleigh, John Henry. *The Plays of Eugene O'Neill.* Carbondale: Southern Illinois University Press, 1965.

Ranald, Margaret Loftus. *The Eugene O'Neill Companion.* Westport, Conn.: Greenwood Press, 1984.

Roberts, Nancy L., and Arthur W. Roberts. *As Ever, Gene: The Letters of Eugene O'Neill to George Jean Nathan.* Rutherford, N.J.: Fairleigh Dickinson University Press, 1987.

Robinson, James A. *Eugene O'Neill and Oriental Thought: A Divided Vision.* Carbondale: Southern Illinois University Press, 1982.

Sanborn, Ralph, and Barrett H. Clark. *A Bibliography of the Works of Eugene O'Neill.* New York: Random House, 1931; rev. ed., New York: Benjamin Blom, 1965.

Scheick, Williams J. "The Ending of O'Neill's *Beyond the Horizon.*" *Modern Drama* 20 (September 1977): 293–98.

Sheaffer, Louis. *O'Neill: Son and Playwright.* Boston: Little, Brown, 1978.

———. *O'Neill: Son and Artist.* Boston: Little, Brown, 1973.

Skinner, Richard Dana. *Eugene O'Neill: A Poet's Quest.* New York: Longmans, Green, 1935.

Smith, Madeline, and Richard Eaton. *Eugene O'Neill: An Annotated Bibliography.* New York: Garland, 1988.

Tiusanen, Timo. *O'Neill's Scenic Images.* Princeton: Princeton University Press, 1968.

Törnqvist, Egil. *A Drama of Souls: Studies in O'Neill's Super-Naturalistic Technique.* New Haven: Yale University Press, 1969.

Van Lamm, Thomas F. "Singing in the Wilderness: The Dark Vision of Eugene O'Neill's Only Mature Comedy." *Modern Drama* 22 (March 1979): 9–18.

Wasserstrom, William. "Notes on Electricity: Henry Adams and Eugene O'Neill." *Psychological Review* 1 (Spring 1977): 161–78.

Whitman, Robert. "O'Neill's Search for a Language of Theatre." *Quarterly Journal of Speech* 46 (April 1960): 153–70.

Winther, Sophus Keith. *Eugene O'Neill: A Critical Study.* New York: Random House, 1934.

Rice, Elmer

Durham, Frank. *Elmer Rice.* New York: Twayne, 1970.

Hogan, Robert G. *The Independence of Elmer Rice.* Carbondale: Southern Illinois University Press, 1965.

Palmieri, Anthony. *Elmer Rice: A Playwright's Vision.* Rutherford, N.J.: Fairleigh Dickinson University Press, 1980.

Saroyan, William

Calonne, David S. *William Saroyan: My Real Work Is Being.* Chapel Hill: University of North Carolina Press, 1983.

Floan, Howard R. *William Saroyan.* New York: Twayne, 1966.

Lee, Lawrence, and Barry Gifford. *Saroyan: A Biography*. New York: Harper & Row, 1984.

Saroyan, Aram. *William Saroyan*. New York: Harcourt Brace, Jovanovich, 1983.

Sherwood, Robert E.

Brown, John Mason. *The Ordeal of a Playwright: Robert E. Sherwood and the Challenge of War*. New York: Harper & Row, 1970.

————. *The Worlds of Robert E. Sherwood: Mirror to His Time*. New York: Harper & Row, 1965.

Meserve, Walter J. *Robert E. Sherwood, Reluctant Moralist*. New York: Pegasus, 1970.

Shuman, Robert B. *Robert E. Sherwood*. New York: Twayne, 1964.

Steinbeck, John

Benson, Jackson J. *The True Adventures of John Steinbeck*. New York: Viking, 1984.

Fontenrose, Joseph E. *John Steinbeck: An Introduction and Interpretation*. New York: Holt, Rinehart & Winston, 1963.

French, Warren. *John Steinbeck*. New York: Twayne, 1961.

Goldhurst, William. "Of Mice and Men: John Steinbeck's Parable of the Curse of Cain." *Western American Literature* 8 (Summer 1971): 123–35.

Lisca, Peter. *The Wide World of John Steinbeck*. New Brunswick, N.J.: Rutgers University Press, 1958.

McCarthy, Paul. *John Steinbeck*. New York: Ungar, 1980.

Thurber, James

Bernstein, Burton. *Thurber: A Biography*. New York: Dodd, Mead, 1975.

Holmes, Charles, ed. *Thurber: A Collection of Critical Essays*. Englewood Cliffs, N.J.: Prentice-Hall, 1974.

Morsberger, Robert E. *James Thurber*. New York: Twayne, 1964.

Wilder, Thornton

Burbank, Rex. *Thornton Wilder*. New York: Twayne, 1961.

Goldstein, Malcolm. *The Art of Thornton Wilder*. Lincoln : University of Nebraska Press, 1965.

Goldstone, Richard H. *Thornton Wilder: An Intimate Portrait*. New York: Saturday Review Press, 1975.

Harrison, Gilbert A. *The Enthusiast: A Life of Thornton Wilder*. New Haven: Ticknor & Fields, 1973.

Index

Abbey Theatre (Dublin), ix, 3, 41

Abbott, George, 224–26

Abe Lincoln in Illinois (Sherwood), 122, 146–47, 197

Abie's Irish Rose (Nichols), 204

Abortion (O'Neill), 39, 41

Abraham Lincoln (Drinkwater), 146

Act One (Hart autobiography), 214, 218

Actor Prepares, An (Stanislavsky), 102

Actors' strike, 2

Actors' Studio, 105, 281n4

Adams, Henry, 86

Adams, Maude, in *Peter Pan*, 228n1

Adding Machine, The (Rice), 36, 159–63, 167, 213, 264

Adler, Luther and Stella, 105

Aeschylus, 88, 89

Aesthetic distance, maintaing in realism, 170

Agitprop theater, 115–18

Ah, Wilderness! (O'Neill), 47, 61, 93–95, 264; staged with *Long Day's Journey into Night*, 280n40

Akins, Zoë, 13, 24, 272n6

Alexander, Doria, 82

Algonquin Roundtable, 217

Alien Corn (S. Howard), 139

Alienation in realism, 170

Alison's House (Glaspell), 18

All God's Chillun Got Wings (O'Neill), 15, 65–67, 71, 99, 251; character names 277n17

Allegory, in *Golden Boy*, 183; in *Here Come the Clowns* and *Hotel Universe*, 235; in *Of Mice and Men*, 207; in *Petrified Forest*, 144; in *Tomorrow and Tomorrow*, 235

American Landscape (Rice), 167

American Way, The (Kaufman and Hart), 218

Ames, Winthrop, x, 3

Ancient Mariner, The (O'Neill), 64, 71, 274n19

Anderson, John, on *Strange Interlude*, 84

Anderson, Judith, in *Strange Interlude*, 278n28

Anderson, Maxwell, viii, 6, 36, 103, 121, 122–33, 283n6, 283n8; as tragic writer, 127, 130; compared with O'Neill, 122–23; dramatization of warfare, 123–25; Tudor plays, 125–27

Anderson, Robert, 286n12

Angel That Troubled the Waters, The (Wilder), 236

Animal Crackers, (Kaufman), 220

Animal Kingdom, The (Barry), 222–23

Anna Christie (O'Neill), 48, 58–60, 67; film version 277n18

Anne of the Thousand Days (Anderson), 125, 127

Anouilh, Jean, 282n2

Ansky, Solomon, 5

Antigone (Anouilh), 283n5

Antoine, André, ix

Antoinette Perry Award (the Tony), for *Our Town*, 237

Archibald, William, 286n13

Ardrey, Robert, 105

Arena (Flanagan book), 281n6

Aria da Capo (Millay), 19–20, 35, 99; as fantasy, 233

Aristophanes, 233

Aristotle, 210

Armory exhibition, x–xi

Art theaters. *See* Little Theater movement

Arthur, Helen, 6

As Husbands Go (Crothers), 23

Atkinson, Brooks, on Kingsley 191; on *Life with Father*, 227; on *Outward Room*, 197

Austen, Jane, 13

Awake and Sing (Odets), 104, 174, *175–77*

Back to Methusala (Shaw), 282n2

Bad Seed (Anderson), 283n8

Baker, George Pierce, 9, 49; 47 Workshop, 4, 6, 39

Balderston, John, 233

Bandbox Theatre, 12

Bankhead, Tallulah, in *Little Foxes*, 203

Barefoot in Athens (Anderson), 283n8

Barrie, J. M., 232

Barry, Philip, 37, 211, 288n6; high comedy of, 221–23; fantasy of, 234–36

Barrymore, Ethel, 6, 219

Barrymore, John, 5, 219

Barrymore, Lionel, 219

Basic Training of Pavlo Hummel, The (Rabe), 282n4

Basshe, Emanual (Em Jo), 100, 101

Be Yourself (Kaufman and Connelly), 213

Beach, Lewis, 250

Beautiful People, The, (Saroyan), 244

Before Breakfast (O'Neill), 41

Beggar on Horseback (Kaufman and Connelly), 213–14

Behold the Bridegroom (Kelly), 189–90

Behrman, S. N., 37, 121, *148–58*, 211, 221

Bel Geddes, Norman, 194

Belasco, David, 2, 29, 190–91, 249

Bell, The (Sifton), 101

Ben-Ami, Jacob, 6

Benavente, Jacinto, 20, 35

Bentley, Eric, 273n5; on artistic interpretation, 170–71; on melodrama, 198

Berkeley Square (Balderston), 233–34, 235

Bernice (Glaspell), 17

Between Two Worlds (Rice), 167

Bewitched (Howard and Sheldon), 134

Beyond the Horizon (O'Neill), 40, 48–52, 58, 67, 72, 75, 264

Bigsby, C. W. E., on alienation, 170

Biography (Behrman), *153–55*

Birth of Tragedy, The (Nietzsche), 85

Black actors, in *All God's Chillun*, 65; in *Dreamy Kid*, 53; in *Emperor Jones*, 53; in *Green Pastures*, 258–59; in

Mamba's Daughters, 257; in *Porgy*, 254–56; in "voodoo" *Macbeth*, 109, 111
Black Pit (Sklar), 116
Blair, Mary, in *Diff'rent*, 35
Bland, James A., 249
"Blind Alley Guy" (O'Neill), 275nl
Blitzstein, Marc, 112
Bogard, Travis, on *Emperor Jones*, 58
Bogart, Humphrey, in *Petrified Forest*, 284n12
Bonds of Interest (Benavente), 20, 35
Boni, Charles and Albert, 11
Boothe, Clare, 211, 226–27, 231
Both Your Houses (Anderson), 131
Boulton, Agnes, 61, 88
Bound East for Cardiff (O'Neill), 9, 39–40, 41, 43
Boy Meets Girl (Spewack), 226
Boyce, Neith, 8, 9
Boyd, William, in *What Price Glory?* 283n5
Bradford, Roark, 257
Brand, Millen, 197
Bravo (Kaufman and Ferber), 220
Bread and Butter (O'Neill), 274n13
Bridge of San Luis Rey (Wilder), 236
Brief Moment (Behrman), 156
Broadway (Abbott and Weaver), 225, 264
Brontës, 13
Brother Rat (Monks and Finklehoffe), 230
Broun, Heywood, on *Bound East for Cardiff*, 40
Browder, Earl, 115
Brown, Gilmore, 3
Brown, John Mason, on Welles's *Julius Caesar*, 113; on George Kelly, 286n7
Brown, Maurice, x, 3
Browning, Elizabeth Barrett, 13
Browning, Robert, 233
Bryant, Louise, 9
Büchner, George, 114
Bury the Dead (Irwin Shaw), viii
Butter and Egg Man, The (Kaufman), 213

Cabinet of Dr. Caligari, The, 273n7
Cagney, James, in *What Price Glory?* film, 283n5
Caldwell, Erskine, 260
Calms of Capricorn, The (O'Neill), 278n22
Camera Work (Stieglitz), xii
Candle in the Wind (Anderson), 131
Carlin, Terry, 8
Carnovsky, Morris, 76, 105
Carolina Playmakers, 249
Carpenter, Frederick, on *Strange Interlude*, 79
"Carry Me Back to Old Virginny" (song), 249
Carter, Jack, 112
Censorship, *All God's Chillun*, 65, 277n16; *Children's Hour*, 199, 200, 286n12; *Desire under the Elms*, 71, 277n20; *Ethiopia*, 107; *Hairy Ape*, 61, 63, 277n16; *Mrs. Warren's Profession*, 273n8; NEA, 282n9; *Strange Interlude*, 278n25
Centuries, The (Basshe), 101
Chains of Dew (Glaspell), 18
Chase, Mary, 245–46
Chekhov, Anton, ix, 5, 13; compared to Odets, 174–75, 184
Children of the Sea (O'Neill), 9, 39, 274n13
Children's Hour, The (Hellman), 199–201, 205; censorship attempts, 286n12; film version 286n12
Chris. See Anna Christie
Chris Christopherson. See Anna Christie
Circle-in-the-Square, 78
Citizen Kane (Welles film), 114
City, The (Fitch), 29
Civic Repertory Theatre, 18, 25, 104, 117
Claire, Ina, 156
Clash by Night (Odets), 184
Cleveland Playhouse, 3
Climbers, The (Fitch), 29
Clod, The (Beach), 250
Close the Book (Glaspell), 16
Clurman, Harold, 102, 104

Cocoanuts, The (Kaufman and Ryskind), 220

Cohan, George M., in *Ah, Wilderness!* 93; in *I'd Rather be Right*, 216

Coleridge, Samuel Taylor, 30

Collier, Jeremy, vii

Comedy defined, 210–11

Comedy Theatre, 12, 13; becomes Mercury, 113

Commedia dell'arte, aspects in *Aria da Capo*, 19

Communist Manifesto, 118, 196

Communism, cell in Group Theatre, 104; in Odets, 171–74; Stalin-Hitler pact, 117; support of agitprop, 115–16, 118

Congreve, William, 10, 148

Conklin, E. P., 146

Connelly, Marc, 257–59; as Kaufman collaborator, 213–14

Conrad, Joseph, O'Neill compared to, 274n13

Constancy (Boyce), 9

Cook, George Cram, 8, 11, 15, 46, 48, 55

Coolidge, Calvin, 99

Cornell, Katharine, 111, in *No Time for Comedy*, 157

Coughlin, Father, 108

Count of Monte Cristo, The x, 45, 274n15

Country Girl, The (Odets), 184; film 285n6

Cradle Will Rock, The (Blitzstein), 112–13, 172, 264; revival 1983, 282n11

Craig's Wife (Kelly), 187, 188–89, 264

Crane, Stephen, 123

Crawford, Cheryl, 25, 102, 105, 281n4

Cronyn, Hume, in *Madame Will You Walk*, 139

Crosby, Bing, in *High Society*, 223; in film of *Country Girl*, 285n6

Crothers, Rachel, 21–24

Crouse, Russell, 227

Crucible, The (Miller), 286n13

Cue for Passion (Rice), 167

Daily Worker, 101, 115

Daisy Mayme (Kelly), 189

Dakota Playmakers, 249

Daly, Augustin, 273n8

Danton's Death (Büchner, Welles production), 114

Daring Young Man on the Flying Trapeze, The (Saroyan), 242

Davis, Bette, in *Petrified Forest* film, 284n12

Davis, Owen, 150

Davy Crockett (Murdoch), 249

Day, Clarence, 227

Day, Cyrus, 86

Days to Come (Hellman), 201

Days without End (O'Neill), 24, 47, 95–96

Dead End (Kingsley), 194–96, 197

Déclassé (Akins), 24

Deep Mrs. Sykes, The (Kelly), 190

Dekker, Thomas, 114

Dell, Floyd, xi

Desire under the Elms (O'Neill), 67–71, 75, 136, 253; censorship of, 277n20; character names, 277n19; film version, 277n20; parallels to Greek tragedy, 68; rivivals, 277n20

Detroit Arts and Crafts Theatre, 3

Deutsch, Helen, 8

DeVoto, Bernard, on Nobel award to O'Neill, 96

Dewhurst, Colleen, in *Ah, Wilderness* and *Long Day's Journey*, 280n40; in *Desire under the Elms*, 277n20

Dickinson, Emily, 14, 18

Diff'rent (O'Neill), 58

Digges, Dudley, 35

Dinner at Eight (Kaufman and Ferber), 219

Dirksen, Everett, and Federal Theatre Project, 281n9

Dodsworth (Howard), 139

Doll's House, A (Ibsen), viii

Dome, plaster, construction of by Provincetown, 55–56; use in plays *The Verge*, 17 and *Emperor Jones*, 56

Dos Passos, John, 37, 100

Drama Critics Circle Award, for *My Heart's in the Highlands*, 243; *Of Mice and Men*, 206; *Patriots*, 197; *Watch on the Rhine*, 203; *Winterset*, 130

Dramatists' Guild, 139

Draper, Ruth, 6

Dream Girl (Rice), 167

Dream Play, The (Strindberg), 33, 214

Dreamy Kid, The (O'Neill), 45, 53

Drinkwater, John, 146

Dulcy (Kaufman and Connelly), 213

Duncan, Augustin, 35

Duncan, Isadora, xi

Duncan, Sandy, in *Peter Pan*, 288n1

Dunlap, William, 233

Dunning, Philip, 225

Dunsany, Lord, 5, 12

Dybbuk, The (Ansky), 5

Dynamo (O'Neill), 83, 86–87; and Lawson's *Nirvana*, 281n2; intended sequels, 279n34

Eastman, Max, 9

Eaton, Walter Prichard, on the Theatre Guild, 35, 38

Electra complex, 88

Eliot, George, 13

Elizabeth the Queen (Anderson), 125–26

Emperor Jones, The (O'Neill), 10, 11, 15, 52–58, 75, 111, 215, 251, 264; film and opera versions, 276n10

End of Summer (Behrman), 156

Enemy at the Door, British TV production of German occupation, 287n18

Engel, Edward, 79, 91

Ensemble acting, 102

Erlanger, A. L., 2

Ervine, St. John, 35

Essence of Tragedy, The (Anderson), 123, 127

Ethan Frome (Wharton), 253

Ethiopia (Federal Theatre), 107, 109

Eugenically Speaking (Goodman), 12

Eve of St. Mark, The (Anderson), 132–33; London production, 283n7

Exorcism (O'Neill), 45

Experimental Theatre, Inc., 10

Expressing Willie (Crothers), 22

Expressionism, 33–34; differences from fantasy, 288n2

Expressionistic staging, in *Adding Machine*, 159–63; in *All God's Chillun*, 66; in *Aria da Capo*, 19–21; in *Beggar on Horseback*, 213–14; in *Emperor Jones*, 55–57; in *Hairy Ape*, 62–63; in *Johnny Johnson*, 254; in *Machinal*, 25; in *Verge*, 17

Fabulous Invalid, The (Kaufman and Hart), 216

Faith Healer, The (Moody), as fantasy, 233

Falk, Doris, on Hellman's plays, 205, 287n15

Fall Guy, The (Abbott and Gleason), 225

Fanchois, René, 139

Fantastic, as different from fantasy, 232

Fantasy, 232–46

Faragan, Frances, 100

Fashion (Mowatt), 14

Fatal Weakness, The (Kelly), 190

Father, The (Strindberg), 273n6

Faust (Goethe), 75, 96; as fantasy, 233

"Feathertop" (Hawthorne), as fantasy, 233

Federal Bureau of Investigation, 115

Federal Theatre Project, 18, 25, 105–10, 117, 118, 158, 206, 264; Negro unit, 109; opposed by Dirksen, 281n9; radio division, 109

Feminism, in Crothers, 22

Ferber, Edna, as collaborator with Kaufman, 219–20

Field God, The (Green), 252–53

First Man, The (O'Neill), 61

Fiske, Minnie Maddern, 2

Fitch, Clyde, ix, 29

Fitzgerald, Eleanor, 10

Fitzgerald, F. Scott, 236

Flanagan, Hallie, 25, 106–7; author of *Arena*, 281n6

Flexner, Elizabeth, on Kelly, 285n7

Flight to the West (Rice), 167

Fog (O'Neill), 39, 41, 274n13

Fonda, Jane, in *Julia*, 286n10

Fontanne, Lynn, in *Taming of the Shrew*, 37; in *Strange Interlude*, 278n28

For the Defense (Rice), 159

Folk drama, defined, 247; discussion of plays, 247–61; sources in America, 247–48

47 Workshop, 4, 6, 41, 134, 221, 224

Foster, Stephen, 249

Fountain, The (O'Neill), 71, 77, 86

Freie Bühne (Germany), ix

Freud, Sigmund, 82

Freudianism, 86, 88

From Morn to Midnight (Kaiser), 34

Front Page, The (Hecht and MacArthur), 224, 226

Frontier plays, 248–49

Full Metal Jacket (film), 283n4

Gable, Clark, in *Strange Interlude* film, 279n28

Gale, Mrs. Lyman, 3

Gale, Zona, 24

Galsworthy, John, 5, 49

Garbo, Greta, in *Anna Christie*, 277n18

Garrick Theatre, 11, 35, 36

Gas trilogy (Kaiser), 34

Gassner, John, on O'Neill's craft, 97

Gate, Theatre, Dublin, 111

George Washington Slept Here (Kaufman and Hart), 216

Gershwin, George and Ira, 220, 256

Gerstenberg, Alice, 13, 24

Gilbert and Sullivan, 10

Gillette, William, 273n8

Gillmore, Margalo, in *Marco Millions*, 76; in *No Time for Comedy*, 157

Gilpin, Charles, in *Emperor Jones*, 11, 53

Girl of the Golden West, The (Belasco), 249

Glaspell, Susan, 8, 11, 13, *14–19*, 24, 39, 250

Gleason, James, 225

Glencairn cycle (O'Neill), *40–44*, 75, 274n13

Glittering Gate, The (Dunsany), 12

Gods of the Lightning (Anderson and Hickerson), 128

Gold (O'Neill), 58

Gold, Michael, 100, 115

Golden Boy (Odets), 105, *181–83*; 264

Goldman, Emma, xii, 271n3

Gone With the Wind, 133

Good Gracious Annabelle (Kummer), 24

Goodman, Edward, 12

Gorelik, Mordecai, 105

Grand Street Follies, 5, 98

Great Divide, The (Moody), ix, 23, 249

Great God Brown, The (O'Neill), 37, 71–75, 76, 77, 86, 264

Green, Paul, 37, 103, 105, 109, 252–54

Green Grow the Lilacs (Riggs), 289nl

Green Pastures, The (Connelly), 257–59, 289n2

Greenwich Village Players, 40

Greenwich Village Theatre, 10, 60 272n4

Gregory, Lady Isabella, ix

Gropius, Walter, xiii

Group Theatre, 25, 37, *101–5*, 117, 118, 171, 175, 243

Guilbert, Yvette 6

Guild Theatre, 36

Gypsy (Anderson), 125

Hairy Ape, The (O'Neill), 10, 15, *61–64*, 71, 88, 99, 213, 264; censor efforts, 64; critical attack in *Billboard*, 276n13; explanation of subtitle, 276n15

Hamilton, Clayton, 39

Hammett, Dashiell, 198

Hanau, Stella, 8

Hapgood, Hutchins, 8, 39

Happy Journey, The (Wilder), 236–37

Harrison, Hubert, 57

Harrison, Richard B., in *Green Pastures*, 259

Hart, Moss, as collaborator with Kaufman, 214–18

Harvard Dramatic Club, 250

Harvard 47 Workshop. *See* 47 Workshop

Harvey (Chase), 245–46, 264

Having Wonderful Time (Kober), 230

Hawthorne, Nathaniel, 13, 14, 233

He and She (Crothers), 21–22

Heartbreak House (Shaw), 114, 273n10

Hecht, Ben 224

Helburn, Theresa, 11, 25, 38

Hell-Bent fer Heaven (Hughes), 251; compared to *Tobacco Road*, 260

Hellman, Lillian, 198–206, book awards, 286n10; statement on realism, 199

Henrietta, The (B. Howard), 272n1

Henry Street Settlement House, 5

Hepburn, Katharine, in *Philadelphia Story*, 223

Here Come the Clowns (Barry), 235–36

Hernani (Hugo), vii

Herne, James A., ix, 29, 272n2

Heyward, DuBose and Dorothy, 37, 254

Hickerson, Harold, 128

High comedy, defined 149; in Barry, 221–23; in Behrman, 149–58

High Society, film version of *Philadelphia Story*, 223

High Tor (Anderson), 130–31

Hirsch, Foster, on Kelly, 285n7

Hoffman, Dustin, as Method actor, 281n4

Holiday (Barry), 221–22

Holloway, Baliol, in *Marco Millions*, 76

Holm, John Cecil, 225

Hopkins, Harry, 107

Hotel Universe (Barry), 234–35, 264

House of Connelly, The (Green), 103, 253

House Un-American Activities Committee (HUAC), 110, 115, 185,282n13

Houseman, John, 111, 112, 113

Howard, Bronson, 60, 272n1; dramatic "laws," 28

Howard, Leslie, in *Petrified Forest*, 284n12

Howard, Sidney, 5, 36, 121, 133–39

Hughes, Hatcher, 251

Hughes, Langston, 166

Hugo, Victor vii

Hume, Sam, 3

Hylan, John, New York mayor attempts to censor *All God's Chillun*, 277n16

Hyland, Lilly May, 6

Hymn to the Rising Sun (Green), 253

Ibsen, Henrik, 13, 16, 30, 31, 32, 37, 94

Iceman Cometh, The (O'Neill), 9, 78, 97; compared to *Time of Your Life*, 289n6

I'd Rather Be Right (Kaufman and Hart), 216

Idiot's Delight (Sherwood), 144–46

"If Men Played Cards as Women Do" (Kaufman), 287n3

Ile (O'Neill), 40, 44

In a Garden (Barry), 221

In Abraham's Bosom (Green), 252, 264

In the Zone (O'Neill), 13, 40, 42, 43, 274n15

Industrial Workers of the World (IWW), 276n12

Ingram, Rex, in film version of *Green Pastures*, 259

Inheritors (Glaspell), 17

Innocents, The (Archibald), 286n13

Interiors (Maeterlinck), 12

International, The (Lawson), 101

International Ladies' Garment Workers' Union, 117

It Can't Happen Here (Lewis), 108–9

It Is the Law (Rice and Talbot), 159

Ives, Burl, in *Desire under the Elms* film, 277n20

Jackson, Glenda, in *Strange Interlude*, 278n28

James, Henry, 206, 233, 286n13

Jane Eyre, 84

Jephthah's Daughter, 5

Joan of Lorraine (Anderson), 283n6, 283n8

John (Barry), 288n6

John Ferguson (Ervine), 35–36

Johnny Johnson (Green), 105, 254

Jolson, Al, 57
Jones, Robert Edmond, 10, 11, 71, 99
Joyous Season, The (Barry), 235
Judgment Day (Rice), 167
Julia, film on Hellman's life, 286n10
Julius Caesar (Welles production), 113

Kaiser, Georg, 34
Kaufman, George S., 206, 211–20; books about, 287n2, 287n3
Kazan, Elia, 281n4
Kelly, George, 185–90, 212; criticism of style, 285n7
Kelly, Grace, 186; in *High Society*, 233; in *Country Girl* film, 285n6
Kelly, Walter, 186
Key Largo (Anderson), 131
King's Henchman, The (Millay), 21
Kingsley, Sidney, 104, 190–98, statement on abortion, 286n9
Kirkland, Jack, 260
Kiss the Boys Goodbye (Boothe), 231
Klaw, Marc, 2
Kleines Theatre (Berlin), ix
Knickerbocker Holiday (Anderson), 122, 131
Kober, Arthur, 220
Koch, Frederick, 249
Kotzebue, August von, 233
Krutch Joseph Wood, on high comedy in Behrman, 157–58; on Kelly, 285n7; on *Little Foxes*, 203; on Neighborhood Playhouse, 7; on *Strange Interlude*, 84; on *Tobacco Road*, 260
Kummer, Clare, 24

Labor Stage, 117–18
Lady in the Dark (Hart), 218
Lafayette Theatre, 109, 111
Land is Bright, The (Kaufman and Ferber), 220
Langner, Lawrence, 11, 12, 35, 38
Language, in soldier plays, 282n4
"Last Conquest, The" (O'Neill), 275n1

Late Christopher Bean, The (Howard), 139
Late George Apley, The (Kaufman and Marquand), 220
Lawrence, Basil (pseud). *See* Langner, Lawrence
Lawson, John Howard, 37, 100, 101, 116, 280n2
Lazarus Laughed (O'Neill), 84–86; O'Neill's description of masks, 279n32
Le Gallienne, Eva, 18, 25, 37
League of Workers' Theaters, 116
Left Bank, The (Rice), 167
Leigh, Vivien, in *Waterloo Bridge* film, 141
LeMoyne, Sara Cowell, 6
Let Us Be Gay (Crothers), 22
Lewis, Bobby, 281n4
Lewis, Sinclair, 108, 139
Lewisohn, Alice, 4–5, 6, 7, 13, 46
Lewisohn, Irene, 4–5, 7
Licensed (Langner), 12
Life with Father (Lindsay and Crouse), 227–28 264
Light, James, 10
Lighting, as adjunct to realism, 30
Lindsay, Howard, 227, 230
Little Clay Cart, The, 5
Little Foxes, The (Hellman), 201–3, 205
Little Theatre, in Chicago, Indianapolis, New York, 3; in Los Angeles, 4
Little theater movement, 2–13, 98; academic, 47 Workshop, 4; early professional companies, 3–4; Neighborhood Playhouse, 4–7; Provincetown Players, 7–11; Washington Square Players, 11–13
Living Newspaper, Federal Theatre Project, 107–8, 109, 206
Living Theater, The (Rice book), 163
Long, Huey, 108
Long, John Luther, 29
Long Christmas Dinner (Wilder), 237
Long Day's Journey into Night (O'Neill), 59, 92, 94; staged with *Ah, Wilderness*, 280n40

Long Night, The (Powell), 103
Long runs on Broadway, 264
Long Voyage Home, The (O'Neill), 40, 43; film version, 42
Longfellow, Henry Wadsworth, 200
Loren, Sophia, in *Desire under the Elms* film, 277n20
Lost Colony, The (Green), 109
Lost in the Stars (Anderson), 283n8
Loud Speaker (Lawson), 101
Love'em and Leave'em (Abbott and Weaver), 225
Love Nest, The (Sherwood), 140
Lucky Sam McCarver (Howard), 138
Lunt, Alfred, in *Marco Millions*, 76; in *Taming of the Shrew*, 37

MacArthur, Charles, 224
Macbeth. See voodoo *Macbeth*
Macgowan, Kenneth, 10, 11, 71, 99
Machinal (Treadwell), 25
MacKaye, Percy, 233, 250
McKaye, Steele, 30
McLaglen, Victor, in *What Price Glory?* film, 283n5
MacLeish, Archibald, 111
Madame Butterfly (Belasco), 29
Madame Will you Walk (Howard), 139
Maeterlinck, Maurice, 12
Maggie the Magnificent (Kelly), 190
Malden, Karl, in *Desire under the Elms*, 277n20
Male Animal, The (Thurber and Nugent), 229–30
Maltz, Albert, 116
Mamba's Daughters (Heywards), 257
Man and the Masses (Toller), 34
Man Who Came to Dinner, The (Kaufman and Hart), 217–18
Mantle, Burns, on *Days without End*, 95
March of Time, The, 107
Marching Song (Lawson), 116
Marco Millions (O'Neill), 36, 38, 76–78, 88
Margaret Fleming (Herne), ix, 29, 272n2

Maria Stuart (Schiller), 126
Marlowe, Christopher, 111
Marquand, John P., collaborator with Kaufman, 200
Marshall, Armina, 25
Martin, Mary, in *Peter Pan*, 288n1
Mary of Scotland (Anderson), 125, *126*
Mary the Third (Crothers), 22
Marx Brothers, 220, 225
M*A*S*H, 192
Masks, use by O'Neill, in *All God's Chillun*, 66; in *Ancient Mariner*, 71, in *Days without End*, 96; in *Great God Brown*, 71–74; in *Hairy Ape*, 71
Masque of Kings, The (Anderson), 131, 141
Masses, The (journal), xi, 9, 115
Matchmaker, The (Wilder), 289n5
Maxine Elliott Theatre, 111, 113
Melville, Herman, 13
Men in White (Kingsley), 104, 172, *191–94,* 197, 285n8
Merchant of Yonkers, The (Wilder), 289n5
Mercury Theatre, *113–14,* 118
Meredith, Burgess, in *Winterset*, 128
Merrily We Roll Along (Kaufman and Hart), 216
Merton of the Movies (Kaufman and Connelly), 213
Meserve, Walter, on Howard, 133
Metamora (Stone), 249
Method acting, 102, 281n4
Metropolitan Museum of Art, 7
Metropolitan Opera, 21
Middle genre, 31
Midsummer Night's Dream, A (Shakespeare), as fantasy, 233
Midwest Play Bureau, Federal Theatre Project, 19
Mielziner, Jo, setting for *Winterset*, 128
Miller, Arthur, 187, 286n13
Millay, Edna St. Vincent, 9, *19–21,* 35, 99, 233

Milwaukee Repertory Theatre, stages *Ah, Wilderness* and *Long Day's Journey*, 280n40
Minick (Kaufman and Ferber), 219
Minority Report (Rice book), 166
Miss Lulu Bett (Gale), 24
Moeller, Philip, 11
Molière, 10, 13
Monroe, Harriet, xi
Monte Cristo Cottage, 94
Monterey, Carlotta, 82, 88
Moody, William Vaughn, ix, 23, 30, 233, 247
Moon Is Down, The (Steinbeck), 208
Moon of the Caribbees (O'Neill), 40, 44, 52
More Stately Mansions (O'Neill), 278n22
Morgan, Agnes, 6
Morgenthau, Rita, 7
Moscow Art Theatre, ix, 37, 102, 106, 175
Mother Earth (journal), xii
Mourning Becomes Electra (O'Neill), 88–93, 128, 220, 264
Movie Man, The (O'Neill), 39, 41
Mowatt, Anna Cora, 14
Mrs. Warren's Profession (Shaw), 273n8
Murdoch, Frank, 249
Musset, Alfred, 13
Mussolini, Benito, 107
My Heart's in the Highlands (Saroyan), 105, 243
My Life in Art (Stanislavsky), 102
Mythic parallels, in *Desire under the Elms*, 68; in *Mourning Becomes Electra*, 88–89; in *Wingless Victory*, 128

Nathan, George Jean, 38, 48
National Endowment for the Arts (NEA), Congressional criticism of, 282n9
Native Son (Green and Wright), 254
Naturalism, 31–32, 208–9; in *Dead End*, 195–96; in *Desire under the Elms*, 69–70; in *Men in White*, 192; in *Street Scene*, 166; in *Tobacco Road*, 260; in *World We Make*, 197; statement by Bentley, 170

Ned McCobb's Daughter (Howard), 138
Negro unit, Federal Theatre Project, 109
Neighborhood Playhouse, 4–7, 8, 14, 46, 98
New Playwrights' Theatre, 100–101, 118
New spirit, xi
New Theatre, 3
New Theatre League, 117, 172
Newsboy (Workers Laboratory Theatre), 116
Newspaper Guild of America, 107
Nice People (Crothers), 22
Nichols, Anne, 264
Nietzsche, Friedrich, 82, 85
Night Music (Odets), 105, 184
Night over Taos (Anderson), 103, 127
1931 . . . (Sifton), 103
Nirvana (Lawson), 281n2
No Time for Comedy (Behrman), 157
Nobel Prize, to O'Neill, 47, 95, 96–97; to Steinbeck, 208
Now I Ask You (O'Neill), 274n13
Nude Descending a Staircase (Duchamps painting), xi
Nugent, Elliott, 229

Odets, Clifford, 102, 104, 105, *171–85*; compared to Chekhov, 174–75; contrasted to Kingsley, 196–97
Oedipus complex, 88
Oenslager, Donald, 105
Of Mice and Men (Steinbeck), 206–8
Of Thee I Sing (Kaufman and Ryskind), 220
Oklahoma! (Rodgers and Hammerstein), 289n1
"Ol' Man Adam and His Chillun" (Bradford), 257
Old Maid, The (Akins), 24
"Ole Black Joe" (Foster), 249
Old Davil, The. *See Anna Christie*
Olivier, Laurence, in *No Time for Comedy*, 157; to Hoffman on Method acting, 281n4
On Trial (Rice), 168–69

Once in a Lifetime (Kaufman and Hart), 214–15, 219, 226

O'Neill, Eugene, 15, 19, 24, 37–96, 98, 99, 111, 157; and Abbey Theatre, 3; and Guild, 27, 28, 34, 36; arrival at Provincetown, 8, 9, 39; artistic growth and unfinished plays, 275n1; as actor, 274n14; as tragic writer, 88–90, 92; as turning point in American drama, x; biographical aspects of plays, 82, 93, 96, 273n12; black dialect of *Jones* and *Dreamy Kid*, 276n6; career 1916–1920, 37–45; career 1920–1934, 46–96; compared to Anderson, 122–23; compared to Conrad, 274n13; compared to Kelly, 186, first production, 39; first publication, 39–40; first reviews, 40; impact, 120; lack of imitators, 120–21; on board of *The Masses*, 115; parodied by Neighborhood, 5; produced by Washington Square, 13; reaction to criticism, 275n2; receives Nobel Prize, 96–97; treatment of Blacks, 251

O'Neill, Eugene, Jr., 280n35

O'Neill, James, 40, 49, 58, 274n15

One-third of a Nation (Living Newspaper), 108

Oresteia, The (Aeschylus), adapted by O'Neill, 88

Otley, Roi, on voodoo *Macbeth*, 111

Our Town (Wilder), 237–40, 264; London production, 288n3

Outside, The (Glaspell), 16

Outside Looking In (Anderson), 125

Outward Room, The (Brand novel), 197

Overtones (Gerstenberg), 24

Page, Geraldine, in *Strange Interlude*, 278n28

Panic (MacLeish), 111

Paradise Lost (Odets), 105, 174, 177–81

Paris Bound (Barry), 221, 222

Pasadena Playhouse, 3, 84

Patriots, The (Kingsley), 197

Peabody, Josephine Preston, 233

Peace on Earth (Maltz and Sklar), 116

Peck, Esther, 6

Pentimento (Hellman book), 286n10

Perkins, Tony, in *Desire under the Elms* film, 277n20

Personal Equation, The (O'Neill), 274n13

Petit théâtre du Vieux Carré, 3

Petrified Forest, The (Sherwood), 142–44, film 284n12

Philadelphia Story, The (Barry), 223; film versions, 223

Philip Goes Forth (Kelly), 190

Pins and Needles (Garment Workers' Union), 117–18

People, The (Glaspell), 16

Peter Pan (Barrie), as fantasy, 232; modern productions, 288n1

Phoenix Theatre, 111

Piper, The (Peabody), 233

Platoon (film), 283n4

Playboy of the Western World, The, (Synge), ix

Playwrights' Company, 37; organization of, 121–22; summary of, 169; writers of, *See entries under Anderson, Behrman, Howard, Rice, Sherwood*

Playwrights' Theatre, 9–10, 15, 40

Poetic drama, in Anderson, 125–30; in Millay, 19; in O'Neill, 71

Poetics, The (Aristotle), 210

Poetry: A Magazine of Verse, xi

Porgy (Heywards), 254–56

Porgy and Bess (Gershwin & Heyward), 256–57, 289n1

Pound, Ezra, xi, 5

Powell, Dawn, 103

Power (Living Newspaper), 108

Princess Marries the Page, The (Millay), 21

Problem play, 31

Processional (Lawson), 281n2

Production totals, New York theaters, 1919–1940, 280n1

Prohibition, 99

Proletbühne (Proletarian Stage), 116

Prologue to Glory (Conklin), 146

Provincetown, The (Glaspell book), 8

Provincetown Players (Playhouse), 7–11, 46, 99; construction of plaster dome, 55–56; first meeting with O'Neill, 9, 39; first production of O'Neill, 39

Psychodrama, in Barry, 234–36

Public Works Administration (PWA), 281n5

Pulitzer Prize, 25, 47, 197, 263–64; winners of, Akins, 24; Anderson, 131; Chase, 245; Connelly, 259; Gale, 24; Glaspell, 18; Green, 252; Hughes, 251; Kaufman and Hart, 216; Kaufman and Ryskind, 200; Kelly, 188; Kingsley, 191; Millay, 21; O'Neill, 49, 58, 78; Rice, 163; Saroyan, 243; Sherwood, 144, 146, 147, 284n13; Wilder, 236, 237

Pullman Car Hiawatha (Wilder), 237

Queen's Husband, The (Sherwood), 141

Quintero, José, 78, 277n20, 280n40

Quintessence of Ibsenism, The (Shaw), 273n3

Rabe, David, 282n4

Rathbun, Stephen, 40

Rauh, Ida, 9

Realism, 15–16, 29–31, 32, 169–71, 208–9

Recklessness (O'Neill), 39

Red Badge of Courage, The (Crane), 123

Reed, John, 9, 13, 99, 284n4

Reed, Mark, 230

Reflected Glory (Kelly), 190

Reinhardt, Max, ix

Renascence (Millay poems), 19

Reunion in Vienna (Sherwood), 141–42

Rice, Elmer, 13, 36, 37, 121, 158–68

Riggs, Lynn, 289n1

Road to Rome, The (Sherwood), 140, 141

Road to the Temple, The, (Glaspell book), 8, 15

Robards, Jason, in *Julia*, 286n10; in *Ah, Wilderness* and *Long Day's Journey*, 280n40

Robeson, Paul, in *Emperor Jones*, 57

Robinson, James, on *Strange Interlude*, 82

Rocket to the Moon (Odets), 105, 181, 183–84

Rockwell, Norman, 94, 239

Romanticism, 32

Room Service (Abbott), 225

Roosevelt, Franklin D., 100, 106, 118

Roosevelt, Theodore, xii

Rope, The (O'Neill), 41, 44

Royal Family, The (Kaufman and Ferber), 219

Rugged Path, The (Sherwood), 284n13

Russia, events in and American views between wars, 285n4

Ryskind, Morrie, as Kaufman collabortor, 220

Sacco, Nicola, 99

Sacco-Vanzetti case, 99; reflected in *God of the Lightning* and *Winterset*, 128; in *Male Animal*, 229

Salon des impressionistes, xi

Saroyan, William, 105, 242–45

Satire, in Kaufman plays, 211–220 *passim;* in *Harvey*, 245–46 in *Marco Millions*, 78

Saturday's Children (Anderson), 125

Savoy Theatre (London), 30

Sayler, Oliver, on *Emperor Jones*, 57

Scarecrow, The (MacKaye), as fantasy, 233

Schiller, Friedrich, 126, 283n6

Schopenhauer, Arthur, 82

Scott, George C., in *Desire under the Elms*, 277n20

Scott, Maibelle, 94

Scoundrel Time (Hellman book), 286n10

Seagull, The (Chekhov), ix

Searching Wind, The (Hellman), 203

Second Engineer, The (O'Neill), 274n13

Second Man, The (Behrman), 150–53

Secret Service (Gillette), 273n8

See Naples and Die (Rice), 163

Selaissie, Haile, 107

"Sense of the Past, A" (James), 233

Serling, Rod, 232

Servitude (O'Neill), 41

Shame Woman, The (Vollmer), 250

Shand, John, 57

Shaw, George Bernard, 5, 13, 30, 99, 273n10, 282n2; censored for American production of Mrs. Warren's Profession, 273n8; produced by Guild, 36; staged by Welles, 114; Supporter of Ibsen, 273n3

Shaw, Irwin, viii

She Loves Me Not (Lindsay), 230

Shearer, Norma, in Strange Interlude film, 279n28

Sheldon, Edward, ix, 134

Shell Shock (O'Neill), 274n13

Shenandoah (B. Howard), 272n1

Sheridan, Richard Brinsley, 5

Sherwood, Robert, E., 36, 121, 139–48, 204; postwar plays, 284n13

Shoemakers' Holiday, The (Dekker, Welles production), 114

Short View of the Immorality and Profaneness of the English Stage (Collier), vii

Show Boat (Ferber novel), 219

Show-Off, The (Kelly), 187–88, 189, 212

Shuberts, J. J., Lee, Sam, 2

Sifton, Claire, 103

Sifton, Paul, 101, 103

Silver Cord, The (Howard), 136–38, 264

Simonson, Lee, 35, 38

Sinatra, Frank, in High Society, 223

Skin of Our Teeth, The (Wilder), 241–42, 264

Sklar, George, 116

Small War on Murray Hill (Sherwood), 284n13

Solid Gold Cadillac, The (Kaufman and Taubman), 220

Soliloquy-asides in O'Neill, 82–83, 87

Sophocles, 88

Souls (Lawson), 281n2

Spanish-American War, xii

Spewack, Bella and Samuel, 226

Stage Door (Kaufman and Ferber), 220

Stage lighting, 273n4

Stalin-Hitler non-aggression pact, 117

Stallings, Laurence, viii, 6

Spirochete (Living Newspaper), 108

Stanislavsky, Konstantin, ix, 102

Star Wagon, The (Anderson), 283n8

Star Wars, as example of fantastic, 233

Steinbeck, John, 206–8

Steiner, George, on tragedy, 89

Stevedore (Maltz and Sklar), 116

Sticks and Bones (Rabe), 283n4

Stieglitz, Alfred, xii

Stone, John Augustus, 248

Storm Operation (Anderson), 131

Stowe, Harriet Beecher, 14, 272n5

Strange Interlude (O'Neill), 78–84, 88, 91, 234, 235, 264; actresses performing Nina, 278n28; and Lawson's Souls, 281n2; staged with dinner break, 278n25

Strasberg, Lee, 102, 105

Straw, The (O'Neill), 38, 60–61, 76

Street Scene (Rice), 163–66, 167, 234, 264

Strictly Dishonorable (Sturges), 230

Strindberg, August, 10, 33, 34, 39, 41, 214, 273n6; influence on O'Neill, 55

Sturges, Preston, 230

Subway, The (Rice), 163

Success Story (Lawson), 103

Sun-Up, (Vollmer), 25, 250–51; compared to Tobacco Road, 260

Suppressed Desires (Glaspell), 9, 15

Supreme Court, ruling on AAA and NRA, 281n7

Susan and God (Crothers), 23

Suspension of disbelief, 30

Swinburne, Algernon, 94

Swing Mikado, The (Federal Theatre), 109

Swords (Howard), 134

Synge, John Millington, ix

Talbot, Hayden, 159

"Tale of Possessors Self-Dispossessed, A" (O'Neill), 97, 278n22

Talmud, Blanche, 6

Taming of the Shrew, The (Shakespeare), Guild production, 37

Tamura, 5

Tandy, Jessica, in *Madame Will You Walk*, 139

Tao House, 77

Taubman, Howard, as collaborator with Kaufman, 200

Taylor, Deems, 21

Taylor, Robert, in *Waterloo Bridge* film, 141

Tea and Sympathy (R. Anderson), 286n12

Teapot Dome scandal, 99

Teichman, Howard, on Kaufman, 212

Tempest, The (Shakespeare), as fantasy, 233

Ten Days That Shook the World (Reed book), 9, 99, 285n4

Ten Million Ghosts (Kingsley), 196–97

Tennessee Valley Authority, 108

Terry, Ellen, 6

Theatre Collective, 116

Theatre Guild, 10, 11, 27, 28, 34–37, 98, 100, 101; becomes O'Neill producer, 38, 76; declines to produce *Lazarus Laughed*, 84; discovers Behrman, 150; problems with leading to formation of Playwrights' Company, 121

Théâtre Libre (Paris), ix

Theatre of Action, 116

Theater syndicates, 2

Theatre Union, 116

Theory and Technique of Playwriting (Lawson), 101

There Shall Be No Night (Sherwood), 147–48, 204

These Three, film version of *Children's Hour*, 286n12

They Knew What They Wanted (Howard), 36, 134–36, 264; film versions 284n11

They Knew What They Wanted Under the Elms, 6

Thirst (O'Neill), 41, 274n13

Thirst and Other One-Act Plays (O'Neill), 39

This Fine Pretty World (MacKaye), 250

This Is New York (Sherwood), 141

Thomas, Augustus, 233

Three Men on a Horse (Abbott and Holm), 225–26

Thunder Rock (Ardrey), 105

Thurber, James, 229

Thus Spake Zarathustra, 85

Tickless Time (Glaspell), 16–17

'Til the Day I Die (Odets), 104, 174

Time of Your Life, The (Saroyan), 243–44; compared to *Iceman Cometh*, 289n6

To the Ladies (Kaufman and Connelly), 213

Tobacco Road (Kirkland/Caldwell), 259–60, 264; compared to *Sun-Up* and *Hell-Bent for Heaven*, 260

Toller, Ernst, 34

Tomorrow and Tomorrow (Barry), 235

Tone, Franchot, 105

Torchbearers, The (Kelly), 156–57, 190, 213

Torn, Rip, in *Desire under the Elms*, 277n20

Touch of the Poet, (O'Neill), 278n22

Toy Theatre (Boston), 3

Tragedy, 67; in *Desire under the Elms*, 78; in *Mourning Becomes Electra*, 88–90, 92; in *Winterset*, 130; lack in modern realism, 170

Tragical History of Dr. Faustus (Marlowe, Federal Theatre), 111

Treadwell, Sophie 25

Trifles (Glaspell), 15–16, 250

Trilling, Lionel, on *Days without End*, 96

Triple-A Plowed Under (Living Newspaper), 108

Triumvirate of Jones, Macgowan, O'Neill, 10, 48

Truckline Cafe (Anderson), 283n8

Tudor plays. See Anderson, Maxwell

Turn of the Screw, The (James), 286n13

"Twilight Zone, The," as fantasy, 232

Two on an Island (Rice), 167

Two Slatterns and a King (Millay), 21

Uncle Tom's Cabin (Stowe), 14, 272n5
Unfinished Woman, An (Hellman book),
  286n10
USA (Dos Passos book), 101
Utopia (More), 288n1

Valley Forge (Anderson), 128
Vanzetti, Bartolomeo, 99
Venice Theatre, houses *Cradle Will Rock*,
  113
Verge, The (Glaspell), 17–18; as fantasy,
  233
"Virgin and the Dynamo, The" (Adams),
  86
"Visit of Malatesta, The" (O'Neill), 275n1
Vollmer, Lulu, 24, 250
Voodoo *Macbeth* (Federal Theatre, 109,
  111
Vorse, Mary Heaton, 9

Waiting for Lefty, 102, 104, 112, 117,
  118, *172–74*
Wald, Lillian, 6
Walk Together Chillun (Federal Theatre),
  109
Walpole, Horace, 157
Walter, Eugene, x
"War of the Worlds, The," Mercury The-
  atre radio production, 114
Warner, Susan, 13
Warnings (O'Neill), 39, 274n13
Warren, Mercy Otis, 14
Washington Square Bookshop, 11
Washington Square Players, 9, *11–13*, 24,
  37, 38, 46, 98; become Theatre
  Guild, 35; produce O'Neill's *In the
  Zone*, 40
Watch on the Rhine (Hellman), 203–5
Waterloo Bridge (Sherwood), 141
Waters, Ethel, in *Mamba's Daughters*, 257
Way of the World, The (Congreve), 148
We the People (Rice), 167
Weales, Gerald, on style, 169
Weaver, John V. A., 225
Web, The (O'Neill), 39, 41

Wedekind, Frank, 13
Weill, Kurt, 105, 166, 218
Welded (O'Neill), *61*, 96
Welles, Orson, 110–14
Wells, H. G., 114
Wertheim, Maurice, 38
Westley, Helen, 11, 38
Wexley, John, 37
Wharf Theatre, 9, 37
Wharton, Edith, 24, 252
What Price Glory? (Anderson and
  Staullings), viii, 6, *123–25*, 133;
  film versions, 283n5
When Ladies Meet (Crothers), 23
Where the Cross Is Made (O'Neill), 41, 44,
  58
White, Sidney Howard, on Howard, 134
White Wings (Barry), 288n6
Whitman, Walt, 13
Why Marry? (Williams), first Pulitzer win-
  ner, 263
Wife for a Life, A (O'Neill), 39, 41
Wilde, Oscar, 13, 94
Wilder Thornton, 236–42, 288n5
Williams, John, 48
Williams, Jesse Lynch, 263
Wills, Arthur, on Kelly, 285n7
Wilson, Woodrow, xi, 99
Wingless Victory, The (Anderson), 127–28
Winterset (Anderson), 103, 125, *128–30*,
  264
Wisconsin Players, 4
Witching Hour, The (Thomas), as fantasy,
  233
Wolheim, Louis, in *Hairy Ape*, 64; in
  What Price Glory, 283n5
Woman's Honor (Glaspell), 16
Women and the Neighborhood Playhouse,
  6, 14
Women, The (Boothe), 226–27
Women playwrights, 13–26; Aiken, 24;
  Boothe, 226–27; Chase, 245–56;
  Crothers, 21–24; Gale, 24;
  Gerstenberg, 24; Glaspell, 14–19;
  Hellman, 198–206; Kummer, 24;
  Millay, 19–21; Vollmer, 24

Woollcott, Alexander, 217

Workers' Laboratory Theatre, 116

Works Progress (Projects) Administration (WPA), 106, 107; refuses *Cradle Will Rock*, 113; accomplishments, 281n5

World War I, influence on Drama, viii-ix, 31; plays based on or influenced by *Aria da Capo*, 19; *Bury the Dead*, viii; *What Price Glory?* 123

World War II, plays based on or influenced by, *Candle in the Wind*, 131; *Eve of St. Mark*, 132–33; *Flight to the West*, 167; *Moon is Down*, 208; *No Time for Comedy*, 157; *Searching Wind*, 203; *Storm Operation*, 131; *There Shall Be No Night*, 147–48; *Watch on the Rhine*, 203–5

World We Make, The (Kingsley), 197

Wright, Frank Lloyd, xii

Wright, Richard, 254

Yale Repertory Theatre, 280n40

Yale University, 4, 47

Yeats, William Butler, ix

Yellow Jack (Howard), 139

Yellow Jacket, The 20

Yes, My Darling Daughter (Reed), 230

You and I (Barry), 221

You Can't Take It With You (Kaufman and Hart), 216–17

Youngest, The (Barry), 221

Zola, Emile, 32

the authors

Jordan Y. Miller, professor emeritus and former chair of the English Department at the University of Rhode Island, received his B.A. from Yale University in 1942 and his Ph.D. from Columbia University in 1957. His doctoral dissertation on Eugene O'Neill led to the publication of *Eugene O'Neill and the American Critic* (1962, 1973). He has written and edited *American Dramatic Literature* (1961), *Playwright's Progress: O'Neill and the Critics* (1965), and *The Heath Introduction to Drama* (1976, 1983, 1988). He is a consultant to the *American Quarterly*, *PMLA*, and the National Endowment for the Humanities; has held a Fulbright lectureship in Bombay (1964–65); and was visiting professor in the School of English and American Studies at the University of East Anglia (1977–78).

Winifred L. Frazer is professor emeritus of the English Department at the University of Florida, where she taught for 26 years. She is the author of *The Theme of Loneliness in Modern American Drama* (1960), *Love as Death in "The Iceman Cometh"* (1967), *E. G. and E. G. O.: Emma Goldman and "The Iceman Cometh"* (1974), and *Mable Dodge Luhan* (1984). She wrote the drama section *American Literary Scholarship* for the volumes 1976–80.